A Word from the Canadian Cancer Society

The Canadian Cancer Society recommends a diet based on Canada's Guidelines for Healthy Eating. These are:

1. Enjoy a *variety* of foods.

2. Emphasize cereals, breads, other grain products, vegetables and fruits.

3. Choose lower-fat dairy products, leaner meats and foods prepared with little or no fat.

4. Achieve and maintain a healthy body weight by enjoying regular physical activity and healthy eating.

5. Limit salt, alcohol and caffeine.

The guidelines were designed to promote well-being and to reduce the risk of developing health problems such as cancer, heart disease, diabetes and obesity. The Canadian Cancer Society believes that a healthy diet is one of your best defenses against cancer. Although it is not known at this time exactly why a diet rich in vegetables, fruits and grains helps to reduce the risk of cancer, the current theory is that the vitamins and other non-nutritive food substances in fruits and vegetables are natural antioxidants that protect against cancer.

The recipes in this cookbook feature lower-fat cooking, emphasize dark green and orange vegetables and orange fruits and provide a wide variety of ideas to incorporate them into every part of the meal from appetizer to dessert. This cookbook will help make it easy for Canadians to follow Canada's Guidelines for Healthy Eating.

Yours in health,

Nutrition Expert Advisory Group
CANADIAN CANCER SOCIETY

The *Vitality* Cookbook

Eating for Great Taste and Good Health — Easy Recipes Abundant with Fruits and Vegetables

MONDA ROSENBERG
and FRANCES BERKOFF

A Lorraine Greey Book
HarperCollins*Publishers*Ltd

We dedicate this book to
Jean Berkoff and Gwen Rosenberg
who define Vitality.

A portion of the proceeds of the sales of this book will go to The Vitality Cancer Research Fund,
a part of The Samuel Lunenfield Research Institute of Mount Sinai Hospital.

With Appreciation

A special thank you goes to Anita Draycott, for her superb editorial advice and for adding her magical
touch to our sometimes awkward phrases.

Among the other people who helped produce this book, we would especially like to thank:
Andrea Emard, whose sterling copyediting skills caught our mistakes and saved us days of work and
worry. Cheryl Frayn, who met impossible deadlines while maintaining accuracy and amazing calm
professionalism. Barbara Dean, for family-testing our recipes, allowing us to turn her kitchen into chaos
and cheerfully giving us her opinion any hour of the night. Jodi Macpherson, supermom, super friend,
super supporter. Trudy Patterson and Marilyn Crowley, from the CHATELAINE Test Kitchen, who freely
gave their expert advice and were the team that tested the CHATELAINE recipes. Julian Armstrong, our
Quebec stringer and food editor of the *Montreal Gazette*, for her always welcome faxes and bites of
wisdom. Karen Hanley, who helped us make the nutritional lingo appealing. Susan Sutherland, of the
Fresh for Flavour Foundation, for her early and constant encouragement and for generously sharing her
invaluable information. Alison Fryer and Jennifer Grange, from The Cookbook Store, for sharing their
top-notch market research. Barbara Selley, who cheerfully churned out the nutritional analysis days,
nights and weekends. Anne Lindsay, for her expert author advice. Carolyn Lake, for sharing her fabulous
palate and appreciation of food. Lucie Cousineau, for her enthusiasm and constant good sense; Lee
Simpson, for her three-star support; Rona Maynard, for her caring encouragement. Marion Hebb, our
meticulous lawyer. Andrew Smith, a great designer and a joy to work with. Lorraine Greey, for her
expert guidance, constant caring, precise editing and for always championing our cause. Our friends,
who always understood when we were too busy to play.

First Edition

Canadian Cataloguing in Publication Data

Rosenberg, Monda
    The vitality cookbook

"A Lorraine Greey book".
ISBN 0-00-638047-6

1. Cookery (Fruit). 2. Cookery (Vegetables).
I. Berkoff, Frances G. II. Title.

TX811.R67 1995 641.6'4 C95-930434-7

95 96 97 98 99 00 ❖ RRD 10 9 8 7 6 5 4 3 2

Produced for HarperCollins Publishers Ltd
by Lorraine Greey Publications Ltd.
Suite 303, 56 The Esplanade
Toronto, Canada M5E 1A7

Design: Andrew Smith

Page layout and composition:
    Joseph Gisini, Andrew Smith Graphics, Inc.

Illustrations: Grant Innes

Printed and bound in the United States

Contents

Eat Your Way to Well-Being

WHEN MOM CAJOLED US TO EAT OUR VEGGIES AND fruit, she was onto something. Fruits and vegetables are definitely the nutritional superstars of the '90s. Scientists have been concentrating for some time on the benefits of eating whole foods and research shows that a diet high in vitamin- and mineral-rich fruits and vegetables may help provide protection against heart disease, certain types of cancers and even some processes of aging. Recently, fruits and vegetables are claiming further attention because they contain both antioxidant vitamins and phytochemicals, and ongoing research in this area holds promise for even more healthy news in the future.

Most produce is rich in minerals, phytochemicals and vitamins, including the antioxidant vitamins — C and beta-carotene (which converts to vitamin A in the body). Scientists are just beginning to unravel the complex interplay of antioxidants and free radicals that roam our bodies. It's a good guy / bad guy scenario. Free radicals — the bad guys — are formed daily in our bodies from the normal stresses of living, as well as from pollutants like smoke and exhaust fumes that we can't escape. It's suspected that these short-lived oxygen-free radicals jet around the body damaging cells. Think of a rocketing pinball that collides with the cushions and bumpers in a pinball machine.* This damage is partly responsible for cell changes that lead to certain cancers. And, that's not all — these free radicals can join forces with oxygen to form compounds that lead to

HOW MUCH IS A SERVING?
Canada's Food Guide to Healthy Eating recommends eating 5 to 10 servings of vegetables and fruit a day to maintain good health.

Servings don't need to be huge but a leaf of lettuce doesn't cut it. So what is a serving?

- 1 cup leafy greens
- ½ cup cooked fruit or vegetables
- ¼ cup dried fruit
- ½ cup (4 ounces) juice
- 1 orange, apple, pear, peach, banana, etc.
- 1 potato — but not potato chips, because they're mostly fat.

Fruit-flavored yogurts don't count because there usually isn't much fruit in them. Remember that lettuce and tomato on your burger don't count as a serving but it's a good beginning.

* The Nutrition Post, September 1994

the buildup of artery-clogging LDL cholesterol. Enter the good guys — the antioxidants. They fight the negative effects of oxidation by capturing, neutralizing or eliminating these damaging free radicals and combat the oxidative hits that damage DNA and cell membranes.

There are phytochemicals naturally found in abundance in every bite of cantaloupe, tomato or broccoli you take. The names of these chemicals — indoles, phenols, flavones and isothiocyanates, to name a few — are a mouthful, but one that is easy to swallow in foods that we enjoy regularly, like carrots, greens and berries. Researchers are exploring the role these potentially protective chemicals may play in helping to neutralize carcinogens or prevent them from forming and in providing protection against some hormone-related cancers, such as breast cancer. It may be partly because of these phytochemicals that straight, drugstore vitamin supplements may not be able to do the protective job as well as whole foods.

OUR TOP 20

All vegetables and fruits are packed with goodness. We've picked 20 that, based on a typical serving size, are rich in vitamin C, beta-carotene and/or other phytochemicals. Here is our top-20 list:

- Apricots
- Berries
- Broccoli
- Brussels Sprouts
- Cabbage
- Cantaloupe
- Carrots
- Cauliflower
- Greens
- Kiwi
- Mangoes
- Oranges
- Papayas
- Peppers
- Potatoes
- Pumpkin
- Spinach
- Squash
- Sweet Potatoes
- Tomatoes

MAKE BREAKFAST COUNT
- Start with juice, grapefruit or an orange.
- Add raisins or a sliced banana to cereal.
- Stir berries into plain yogurt.
- Eat a sliced apple with your muffin.
- Top pancakes with applesauce or rhubarb compote instead of syrup.
- Tuck an apple, pear or low-fat carrot muffin into your pocket, purse or briefcase.

MAKE LUNCH COUNT
- Ask for extra tomato and lettuce on your burger and order a side salad.
- Throw a carrot, tomato, celery sticks or banana into your brown-bag lunch.
- Add spinach leaves to your sandwich.
- Stuff a pita with cut-up vegetables.
- Top tuna salad or peanut butter with shredded carrots.
- Drink a can of fruit or vegetable juice.
- Add leftover dinner vegetables to a can of soup — pack in a thermos or microwave at the office.

MAKE DINNER COUNT
- Add more veggies and less meat to stews or soups.
- Concentrate on the vegetables in a stir-fry.
- Heat whatever vegetables you have on hand in a spaghetti sauce and toss with pasta.
- Double up on vegetables on your pizza.
- Use lean ground meat in a meat loaf and add grated carrots for extra moistness.
- Spruce up chili with chunks of tomato, peppers and mushrooms.
- For express dinners, add fresh vegetables to rice or pasta as it cooks.

MAKE SNACKS COUNT
- Keep baby carrots, cherry tomatoes and cleaned broccoli in vegetable crisper.
- Leave a bowl of fresh fruit on the kitchen counter.
- Stock your glove compartment with boxes of raisins, bags of dried apricots, packets of dried cranberries or cherries, and small cans of vegetable juice.

There seems to be no limit to the good news. Fruits and vegetables are rich in fiber (associated with lowered risk of some cancers) and folic acid (linked to prevention of birth defects and even some cancers). And no matter what benefits scientists uncover, the basic facts remain that fruits and vegetables are filling, virtually fat-free and low in calories. So if you fill up on fruits and vegetables, there's little room or urge to eat a lot of fat-heavy foods.

Which leads us to our last point. We think it's time for a new message — a positive one — not a cut down, cut out, feel guilty one. We want you to replace "I can't" thinking with an "I can eat as much as I want and enjoy it" attitude. We want you to *indulge in fruits and vegetables.* That doesn't mean snacking only on carrot sticks, munching through mountains of steamed broccoli or becoming a strict vegetarian. Our book will show you the payoffs of simply adding more fruits and vegetables to your everyday meals.

While we highlight some of the healthiest vegetables and all the good-for-you reasons to serve them, it is the seductive taste appeal of the recipes — Sweet Potato Vichyssoise with Red Pepper Purée, Blazing Vegetable Curry, Hot Pepper Bouillabaisse with Fresh Coriander, and Rosemary Roast Chicken with Modern Mashed Potatoes and Greens — that we want to be the "carrot".

Bon appétit and indulge!

MONDA ROSENBERG AND FRANCES BERKOFF

NUTRIENT ANALYSIS

Nutrient analysis of recipes was done by Info Access (1988) Inc., Don Mills, Ontario, using the nutritional accounting component of the CBORD Menu Management System.

The nutrient data base was the 1991 Canadian Nutrient File, supplemented with documented data from reliable sources. Updated beta-carotene values were used (Mangels, A.R. et al, Journal of the American Dietetic Association, 93:284-296, 1993).

Analysis is based on Imperial weights and measures, the smaller number of servings (i.e., larger portion) when there is a range, and the first ingredient listed when a choice is given. Optional ingredients are not included.

Nutrient Information On Recipes: Nutrient values have been rounded to nearest whole number. Good and excellent sources of vitamins and minerals have been identified according to criteria established for nutrition labeling (Guide for Food Manufacturers and Advertisers, 1988). A serving which supplies 15% of Recommended Daily Intake (RDI) for a vitamin or mineral (30% for vitamin C) is a good source of that nutrient. An excellent source must supply 25% of the RDI (50% for vitamin C).

Fresh Beginnings

*S*TART YOUR ADVENTURE INTO VITALITY EATING
with this lively collection of garden-fresh nibbles
and beta-carotene-boosting dips. Then, as your dinner
opener, consider one of our soups — some refreshing,
some heartwarming — all based on puréed fruits and
vegetables instead of the traditional butter and cream.

Easy Chicken and Red Pepper Kabobs

Using chutney in the marinade is a fast-fix way of producing an intriguing appetizer. We find guests love these kabobs because they're very flavorful, yet not fat- or calorie-laden.

PREPARATION TIME: 10 MINUTES / BROILING TIME: 16 MINUTES

MAKES: 24 KABOBS

6 chicken breasts, skinned and boned, about 1½ lbs (750 g)
6 peppers, preferably 2 red, 2 green and 2 yellow
½ cup apricot and ginger or mango chutney
2 tbsp soy sauce
1 tbsp each of brown sugar and olive oil
24 (6-inch) bamboo skewers

1. Cut chicken into 1-inch pieces, place in a large bowl and set aside. Core and seed peppers and cut into 1-inch pieces. Set aside in a separate bowl.

2. Purée chutney in a food processor with soy sauce, sugar and oil until smooth. Pour over chicken and toss until coated. Use right away or cover and refrigerate up to 24 hours.

3. Before assembling skewers, soak in water for 30 minutes. Skewer 3 pieces of chicken alternately with 2 pieces each of red, green and yellow pepper on each skewer.

4. Just before serving, preheat barbecue and grease grill or preheat oven broiler. Barbecue skewers for 7 to 8 minutes, turning several times during cooking. If broiling, set skewers on a wire rack in a shallow-sided baking sheet. Set oven rack in center of oven, about 8 inches from broiler. Cook for 16 minutes, turning partway through cooking, until chicken feels springy.

JAZZY HOT PEPPER AND TOMATO BRUSCHETTA

Cut 3 large or 6 plum tomatoes in half. Squeeze out all seeds and juice. Coarsely chop pulp and stir with 1 tablespoon finely chopped jalapeño pepper, 2 sliced green onions, ¼ cup chopped fresh basil or ½ teaspoon dried basil, 2 crushed garlic cloves, 1 tablespoon olive oil, 1 teaspoon balsamic or red-wine vinegar and ¼ to ½ teaspoon salt. Spoon onto small rounds of toasted garlic bread for an appetizer, or toss with pasta and serve with grilled meat. *Makes 3 cups.*

PER KABOB

Calories:	54
Protein:	7 g
Fat:	1 g
Carbohydrate:	5 g
Fiber:	1 g
Excellent source:	Vitamin C

Baked Garlic-Chili Shrimp

Everything you've ever wanted in an appetizer. Plump shrimp on a bed of spinach makes an elegant presentation, and you can prepare it ahead.

PREPARATION TIME: 10 MINUTES
COOKING TIME: 5 MINUTES / BAKING TIME: 12 MINUTES
MAKES: 6 APPETIZER SERVINGS OR 3 MAIN COURSES

1 lb (500 g) fresh or frozen medium-size shrimp, peeled and deveined, or small scallops
1 sweet red pepper, seeded
2 tbsp butter
4 large crushed garlic cloves
½ tsp hot red pepper flakes
2 tbsp freshly squeezed lime juice
¼ tsp salt
2 bunches or a 10-oz (284-g) bag fresh spinach

1. Preheat oven to 400°F. Rinse shrimp or scallops with cold water. If frozen, rinse until ice crystals are melted. Pat dry. Arrange in a single layer, in a shallow baking dish just big enough to hold them snugly. Slice pepper into thin strips and scatter over shrimp.

2. Melt butter in a small frying pan set over medium heat. Stir in garlic, red pepper flakes, lime juice and salt. Cook, stirring often, for 4 to 5 minutes. Pour over shrimp and peppers and stir gently. (If making ahead, refrigerate, covered, for up to 8 hours.) Bake, uncovered, in center of preheated oven until shrimp are pink and firm, about 10 to 12 minutes, or up to 16 minutes for scallops. Stir halfway through.

3. Meanwhile, clean spinach. Place in a large saucepan along with any water that clings to leaves. Stir over medium heat until wilted. Squeeze out all liquid. If making ahead, reheat spinach in microwave. Spread over 6 plates. Arrange shrimp and peppers over top and drizzle with garlic butter. Shrimp are also great over rice or pasta.

BEST SNACKS
When you're in need of a pick-me-up or want to stave off hunger before dinner, consider one of these beta-carotene-rich satisfiers.

• Half a mango
• Dried apricots
• Carrot sticks
• A glass of vegetable juice
• Broccoli florets with a light sour cream dip
• Half a cantaloupe

PER APPETIZER

Calories: 134

Protein: 17 g

Fat: 5 g

Carbohydrate: 5 g

Fiber: 2 g

Excellent source:
Beta-Carotene, Vitamin C, Folic Acid

Good source: Iron

Smoked Salmon Latkes

These appetizer-size latkes are oven-baked in big batches, cutting down on time and fat. With chic smoked salmon, they make elegant party nibblers. A lot of flavor for 21 calories.

PREPARATION TIME: 30 MINUTES / BAKING TIME: 16 MINUTES

MAKES: 60 (2-INCH) LATKES

4 medium potatoes, peeled, about 2 lbs (1 kg)

1 egg

2 tbsp all-purpose flour or matzo meal

½ tsp salt

Pinch of freshly ground black pepper

2-oz (60-g) pkg smoked salmon, finely minced, about ½ cup (optional)

1 cup thinly sliced green onions

3 tbsp olive or vegetable oil

1. Preheat oven to 450°F. Grate potatoes using grating disc of a food processor or medium size on a hand grater. Firmly squeeze grated potatoes in your hand and discard juice. Place grated potatoes in a large mixing bowl.

PER LATKE
WITH SMOKED SALMON

Calories: 21

Protein: 1 g

Fat: 1 g

Carbohydrate: 3 g

Fiber: trace

SMART COCKTAIL CANAPÉS

Instead of wrapped sausages and high-fat pâté at your next cocktail party, consider these nibblers featuring fruits and vegetables.

• Serve Jazzy Hot Pepper and Tomato (page 10) in hollowed-out cherry tomatoes or large mushroom caps.

• Bake mini tea biscuits. Break open and spread with chèvre or Gorgonzola. Abundantly fill with roasted red peppers.

• Serve cold ratatouille in mini pitas or tiny store-bought canapé shells.

• Buy fondue sauce in the refrigerator section of your supermarket. Heat and serve in a chafing or fondue dish, with vegetable crudités, apple and pear wedges for dipping.

• Cook small potatoes. Chill. Shave off bottoms so they will sit flat. Hollow out centers and fill with salsa or caviar.

• Cut small apples and pears into wedges. Squeeze with lemon juice and wrap with strips of prosciutto. Wrap quarters of fresh figs with smoked goose.

2. Whisk egg with flour, salt and pepper. Stir into potatoes until well mixed. Stir in salmon and green onions until evenly distributed.

3. Pour 1 tablespoon oil into a large jelly-roll pan with shallow sides, about 15x10 inches. Tilt pan to evenly coat with oil. Drop 1 slightly rounded tablespoon of potato mixture into oiled pan and flatten with back of spoon. Repeat until pan is full. Latkes do not spread, so they can be placed ½ inch apart. You may need 2 more oiled pans. Bake in center of preheated oven until edges are browned, about 8 minutes. Turn cakes and bake until they are browned as you like, about 8 more minutes. Place on paper towels to soak up excess oil. Serve warm latkes on a large platter with a bowl of light sour cream sprinkled with green onions for dipping.

MAKE AHEAD: *If making latkes ahead, bake for only 4 minutes after turning. They'll keep well in the freezer for at least a month. Reheat frozen latkes, uncovered, on a baking sheet in a preheated 375°F oven until hot and crisp, about 15 minutes.*

SMOKED SALMON DIP

Whirl a 6½-oz (184-g) can salmon with a 4-oz (125-g) package light cream cheese, ¼ cup light sour cream and 2 drops liquid smoke in a food processor. Stir in 2 chopped green onions. Place in bottom of a cylindrical glass dish. Stick asparagus or zucchini spears, peppers and bread sticks in salmon for dipping. *Makes 1½ cups.*

- Cut papaya or firm honeydew melon into bite-size pieces. Squeeze with lime juice and wrap with strips of thinly sliced smoked turkey or smoked salmon. Wrap cantaloupe with prosciutto.
- Blend whipped cream cheese with chutney and curry powder. Make a small slit in whole dried apricots and fill with curried cream cheese.
- Drain a jar of marinated artichokes. Warm in microwave oven. Toss with Parmesan. Serve with toothpicks.

- Spread slices of baguette with chèvre or cream cheese. Top with strawberry halves and small mandarin wedges.
- Cut fruit into cubes and thread onto skewers. Fill center of a cantaloupe half with cream cheese blended with grated tangerine peel and juice. Stick kabobs in cut-side of melon.
- Hollow out firm cherry tomatoes or slice slim zucchini into thick rounds and hollow out centers. Fill with egg salad mixed with smoked salmon, or with curried tuna or turkey salad mixed with finely chopped colorful peppers.

Cactus Jack's Sizzling Salsa

Cactus Jack's is a cozy diner in Carmel, Calif., that makes the best salsas we've ever tasted. They kindly gave us their recipe so it could soar north of the border. A mere 15 minutes of prep gives you salsa for a month. What a wallop of flavor for 5 calories a tablespoon!

PREPARATION TIME: 15 MINUTES / COOKING TIME: 15 MINUTES

MAKES: 7 CUPS

EXPRESS WAYS WITH SALSA

- Combine ¼ cup salsa and ¼ cup white wine in a frying pan. Simmer skinless, boneless chicken breasts in salsa mixture.

- Combine equal amounts of apple juice and salsa. Use as a simmering or baking sauce for pork chops.

- When making burgers, stir ¼ cup salsa into 1 lb (500 g) ground beef along with 1 egg and ½ cup bread crumbs. This salsa is also wonderful on top of steaks, grilled cheese sandwiches or with scrambled eggs.

- Place guacamole in the center of a dish and surround with salsa. Serve with corn chips.

PER ¼ CUP

Calories:	18
Protein:	1 g
Fat:	trace
Carbohydrate:	4 g
Fiber:	1 g

2 (28-oz/796-mL) cans diced (not whole) tomatoes, or 6 cups coarsely chopped, peeled ripe tomatoes and a 7 ½-oz (213-mL) can tomato sauce

¼ to ½ tsp salt

4 fresh jalapeño peppers, seeded and finely chopped, or a 3 ½-oz (114-mL) can diced green chilies, drained

6 crushed garlic cloves

1 tbsp paprika

1 tbsp ground cumin

2 onions, finely chopped

½ cup finely chopped fresh coriander

Juice of 2 limes

1. In a large wide saucepan, place entire contents of canned diced tomatoes and ¼ teaspoon salt. Or combine chopped ripe tomatoes with tomato sauce and ½ teaspoon salt. Then, add peppers, garlic, paprika and cumin. Place over high heat and bring to a boil, stirring often. Reduce heat to medium-low and boil gently, uncovered, stirring often, for 10 minutes.

2. Then, stir in onions and ¼ cup coriander. Cook until most of liquid has evaporated, 5 to 10 more minutes. Stir frequently, especially near end of cooking time. Remove from heat and stir in ¼ cup coriander and 3 tablespoons lime juice. Taste and add more lime juice, if you like. Store in the refrigerator for up to a week or freeze.

Fiery Cream Cheese Veggie Dip

Lighten this dip with beta-carotene-rich red pepper instead of butter, then use as a veggie dip — a double winner.

PREPARATION TIME: 5 MINUTES / MAKES: 2 CUPS

1 large red pepper

2 fresh jalapeño peppers, or ½ (3 ½-oz / 114-mL) can diced green chilies

2 crushed garlic cloves

8-oz (250-g) pkg light or regular cream cheese

2 tbsp finely chopped fresh coriander (optional)

Salt (optional)

1. Seed peppers and cut into 1-inch pieces. Place in a food processor fitted with a metal blade along with garlic and cream cheese. Whirl, using an on-and-off motion, until peppers are coarsely ground. Then, stir in coriander. Taste and add salt, if you wish. Serve right away or cover and refrigerate up to a day. Use as a dip for sliced vegetables, fruit, shrimp or nachos.

BIG DIPPERS

Add color and crunch to your next dip by using any of the following healthy scoopers:

- Clementine wedges
- Broccoli florets
- Cauliflower florets
- Mango slices
- Red and green apple slices
- Red and green pepper strips
- Endive leaves
- Pear slices

PER 2 TABLESPOONS

Calories:	33
Protein:	2 g
Fat:	2 g
Carbohydrate:	1 g
Fiber:	trace
Good source:	Vitamin C

YOGURT CHEESE

At about 20 calories per tablespoon, this makes a wonderfully creamy dip for vegetables or a lean alternative to mayonnaise or cream cheese. We also love it with berries.

Start with a plain yogurt that doesn't contain gelatin (whole-milk yogurt delivers the richest taste, nonfat the tangiest). Line a strainer or colander with a disposable kitchen cloth or cheesecloth. Set strainer in a bowl so cloth is suspended at least 2 inches from bottom. Place yogurt in cloth. Cover with plastic wrap and refrigerate.

Pour off cloudy liquid as it accumulates. Most liquid drains off in the first 12 hours.

You can use right away or continue draining. Over the next 2 days, yogurt will continue to drain a little and thicken. Then, turn cheese out of cloth into a container and cover.

Four cups (1 L) of yogurt will make about 1½ to 2 cups of cheese, depending on fat content of yogurt and draining time. Cheese will keep well for about 1 week in the refrigerator.

For a vegetable dip, stir in chopped fresh herbs or coriander.

For a creamy bagel spread, stir 1 teaspoon finely grated lemon peel and ¼ teaspoon salt into 1½ cups of cheese.

Grilled Vegetable Soup

Grilling adds a seductive smoky flavor to this multi-vegetable puréed soup. A smart start to summer barbecues.

2 large red peppers
2 large yellow peppers
1 hot banana pepper
1 red onion or small Spanish onion
Olive oil
4 large firm tomatoes
2 garlic cloves
½ cup loosely packed, fresh basil leaves
2 cups chicken broth or bouillon

1. Grease grill and preheat barbecue. Seed red and yellow peppers and cut into quarters. Make a lengthwise slit in hot pepper. Lay flat, scrape out seeds and discard. Slice onion into quarters.

2. Generously brush olive oil over vegetables, including whole unpeeled tomatoes. Or stir vegetables with about a tablespoon of oil until lightly coated. Place vegetables on grill. Grill until peppers are golden and onion is soft, about 10 to 15 minutes. Turn vegetables occasionally.

3. Remove onions to plate and place grilled peppers in a paper bag. Close bag and let stand for 10 minutes. (This helps to loosen any charred skin.) Barbecue whole tomatoes until skins become a little charred, about 8 to 10 minutes. Do not remove charred tomato skins. Remove blackened skins from peppers and discard.

4. Place 2 tomatoes, onions, garlic and fresh basil in a food processor. Whirl, using an on-and-off motion, until onion is chopped. Pour into a large bowl. Then, purée remaining tomatoes and peppers, in several batches if necessary, and add to bowl. Stir in chicken broth until soup is as thin as you like.

LIGHT'N'CREAMY SALSA DIP

Stir together equal amounts of light sour cream and bottled salsa. Add sliced green onion or chopped fresh coriander or basil. Dip with sliced peppers, cauliflower and broccoli florets, tortilla chips or pita crisps.

CAULIFLOWER IN THE RAW

Cauliflower, a source of fiber, is a must on your crudité trays with salsa or curried yogurt for dipping. One large floret has fewer calories than a carrot and even after cooking, a cup has more than our daily vitamin C needs.

PER SERVING

Calories: 86

Protein: 4 g

Fat: 3 g

Carbohydrate: 14 g

Fiber: 4 g

Excellent source:
Beta-Carotene, Vitamin C

Good source: Folic Acid

5. You can enjoy this soup right away, but flavor is improved if refrigerated overnight and served cold. This soup will keep well in refrigerator for at least 2 days or in the freezer for several months. For a light dinner, serve with grilled focaccia bread spread with creamy goat's cheese.

Spicy Mango Gazpacho

For a new whirl on gazpacho, let seductive silky mangoes take the place of tomatoes and lace them with lime and coriander.

PREPARATION TIME: 10 MINUTES / REFRIGERATION TIME: 2 HOURS
MAKES: 12 HALF-CUP SERVINGS

3 large very ripe mangoes
1 red pepper
1 to 2 jalapeño or hot banana peppers (optional)
½ English cucumber
½ red or regular cooking onion, or 4 green onions
2 large garlic cloves, coarsely chopped
½ to 1 cup fresh coriander leaves
Grated peel and juice of 2 limes
10-oz (284-mL) can undiluted chicken broth,
    or 1½ cups chicken bouillon
¼ tsp each Tabasco and salt (optional)

1. Peel mangoes with a sharp knife and cut pulp away from pit. Place pulp in a food processor fitted with a metal blade. Seed peppers. Cut into 3 or 4 pieces and add to processor. Slice unpeeled cucumber into 2-inch pieces and add. Cut onion into 2 or 3 wedges, or 1-inch pieces if using green onions. Add onions and garlic to processor. Pulse, just until vegetables are coarsely chopped. Rinse coriander leaves until clean and add wet leaves to food processor. Pulse 2 or 3 times.

2. If processor bowl is large enough, add remaining ingredients and whirl just until mixed. Or pour mango mixture into a large bowl and stir in remaining ingredients. Cover and refrigerate at least until cold. Gazpacho will keep well for two days.

GARDEN-FRESH GAZPACHO

In a food processor, purée 4 peeled tomatoes with 1 small green pepper, ½ English cucumber and generous pinches of dried basil, salt and freshly ground black pepper. Stir in 2 (5½-oz/156-mL) cans of vegetable cocktail juice or tomato juice. Refrigerate until cold. *Makes 12 half-cup servings.*

PER SERVING

Calories:	64
Protein:	2 g
Fat:	1 g
Carbohydrate:	15 g
Fiber:	2 g
Excellent source:	Vitamin C
Good source:	Beta-Carotene

Hot 'n' Fiery Celebration Thai Soup

This is the most addictive soup we know. We love it to start a dinner party — it definitely wakes up the taste buds for the rest of the meal.

6 cups chicken broth, or 4 cups of chicken bouillon plus 2 cups water

¼ cup fish sauce

6 garlic cloves, crushed or minced

1 tsp hot red pepper flakes

2-inch knob fresh ginger

8 green onions

5 stalks lemon grass

2 cups dried whole mushrooms (sold in Oriental stores)

2 red peppers

1 bunch fresh coriander

1 bunch or ½ (10-oz/284-g) bag fresh spinach

1 lb (500 g) medium-size shrimp, fresh or frozen

1 tsp hot Oriental sauce or Sambal Oelek

Juice of 1 large lime

1. To make stock, pour broth and fish sauce into a large saucepan. Add garlic and red pepper flakes. Thinly slice unpeeled ginger and add to saucepan. Cut white part of green onions (saving green parts for later) and lemon grass into ¼-inch slices and add to saucepan. Bring to a boil over high heat.

2. Meanwhile, rinse mushrooms with warm water. Place in a bowl and pour 2 cups boiling water over top. Let stand until softened, about 20 minutes.

YOUR ORIENTAL PANTRY

Many supermarkets now stock Oriental basics from fish sauce to lemon grass.

- Fish sauce is to Thai cooking what soy sauce is to Chinese. A translucent, dark thin sauce made from fermented fish or shrimp, it's very salty and essential to dishes like pad Thai noodles.

- Lemon grass looks like dried-out giant scallions with gray-green leaves. Containing an oil that's found in lemon peel, it gives a sour lemon taste and aroma to soups and other Thai dishes.

- There are many varieties of hot Oriental sauce available. Most are a fiery mixture of ground hot peppers and garlic. They give instant heat to any dish.

PER SERVING

Calories: 173

Protein: 19 g

Fat: 2 g

Carbohydrate: 22 g

Fiber: 4 g

Excellent source:
Beta-Carotene, Vitamin C, Folic Acid

Good source: Iron

3. Once stock comes to a boil, reduce heat to medium and boil gently, uncovered, for 20 minutes. Stock will have a strong taste. Strain and save broth. Discard vegetables. Add mushroom-soaking liquid to broth. Slice mushrooms, discarding stems, and add to broth. If making ahead, broth can now be refrigerated for several days or frozen.

4. Before reheating broth, slice green parts of onions into 1-inch pieces. Thinly slice peppers, then cut into bite-size pieces. Wash coriander and coarsely chop. Shred spinach. If shrimp are frozen, rinse with cold water until ice crystals melt.

5. Just before serving, bring broth to a boil over high heat. Add peppers and green portions of onions. Stir in Oriental sauce and lime juice. Add shrimp and continue boiling gently just until shrimp are bright pink and hot, about 2 minutes. Stir in coriander and spinach and remove from heat. Serve immediately.

HEARTY VEGETABLE SOUPS

WILD MUSHROOM AND CABBAGE SOUP

In a saucepan, whisk a 34-g package of cream-of-wild-mushroom soup mix with 1 cup milk. Add 1½ cups water and 2 diced carrots. Cover and bring to a boil until carrots are almost cooked. Add 4 cups shredded cabbage and 4 sliced green onions. Simmer for about 5 minutes. Stir in a tablespoon of sherry before serving. *Serves 5.*

LAZY LEEK 'N' CABBAGE SOUP

Place a 34-g package of leek soup mix in a large saucepan with 5 cups water and ½ teaspoon dried dillweed. Bring to a boil and stir in a ½ head cabbage, thinly shredded. Cover and cook over medium heat, stirring often, until done as you like, about 10 minutes. *Serves 6.*

FESTIVE SWEET POTATO SOUP

Microwave 2 sweet potatoes on high for 10 minutes. Peel and purée in a food processor. Place purée, 2 (10-oz/284-mL) cans chicken broth, 1 cup water and 1 teaspoon hot pepper relish or ¼ teaspoon Tabasco sauce in a large saucepan. Cook over medium heat, stirring often, until hot. Thin, if needed, with water. Serve topped with a dollop of sour cream and more hot pepper relish. *Serves 6.*

HARVEST PUMPKIN SOUP

In a saucepan, whisk a 14-oz (398-mL) can or 1½ cups puréed pumpkin with 2 cups chicken broth or bouillon, 2 tablespoons maple syrup, ¼ teaspoon each cinnamon, mace and salt. Cook, stirring often, until hot. Then, stir in 1 cup light sour cream. Great with pumpernickel croutons. *Makes 4 cups.*

Golden Curried Moroccan Soup

A mélange of nutrient-rich fruits and vegetables, livened-up with curry and cumin, creates an exceptionally intriguing soup — hot or cold. For a party, serve with peppered pappadams. For a simple soothing dinner, we love a large bowl with thick slices of dark bread. Make up this big batch and store it in your freezer.

PREPARATION TIME: 15 MINUTES / COOKING TIME: 45 MINUTES

MAKES: 10 ONE-CUP SERVINGS

1 tbsp butter
1 large onion, chopped
1 crushed garlic clove
2 tsp curry powder
1 tsp ground cumin (optional)
1 parsnip, peeled and cubed, or 1 cup cubed
   rutabaga
1 large sweet potato, peeled and diced
2 carrots, sliced
2 celery stalks, sliced
½ very ripe fresh pineapple, or a 14-oz
   (398-mL) can undrained crushed pineapple
2 large very ripe bananas
5 cups chicken broth or apple juice
¼ to ½ tsp salt
¼ tsp ground black or white pepper
½ cup light sour cream (optional)
Fresh chives (optional)

1. In a large saucepan, melt butter over medium heat. Add onion and garlic. Sprinkle with curry and cumin. Sauté, stirring often, for 1 minute. Add parsnip, sweet potato, carrots and celery. Cook, stirring frequently, just until vegetables begin to soften, about 10 minutes.

HEALTHY SOUP TIPS

Simple Soup Bases
In addition to chicken broth or bouillon, soups can get a jump-start with frozen puréed squash or a can of diced tomatoes.

Fast Fillers
Add frozen vegetables to a cream soup or broth. Then, add a can of drained salmon or tuna. Thicken soups with puréed leftover vegetables. Shred spinach, romaine or any lettuces, especially the tougher outer leaves, and add to soup just before serving. For instant low-fat creaminess, whisk in a little low-fat sour cream.

Protein and Calcium Boosters
Crumble cheese over soup and you can add enough protein to turn it into a main course. Try blue cheese over creamy soups, Parmesan over vegetable and cheddar on onion or tomato.

PER SERVING

Calories: 111

Protein: 4 g

Fat: 2 g

Carbohydrate: 20 g

Fiber: 3 g

Excellent source:
Beta-Carotene

2. Meanwhile, cut fresh pineapple, if using, and bananas into chunks. When vegetables have begun to soften, add chicken broth, salt and pepper. Stir in fruit and bring to a boil. Then, reduce heat to low and simmer, covered, stirring often, until all vegetables and fruits are very soft, about 30 minutes.

3. Purée soup in several batches in a blender or food processor. Serve with a swirl of sour cream in each bowl and a light sprinkling of fresh chives. Soup will keep for several days and can also be frozen.

Instant Blender Gazpacho

When Anita Draycott, a superb editor and friend, served this 5-minute gazpacho at a pool party, we couldn't believe it was a fast blender number. Keep a batch of this summertime lifesaver in the fridge.

PREPARATION TIME: 5 MINUTES / REFRIGERATION TIME: 2 HOURS

MAKES: 8 HALF-CUP SERVINGS

19-oz (540-mL) can tomatoes, or 4 to 6 fresh
   ripe tomatoes
1 small cucumber, English or regular
1 small onion
1 small green pepper
1 tbsp olive oil
2 tbsp red-wine vinegar
¼ tsp each of salt, Tabasco and
   Worcestershire sauce
½ tsp each of dried basil, oregano, dillweed
   and celery salt

1. Place entire contents of can of tomatoes in a blender or food processor. Or blanch and peel tomatoes and place in a blender. Peel cucumber and onion and add to blender. Seed and core pepper. Cut into chunks and add to blender along with remaining ingredients. Whirl, using an on-and-off motion, until vegetables are chopped as fine as you like. Refrigerate at least until cold, about 2 hours, or overnight.

PER SERVING

Calories: 38

Protein: 1 g

Fat: 2 g

Carbohydrate: 5 g

Fiber: 1 g

Hot and Hearty Borscht

Our ruby borscht brims with tender veggies in a full-bodied broth. A food processor speeds up preparation.

PREPARATION TIME: 30 MINUTES / COOKING TIME: 50 MINUTES
MAKES: 16 ONE-CUP SERVINGS

1 medium onion
½ small head green cabbage
2 to 2 ½ lbs (1 kg to 1.25 kg) fresh beets, about 7
3 carrots
1 small celeriac bulb, or 4 celery stalks
1 tbsp unsalted butter
4 crushed garlic cloves
48-oz (1.36-L) can vegetable cocktail juice
4 cups water
1 cup chopped fresh dill, or 2 tbsp dried dillweed
¼ cup red-wine vinegar
3 tbsp granulated sugar
1 ½ tsp hot red pepper flakes
1 ½ tsp caraway seeds
1 tsp each of salt and freshly ground black pepper
2 bay leaves
Sour cream or feta cheese (optional)

1. Using a knife, or slicer and grating discs of food processor, finely slice onion and cabbage. Peel and grate beets. You should have 6 cups cabbage and 8 cups beets. Grate carrots and celeriac. Slice celery, if using.

2. Melt butter in a large stockpot. Stir in onion and garlic and sauté over medium heat for 5 minutes. Pour in vegetable juice. Then, stir in vegetables and remaining ingredients except sour cream. Vegetables will be stacked high in pot, but will wilt as soup cooks.

3. Cover and bring to a boil. Then, reduce heat to low and simmer for 45 minutes to 1 hour. Stir often. Top with a swirl of sour cream or crumble of feta and sprinkle with more fresh dill. Cover and refrigerate for up to 5 days or freeze.

PER SERVING

Calories: 66

Protein: 2 g

Fat: 1 g

Carbohydrate: 14 g

Fiber: 3 g

Excellent source: Vitamin C

Good source: Beta-Carotene, Folic Acid

Sweet Potato Vichyssoise with Red Pepper Purée

A '90s' gold strike — easy, loaded with beta-carotene and low in fat. Gorgeous swirled with a little Red Pepper Purée.

PREPARATION TIME: 15 MINUTES / COOKING TIME: 55 MINUTES

MAKES: 12 ONE-CUP SERVINGS

3 (10-oz/284-mL) cans undiluted chicken broth, or 7 cups chicken bouillon
4 large sweet potatoes, about 2 lbs (1 kg)
1 tbsp finely minced fresh ginger
1 tbsp ground cumin
3 leeks
1 apple, peeled and cored
Sour cream (optional)
Red Pepper Purée (optional)

1. Place canned chicken broth and 3 cans water, or 7 cups chicken bouillon, in a large wide saucepan. Bring to a boil.

2. Peel potatoes, quarter and add to broth with ginger and cumin. Cover and boil gently, stirring often.

3. Meanwhile, trim root ends from leeks. Slice off and discard all dark green tough portions from leeks. Slice in half, lengthwise. To clean, gently separate top portion of leeks and hold under running water until all sand is washed away. Slice leeks into 1-inch pieces and add to broth. Slice apple into eighths and add to broth.

4. Continue boiling gently, covered, stirring often, until potatoes are very tender, about 45 minutes.

5. Purée soup, in several batches, in a food processor until fairly smooth. Taste and add salt, if needed.

6. Reheat, stirring often, over medium heat. For a vichyssoise texture, stir in sour cream, ¼ cup at a time, until as creamy as you like, then remove from heat. Or, thin with water or chicken broth. Serve in large bowls with swirls of red pepper purée and sour cream.

RED PEPPER PURÉE

Place red peppers on a foil-lined baking sheet. Set sheet 4 inches from broiler. Broil until blackened and blistered on all sides, about 15 minutes. Seal in a paper bag until cool enough to handle. Peel away skin. Core and seed peppers. Then, purée in food processor.

GO FOR SWEET POTATOES

Sweet potatoes sound fattening, but at about 100 calories per 100 g, they contain no more fat or calories than white potatoes. They are one of the best vegetable sources of beta-carotene and a source of fiber. The darker orange the potato, the higher the beta-carotene content.

PER SERVING

Calories: 92

Protein: 5 g

Fat: 1 g

Carbohydrate: 17 g

Fiber: 2 g

Excellent source: Beta-Carotene

Carrot-Butternut Soup with Fresh Coriander

This nutrient-packed hearty soup makes a satisfying, simple Saturday brunch or a sophisticated starter to a big hullabaloo dinner. The recipe can easily be halved, if you wish, and it also freezes well.

PREPARATION TIME: 15 MINUTES / COOKING TIME: 40 MINUTES

MAKES: 12 ONE-CUP SERVINGS

1 butternut squash or small pumpkin, about 3 lbs (1.5 kg)

2 large onions, coarsely chopped

1 tsp olive oil

6 to 8 cups chicken broth or bouillon

1 tbsp ground cumin

1 tsp ground coriander (optional)

1 tsp curry powder

¼ to ½ tsp cayenne pepper

6 carrots

1 cup uncooked red lentils or drained canned lentils (optional)

1 cup orange juice

1 bunch fresh coriander (optional)

Light sour cream or 5% yogurt (optional)

1. To make squash or pumpkin easier to cut, make a small slash in skin with point of a sharp knife. Place whole squash in the microwave and cook, uncovered, on high for 10 minutes.

2. Meanwhile, place onions, oil, 1 cup chicken broth and seasonings in a large saucepan. Bring to a boil over medium heat and cook, uncovered, stirring often, until onions are soft, about 10 minutes.

3. Peel carrots and slice into 1-inch pieces. Rinse lentils, if using. When onions are soft, stir in 5 cups broth, carrots, lentils and orange juice. Cover and bring to a boil.

ALL-SEASON RASPBERRY SOUP

A package of frozen raspberries quickly produces this tangy, full-flavored refreshing soup.

Place entire contents of a 14-oz (425-g) container frozen raspberries in light syrup (no need to thaw) and 1 cup light sour cream in a food processor. Whirl until fairly smooth. Strain through a sieve if you want to remove seeds. Add a generous pinch of cardamom. Thin, if necessary, with water. Covered and refrigerated, soup will keep well for several days. Garnish with fresh mint leaves. *Serves 4.*

PER SERVING

Calories:	96
Protein:	4 g
Fat:	1 g
Carbohydrate:	18 g
Fiber:	4 g

Excellent source: Beta-Carotene

4. Then, cut squash in half. Remove seeds and cut away peel. Cut pulp into 1½-inch pieces or, if soft enough, simply scoop out of skin. Stir pulp into soup. Cover, reduce heat and simmer, stirring often, until lentils and carrots are soft, about 20 to 35 minutes.

5. Then, purée soup in several batches in a food processor or blender until smooth. If thicker than you like, thin with broth, stirring in no more than a ½ cup at a time. Chop most of coriander leaves and stir into soup just before serving. Swirl a little sour cream in center of each bowl and sprinkle with a few coriander leaves. Covered and refrigerated, this soup will keep well for several days and also freezes well.

6-Minute Tomato-Orange Soup

Need a delicious soup in a hurry? Here's your miracle answer and it's brimming with vitamins.

PREPARATION TIME: 5 MINUTES / MICROWAVING TIME: 6 MINUTES

MAKES: 6 ONE-CUP SERVINGS

1 tsp olive oil
1 onion, chopped
1 crushed garlic clove
28-oz (796-mL) can tomatoes, including juice
10-oz (284-mL) can undiluted chicken broth
Finely grated peel and juice of 1 orange
1 tsp each of ground cumin and granulated sugar
Generous grinding of black pepper
1 cup crumbled feta cheese (optional)

1. Place oil, onion and garlic in a 12-cup (3-L) microwave-safe bowl. Microwave, uncovered, on high for 1 minute, until onion is soft. Add remaining ingredients, except feta, to bowl. Break up tomatoes with a fork. Microwave, covered, on high for 5 minutes, to heat and blend flavors. Turn into a food processor and purée until fairly smooth. Sprinkle with crumbled feta.

PER SERVING

Calories: 71

Protein: 4 g

Fat: 2 g

Carbohydrate: 11 g

Fiber: 2 g

Good source: Vitamin C

Cream of Broccoli Soup

Few vegetables are as nutritious as broccoli. Here's a wonderfully creamy yet low-fat way to serve it either as a beginner to a cozy dinner party or, with multigrain bread, as a weekday dinner.

PREPARATION TIME: 20 MINUTES / COOKING TIME: 20 MINUTES
MAKES: 5 ONE-CUP SERVINGS

1 large onion
1 tbsp butter or olive oil
1 large garlic clove, chopped
3 thin carrots, thinly sliced
½ tsp ground cumin, or ¼ tsp curry powder
¼ tsp nutmeg
10-oz (284-mL) can undiluted chicken broth,
  or 1 cup chicken bouillon
2 cups water
1 tsp Dijon mustard
1 large bunch broccoli
½ cup sour cream, light or regular

1. Chop onion. Melt butter in a large saucepan set over low heat. Add onion and garlic and sauté, stirring often, until onion is soft, about 5 minutes. Then, add carrots, cumin and nutmeg to saucepan. Stir in broth, water and Dijon and bring to a boil over medium-high heat. Cover, reduce heat to low and simmer.

2. Meanwhile, trim broccoli. Remove tough areas from stalks. Then, slice stalks into thin rounds and add to simmering soup. Coarsely chop florets. When soup has simmered enough that carrots are tender, stir in florets. Then, boil gently, uncovered, until all vegetables are soft, about 5 to 7 more minutes.

3. Purée soup, in two batches if necessary, in a food processor or blender until fairly smooth. For a perfectly smooth texture, strain soup through a sieve. If soup is thicker than you like, stir in a little hot water or broth. Whisk in sour cream or swirl a little in center of each soup bowl. This soup's flavor is best the same day it is made.

FRESH SPINACH AND PEA SOUP

Light 'n' healthy and a refreshing bright green color — definitely a '90s' pea soup at 56 calories per half cup.

Place 2 cups frozen peas, 2 sliced green onions and 1 cup chicken broth or bouillon in a saucepan. Bring to a boil and cook for 2 minutes. Then, whirl in a food processor until fairly smooth. Pour back into saucepan and add 2 more cups chicken broth or bouillon, 1 teaspoon dried basil and ¼ teaspoon white pepper. Cover and simmer for 5 minutes. Stir in 2 cups shredded spinach and ½ cup light sour cream. Continue simmering just until spinach has wilted. *Serves 4.*

PER SERVING

Calories: 110

Protein: 6 g

Fat: 4 g

Carbohydrate: 14 g

Fiber: 4 g

Excellent source:
Beta-Carotene, Vitamin C

Sassy
Salads

*S*ALADS ARE TAKING A NEW TOSS THESE DAYS.
*Don't expect to find old hat combos here. We've updated
the classics: coleslaw becomes the snowbirds' special with
fat slashed and mangoes added, potato salad
goes international with sweet potatoes and a light
Oriental dressing — more taste, more color, less fat.*

Sweet Potato Salad

This is unlike any potato salad you've ever tasted —
and you'll be asked for the recipe every time you serve it.

PREPARATION TIME: 15 MINUTES

MICROWAVING TIME: 14 MINUTES / MAKES: 6 TO 8 SERVINGS

CARAMELIZED TOMATOES

Line a baking sheet with foil and lightly oil. Slice unpeeled ripe tomatoes about 1 inch thick or slice plum tomatoes in half, lengthwise. Arrange in a single layer on foil. Do not oil. Sprinkle generously with salt and sugar. Bake at 300°F until most of liquid has evaporated and tomatoes have started to caramelize, about 1½ hours. While these are not the prettiest tomatoes you've ever seen, we much prefer them to sun-dried tomatoes. They're flavor-packed and neither tangy nor leathery. Great with chicken or tossed in a salad. Covered, they'll keep in the refrigerator for several weeks and can be frozen. If frozen, they can be used in sauces or stews.

---

4 large sweet potatoes, about ½ lb (250 g) each
Finely grated peel and juice of 1 large orange
2 tbsp olive oil
2 tsp each of sesame oil, brown sugar
   and Dijon mustard
½ tsp each of salt and black pepper
Generous pinch of cayenne pepper
1 small red onion, finely chopped
2 cups thinly sliced celery
¼ cup snipped chives or chopped fresh coriander

1. Sweet potatoes cook quickly, so watch carefully during cooking. If potatoes are overcooked, the salad will be mushy. Slice unpeeled potatoes in half, lengthwise. Place on paper towel in the microwave. Microwave on high until almost fork-tender. Two pounds potatoes will need 10 to14 minutes. Cover and let stand for 5 minutes. Or bake potato halves in a shallow pan in a 375°F oven for 25 to 30 minutes or just until fork-tender. Or cut in half and boil for 20 to 25 minutes.

2. Meanwhile prepare dressing. In a large bowl, whisk orange peel and juice with oils, sugar, Dijon and seasonings. As soon as potatoes are cooked and microwaved potatoes have stood for 5 minutes, run under cold water to stop cooking. Peel potatoes and cut into ¾-inch pieces. Add warm potatoes to dressing as soon as they are cut. Then, stir in onion, celery and chives. Taste and add more salt and pepper, if needed. Salad is wonderful served warm and can be refrigerated for up to 2 days. Cover, once salad is cold. Bring to room temperature before serving. If salad seems dry, stir in 1 to 2 tablespoons orange juice or oil. Sprinkle liberally with chives or coriander. Great with chicken.

PER SERVING

Calories: 149

Protein: 2 g

Fat: 5 g

Carbohydrate: 26 g

Fiber: 4 g

Excellent source:
Beta-Carotene, Vitamin C

Good source: Folic Acid

Roasted Red Pepper, Orange and Broccoli Salad

Open a jar of roasted peppers and you can quickly have a spectacular party salad.

PREPARATION TIME: 10 MINUTES / COOKING TIME: 5 MINUTES

MAKES: 6 TO 8 SERVINGS

2 tbsp olive oil

3 tbsp balsamic or white-wine vinegar

2 tsp Dijon mustard

¼ tsp salt

¼ tsp white or cayenne pepper

2 large heads broccoli

3 small oranges, or 4 tangerines, clementines
   or mandarin oranges

5 thin green onions, thinly sliced

⅓ cup small black olives (optional)

7 ½-oz (250-mL) jar of roasted red peppers,
   or 2 red peppers, roasted, peeled and seeded

Leaf lettuce

1. Whisk olive oil with vinegar, Dijon, salt and cayenne. Set aside or refrigerate if making a day ahead.

2. Cut away and discard tough portions from broccoli stalks. Cut florets from stalks. Peel stalks, then slice into ½-inch rounds. Cut florets into bite-size pieces. Place 2 inches of water in a saucepan and bring to a boil. Add stalks and boil gently, covered, until they start to soften, about 2 minutes. Then, add florets and continue cooking just until they turn bright green, about 2 more minutes. Drain and rinse under cold water until cool.

3. Peel oranges and slice into rounds. Place in a large dish. Add broccoli, onions and olives. Drain peppers and slice into strips. Whisk dressing and drizzle over salad. Toss until evenly coated. Turn salad out onto a bed of lettuce and scatter the peppers over top.

ALL ORANGES ARE NOT EQUAL

All oranges are high in vitamin C, but mandarin oranges and tangerines come with the added bonus of being much higher in vitamin A. An average-size orange has 269 I.U. of vitamin A, a tangerine has 773 I.U. and a ½ cup canned mandarin oranges has 1060 I.U. of vitamin A.

IRON LORE

All the iron we eat is not absorbed equally. You can enhance the absorption of iron found in dark green vegetables, enriched cereal and dried fruit by eating them with a food source of vitamin C. For instance, oranges added to a broccoli salad or fresh strawberries on your breakfast cereal guarantee a better absorption of iron.

PER SERVING

Calories: 94

Protein: 4 g

Fat: 4 g

Carbohydrate: 13 g

Fiber: 4 g

Excellent source: Vitamin C, Folic Acid

Good source: Beta-Carotene

Snowbirds' Low-Fat Slaw

The ultimate guilt-free salad — this high-fiber, low-fat coleslaw bursts with flavor from hot peppers, ginger and tropical mangoes — and it keeps in the refrigerator for days.

PREPARATION TIME: 15 MINUTES / STANDING TIME: 1 HOUR
MAKES: 15 ONE-CUP SERVINGS

WINTER COLESLAW

Cabbage contains a lot more nutrients than leaf lettuce and costs about half the price in the depth of winter. Coarsely grate cabbage and spice it up with hot peppers, slices of mango, dried apricots and raisins.

CREOLE SALAD

Coarsely chop 3 tomatoes, 1 green pepper and 4 stuffed green olives. Toss with 2 tablespoons olive oil, 1 tablespoon vinegar, ½ teaspoon dried basil, ¼ teaspoon garlic powder, ¼ teaspoon dried leaf thyme and ⅛ teaspoon cayenne pepper. *Makes 3 cups.*

8 cups shredded green cabbage, about ½ medium-size head

2 red peppers, seeded and thinly sliced

2 large carrots, coarsely grated

4 green onions, thinly sliced

½ cup chopped fresh coriander, arugula or parsley

½ cup rice vinegar or white vinegar

¼ cup granulated sugar

2 tbsp grated fresh ginger, or 1 tsp dried ground ginger

½ tsp salt

½ to 1 tsp hot red pepper flakes

2 large firm ripe mangoes

1. In a large bowl, mix cabbage with red peppers, carrots, green onions and coriander. Whisk vinegar with sugar, ginger, salt and ½ teaspoon crushed red pepper. Pour over vegetables and toss until coated.

2. Using a sharp knife, remove peel from mangoes. Cut pulp from stones. Then, slice pulp into thin strips and stir into salad.

3. Taste and add more red pepper flakes, if you like a fiery salad. Cover and let stand at room temperature for at least 1 hour or for up to 3 days in the refrigerator.

PER SERVING

Calories:	60
Protein:	1 g
Fat:	trace
Carbohydrate:	15 g
Fiber:	2 g

Excellent source:
Beta-Carotene, Vitamin C

Good source: Folic Acid

Mixed Greens with a Warm Orange-Sherry Dressing

A warm dressing of amber sherry simmered with freshly squeezed orange juice smoothly coats this colorful salad. This recipe can be easily halved.

PREPARATION TIME: 15 MINUTES / COOKING TIME: 10 MINUTES

MAKES: 8 SERVINGS

16 cups torn mixed salad greens, such as spinach, romaine, leaf lettuce and arugula

2 cups very thinly sliced red cabbage or torn radicchio

½ cup freshly squeezed orange juice, about 1 medium orange

¼ cup sherry

1 tbsp Dijon mustard

1 crushed garlic clove

¼ tsp each of salt and sugar

¼ cup olive oil

1. Place salad greens and cabbage in a large salad bowl. (While 16 cups may seem like a lot, you'll need that much for 8 servings.) Toss, using 2 large spoons or your hands, until evenly mixed.

2. In a small saucepan, whisk orange juice with sherry, Dijon, garlic, salt and sugar. Bring to a boil over medium heat and continue boiling gently, stirring occasionally, until reduced by half, about 8 minutes. Remove from heat and slowly whisk in ¼ cup olive oil.

3. Pour warm dressing over greens and toss until evenly coated. Serve immediately.

GO FOR DARK GREEN SALAD GREENS

Romaine lettuce has not only 4 times as much vitamin C and beta-carotene as iceberg lettuce but also twice the folic acid. Spinach, watercress, arugula and dandelion greens are other nutritious greens.

ARUGULA IS FOR BITE

Arugula is a trendy green that gives kick to any salad. It has bright-green, flat serrated leaves about the size of a large basil leaf. Add a little to your next salad or Italian sandwich for an appealing, slightly bitter yet spicy tang. Arugula is a rich source of beta-carotene and calcium.

PER SERVING

Calories:	98
Protein:	2 g
Fat:	7 g
Carbohydrate:	6 g
Fiber:	2 g

Excellent source:
Beta-Carotene, Vitamin C, Folic Acid

Magnificent Mango Salad

Monda tasted Wandee Young's salad over 20 years ago at a tiny Thai restaurant in Toronto. It started her Thai love affair that has grown to an addiction, now satisfied at Wandee's elegant new Young Thailand Restaurant II on Church Street. This salad is wonderful with everything from grilled steak to a turkey dinner, or add ground chicken and make it a main course.

PREPARATION TIME: 30 MINUTES / COOKING TIME: 5 MINUTES

MAKES: 4 TO 6 SERVINGS

2 limes
2 tbsp fish sauce
2 tbsp granulated sugar
1 tsp hot red pepper flakes
¼ tsp salt
2 large or 3 small firm, but ripe mangoes
1 large red pepper
½ small red onion
½ cup finely chopped fresh mint
1 cup chopped fresh coriander
½ lb (250 g) ground chicken (optional)
1 tsp sesame oil (optional)

1. Squeeze juice from limes and place 3 tablespoons in a large bowl. Add fish sauce, sugar, red pepper flakes and salt and whisk until sugar is dissolved.

2. Peel mangoes. Slice pulp from stone, then cut into bite-size julienne strips. Slice pepper into very thin, bite-size julienne strips. Combine mangoes and pepper in a bowl. Finely chop onion and add along with mint and about half of chopped coriander. If making ahead, salad and dressing can be covered separately and left at room temperature for several hours or refrigerated overnight.

NEW SALAD SPRINKLES

Give your tosses extra oomph by sprinkling with:

- Homemade croutons made from cheese bread, pumpernickel or pitas
- Finely chopped fresh herbs
- Finely grated orange, lemon or lime peel
- Finely chopped hot peppers, hot red pepper flakes or coarsely ground peppercorns
- Crumbled feta, Stilton or goat's cheese
- Grated old cheddar, Asiago, or smoked cheese
- Toasted pine nuts, sesame seeds or hazelnuts

PER SERVING

Calories: 100

Protein: 1 g

Fat: trace

Carbohydrate: 25 g

Fiber: 3 g

Excellent source: Beta-Carotene, Vitamin C

3. About 1 hour before serving, whisk dressing and toss with salad. Taste and add more lime juice, if you like. The flavor improves if salad sits at room temperature for at least 1 hour. If adding chicken, sauté in sesame oil in a large frying pan set over medium heat until chicken is done as you like, about 5 to 8 minutes. Stir often with a fork to keep chicken separated. Toss warm chicken with salad. Sprinkle with remaining coriander. Serve right away or refrigerate. Covered and refrigerated, salad will keep well for at least 1 day.

Creamy Low-Fat Spinach Salad

Buttermilk, with less fat than 2% milk and a remarkable thickness, makes a great stand-in for high-fat cream. Just check out this satisfying creamy salad at 39 calories per serving.

PREPARATION TIME: 10 MINUTES / MAKES: 6 SERVINGS

¼ cup light sour cream

¼ cup buttermilk

1 tbsp chopped fresh dill, or ¼ tsp dried dillweed

Generous pinches of salt and freshly ground black pepper

2 large bunches or a 10-oz (284-g) bag fresh spinach, about 7 cups

2 ripe tomatoes

¼ small red onion

1. Combine sour cream and buttermilk in a small bowl. Stir in dill, salt and pepper. Tear spinach into large bite-size pieces and place in a salad bowl. Coarsely chop tomatoes. Thinly slice red onion and separate into rings. Add to spinach. Drizzle salad with dressing. Toss well and serve immediately.

TOMATO SUGAR AND SLICE

A pinch of sugar balances the acid in tomatoes and rounds out the flavor. Contrary to the popular approach of slicing crosswise (along the equator), you'll save more juice if you slice lengthwise with a serrated knife.

WATCH THAT DRESSING

While salad vegetables are generally low in calories, what you toss them with can dramatically increase their fat and calorie content. A mere tablespoon of regular dressing can triple a salad's calories. To minimize calories while maximizing flavor, spritz your salad with flavored vinegar. Or for a creamy dressing, season buttermilk or low-fat yogurt with herbs and thicken with a little low-fat mayonnaise.

PER SERVING

Calories: 39	
Protein: 3 g	
Fat: 1 g	
Carbohydrate: 6 g	
Fiber: 2 g	

Excellent source: Beta-Carotene, Folic Acid

Good source: Vitamin C

Papaya and Shrimp Thai Salad

An intriguing salad that's as good as any you'll be served in a Thai restaurant — and it proves again you don't have to add fat for flavor.

PREPARATION TIME: 20 MINUTES / STANDING TIME: 30 MINUTES

MAKES: 8 SERVINGS

2 firm papayas
2 large ripe tomatoes
¼ head green cabbage, finely shredded
1 lb (454-g bag) cooked baby shrimp
Finely grated peel of 1 lime
⅓ cup freshly squeezed lime juice
1 tsp hot red pepper flakes
⅓ cup fish sauce
½ cup brown sugar
1 cup finely chopped fresh coriander
4 green onions, thinly sliced

1. Peel and seed papayas. Thinly slice papayas, then cut into 2-inch strips. Slice tomatoes in half. Squeeze out seeds and juice. Chop tomato pulp into ⅓-inch pieces. Stir with papaya, cabbage and shrimp. Stir remaining ingredients together. Toss with salad and let stand at room temperature for 30 minutes or refrigerate up to 2 hours before serving.

PRETTY PAPAYAS

Papayas don't darken after cutting, so they're great for salads and desserts. Cut, they'll keep well for at least 5 hours. Covered with plastic wrap and refrigerated, they'll keep beautifully overnight. Half a medium papaya contains about 60 calories. Papayas are almost fat-free, very high in vitamin C, and are a source of potassium and fiber.

PER SERVING

Calories:	191
Protein:	18 g
Fat:	2 g
Carbohydrate:	28 g
Fiber:	3 g
Excellent source:	Vitamin C
Good source:	Iron

SALAD SANDWICHES

Here are some smart, new, veggie-packed sandwich fillings to expand your repertoire.

TROPICAL SANDWICHES

Peel 1 mango and cut pulp from stone. Slice half of pulp into strips. Purée remaining mango or mash with a fork and stir with ¼ cup light mayonnaise, yogurt cheese or light sour cream. In 6 pitas, layer slices of chicken, sliced mango and roasted red pepper. Drizzle with mango cream and top with shredded lettuce. For appetizer sandwiches, spread mango cream over slices of baguette. Top with slices of chicken, then a crisscross of mango and roasted red pepper slices. Add a dollop of mango cream.

Fiesta Bean Salad

A fragrant mix of Mexican spices delivers bold fiery flavor in this bright, beautiful no-cook salad.

PREPARATION TIME: 10 MINUTES / MAKES: 16 HALF-CUP SERVINGS

19-oz (540-mL) can each of chick-peas
　　and kidney beans, rinsed and drained
12-oz (341-mL) can kernel corn, drained,
　　or 1 cup frozen kernel corn, cooked
3 ½-oz (114-mL) can diced green chilies
2 peppers, preferably 1 red and 1 green
4 green onions, sliced
2 ripe tomatoes, seeded and chopped (optional)
½ cup chopped fresh coriander (optional)
3 tbsp red-wine vinegar
2 tbsp vegetable or olive oil
1 ½ tsp each of chili powder and ground cumin
1 tsp dried leaf oregano
¼ tsp salt

1. In a large bowl, stir chick-peas with beans, corn and drained chilies. Finely chop peppers. Stir into bean mixture with onions, tomatoes and coriander.

2. Whisk remaining ingredients together. Taste and, if you wish, stir in an additional ½ teaspoon chili powder. Gently stir into salad. Serve immediately or cover and refrigerate up to 2 days. Serve garnished with tortilla chips.

DRESSY TOMATO DISHES

Scooped-out tomato halves make healthy holders for:

• Bean salad, potato salad or pasta salad sprinkled with green onions

• Cold ratatouille topped with coarsely grated Parmesan cheese

• Store-bought seafood salad

• Rice salad or couscous salad

PER SERVING

Calories:	98
Protein:	4 g
Fat:	2 g
Carbohydrate:	16 g
Fiber:	4 g
Good source:	Vitamin C, Folic Acid

GREEK SALAD

Stir 2 seeded and chopped ripe tomatoes with ¼ cup crumbled feta cheese, 1 tablespoon yogurt, 1 tablespoon light mayonnaise, 1 tablespoon chopped fresh basil or ¼ teaspoon dried basil, pinch of dried leaf oregano and 1 crushed garlic clove. Spoon into whole wheat pitas. *Makes 1 cup.*

FAJITA SALAD SANDWICH

Combine ½ cup chopped roast beef or leftover barbecued steak with ½ cup chopped green pepper, ¼ cup chopped ripe tomato, 1 sliced green onion, 2 tablespoons light sour cream and 1 tablespoon salsa. Stir in pinches of chili powder and cayenne pepper. Roll up in warm tortillas. *Makes ¾ cup.*

COMPARING RAW GREENS (3.5 OUNCES)

Type	Beta-carotene (RE)	Vitamin C (mg)	Folic Acid (mcg)	Iron (mg)	Calcium (mg)	Comments
ARUGULA (roquette or rocket)	578	*	97	*	160	Has a peppery nutty flavor similar to watercress, but a larger leaf. Spices up salads and perks up puréed soups.
COLLARDS	335	23	12	.2	29	Have a mild cabbage taste. Sautée, steam or cook in broth.
DANDELION GREENS	*	35	27	3.1	187	Extremely nutritious and high in fibre. Pleasant bitter flavor. Toss tender small leaves in salads or sauté.
ICEBERG LETTUCE	80	4	56	.5	19	Least nutritious lettuce.
KALE	785	120	29	1.7	135	Very nutritious and high in fiber. Remove center ribs and braise, or simmer in stews.
LEAF LETTUCE	200	18	50	1.4	68	Red- or green-tipped varieties are more nutritious than other varieties.
RADICCHIO	3	8	60	.3	19	Radicchio looks like a small red cabbage. It has an agreeably bitter taste.
ROMAINE LETTUCE	318	24	136	1.1	36	Dark leaves are most nutritious.
SPINACH	685	28	195	2.7	99	High in oxalates, so its iron and calcium are poorly absorbed. Use raw in salads, microwave until wilted, or slice and add to stir-fries or soups.
SWISS CHARD	609	30	14	1.8	51	Really a beet, but we eat only the stems and leaves. Ranges in color from light to dark green and red.
WATER-CRESS	*	43	9	2	120	Look for dark green, unyellowed leaves. Great in salads, or sauté with spinach or other greens.

* Data not available.

The Main Event

*Y*OUR FAVORITE, SOUL-SATISFYING DINNER DISHES —
*from a comforting oven dinner of rosemary chicken
with garlic mashed potatoes and wilted greens to a light
veal stew that is ready in a half hour, or a satisfying, yet
fast, weekday creole pasta — all spiced up and
embellished with a healthful cache
of fruits and vegetables.*

Sautéed Chicken and Colorful Peppers

A Dijon honey sauce gives a fast sense of elegance to this easy sauté, and the peppers add a peck of beta-carotene and vitamin C.

PREPARATION TIME: 5 MINUTES / COOKING TIME: 30 MINUTES

MAKES: 4 SERVINGS

1 tsp butter
4 skinless boneless chicken breasts
1 cup chicken broth or bouillon
1 tbsp each of Dijon mustard and honey
¼ tsp cayenne pepper
2 red peppers
¼ to ½ cup light sour cream (optional)

1. Melt butter in a large nonstick frying pan set over medium-high heat. Tip pan until it's evenly coated with butter. Add chicken and cook, uncovered, until lightly browned, about 5 minutes per side.

2. Add broth, Dijon, honey and cayenne. Stir until mixed. Cover, reduce heat to medium-low and boil gently until chicken feels springy, about 10 to 12 minutes. Turn halfway through.

3. Meanwhile seed peppers and slice into bite-size julienne strips. When chicken is done, remove to a platter and cover to keep warm. Add peppers to pan. Increase heat to high. Boil rapidly, uncovered, stirring often, until sauce has turned a golden color and is reduced to about a half cup, about 8 minutes. Pour any juices that have collected from chicken back into sauce. Add sour cream, if you like, and stir constantly just until evenly blended, about 1 minute. Spoon over chicken and serve.

LIGHT SOUR CREAM — A GOOD CHOICE

Light sour cream and 5% yogurt are wonderful thickeners for pasta sauces, stews, soups, or sauces to go over burgers or chicken.

A tablespoon of either light sour cream or yogurt adds approximately 17 calories, but if you thicken with a butter-flour mixture, each tablespoon adds about 70 calories.

PER SERVING

Calories: 183

Protein: 29 g

Fat: 3 g

Carbohydrate: 9 g

Fiber: 1 g

Excellent source: Vitamin C

Good source: Beta-Carotene

Express Curried Chicken Dinner

A hearty warming dinner — low in fat and high in flavor — in less than an hour.

PREPARATION TIME: 10 MINUTES / ROASTING TIME: 45 MINUTES
MAKES: 4 SERVINGS

4 chicken breasts, bone-in
2 tbsp each of Dijon mustard, liquid honey,
    and ketchup or tomato sauce
1 tbsp each of melted butter and curry powder
4 baking potatoes
Olive oil or melted butter
Freshly ground black pepper, crushed
    dried rosemary and cinnamon
2 acorn squashes

1. Preheat oven to 375°F. Remove skin from chicken. Stir Dijon with honey, ketchup, butter and curry powder. Smear curry mixture over both sides of chicken and place, bone side down, without overlapping, in a shallow casserole dish. Save any remaining curry mixture. Lay a piece of foil over dish and place chicken in preheated oven. Bake for 30 minutes.

2. Slice potatoes in half and rub with oil or melted butter. Sprinkle with black pepper and crushed rosemary. Place on a large cookie sheet beside or under roasting chicken and roast for 25 to 30 minutes.

3. To make squash easier to cut, microwave, uncovered, on high for 2 minutes. Then, slice into quarters and remove seeds. Lightly rub with some of remaining curry mixture and sprinkle with cinnamon. Place beside roasting potatoes.

4. After chicken has roasted for 30 minutes, remove foil and brush with pan juices, then any remaining curry mixture. Continue roasting until chicken and vegetables are done as you like, about 15 to 20 more minutes.

FRESH CORIANDER SALSA

This easy salsa is all you need to add fresh glamour to chicken or everyday barbecued burgers. Dice 3 ripe tomatoes and finely chop ½ red onion. Stir with ¼ cup chopped fresh coriander, 2 tablespoons olive oil, 1 tablespoon red-wine vinegar, ⅛ teaspoon Tabasco sauce and pinches of salt and freshly ground black pepper. *Makes 3 cups.*

PER CHICKEN BREAST, POTATO AND HALF SQUASH

Calories: 461	
Protein: 33 g	
Fat: 7 g	
Carbohydrate: 70 g	
Fiber: 9 g	

Excellent source: Beta-Carotene, Vitamin C, Iron

Good source: Folic Acid

Curried Treasures

When a glance into the fridge reveals cooked chicken or meat and some veggies, stir together this curry and you'll be adding a blast of nutrition as well as taste.

PREPARATION TIME: 15 MINUTES / COOKING TIME: 50 MINUTES

MAKES: 4 TO 6 SERVINGS

2 tsp butter

1 onion, chopped

4 carrots, peeled and thinly sliced

1 apple, peeled and chopped

2 crushed garlic cloves

1 tbsp curry powder

1 ½ tsp ground cumin

19-oz (540-mL) can tomatoes, including juice

1 cup apple juice

1 bay leaf

½ tsp salt

¼ tsp freshly ground black pepper

2 ½ to 3 cups bite-size pieces roasted turkey, chicken, lamb or beef, or vegetables, such as squash, potatoes or sweet potatoes

2 cups cauliflower florets, or 1 large green pepper, chopped

Chopped fresh coriander or parsley (optional)

1. Heat butter in a large saucepan set over medium heat. Stir in onion, carrots, apple and garlic. Sprinkle with curry and cumin. Cook, stirring frequently, until onion begins to soften, about 2 minutes.

2. Add entire contents of canned tomatoes and apple juice. Stir in bay leaf, salt and pepper. Bring to a boil over high heat, breaking up tomatoes with a spoon.

OIL-FREE TOMATO SAUCE

You can cut the oil called for at the beginning of tomato sauces by pouring a little juice from canned tomatoes into the pan, then adding onions and garlic. Boil gently until onions are softened and most of the juice is absorbed.

PER SERVING
WITH CHICKEN

Calories: 216

Protein: 19 g

Fat: 6 g

Carbohydrate: 21 g

Fiber: 4 g

Excellent source:
Beta-Carotene, Vitamin C

Good source: Folic Acid, Iron

3. If using lamb or beef, potatoes, sweet potatoes or squash, stir into curry. Cover and reduce heat to low. Simmer, stirring occasionally, until meat or vegetables are fork-tender and flavor has developed, about 45 minutes. If using turkey or chicken, stir into curry after it has simmered for 30 minutes. Then, simmer for 15 more minutes. Cauliflower or green pepper should be added for last 10 minutes of simmering. Remove bay leaf. Spoon over steamed rice and sprinkle with chopped coriander.

Rosemary Roast Chicken with Modern Mashed Potatoes and Greens

A more comforting dinner you'll not find.

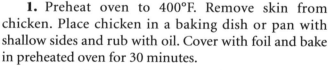

PREPARATION TIME: 5 MINUTES / ROASTING TIME: 45 MINUTES

MAKES: 4 SERVINGS

4 large chicken breasts, bone-in
1 tsp olive oil
2 oranges
2 tsp dried rosemary
Modern Mashed Potatoes (page 94)
Wilted Greens (page 93)

1. Preheat oven to 400°F. Remove skin from chicken. Place chicken in a baking dish or pan with shallow sides and rub with oil. Cover with foil and bake in preheated oven for 30 minutes.

2. Meanwhile, finely grate peel from oranges and place in a dish. Using your fingers, crush rosemary into orange peel. When chicken has baked for 30 minutes, remove foil and sprinkle peel and rosemary over top. Then, baste with pan juices. Continue roasting, uncovered, basting often with pan juices, until chicken is golden, about 15 to 25 minutes.

3. Meanwhile, prepare Modern Mashed Potatoes and Wilted Greens.

PER CHICKEN BREAST
WITH MASHED POTATOES
AND GREENS

Calories: 360

Protein: 34 g

Fat: 4 g

Carbohydrate: 47 g

Fiber: 7 g

Excellent source: Beta-Carotene, Vitamin C, Iron

Good source: Folic Acid

Classy Harvest Stew

Pumpkin or squash gives it substance and mint adds an unexpected twist — unlike any stew you've ever tasted.

PREPARATION TIME: 10 MINUTES / COOKING TIME: 1 TO 2 HOURS

MAKES: 10 ONE-CUP SERVINGS

2 lbs (1 kg) lean tender beef, lamb or veal

1 tbsp olive oil

2 large onions

4 large garlic cloves

2 hot banana peppers, or 1 jalapeño pepper, seeded

28-oz (796-mL) can tomatoes, drained

10-oz (284-mL) can undiluted chicken broth

1 cup red wine

1 small pumpkin or butternut squash, or 2 lbs (1 kg) hubbard or acorn squash

¾ cup chopped fresh mint or coriander

1 tsp paprika

½ tsp each of salt and freshly ground black pepper

¼ tsp cayenne pepper

19-oz (540-mL) can white kidney beans or chick-peas (optional)

1. Trim excess fat from meat, then cut into 1½-inch cubes. Heat oil in a large saucepan set over medium-high heat. Add half of meat and cook, stirring often, until lightly browned, about 5 to 8 minutes. Remove each piece to a dish as soon as it is browned. Repeat with remaining meat, adding more oil if needed.

2. Meanwhile, slice onions into rings, crush garlic and chop hot peppers. After meat has browned, add onion mixture to pan. Cook, stirring often, for 2 minutes. Then, add drained tomatoes, breaking them up with a fork. Stir in chicken broth and wine. Return meat and any juices to pan. Bring to a boil over medium-high heat. Cover, reduce heat to low and simmer, stirring often, for 30 minutes.

SMART THICKENING

Instead of thickening a stew with flour and oil, simply add lots of vegetables and boil gently, uncovered, until some vegetables are soft and naturally thicken the broth. Instead of thickening a vegetable sauce with a butter-and-flour combination, gently boil vegetable mixture until thickened. Or, remove part of it and purée in a blender.

PER SERVING

Calories: 270

Protein: 25 g

Fat: 9 g

Carbohydrate: 22 g

Fiber: 4 g

Excellent source: Beta-Carotene

Good source: Vitamin C, Folic Acid, Iron

3. Meanwhile, prepare pumpkin or squash. For easy peeling, pierce peel and place in the microwave. Cook on high for 5 minutes, until easy to cut. Slice off peel. Scoop out seeds and slice into ½-inch cubes. They will measure about 4 cups.

4. After meat has simmered 30 minutes, stir in pumpkin, ½ cup chopped mint, seasonings and beans, if using. Cover and continue simmering, stirring occasionally, until meat and pumpkin are done as you like. Lamb and veal will probably need an hour of cooking, while beef may take up to 2 hours. Then, stir in remaining ¼ cup chopped fresh mint. Great with rice or couscous. Refrigerated, this stew will keep well for at least a day and can be frozen.

Always-Ready Stir-Fry Sauce

A stir-fry has great appeal any night of the week. Keep a jar of your own homemade sauce in the refrigerator and you always have the basis for a clean-out-the-fridge dinner.

PREPARATION TIME: 5 MINUTES / MAKES: 1½ CUPS

¾ cup soy sauce, preferably light
½ cup vegetable or chicken broth or bouillon
¼ cup dry sherry, or 3 tbsp ketchup
3 tbsp brown sugar
¼ cup cornstarch
4 crushed garlic cloves
2 tbsp chopped fresh ginger, or 1 tsp
    ground ginger

1. Place all ingredients in a jar with a tight-fitting lid. Seal and shake until evenly combined. Refrigerate until ready to use. This sauce will keep well for up to 3 weeks. Remember to shake well before using. (See page 45 for uses.)

INSTANT ORIENTAL SAUCE

For an even faster refrigerator stir-fry sauce, simply stir ½ cup soy sauce with 2 tablespoons sesame oil, 2 tablespoons ketchup and 4 crushed garlic cloves. Store in the refrigerator for up to 3 weeks and use as you would the Always-Ready Stir-Fry Sauce. This sauce also makes a wonderful marinade for chicken, pork chops or steak. *Makes ¾ cup.*

PER ¼ CUP	
Calories: 77	
Protein: 2 g	
Fat: trace	
Carbohydrate: 16 g	
Fiber: trace	

Ginger Beef Stir-Fry with Pasta

A fresh garlic-and-ginger marinade turns lean, economical steak into a stir-fry star.

PREPARATION TIME: 15 MINUTES / COOKING TIME: 20 MINUTES

MAKES: 4 TO 6 SERVINGS

2 onions

3 garlic cloves

1 tbsp soy sauce

¼ cup coarsely chopped fresh ginger, or 2 tsp ground ginger

1 jalapeño or small hot pepper

1 tsp chili powder

1 lb (500 g) flank or sirloin steak

3 green peppers

4 carrots

2 large ripe tomatoes

¼ cup each of soy sauce and spicy salsa

1 tbsp brown sugar

½ tsp salt

Pinch of cayenne pepper

4 tsp peanut or vegetable oil

4 cups hot cooked pasta or rice

1. Slice 1 onion into quarters. Place in a food processor along with garlic, 1 tablespoon soy sauce, ginger, jalapeño and chili powder. Process, stopping and scraping down sides of bowl as necessary, until very finely chopped. Or chop with a sharp knife. Place mixture in a large mixing bowl.

2. Cut steak diagonally, across the grain, into very thin bite-size strips. Add strips to onion mixture and toss until evenly coated.

PER SERVING

Calories: 372

Protein: 24 g

Fat: 10 g

Carbohydrate: 47 g

Fiber: 6 g

Excellent source:
Beta-Carotene, Vitamin C

Good source: Folic Acid, Iron

3. Thickly slice remaining onion. Seed and cut green pepper into 1-inch triangular pieces. Slice carrots into thin julienne pieces or very thin slices. (This will help them cook quickly.) Coarsely chop tomatoes. Stir ¼ cup soy sauce with salsa, brown sugar, salt and cayenne.

4. Heat 1 teaspoon oil in a large nonstick pan set over medium heat. Add one-third of beef and stir-fry just until meat is lightly browned, about 4 minutes. Remove and cover to keep warm. Repeat with remaining oil and meat.

5. Then, add remaining teaspoon of oil to pan. Add onion and carrots plus any remaining onion-garlic mixture. Sauté until onion softens, about 5 minutes. Add green pepper and tomatoes. Stir-fry until hot, about 3 minutes. Stir in soy mixture. When bubbly, toss with hot pasta, then scatter with beef strips.

MORE STIR-FRIES

FRESH VEGETABLE STIR-FRY

Cut vegetables, such as onions, broccoli, celery, cauliflower, peppers and snow peas, into bite-size pieces. If using carrots, slice very thinly so they will cook quickly. For 6 cups of sliced vegetables, heat 1 to 2 tablespoons vegetable oil in a large frying pan or wok. (For extra flavor, use 1 teaspoon dark sesame oil and 2 teaspoons vegetable oil.) Add vegetables all at once. Sprinkle with ¼ cup water and toss frequently until vegetables are hot, about 3 minutes. Stir in ½ cup Always-Ready Stir-Fry Sauce. Cook, stirring constantly, until vegetables are done as you like and sauce is clear, about 4 to 6 minutes. Serve over hot rice. Sliced cooked chicken, beef or shrimp can also be added to stir-fry. *Serves 4.*

QUICK TOFU STIR-FRY

Drain, press and cube half of a 19-oz (550-g) package tofu. Heat 1 tablespoon oil in a large frying pan set over medium-high heat. Add tofu and stir until hot, about 3 minutes. Or add ½ lb (250 g) thinly sliced bite-size pieces beef, pork or chicken and cook, stirring frequently, until lightly browned, about 5 minutes. Then, add a 1-lb (500-g) package frozen stir-fry vegetables, about 5 cups, and ½ cup Always-Ready Stir-Fry Sauce to pan. Cook, stirring frequently, until vegetables are done as you like, about 8 to 10 minutes. Serve over hot rice or pasta. *Serves 2 to 4.*

Anything Goes Stir-Fry

We guarantee this will become a "count-on" dinner, since kitchen staples create a flavorful sauce for whatever's stashed in your fridge. It's a delicious way to clean out the crisper bin.

SAUCE

½ cup water

¼ cup soy sauce

1 tbsp cornstarch

1 tbsp brown sugar or honey

¾ tsp ground ginger

½ tsp chili powder

¼ tsp garlic powder

¼ tsp black pepper

STIR-FRY

1 lb (500 g) skinless boneless chicken breasts, beef sirloin or pork tenderloin

2 tbsp vegetable or peanut oil

8 cups thinly sliced, mixed fresh vegetables, such as broccoli, bell peppers, onions, carrots, cauliflower, celery and green beans, or 2 (1-lb/500-g) bags frozen stir-fry vegetables

1. Stir all sauce ingredients together and let stand while preparing stir-fry. For easy slicing, firm chicken or meat by placing in freezer for 30 minutes or use partially defrosted meat. With a sharp knife, thinly slice into ¼-inch-wide strips. Then, cut into bite-size pieces.

2. Heat oil in a wok or large frying pan set over medium-high heat. Add meat and stir-fry until lightly browned, about 3 minutes. Then, stir sauce and add to wok along with vegetables. Stir-fry until vegetables are hot but still crisp, about 5 to 8 minutes. If using fresh vegetables, cover pan between stirrings to steam them. Don't cover frozen vegetables. Serve over noodles or rice.

BROCCOLI TIPS

Buy:
Select compact florets that are dark green with a slightly purplish hue. Stalks should be firm and core compact.
Prepare: Slice off stalks, leaving about 1 inch on florets. Cut away any tough portion from stalks, then slice into ½-inch rounds.

Boil:
Cook stalks, uncovered, in boiling water, for about 3 minutes. Then, add florets and continue cooking until bright green, about 2 minutes.

Microwave:
Arrange stalks around outside of a pie plate. Place florets in center. Drizzle with 2 tablespoons water. Microwave, covered, on high for 2 to 3 minutes for a small head of broccoli.

PER SERVING

Calories:	201
Protein:	19 g
Fat:	8 g
Carbohydrate:	14 g
Fiber:	3 g

Excellent source:
Beta-Carotene, Vitamin C

Good source: Folic Acid, Iron

Herbed Pork Tenderloin with Glazed Vegetables

*Dress up your Sunday roast with everyday ingredients
and boost your beta-carotene along the way.*

PREPARATION TIME: 5 MINUTES / COOKING TIME: 20 MINUTES

MAKES: 4 SERVINGS

2 pork tenderloins, about ¾ lb (375 g) each, or
   1 lb (500 g) boneless, center-cut pork loin chops
1 tsp dried rosemary, well crushed
½ tsp dried leaf thyme
¼ tsp each of salt and freshly ground black pepper
1 to 2 tsp vegetable oil
6 carrots, sliced
1 cup orange juice
1 large green pepper
2 tbsp sherry or brown sugar (optional)

1. Place tenderloins or chops on a plate. Stir seasonings together and sprinkle half over pork. Press into meat to evenly coat. Turn pork and repeat. Heat oil in a large wide frying pan or wide saucepan set over medium heat. Add meat and cook, turning often, until lightly and evenly browned, about 4 to 6 minutes.

2. Meanwhile, slice carrots lengthwise into eighths. Then, cut into 1½-inch pieces. Add orange juice to browned pork. Stir to loosen browned bits from pan. Add carrots. Bring to a boil. Cover and cook over medium heat, turning meat several times, until it feels springy to the touch, about 10 to 12 minutes.

3. Meanwhile, slice pepper into julienne strips and add to pork. Move cooked tenderloins to a cutting board and cover to keep warm. Add pepper to juice. Increase heat to medium-high. Boil juice, stirring carrots frequently, until done and most of liquid has evaporated. Then, stir in sherry, if using. Or taste and stir in 1 to 2 tablespoons brown sugar as needed. Turn into center of a platter. Slice tenderloins into medallions and arrange around carrots. Serve with couscous or baked potatoes.

CHOOSE COLORFUL PRODUCE

For the most nutrient-dense produce — go for bright orange and yellow produce — carrots are far more nutritious than celery, cantaloupe than cucumber, and berries than grapes. Remember that dark leafy greens, spinach and romaine lettuce, for example, are richer in nutrients than paler iceberg lettuce.

PER SERVING

Calories: 288	
Protein: 38 g	
Fat: 5 g	
Carbohydrate: 21 g	
Fiber: 4 g	
Excellent source: **Beta-Carotene, Vitamin C**	
Good source: Folic Acid, Iron	

Veal and Hot Pepper Paprikash

Monda's neighbor, Eva Kuhn, is as superb a cook as she is a gardener. When she first served us this fabulous twist on paprikash on her patio, we thought it was one of the best stews we'd ever eaten — even in the heat of summer. And while it's relatively low in fat and enriched with yogurt, it still tastes rich, creamy and decadent.

PREPARATION TIME: 20 MINUTES / COOKING TIME: 30 MINUTES

MAKES: 6 ONE-CUP SERVINGS

2 large onions

3 garlic cloves

2 tsp vegetable oil

2 lbs (1 kg) stewing veal, veal shanks or lean beef

2 tbsp paprika, preferably Hungarian paprika

¼ tsp salt

3 to 4 large ripe tomatoes, or a 28-oz (796-mL) can tomatoes, drained

1 green pepper, seeded and finely chopped

1 to 2 jalapeño peppers, seeded and finely chopped, or ¼ tsp cayenne pepper

¼ cup Veloutine (lump-free sauce thickener)

¾ cup or a (6-oz/175-g) container 5% yogurt or light sour cream

1. Chop onions and mince garlic. Heat just enough oil in a large wide saucepan to coat bottom. Add onions, garlic and 2 tablespoons water and sauté over medium heat until onions are soft, about 5 minutes.

2. Meanwhile, slice veal into ½-inch-thick slices, then into bite-size pieces. Remove pan from heat. Stir in paprika and salt. Then, add meat but do not return to burner. Peel tomatoes, if you wish. Chop tomatoes and stir into pan along with any juice and seeds. Or stir in drained canned tomatoes, breaking them up with a fork. Stir in chopped peppers.

GRILLED TOMATO RELISH

Make this smoky-flavored relish once and it will become a must-have when grilling steak. Slice 10 plum tomatoes in half, lengthwise, and brush both sides with olive oil. Place, round-side down, on a hot grill. Barbecue for 5 minutes. Turn and continue barbecuing until hot, but not soft, about 3 to 5 more minutes. Remove to a cutting board and chop into ¼-inch pieces. Place in bowl along with 3 sliced green onions. Drizzle with olive oil and balsamic vinegar. Sprinkle with salt and pepper and toss well. Terrific with steak, burgers or chicken. *Makes 3 cups.*

PER SERVING

Calories: 285

Protein: 32 g

Fat: 10 g

Carbohydrate: 17 g

Fiber: 3 g

Excellent source: Vitamin C

Good source: Iron

3. Return pan to medium heat. Stir often until mixture starts to simmer. Then, reduce heat to low and simmer, covered, stirring often, until veal is tender, about 20 to 30 minutes. Then, stir paprikash while gradually adding Veloutine. Stir until thickened, about 3 to 4 minutes. Stir in yogurt or sour cream and just heat through. Don't boil. Serve over broad noodles or rice.

Oriental Salmon with Cucumber and Hot Pepper Salsa

A sublime and easy way to prepare world-class Canadian salmon any time of the year. Serve hot salmon with our refreshing salsa or on chilled summer greens. And you don't have to add an oily salad dressing either way.

PREPARATION TIME: 10 MINUTES / MARINATING TIME: 2 HOURS
COOKING TIME: 10 MINUTES / MAKES: 4 SERVINGS

SALMON
4 salmon steaks, each about 1 inch thick
¼ cup hoisin sauce (optional)
2 tbsp each of soy sauce and freshly squeezed lime or lemon juice
2 tbsp dry sherry

SALSA SALAD
1 small English cucumber
1 red pepper, seeded
2 jalapeño peppers, seeded (optional)
½ cup finely chopped red or green onion
½ cup chopped fresh dill, or 1½ tsp dried dillweed
4 tbsp freshly squeezed lime or lemon juice
2 tbsp granulated sugar
¼ tsp salt
8 cups salad greens, preferably a mix of romaine, spinach and arugula

PER SERVING

Calories: 322

Protein: 34 g

Fat: 11 g

Carbohydrate: 22 g

Fiber: 3 g

Excellent source:
Beta-Carotene, Vitamin C,
Folic Acid

Good source: Iron

BARBECUE SMARTS

For barbecuing or grilling, marinades add extra flavor and moistness and tenderize meats. But, they often call for a large quantity of fat. If you marinate chicken breasts, pork or lamb for at least 4 hours (or preferably overnight) in white wine or apple juice mixed with herbs, the liquid will be soaked up and the chicken or meat will be wonderfully moist with no oil needed. Instead of oiling the grill before heating, coat with a non-stick cooking spray. Instead of basting the food with oil throughout the barbecuing, just lightly brush the outside of the chicken or meat with oil before placing it on the grill.

1. Pat salmon steaks dry. Whisk remaining salmon ingredients together. Brush over both sides of salmon. If time is short, you can cook salmon right away but it's best to marinate, covered, in the refrigerator, for at least 2 hours.

2. Prepare salsa by finely dicing unpeeled cucumber and peppers. Place in a bowl and add onion and fresh dill, if using. Stir lime juice with sugar, salt and dried dill, if using, until sugar is dissolved. Then, stir into salsa until well mixed. For best flavor, let stand at room temperature for a couple of hours or up to a day.

3. Remove salmon from marinade and save for basting. Place salmon on a greased grill and barbecue, basting several times with marinade, until a knife point inserted into center feels warm, about 5 to 7 minutes per side. Or grill in the oven, 4 inches from broiler element, for 5 to 7 minutes per side, basting several times with marinade.

4. Salmon is delicious with salsa spooned over top. Or toss salsa and all salsa liquid with salad greens. Arrange on dinner plates and place hot grilled salmon on top. Sprinkle with additional chopped fresh dill and serve immediately.

MORE SALSAS

NECTARINE, PLUM AND FRESH MINT SALSA

This vitamin-rich salsa is wonderful with grilled chicken, tossed with greens or on top of cottage cheese. Finely chop 3 nectarines and 2 plums. Mix with ¼ cup chopped fresh mint, 2 tablespoons liquid honey and 1 tablespoon freshly squeezed lime or lemon juice. Serve at room temperature. Salsa is best served the same day it is made. *Makes 3 cups.*

PAPAYA-CORIANDER SALSA

A luscious, nutrient-rich fat-free way to add glamour to grilled chicken, fish, steaks and lamb. Peel, seed and finely chop 1 large papaya. Mix with 2 sliced green onions, ¼ cup chopped fresh coriander, 1 tablespoon finely diced jalapeño pepper, 1 teaspoon lime juice, ½ teaspoon sugar and a pinch of salt. *Makes 2 cups.*

Weekday Creole Pasta

This is a heartwarming and zesty dish for chilly nights and roaring fireplaces. And you probably have all the ingredients on hand.

PREPARATION TIME: 20 MINUTES / COOKING TIME: 20 MINUTES
MAKES: 2 TO 3 SERVINGS

1 onion, finely chopped

1 crushed garlic clove

28-oz (796-mL) can tomatoes, including juice

2 celery stalks, chopped

1 green pepper, chopped

2 tsp chili powder

½ tsp dried leaf oregano

¼ tsp paprika

Freshly ground black pepper

½ tsp granulated sugar

½ lb (250 g) fresh or frozen shrimp, or a 6 ½-oz (184-g) can tuna (optional)

¼ lb (125 g) linguine or penne

⅓ cup freshly grated Parmesan or Asiago cheese

1. Place onion and garlic in a large nonstick pan. Drain juice from tomatoes into pan. Bring to a boil over medium heat. Then, boil gently, stirring often, until onion is soft and most of liquid has evaporated, about 5 minutes.

2. Then, add tomatoes, breaking up with a fork. Stir in celery, green pepper, seasonings and sugar. Return to a boil and boil gently, uncovered, stirring often, until thickened, about 10 to 15 minutes.

3. Then, if using shrimp or tuna, stir into sauce. Cover and reduce heat to low. Simmer just until shrimp are firm, about 2 to 4 minutes.

4. Meanwhile, cook linguine according to package directions. Drain but do not rinse. Toss pasta with sauce and Parmesan.

SPEEDY PASTA SAUCES

- Stir chopped ripe tomatoes, finely chopped hot pepper and fresh basil into store-bought spaghetti sauce. Heat and toss with pasta and grated Parmesan cheese.

- Stir chopped ripe tomatoes, diced zucchini and sweet pepper into store-bought salsa. Heat and toss with pasta.

- Toss chopped ripe tomatoes with a drizzle of olive oil and lots of chopped garlic and chives. Heat and toss with pasta and lots of grated Parmesan.

- Chop and lightly steam or sauté spinach with a crushed garlic clove. Toss with hot pasta, olive oil and grated Asiago or Romano cheese.

PER SERVING

Calories: 424
Protein: 18 g
Fat: 6 g
Carbohydrate: 77 g
Fiber: 8 g

Excellent source:
Beta-Carotene, Vitamin C

Good source: Folic Acid, Iron, Calcium

Primavera Fish Steaks and Pasta à Deux

We've lightly stir-fried spring vegetables to maintain garden-fresh taste and al dente texture. They provide lively contrast to satiny pasta and whatever steak is the best buy at the fish counter.

PREPARATION TIME: 15 MINUTES / COOKING TIME: 20 MINUTES

MAKES: 2 SERVINGS

¼ lb (125 g) fettuccine or spaghetti

1 lemon

1 ½ cups white wine

1 tbsp drained capers

2 tsp butter

4 crushed garlic cloves

2 fish steaks, such as kingfish, swordfish or halibut, each about 4 oz (125 g) and 1 inch thick

Pinches of salt and white pepper

1 large bunch asparagus, or 1 green pepper

2 red peppers

4 green onions

⅓ cup finely chopped or thinly shredded fresh basil

1. To cook pasta, bring a large pot of water to a boil. When boiling rapidly add pasta and cook, stirring often, until al dente, about 10 minutes.

2. Meanwhile, finely grate peel from lemon, then cut lemon in half. Combine white wine, capers, butter, garlic and lemon peel in a large nonstick frying pan. Bring to a boil over medium heat. Add fish and squeeze lemon juice over top and into wine mixture. Sprinkle with salt and pepper. Partially cover and boil gently over medium heat for 10 minutes. Turn fish after 5 minutes.

TWO FOR ONE — VITAMIN C PLUS BETA-CAROTENE

Many fruits and vegetables are sources of both vitamin C and beta-carotene — a double payoff. Here are just a few examples of produce that contains beta-carotene and as much vitamin C as an orange — enough to meet our daily needs:

- A mango
- A red pepper
- Half a cantaloupe
- One cup cooked brussels sprouts

PER SERVING

Calories:	511
Protein:	34 g
Fat:	10 g
Carbohydrate:	62 g
Fiber:	7 g

Excellent source:
Beta-Carotene, Vitamin C, Folic Acid, Iron

3. Meanwhile, break off tough ends from asparagus, and cut into 2-inch pieces. Seed peppers and cut into julienne strips. Thinly slice green onions.

4. When fish has simmered for 10 minutes, use a slotted spatula to lift fish to dinner plates. Place drained pasta beside fish. Cover to keep warm.

5. Return pan to burner and increase heat to high. Boil sauce, uncovered, for 5 minutes. Add all vegetables, ¼ cup chopped basil and stir until hot, about 2 to 4 minutes. Use a slotted spatula to place vegetables on pasta and fish. Then, boil sauce until thick, about 2 minutes. Pour over pasta and fish. Sprinkle with basil.

10-Minute Salsa Fillets and Creamy Spinach

Keep fish fillets and spinach in the freezer and you have the makings for a healthy dinner any day of the week.

PREPARATION TIME: 10 MINUTES / COOKING TIME: 10 MINUTES

MAKES: 2 TO 3 SERVINGS

10-oz (280-g) pkg frozen fish fillets, thawed
½ cup salsa sauce
2 tbsp grated Parmesan or Asiago cheese
10-oz (300-g) pkg frozen chopped spinach
¼ cup light sour cream

1. Preheat oven to 425°F. Arrange fillets in a 9-inch (1-L) pie plate, overlapping ends. Spoon salsa evenly over top, then sprinkle with Parmesan. Bake, uncovered, in preheated oven for 8 to 12 minutes or until cheese is bubbly.

2. Meanwhile, cook spinach according to package directions. Drain well. Stir in sour cream. Serve with microwaved baked potatoes.

PER SERVING

Calories: 149

Protein: 22 g

Fat: 3 g

Carbohydrate: 8 g

Fiber: 3 g

Excellent source: Folic Acid

Good source: Vitamin C, Calcium

Blazing Vegetable Curry

We're crazy about curry, especially this big-batch number. The most assertive spices and best winter vegetables combine to deliver a blast of healthy taste in every bite. You can make up this big batch and freeze part of it.

PREPARATION TIME: 15 MINUTES / COOKING TIME: 1½ HOURS
MAKES: 8 TWO-CUP SERVINGS

2 large onions
1 tbsp olive oil
4 crushed garlic cloves
2-inch knob fresh ginger, or 1 tsp ground ginger
2 tbsp curry powder
1 tbsp ground cumin (optional)
2 tsp ground coriander (optional)
½ to 1 tsp hot red pepper flakes
½ tsp each of cinnamon, salt and black pepper
¼ tsp each of allspice and dry mustard (optional)
2 (28-oz/796-mL) cans plum tomatoes,
  including juice
2 cups vegetable or chicken broth
1 butternut squash or small pumpkin
6 carrots
1 tbsp sugar (optional)
2 green peppers
1 head cauliflower
Light sour cream
1 bunch fresh coriander, chopped,
  or 3 green onions, sliced

1. Coarsely chop onions. Heat oil in a large wide saucepan set over medium heat. Add onions and garlic and cook, stirring often, until onions start to soften, about 5 minutes. Meanwhile, peel ginger. Grate ginger or finely chop in a mini food processor. Stir into onions along with all seasonings. If not using cumin and coriander, use 3 tablespoons curry powder.

PUMPKIN PREP

Don't be intimidated by a pumpkin's size, it's as simple to cook as squash. To bake: Slice pumpkin in half. Remove seeds and stringy membranes. Place cut-side down on an oiled baking pan. Bake at 325°F until very tender, about 1 hour. Spoon pulp into a food processor and purée. Drain well. A 5-lb (2.5-kg) pumpkin gives about 3½ cups purée. Extra purée can be frozen.

To steam: Cut pulp into 1-inch chunks. Place in a vegetable steamer set over 1 inch of boiling salted water. Cook, covered, for 15 to 20 minutes, until tender. Purée. Add butter and a squeeze of lemon if serving as a vegetable.

Half a cup, boiled and mashed, has a mere 25 calories and a whopping amount of beta-carotene.

PER SERVING

Calories: 209

Protein: 8 g

Fat: 3 g

Carbohydrate: 43 g

Fiber: 11 g

Excellent source:
Beta-Carotene, Vitamin C,
Folic Acid, Iron

Good source: Calcium

2. Add tomatoes and juice to saucepan, breaking up tomatoes with a fork. Add broth. Bring to a boil over medium-high heat, then reduce heat to low and simmer gently, covered, while preparing remaining vegetables.

3. To make squash or pumpkin easier to cut, pierce skin and place in microwave and cook on high for 5 minutes. Meanwhile, peel carrots and slice into 1/3-inch-thick pieces. Stir into simmering curry.

4. Slice squash in half and remove seeds. Slice off peel. Cut into bite-size pieces and stir into curry. Taste and add up to 1 tablespoon sugar, if needed. Cover and continue simmering until vegetables are tender, about 1 hour. If making ahead, curry can be refrigerated or frozen at this point.

5. Seed peppers and coarsely chop. Cut cauliflower stalks and florets into bite-size pieces.

6. When squash is tender, stir in peppers and cauliflower. Cover and continue cooking, stirring often, until cauliflower is done as you like, about 5 more minutes. Just before serving, stir in sour cream and coriander. Or serve with a spoonful of sour cream on top, sprinkled with coriander. Refrigerated curry will keep for several days.

No-Stress Cabbage Roll Casserole

CABBAGE PATCH
Two new cabbage varieties are gaining popularity at the produce counter. Savoy cabbage with its crimped, curly yellow-green leaves has a mild flavor and makes an edible presentation bowl for dips, salads, etc. Napa looks similar to romaine lettuce but is white to light green in color. It too has a mild, delicate taste and makes a delicious side dish when steamed.

This recipe, adapted from Rose Murray, a wonderful cookbook author and even better friend, dishes up all the hearty taste of cabbage rolls for a fraction of the work and no extra fat. Use a food processor for slicing and you can make this comfy dinner in less than 20 minutes. If you want to go vegetarian, skip the meat. You'll never miss it.

PREPARATION TIME: 15 MINUTES / BAKING TIME: 1½ HOURS
MAKES: 6 TWO-CUP SERVINGS

½ large head cabbage
4 large carrots
1 to 2 green peppers, seeded
2 hot peppers, seeded (optional)
1 cup uncooked long-grain rice
1 large onion, finely chopped
3 crushed garlic cloves, or 1 tbsp minced garlic
½ tsp each of salt and freshly ground
    black pepper
½ lb (250 g) ground chicken or beef (optional)
2 (14-oz/398-mL) cans tomato sauce
¼ cup cider vinegar
2 tbsp packed brown sugar
1 tbsp dry mustard

PER SERVING
WITHOUT MEAT

Calories: 248

Protein: 7 g

Fat: 1 g

Carbohydrate: 56 g

Fiber: 7 g

Excellent source:
Beta-Carotene, Vitamin C

Good source: Folic Acid, Iron

1. Slice vegetables using the slicing blade of a food processor. If chopping by hand, coarsely chop cabbage. Thinly slice or finely chop carrots. Chop sweet peppers and finely chop hot peppers. Combine vegetables and set aside.

2. Mix uncooked rice with onion, garlic, salt and black pepper. If using meat or chicken, crumble over top and stir gently until evenly mixed. In another bowl, stir tomato sauce with vinegar, sugar and mustard.

3. Preheat oven to 350°F. Cover bottom of a large (12-cup/3-L) deep casserole dish with tight-fitting lid, with one-third of cabbage mixture. Then, top with half of rice mixture. Repeat layers, ending with cabbage layer. Pour tomato mixture over top. Do not stir.

4. Cover and place in preheated oven. Bake, without stirring, for 45 minutes. Then, remove cover and gently push a spoon down side of dish and baste some of accumulated liquid over top. Do not stir. Cover and continue baking until rice is cooked, about 30 to 45 more minutes. Remove from oven. Top will not look nice. Stir until tomato mixture is evenly mixed with vegetables and rice. Serve with light sour cream, if you wish. Covered and refrigerated, baked casserole will keep well for up to 2 days. If frozen, flavor will not be affected but vegetables will lose some of their texture.

MAKE AHEAD: *Casserole can be made ahead and refrigerated for a couple of hours before baking. If not using chicken or beef, it can be refrigerated, unbaked, for a day.*

Easy-Make Veggie Pizza

Two minutes in a food processor creates a "ready-to-use" yeasty pizza crust. Just roll out, place in pan, top with your favorite veggies and bake.

PREPARATION TIME: 15 MINUTES / COOKING TIME: 6 MINUTES

BAKING TIME: 15 MINUTES / MAKES: 8 WEDGES

DOUGH
1 tbsp liquid honey
¾ cup lukewarm water
1 pkg or 1 tbsp traditional or instant dry yeast
2 ¼ cups all-purpose flour
¾ tsp salt
1 tbsp olive oil

PER WEDGE	
Calories: 257	
Protein: 9 g	
Fat: 9 g	
Carbohydrate: 34 g	
Fiber: 2 g	
Excellent source: Vitamin C	
Good source: Folic Acid, Iron	

FRESH TOMATO PIZZA

Stir 3 seeded chopped tomatoes with 4 sliced green onions and ¼ teaspoon each of dried leaf oregano and basil. Scatter over a regular-size store-bought pizza crust. Sprinkle with ½ cup grated mozzarella or 4 oz (125 g) crumbled goat's cheese. Bake at 425°F for 15 minutes. *Serves 4.*

PIZZA CHEESES — MOVE OVER MOZZARELLA

For taste pizazz, replace mozzarella cheese with:

Ready-to-Use Blends
Look for bags of thickly grated cheese in the dairy section of supermarkets. Four-cheese blends add the most flavor and the price is about the same as if you buy a block of cheese.

Nippy Italian
Many semihard and firm cheeses besides Parmesan have lots of flavor punch. Our favorites: Asiago, sharper and saltier than Parmesan; aged provolone, like a strong-tasting mozzarella; and Pecorino Romano, tangy and pungent.

TOPPING

2 tsp olive oil

1 to 2 large crushed garlic cloves

3 cups thinly sliced vegetables, such as sweet peppers, hot peppers, onions and mushrooms

7 ½ oz (213-mL) can tomato sauce, or 1 cup spaghetti sauce

1 tsp dried basil

½ tsp dried leaf oregano

½ cup grated mozzarella or Asiago cheese

½ cup creamy goat's cheese

1. Preheat oven to 450°F. To make dough, lightly oil a 14-inch pizza pan. In a small dish, stir honey with ½ cup lukewarm water. Sprinkle with yeast, but do not stir. Let stand until foamy, about 5 to 8 minutes. Then, place flour and salt in bowl of a food processor. With machine running, pour in yeast mixture, then oil and remaining ¼ cup hot water. Whirl, stopping and scraping sides of bowl when necessary. If dough is too thick, continue whirling and gradually add water, a tablespoon at a time, until dough cleans sides of bowl and balls up. If dough becomes too sticky, add an additional tablespoon of flour while machine is running. Form dough into a ball. Place on a counter or plastic cutting board. Flatten into a disk.

2. To make topping, heat oil in a large frying pan over medium-high heat. Add garlic and vegetables and sauté, stirring often, until they begin to soften, about 3 minutes. Add sauce and seasonings and cook, stirring often, until sauce is thick and vegetables are almost as tender as you like, about 3 to 4 minutes.

3. Then, using a heavy rolling pin, roll dough out to form a thin circle at least 14 inches wide. Turn over at least once while rolling out. Place on oiled pan and with oiled fingers, firmly press dough around edges to form a thicker rim. Spread vegetable sauce over crust, sprinkle with mozzarella and dot with goat's cheese. Immediately bake on bottom rack of preheated oven until golden, about 15 to 20 minutes. Cut into wedges with kitchen shears.

Spaghetti Squash with Fresh Tomato-Basil Sauce

By cleverly replacing pasta with squash, you up the fiber and slash the calories. For extra punch, grate lots of Asiago cheese over top.

PREPARATION TIME: 15 MINUTES / BAKING TIME: 35 MINUTES

COOKING TIME: 15 MINUTES / MAKES: 4 SERVINGS

3-lb (1.5-kg) spaghetti squash
1 to 2 tsp olive oil
1 small onion, finely chopped
1 crushed garlic clove
4 large ripe tomatoes, peeled and seeded
1 small green pepper, cored and seeded
2 tbsp chopped fresh basil, or 1 tsp dried basil
½ tsp dried leaf oregano
¼ tsp dried leaf thyme
Pinches of salt and freshly ground black pepper
1 tsp granulated sugar
Asiago or Parmesan cheese, grated (optional)

1. To cook squash, preheat oven to 350°F. Pierce squash in several places and place on a baking sheet. Bake, turning halfway through, until tender when pierced with a fork, about 35 minutes. Or microwave on high for 15 minutes. Let stand, covered, for 5 minutes.

2. Meanwhile, prepare sauce by heating oil in a wide frying pan set over medium heat. Add onion and garlic and sauté about 5 minutes. Chop tomatoes and green pepper and add to onion mixture. Then, add seasonings and sugar. Simmer, uncovered, stirring often, over medium heat until sauce is thickened, about 10 minutes.

3. Cut squash in half, scoop out and discard seeds. Draw a fork through pulp and it will separate into spaghetti-like strands. Spoon onto a large platter. Top with tomato sauce, and sprinkle with cheese.

TOMATO FREEZING SAVVY

If you have lots of ripe tomatoes, you can quickly turn them into tomato sauce to store in the freezer. Peel tomatoes and coarsely chop. Then simmer, uncovered, with garlic, onions and chopped peppers until thick. Freeze, so you'll always have pasta sauce on hand.

Or, even faster: Wash and dry whole tomatoes. Seal in freezer bags. Add frozen whole tomatoes to stews, soups and chilies. Skins will burst during cooking and float to surface so you can simply skim them off.

PER SERVING

Calories: 134

Protein: 4 g

Fat: 2 g

Carbohydrate: 28 g

Fiber: 3 g

Excellent source:
Beta-Carotene, Vitamin C

Good source: Folic Acid

Winning 3-Alarm Bean Chili

This classy chili from apprentice chefs Damian Harrington and Ian Riddick of Toronto scooped up first prize in The Great Canadian Chili Contest. It's a smart make-ahead party dish. Top with Hot Pepper and Coriander Salsa.

PREPARATION TIME: 10 MINUTES / COOKING TIME: 45 MINUTES
MAKES: 7 TWO-CUP SERVINGS

1 to 2 tbsp butter or olive oil
4 onions, chopped
6 large crushed garlic cloves
2 tbsp chili powder
1 tsp each of cinnamon and dried leaf oregano
½ tsp each of salt, black pepper and
  cayenne pepper
¼ tsp allspice
28-oz (796-mL) can diced tomatoes
7 ½-oz (213-mL) can tomato sauce
2 cups beef or chicken bouillon, or a 10-oz
  (284-mL) can beef or chicken broth plus
  ¾ cup water, or 2 cups vegetable broth
6 peppers, preferably red, green and yellow
1 bunch fresh coriander or parsley (optional)
2 (19-oz/540-mL) cans red kidney beans, drained

1. Melt butter in a large wide saucepan set over medium-high heat. Add onions, garlic and seasonings. Stir frequently until onions have softened, about 5 minutes.

2. Stir in tomatoes, tomato sauce and broth. Bring to a boil, then reduce heat to low and simmer to develop flavors, at least 30 minutes. Stir often.

3. Then, coarsely chop peppers and coriander and stir in along with beans. Add salt, if you wish. Cook, uncovered, until peppers are as you like, about 10 more minutes. Chili can be refrigerated up to 3 days or frozen.

HOT PEPPER AND CORIANDER SALSA

Seed and finely chop 6 jalapeño peppers. Place in a bowl. Cut 4 large ripe tomatoes in half and squeeze out all seeds and juice. Chop pulp and add to peppers along with 2 tablespoons olive oil, 1 tablespoon white vinegar and ¼ teaspoon each of salt and black pepper. Stir until evenly combined. Then, stir in ½ cup chopped fresh coriander. Serve right away or refrigerate until ready to serve. *Makes 1 cup.*

PER SERVING

Calories: 231

Protein: 14 g

Fat: 2 g

Carbohydrate: 44 g

Fiber: 15 g

Excellent source:
Beta-Carotene, Vitamin C,
Folic Acid, Iron

Elegant Entertaining

WHETHER YOU'RE THROWING A CHIC LITTLE DINNER
for four or a grand party, these luxurious dishes overflow
with a cache of wonderful vegetables and the added
bonus of antioxidants in every bite. Dazzle them with a
bouillabaisse that can be completely made ahead,
except for stirring in the tender seafood, a whole side of
salmon that's baked in 20 minutes then dressed
with a fresh ginger-dill wine sauce, or an intriguing
Moroccan couscous.

Tagine Marrakech

A Moroccan mélange of winter vegetables and tender chicken or lamb in a superb saffron sauce. Serve around a mound of couscous and sprinkle liberally with coriander.

PREPARATION TIME: 10 MINUTES / COOKING TIME: 50 MINUTES

MAKES: 5 TWO-CUP SERVINGS

2 lbs (1 kg) boneless chicken breasts or leg of lamb
¼ cup all-purpose flour
1 to 2 tbsp olive oil
2 large onions
4 large garlic cloves
1 cup white wine
2 tsp ground cumin
½ tsp saffron threads
1 tsp cinnamon
½ tsp salt
1 large acorn squash, or 2 lbs (1 kg) butternut
   or hubbard squash
8 thin carrots
2 cups chicken broth or bouillon
1 cup raisins
Finely grated peel of 1 large orange
¼ cup dry sherry or port (optional)

1. Cut chicken into bite-size pieces or slice lamb into ⅓-inch-thick strips and then into 1- or 1½-inch pieces. Place in a bowl, add flour and toss until coated. Heat 2 teaspoons oil in a very large heavy-bottomed saucepan set over medium heat. Add about ⅓ of chicken or lamb and cook, stirring frequently. Remove chicken as soon as it loses its pink color on surface or lamb as soon as it starts to brown. Repeat with remaining meat, adding more oil if necessary.

2. While meat is browning, coarsely chop onions and mince or crush garlic. When all meat is browned, leave lamb at room temperature but refrigerate chicken.

3. To avoid using more oil, add ½ cup wine to pan and stir to remove brown bits from bottom. Then, add onions, garlic and seasonings. Cook, uncovered, stirring often, over medium heat until onions are soft, at least 10 minutes.

4. Meanwhile, for easy cutting, pierce whole squash and place in the microwave. Cook on high for 5 minutes. Remove from oven. Slice in half and spoon out seeds. Peel and cut pulp into 1-inch pieces. Peel carrots and cut into ½-inch pieces.

5. Once onions have softened, add remaining ½ cup wine and chicken broth. Bring to a boil and stir in lamb and any juices that have accumulated. Do not add chicken at this point. Stir in carrots, squash, raisins and orange peel.

6. Simmer on top of stove, covered, stirring often, for 30 to 40 minutes, or cover and bake in a 350°F oven, stirring occasionally, for 30 to 40 minutes, until vegetables are done as you like. Stir in chicken for last 15 minutes of cooking. Stir in sherry just before serving. Spoon over couscous or rice. Sprinkle with sliced green onion or coriander, if you wish.

SQUASHED TO PIECES

Ever wrestled with a large hard-shelled squash trying to cut it into pieces? Here's an easy method. First, split off stem. Then, with a large sharp knife score squash where you want to cut it. Insert knife into squash and tap it several times with a hammer or meat mallet. Voilà! Squash will split on its own. Or even easier, briefly microwave whole squash, just until skin softens enough to cut through, about 2 minutes.

EXPRESS ENTERTAINING VEGGIES

Here are easy ways to add pizazz to these nutritional all-star veggies. All recipes serve 4.

PEPPERED SPROUTS

Cook 3 cups brussels sprouts until tender. Toss with 1 finely chopped red pepper, 1 to 2 teaspoons butter and freshly grated nutmeg.

CARAWAY CARROTS

Cook 4 cups sliced carrots until tender-crisp. Toss with butter and a light sprinkling of caraway seeds.

CREAMY PEAS

Cook 3 cups frozen peas. Add ½ cup light sour cream and ¼ teaspoon curry powder. Heat through.

FESTIVE SQUASH

Cook a 13-oz (400-g) package frozen puréed squash until hot. Stir in a small dab of butter, light sprinkling of brown sugar and pinch of ground ginger.

CANDIED SWEET POTATOES

Heat a 19-oz (540-mL) can drained sweet potatoes or yams. Mash with 1 teaspoon butter and 1 teaspoon brown sugar. Add a little grated orange peel or juice, if you like.

TURNIP TOSS

Cut medium-size turnip into small cubes. Cook until tender. Toss with ¼ cup light sour cream and ½ teaspoon dried dillweed.

The Great Barbecued Steak Dinner

Christopher Thomas, besides being a popular Newsworld host, is also an avid gardener and barbecuer. Here's his favorite robust steak and grilled garden-vegetable toss — a complete barbecued dinner. The grilled sweet potatoes are an unexpected treat.

PREPARATION TIME: 15 MINUTES / MARINATING TIME: 1 HOUR
MICROWAVING TIME: 14 MINUTES / BARBECUING TIME: 12 MINUTES
MAKES: 4 SERVINGS

4 rib-eye steaks, each at least 1½ inches thick

1 tbsp each of Dijon mustard, Worcestershire sauce and coarsely ground black pepper

4 large crushed garlic cloves

4 large sweet potatoes, about ½ lb (250 g) each, or 4 regular baking potatoes

2 hot banana peppers

6 medium-size firm ripe tomatoes

6 sweet peppers, preferably a mix of red, yellow and green

3 tbsp balsamic vinegar

1 tsp Dijon mustard

½ tsp sugar

¼ tsp each of salt and black pepper

Olive oil

Dried rosemary

½ cup chopped fresh basil

1. Trim fat from steaks and nick edges in several places to avoid curling during grilling. Stir 1 tablespoon Dijon with Worcestershire, pepper and 2 garlic cloves. Firmly press into both sides and edges of steaks. Then, let stand at room temperature for about an hour, or refrigerate for up to a day.

BARBECUED TROPICAL FRUIT KABOBS

Slice peel from a pineapple. Then, slice into thick rings. Remove core. Slice into 1½-inch pieces. Place in a large bowl. Hull 1 pint large, firm strawberries. Slice 2 firm bananas into 1-inch pieces. Stir with pineapple and juice from 1 lime and 2 tablespoons sugar. Thread fruit on skewers, about 5 to 6 pieces per skewer. Place on a greased grill and barbecue, turning often and basting with juices from bowl, just until hot. *Makes 12 skewers.*

PER SERVING

Calories: 570

Protein: 39 g

Fat: 19 g

Carbohydrate: 63 g

Fiber: 11 g

Excellent source:
Beta-Carotene, Vitamin C, Folic Acid, Iron

2. Peel potatoes and slice in half lengthwise. Precook on a piece of paper towel in the microwave, uncovered, on high until almost fork-tender. Two pounds sweet potatoes will need 14 to 16 minutes, regular baking potatoes will need 12 to 14 minutes. Cover until ready to barbecue. Slice hot peppers in half and seed. Slice unpeeled tomatoes in half and squeeze out seeds and juice. Seed sweet peppers and slice, lengthwise, into thirds. In a large bowl, whisk vinegar with 1 teaspoon Dijon, remaining 2 garlic cloves, sugar, salt and pepper.

3. When ready to barbecue, oil grill and set heat to medium-high. Slice potatoes, lengthwise, into 1-inch-thick slices and brush with oil. Generously sprinkle with rosemary and place on grill. Oil peppers and tomatoes and place on grill. Then, add steaks to grill and barbecue for 6 to 8 minutes per side for medium-rare.

4. Turn vegetables and steaks after 5 minutes. As soon as tomatoes are hot and skins have started to brown and curl, remove to a cutting board and coarsely chop. Whisk dressing. Stir in tomatoes and sprinkle with basil. Remove hot peppers. Finely dice and add to tomatoes. When sweet peppers are lightly browned, cut into bite-size pieces and immediately stir into tomatoes. Remove potatoes when golden.

5. Serve barbecued steak, grilled potatoes and tossed, warm grilled vegetables immediately.

RED HOT TOMATO SAUCE

A spiced-up chili sauce for the '90s adds a jolt of wake-up taste to just about anything — from grilled steak to eggs. And no oil is added.

Seed 6 hot red peppers, such as red jalapeño or Anaheim. Finely chop and place in a large saucepan. Peel, core and chop 12 ripe tomatoes. Add to saucepan, along with 2 cups white vinegar. Stir in ½ cup granulated sugar and 1½ teaspoons salt. Tie 1 tablespoon pickling spices in a cheesecloth bag and add to saucepan. Simmer, uncovered, stirring frequently, over medium-low heat, until mixture is quite thick, about 30 to 45 minutes. Store in the refrigerator or freezer. *Makes 4 cups.*

TRUMPETING TOMATOES

You can never have too many ways to serve tomatoes. And remember, half a tomato has only 13 calories and 12 mg of vitamin C.

GARLIC TOMATO BAKE

Slice 2 large firm tomatoes in half and place cut side up, in an oiled baking dish. Brush cut sides with olive oil. Cut 2 large garlic cloves into slivers and insert into tops of tomatoes. Sprinkle with basil, thyme, pepper and salt. Bake, uncovered, at 350°F until hot, about 20 minutes. *Serves 4.*

CAESAR TOMATOES

Slice 2 ripe tomatoes in half. Stir 2 tablespoons light, creamy Caesar dressing with 2 tablespoons Parmesan cheese. Thickly spread over tomatoes. Grill, about 7 inches from broiler, until bubbly. Great with steak. *Serves 4.*

HERBED GARDEN RICE

Cook 1 cup rice. About 5 minutes before rice is cooked, stir in 3 chopped ripe tomatoes, ½ teaspoon dried basil and ¼ teaspoon dried leaf oregano. *Makes 4 cups.*

Rack of Lamb with Moroccan Vegetable Couscous

Herbed-crusted racks of lamb make a beautiful marriage with fragrant couscous and fall vegetables.

PREPARATION TIME: 30 MINUTES / COOKING TIME: 15 MINUTES

ROASTING TIME: 25 MINUTES / MAKES: 4 SERVINGS

WHAT IS COUSCOUS?

Couscous is a form of semolina, the milled center of durum wheat. Pale gold and granular, it's high in protein, making it a good choice for vegetarians. The quick-cook variety of couscous that is widely available takes only 5 minutes to make and has a firmer texture than rice. One cup of couscous contains 200 calories, 42 g carbohydrate, 7 g protein, a trace of fat and no cholesterol.

PER SERVING

Calories: 630

Protein: 37 g

Fat: 13 g

Carbohydrate: 93 g

Fiber: 9 g

Excellent source: Beta-Carotene, Vitamin C, Folic Acid, Iron

Good source: Calcium

LAMB
2 racks lamb
2 tbsp Dijon mustard
2 tsp olive oil
3 crushed garlic cloves
1 tsp dried rosemary, crumbled
½ tsp cracked black pepper

COUSCOUS
2-lb (1-kg) butternut squash
2 cups chicken broth or bouillon
¼ to ½ cup dark raisins
½ cup coarsely chopped clementines or tangerines
1 tbsp each of butter and brown sugar
2 tbsp fresh thyme leaves, or 1 tsp dried leaf thyme
1 tsp each of cinnamon and ground cumin
½ tsp turmeric (optional)
¼ tsp salt
1½ cups couscous
4 green onions, thinly sliced

1. To prepare lamb, trim off any excess fat. Stir Dijon with oil, garlic and seasonings. Spread over meaty sides of racks. Place, coated-side up, on an oiled pan with shallow sides. To prevent tips of bones from burning, wrap top ½ inch with foil. Bring meat to room temperature. Then, roast in a preheated 400°F oven for 25 to 30 minutes for medium-rare lamb. Let stand for 5 minutes before slicing into chops.

2. For couscous, make a small slit in squash and microwave on high, uncovered, for 10 minutes. In a large saucepan, combine chicken broth, raisins, clementines, butter, sugar and seasonings. Place over high heat. Cover and bring to a boil. Then, stir in couscous. Turn off burner and let stand for 5 minutes.

3. Meanwhile, slice cooked squash in half. Remove seeds and peel. Cut into bite-size chunks. Once couscous has stood for 5 minutes, stir with a fork to fluff. Gently stir in green onions and squash. Serve in center of a large platter surrounded with lamb chops. Sprinkle with sprigs of coriander and fresh thyme.

FAST 'N' EASY COUSCOUS

Bring 1¼ cups water to a boil. Stir in 1 cup couscous, 1 tablespoon butter and about ¼ teaspoon salt. Cover and let stand for 5 minutes. Fluff with a fork and serve. *Serves 3 to 4.*

Spanish Chicken

This robust chicken-and-rice bake brings to mind all the flavors of sensuous Spanish cooking — baked garlic, herbed rice and tomatoes, olives and heady capers. Just uncork a bottle of Rioja and enjoy.

PREPARATION TIME: 30 MINUTES / COOKING TIME: 20 MINUTES
BAKING TIME: 45 MINUTES / MAKES: 6 SERVINGS

6 chicken breasts, or 8 chicken thighs
¼ cup all-purpose flour
2 tsp olive oil
1 head garlic
4 large sweet peppers, 2 red and 2 green
28-oz (796-mL) can tomatoes, or 4 large ripe tomatoes, coarsely chopped
½ cup pimiento-stuffed green olives
19-oz (540-mL) can chick-peas (optional)
2 cups long-grain rice
3 cups chicken broth or bouillon
1 tbsp drained capers
2 tsp paprika
¼ tsp salt
½ cup raisins (optional)

PER SERVING

Calories:	466
Protein:	37 g
Fat:	6 g
Carbohydrate:	64 g
Fiber:	4 g
Excellent source:	Vitamin C
Good Source:	Beta-Carotene, Iron

1. Preheat oven to 400°F. Remove skin from chicken. Pour flour into a plastic bag or shallow bowl. Heat olive oil in a large nonstick frying pan set over medium-high heat. Place 2 pieces of chicken in plastic bag and shake until coated with flour. Place chicken, bone-side up, in frying pan. Repeat with 2 more pieces. Sauté until well browned on all sides, about 10 minutes. Remove chicken to a plate and repeat with remaining pieces, adding more oil only if needed.

2. Meanwhile, get out a large (16-cup/4-L) casserole dish with a tight fitting lid. Rub off any loose skin from head of garlic but do not peel or separate cloves. Coarsely chop peppers. Drain juice from tomatoes and cut each tomato into 2 or 3 pieces. Measure out ½ cup olives, then thickly slice. Drain chick-peas.

3. When chicken is removed from pan, add uncooked rice and stir in pan juices until coated, scraping up any browned bits from bottom. Add bouillon to pan and bring to a boil. Then, pour rice mixture into casserole dish. Stir in peppers, tomatoes, olives, capers and seasonings. Add chick-peas and raisins, if using. Stir until seasonings are evenly distributed. Tuck whole head of garlic, root-side down, in center of mixture. Arrange chicken over top with thickest parts of chicken toward outside of pan. Pour in any chicken juices.

4. Cover casserole dish tightly and bake in center of preheated oven until rice is done as you like, about 40 to 45 minutes. If not all liquid is absorbed, remove lid and continue baking for 5 more minutes. Or if all liquid is absorbed and rice is not as tender as you like, add ¼ cup water, cover and continue baking for 5 to 10 more minutes. Remove chicken. Then remove whole head of garlic. Squeeze garlic cloves out of their skins, and mash with a fork. Then, stir into rice mixture. Or serve each guest several whole garlic cloves which can be easily squeezed out of skins. Baked this way, garlic becomes soft and sweet and is wonderful to eat along with the chicken.

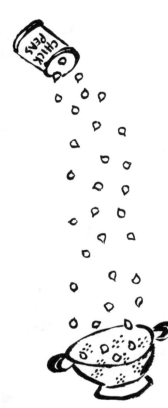

Barbecued Lamb Dinner

Our easy marinade delivers incredibly succulent lamb chops every time. Grill with Garden Vegetable Kabobs, Golden Cayenne Potatoes and, for dessert, Barbecued Tropical Fruit Kabobs (page 64).

PREPARATION TIME: 30 MINUTES / MARINATING TIME: 6 HOURS
GRILLING TIME: 15 MINUTES / SERVES: 4

LAMB

8 loin lamb chops, each 1 inch thick
1 cup white wine or apple juice
2 tbsp olive oil
¼ cup soy sauce
8 crushed garlic cloves
2 tsp dried rosemary, crushed
¼ tsp black or cayenne pepper

GARDEN VEGETABLE KABOBS

4 thin zucchini, preferably 2 green and 2 yellow
2 large peppers, seeded
1 box cherry tomatoes
2 tbsp freshly squeezed lemon juice
1 tbsp butter
1 tsp dried basil

1. Trim fat from lamb chops. Combine remaining lamb ingredients in a large self-sealing bag or bowl. Stir until mixed. Add meat and stir, or manipulate bag, until well coated. Refrigerate at least 6 hours, preferably overnight. Barbecue over hot coals or under oven broiler for 4 to 5 minutes per side for medium lamb.

2. For kabobs, slice zucchini into 1-inch rounds and peppers into 1-inch pieces. Thread alternately on skewers with tomatoes. Combine remaining ingredients in a small heat-proof dish. Set on barbecue to melt butter or melt in microwave. Brush over kabobs. Barbecue or broil until vegetables begin to brown, about 10 to 15 minutes. Turn often and brush with marinade.

GOLDEN CAYENNE POTATOES

Slice 4 potatoes in half, lengthwise. Precook by microwaving, uncovered, on high for 7 minutes, or bake at 350°F for 30 minutes. Potatoes should still be fairly firm. Slice lengthwise into ½-inch-thick slices. Place in a bowl. Drizzle with just enough olive oil to lightly coat. Liberally sprinkle with black pepper, cayenne pepper, salt and ground cumin or chili powder. Barbecue or grill until potatoes are golden, turning often and basting with more oil if they become dry. *Serves 4.*

PER SERVING OF LAMB, POTATO, VEGETABLE AND FRUIT KABOBS

Calories: 271	
Protein: 26 g	
Fat: 12 g	
Carbohydrate: 17 g	
Fiber: 5 g	
Excellent source: Vitamin C	
Good source: Beta-Carotene, Folic Acid, Iron	

Hot Hunan Lamb

A fiery, colorful lamb stir-fry that makes your mouth tingle. Not for the faint of heart. It's a perfect party dish that you can prepare in advance. Just toss in veggies at the last minute. Don't leave out the beer...it's the secret ingredient.

PREPARATION TIME: 30 MINUTES / COOKING TIME: 20 MINUTES

MAKES: 6 TO 8 SERVINGS

2 tbsp ground or minced fresh peeled ginger

8 large garlic cloves, crushed or minced

1 tsp hot red pepper flakes

1½ to 2 lbs (750 g to 1 kg) boneless leg of lamb

1 tbsp peanut oil, or ½ tbsp each of sesame oil and peanut oil

12-oz (341-mL) bottle regular beer

3 tbsp soy sauce

¼ to ½ tsp cayenne pepper

½ tsp salt

2 tbsp sherry (optional)

2 large peppers, preferably yellow

8 green onions

4 small ripe tomatoes

6 cups shredded fresh spinach, about 2 bunches or a 10-oz (284-g) bag

1. Mix ginger, garlic and red pepper flakes together until evenly blended. Trim all fat and any tough white fell from lamb. Slice lamb into ⅓-inch-thick strips, then into bite-size pieces. Toss lamb with garlic-ginger mixture until evenly coated.

2. Heat ½ tablespoon peanut oil or 1 teaspoon each of sesame oil and peanut oil in a large wide saucepan or wok set over medium-high heat. When piping hot, add half of meat and cook, stirring constantly, just until meat loses its red color, about 2 minutes. Remove to a plate. Repeat with remaining oil and meat.

THE FLAVORS OF OIL

When sautéing, use an oil that delivers flavor. Butter and olive oil add appealing taste, yet they contain roughly the same amount of fat and calories as less tasty vegetable oil. Sesame oil has a wonderful roasted sesame seed flavor. Since it smokes at high temperatures, it's best blended with a good frying oil such as peanut oil.

PER SERVING

Calories: 161

Protein: 17 g

Fat: 6 g

Carbohydrate: 10 g

Fiber: 3 g

Excellent source:
Beta-Carotene, Vitamin C, Folic Acid

Good source: Iron

3. Immediately add beer, soy sauce, cayenne, salt and sherry, if using. Return all meat and any accumulated juices to pan. Reduce heat and boil gently, uncovered, stirring often, for about 10 minutes. Liquid will be reduced by about ½ cup. (If making ahead, mixture can now be refrigerated, for up to one day. Reheat gently when ready to proceed.)

4. Meanwhile, seed peppers and cut into ½-inch pieces. Diagonally slice onions into 1-inch pieces. Cut unpeeled tomatoes into 8 wedges.

5. Just before serving, increase heat to high. When boiling, stir in peppers and onions. Cook, stirring often, for 2 minutes. Then, add spinach and tomatoes. Continue stirring just until spinach has wilted and tomatoes are hot. Don't let them get soft. Serve immediately over rice or glass noodles. Great with cold beer.

Salmon with a Fresh Ginger-Dill Vinaigrette

A glamorous way to present a whole side of salmon — on a bed of wilted spinach, bathed with a light and elegant dressing.

PREPARATION TIME: 10 MINUTES / COOKING TIME: 15 MINUTES
BAKING TIME: 20 MINUTES / MAKES: 8 TO 10 SERVINGS

1 cup white wine
½ cup finely chopped shallots
¼ cup finely grated, peeled fresh ginger, or
   2 tbsp bottled minced ginger
2 tbsp sesame oil, preferably dark (optional)
¼ tsp each of salt and freshly ground white pepper
2 tbsp freshly squeezed lemon juice
1 cup finely chopped fresh dill
1 whole boneless salmon fillet, about 4 lbs (2 kg),
   or 8 salmon steaks, each about 1 inch thick
Vegetable oil
6 bunches or 3 (10-oz/284-g) bags fresh spinach
1 bunch green onions

GREAT GINGER

Choose gingerroot that is firm and fresh looking with the least number of protruding knobs.

Gingerroot will keep well, uncovered, in the refrigerator for about 2 weeks — then it starts to dry out. For longer storage, you can peel, cut into pieces, place in a jar and cover with sherry. Seal and keep refrigerated. But, the easiest way to store ginger is to pop it into the freezer. Cut or break off the amount you want to use. If large, defrost in the microwave. Peel, then grate or chop frozen ginger.

Since we despise grating ginger, we usually peel, coarsely chop the root then press through a garlic press. Discard the woody pulp that won't easily go through the press.

PER SERVING

Calories:	325
Protein:	38 g
Fat:	15 g
Carbohydrate:	6 g
Fiber:	2 g

Excellent source: Beta-Carotene, Folic Acid, Iron

GREAT SALMON GRILLS

Here are easy ways to add pizazz to 4 one-inch thick salmon steaks.

French Oriental

Whisk 3 tablespoons teriyaki sauce with 1 tablespoon oil, 1 tablespoon Dijon mustard, ¼ teaspoon ground ginger and 1 crushed garlic clove. Brush over salmon. Grill on barbecue 5 minutes per side, basting occasionally.

Spicy Cajun

Brush steaks with oil. Generously sprinkle with a mix of 1 teaspoon each of chili powder and cumin and ¼ teaspoon each of cayenne pepper and garlic powder. Broil 5 minutes per side.

Teriyaki Glaze

Stir 2 tablespoons each of soy sauce and dry sherry with 1 tablespoon brown sugar, 1 teaspoon grated fresh ginger and 1 crushed garlic clove. Brush over salmon. Broil 5 minutes per side, basting often.

1. Preheat oven to 450°F. To prepare sauce, place wine, shallots, ginger, 1 tablespoon sesame oil, salt and pepper in a saucepan set over medium-high heat. Bring to a boil. Then, reduce heat to low, cover and simmer for 15 minutes. Remove from heat. Stir in lemon juice and dill. Vinaigrette will taste very strong at this point, but will mellow on fish.

2. Meanwhile, prepare salmon by measuring fillet's height at its thickest point. Place fish, skin-side down, on a well-greased baking sheet. Rub top of salmon with vegetable oil. Bake, uncovered, for 10 minutes per inch of thickness, until fish flakes easily with a fork. A 2-inch-thick side of salmon that weighs about 4 pounds (2 kg) will need about 20 minutes. If using frozen fish, do not thaw; simply double baking time. For steaks, rub salmon with oil and place on a well-greased baking sheet. Bake, uncovered, for 10 to 14 minutes or until a knife inserted into center feels warm.

3. While salmon is baking, trim tough leaves from spinach. Wash spinach but don't dry. Slice green onions into ½-inch pieces. Pour about 2 teaspoons sesame oil into bottom of a large saucepan and move pan so oil coats bottom. Place over high heat. Immediately add onions and enough spinach leaves to cover bottom. Add spinach, a handful or 2 at a time, until it all fits into pot. Sprinkle with salt. Continue stirring until spinach is wilted and hot. Turn into a colander to drain. Drizzle with a little sesame oil. Stir in. Then, taste and add more oil, if needed. Spread over platter.

4. When fish is done, use a long wide spatula to transfer to platter covered with wilted spinach, leaving skin from fillet on baking sheet, if you can. Immediately pour warm vinaigrette over salmon and serve.

10-Minute Make-Ahead Chicken Cacciatore

This is the ultimate, weekday entertaining dish. Spend 10 minutes the night before, and all that's left to do is move the dish from the refrigerator to the oven.

PREPARATION TIME: 10 MINUTES / MARINATING TIME: OVERNIGHT
BAKING TIME: 1 HOUR / MAKES: 6 TO 8 SERVINGS

8 skinless boneless chicken breasts
½ lb (250 g) large mushrooms
2 green peppers
1 onion
1 cup white wine
5 ½-oz (156-mL) can tomato paste
28-oz (796-mL) can tomatoes, well drained
4 crushed garlic cloves
1 tsp dried basil, or ¼ cup chopped fresh basil
½ tsp dried leaf oregano
1 tsp salt
¼ tsp freshly ground black pepper
2 bay leaves

1. Place chicken in a lasagna-style dish or casserole that will hold at least 16 cups (4 L). Thickly slice mushrooms. Coarsely chop peppers and finely chop onion. Scatter over and around chicken.

2. Pour wine into a medium-size bowl. Add tomato paste and whisk until evenly blended. Cut tomatoes in half. Stir into wine mixture along with remaining ingredients. Pour over chicken, cover with plastic wrap and refrigerate overnight to allow flavors to blend.

3. When ready to bake, remove casserole dish from refrigerator. Remove plastic wrap and cover with heavy foil. Place in oven and turn heat to 350°F. Bake for 1 to 1¼ hours, or until chicken is cooked.

4. Remove chicken to a serving dish. Discard bay leaves. Stir sauce and spoon over chicken. Serve with rotini noodles, rice or couscous.

PER SERVING

Calories: 185

Protein: 30 g

Fat: 2 g

Carbohydrate: 12 g

Fiber: 3 g

Excellent source: Vitamin C

Good source: Iron

Scallops with Hot and Sweet Red Peppers

Monda first cooked this outstanding dish with Bonnie Stern for a charity dinner. The money it raised couldn't begin to compare with the impression it made. It's wonderful as an entrée over glass noodles, rice or wilted greens or as is for a chic first course.

PREPARATION TIME: 15 MINUTES / COOKING TIME: 6 MINUTES

MAKES: 4 ENTRÉES OR 6 TO 8 APPETIZER SERVINGS

20 dried, whole black mushrooms
  (sold in Oriental stores)
8-oz (237-mL) can strips of bamboo shoots
10-oz (284-mL) can sliced water chestnuts
2 red peppers
2 jalapeño peppers or fresh hot peppers (optional)
¼ lb snow peas (optional)
⅓ cup each of low-sodium soy sauce, rice-wine
  vinegar and light-brown sugar
½ tsp hot red pepper flakes
2 egg whites
2 tbsp cornstarch
1 lb (500 g) scallops, preferably bay scallops,
  or medium-size shrimp, shelled and deveined
Peanut oil

1. When making this recipe for entertaining, all steps except stir-frying can be done ahead. Place mushrooms in a bowl and cover with boiling water. Let stand for at least 15 minutes. When plumped and softened, drain off water. Cut mushroom cap in half, then cut away firm stem portion and discard. Slice moist mushroom caps into ¼-inch strips and set aside.

DRIED MUSHROOMS

Most Oriental foods shops sell large cellophane bags of whole dried mushrooms at a fraction of gourmet store prices.

PER APPETIZER SERVING

Calories: 158

Protein: 8 g

Fat: 4 g

Carbohydrate: 25 g

Fiber: 2 g

Excellent source: Vitamin C

2. Meanwhile, drain bamboo shoots and water chestnuts. (If you purchase whole bamboo shoots and water chestnuts, julienne shoots and slice chestnuts.) Seed sweet pepper and cut into thin strips. Seed and finely dice jalapeños. Combine bamboo shoots, chestnuts and peppers in a bowl and set aside. Remove tips from snow peas and set aside separately.

3. Prepare sauce by blending soy sauce, vinegar, brown sugar and red pepper flakes. A scant ½ teaspoon makes this a fiery party dish. You may want to start with ¼ teaspoon the first time you make it, especially if you've used fresh hot peppers as well. Set sauce aside.

4. About 15 minutes before serving, stir mushroom slices into sauce so they will absorb some of its flavor.

5. When ready to cook, whisk egg whites and cornstarch together in a large bowl. If scallops are large, cut in half. Pat scallops or shrimp dry with paper towels. Then, stir into cornstarch mixture until evenly coated. (This acts as a sealer around seafood, keeping it moist during cooking.) Place coated scallops on waxed paper so excess cornstarch mixture will drain off.

6. Generously coat a wok or large heavy-bottomed frying pan with peanut oil. Warm over high heat. Add about a quarter of scallops and stir-fry over high heat for 30 seconds. Then, using a slotted spoon, remove to paper towels to drain. Repeat with remaining scallops, adding more oil as needed. (Trying to cook more than ¼ pound of seafood at one time cools oil too much and will cause scallops to cook unevenly.)

7. Then, add a scant tablespoon of oil to pan for cooking vegetables. When sizzling hot, add water chestnuts, bamboo shoots and peppers, all at once. Stir-fry over high heat for about 2 minutes. Immediately add mushrooms, sauce, scallops and snow peas. Stir constantly, just until scallops are done as you like, about 2 to 3 minutes.

COOK SMART

Cooking of any kind destroys some nutrients — especially vitamin C and some B vitamins. So cook for the shortest time possible.

- Stir-frying, microwaving and steaming are quick methods that retain the most nutrients.

- When boiling, use as little water as possible so nutrients stay in vegetables instead of going out into cooking water. Don't add veggies until water is boiling rapidly, then cover. An inch of water in the pot is enough. Leafy vegetables, however, need only the water that clings to them after washing.

- Cook vegetables whole and unpeeled, and serve as soon as they're cooked.

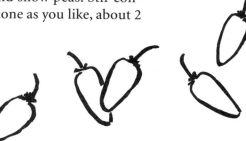

Amazingly Creamy Light Risotto

We guarantee this to be one of the richest-tasting risottos you've ever stirred up, and it has only one teaspoon of butter per serving. With the shrimp, it makes a grand starter or impressive low-cal main course. Without the shrimp it's a wonderful complement to chicken or fish. Asparagus, snow peas and fresh green peas would also be nice additions.

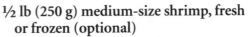

PREPARATION TIME: 10 MINUTES / COOKING TIME: 35 MINUTES

MAKES: 3 TO 4 MAIN COURSE OR 6 TO 8 APPETIZER SERVINGS

½ lb (250 g) medium-size shrimp, fresh or frozen (optional)

2 large peppers, preferably 1 red and 1 yellow

2 tbsp butter

3 crushed garlic cloves

Generous pinch of cayenne pepper

1 onion, finely chopped

1 ¼ cups rice, preferably short-grain Italian Arborio

1 cup finely chopped mushrooms

½ cup dry white wine

¼ tsp hot red pepper flakes

10-oz (284-mL) can undiluted chicken broth

2 (10-oz/284-mL) cans water

¼ cup freshly grated Parmesan cheese

½ cup coarsely chopped fresh coriander

PER APPETIZER SERVING WITH SHRIMP

Calories: 210

Protein: 10 g

Fat: 5 g

Carbohydrate: 30 g

Fiber: 1 g

Excellent source: Vitamin C

1. Clean and devein shrimp. If frozen, do not thaw but rinse under cold water. Seed peppers. Dice or slice into thin julienne strips, then cut into 1-inch pieces.

2. Melt butter in a large wide saucepan set over medium heat. Add shrimp and 2 garlic cloves. Sprinkle with cayenne. Stir-fry just until shrimp are pink, about 2 minutes. Remove to a plate. Add peppers. Stir-fry for 1 minute, then remove to plate. Add onion and remaining garlic clove to pan. Sauté, stirring often, until onion has softened, about 3 minutes. Then, add rice and stir until coated with butter.

3. While constantly stirring rice mixture, immediately add mushrooms, wine and red pepper flakes. Stir gently until rice absorbs wine.

4. Then, add chicken broth. Stir frequently and wait until liquid is absorbed before adding water. (This process is necessary to produce a creamy textured rice.) Add 1 can of water and continue stirring until all is absorbed. Add remaining can of water. Stir frequently until most of water is absorbed and rice is tender but not mushy, about 25 to 35 minutes. (Most people prefer risotto soupy.) Remove from heat.

5. Stir in cheese until evenly distributed, then stir in half of shrimp and peppers. Taste and add salt and white pepper, if needed. Serve immediately in wide shallow soup bowls or deep plates. Scatter remaining peppers over top. Arrange shrimp in a pinwheel shape on top and sprinkle with chopped coriander.

MAKE AHEAD: *After last can of water is added, continue cooking until half of it is absorbed. Cover and refrigerate. Refrigerate shrimp and peppers separately. To finish cooking, reheat over medium heat, stirring often until water is absorbed, and proceed as above.*

GOOD CHOICE PARMESAN

For 25 calories a tablespoon, grated Parmesan provides a lot of taste. A light sprinkle perks up rice dishes or pizza without adding a lot of fat. Or, cut the fat in traditional cheese dishes, such as macaroni and cheese or lasagna, by substituting Parmesan for some of the cheddar or mozzarella.

RICE

Hot Pepper Bouillabaisse with Fresh Coriander

Shellfish in a luxurious hot pepper broth, spiked with lime for an island taste, is our favorite way to serve a crowd. Pass around a basket of oven-toasted thinly sliced baguette brushed with garlicky olive oil.

PREPARATION TIME: 30 MINUTES / COOKING TIME: 50 MINUTES
MAKES: 8 SERVINGS

1 large onion, preferably Spanish

4 hot jalapeño peppers, or 2 (3 ½-oz/114-mL) cans drained green chilies

2 tsp olive oil

8 large garlic cloves, minced

6 cups coarsely chopped, peeled ripe tomatoes, or 2 (28-oz/796-mL) cans plum tomatoes, including juice

8-oz (237-mL) bottle clam juice

1 cup dry white wine

Finely grated peel and juice of 1 small lime

1 tbsp granulated sugar

1 tsp saffron threads

1 tsp dried basil, or ¼ cup chopped fresh basil

½ tsp dried leaf thyme

½ tsp freshly ground black pepper, or ¼ tsp ground white pepper

1 cup chopped fresh coriander

12 littleneck clams, or 2 lbs (1 kg) mussels

1 lb (500 g) firm fish fillets, such as monkfish

1 lb (500 g) shrimp, fresh or frozen

1. Chop onion. Seed and finely chop hot peppers. Pour oil in a large wide saucepan and tilt until bottom is coated. Add onion, peppers, garlic and ¼ cup water. Cook over medium heat, stirring often, until onion is soft, about 10 minutes.

PER SERVING

Calories: 196

Protein: 26 g

Fat: 4 g

Carbohydrate: 13 g

Fiber: 2 g

Excellent source: Vitamin C, Iron

Good source: Beta-Carotene

2. Add tomatoes, clam juice, wine, about 2 table-spoons lime juice, peel, sugar and seasonings. If using canned tomatoes, break into several pieces. Bring to a boil, then stir in half of coriander. Boil gently, uncovered, for 30 minutes to develop flavors and reduce liquid until soup is fairly thick. Stir often. Taste and add salt, if needed. (If making ahead, bouillabaisse can be made up to this point and refrigerated for up to 2 days. Reheat before continuing.)

3. Scrub clams, cut fish into 2-inch pieces, and shell and devein shrimp. Add clams and fish to hot tomato base. Cover and cook for 5 to 6 minutes or until fish starts to firm and clams open. Do not stir but baste fish and clams periodically with tomato mixture.

4. Nestle shrimps in between fish and clams. Cover again and simmer gently, without stirring, until shrimp have firmed and turned pink, about 2 to 4 minutes. Continue basting with tomato mixture.

5. Ladle into warmed soup bowls and serve sprinkled with remaining coriander. Spoon a little mashed roasted garlic into center of each bowl.

LOW-FAT STARTERS
To start a recipe, you don't have to use fat for cooking onions or an onion, celery and carrot mixture. Instead, simmer them in ¼ cup water, broth or wine.

7 Vegetable Paella

Monda's college roommate, Carolyn Lake, discovered on a recent holiday in Spain that there were over 100 variations on paella. This one, courtesy of Carolyn, is the easiest and lightest version we've ever made and it is an impressive vegetarian entrée or a great side dish with chicken or fish.

PREPARATION TIME: 20 MINUTES / COOKING TIME: 30 MINUTES

MAKES: 7 TWO-CUP SERVINGS

4 cups chicken bouillon or vegetable broth, or 2 (10-oz/284-mL) cans undiluted chicken broth and 1½ cups water

1 large onion, chopped

4 garlic cloves, minced

½ tsp saffron threads

PER SERVING

Calories: 295

Protein: 12 g

Fat: 2 g

Carbohydrate: 59 g

Fiber: 6 g

Excellent source: Beta-Carotene, Vitamin C, Folic Acid

Good source: Iron

2 tsp paprika
1 tsp dried leaf thyme
½ tsp salt
½ tsp hot red pepper flakes (optional)
2 large red peppers
2 cups uncooked long-grain rice
2 small thin zucchini
14-oz (398-mL) can artichoke hearts, or
   2 (6-oz/170-mL) jars marinated
   artichoke hearts
4 tomatoes, fresh or canned
6 thin green onions
1 cup peas, fresh or frozen

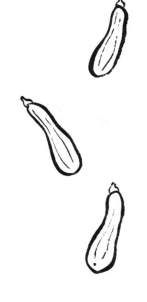

1. Pour chicken bouillon into a large, very wide saucepan. Add onion, garlic and seasonings. Cover and bring to a boil over medium-high heat.

2. Meanwhile, seed peppers and cut into ½-inch pieces. Once broth is boiling, stir in rice and peppers. Cover, reduce heat to medium-low and simmer, without stirring, for 20 minutes.

3. Meanwhile, dice unpeeled zucchini. Drain canned or marinated artichokes well. Rinse with cold water and cut into halves or quarters. Chop tomatoes. Thinly slice green onions.

4. Once rice has simmered for 20 minutes, stir in tomatoes and all remaining vegetables. Cover tightly and continue cooking over low heat until vegetables are hot and rice is done as you like, about 5 to 10 more minutes.

OTHER VEGETABLES: *Depending on the season, you may want to add 2-inch pieces of tender thin asparagus, a cup or two of snow peas or slices of baby carrots at the same time you add tomatoes.*

PLUS SHRIMP AND CHICKEN: *Add thin strips of boneless raw chicken or shrimp along with vegetables for last 5 to 10 minutes of cooking.*

Tantalizing Thai Salad

Thai food generally excites us and one of the fastest ways to satisfy a craving is to toss greens and veggies with a complex, fiery sesame dressing. It goes well as a separate party course or with anything that's barbecued.

PREPARATION TIME: 20 MINUTES / MAKES: 12 SERVINGS

DRESSING

2 tbsp minced or grated fresh ginger

2 large garlic cloves, minced

2 tbsp brown sugar

1 tbsp fish sauce (optional)

2 tbsp sesame oil

⅓ cup peanut or vegetable oil

Freshly squeezed juice of 1 large lime, about 3 tbsp

2 tsp hot chili-garlic paste, such as Sambal Oelek

½ tsp salt

GREENS

2 mangoes, or 2 lbs (1 kg) thin stalks asparagus or snow peas

1 small head leafy green lettuce

1 head romaine lettuce

1 large bunch or ½ (10-oz/284-g) bag fresh spinach

1 small head of radicchio

2 large peppers, 1 red and 1 yellow

2 cups fresh bean sprouts

1 bunch green onions

2 bunches fresh coriander

1. Prepare dressing, preferably a day before using, to give flavors a chance to mingle. Place all dressing ingredients in a jar with a tight-fitting lid and shake until blended. Taste and add more sugar or lime juice, if needed, 1 teaspoon at a time. Let stand at room temperature for up to a day or refrigerate for up to 3 days.

POPEYE SAYS....

Spinach is a source of iron and calcium, and a whole cup has only 12 calories.

- Shred spinach and add to hot pasta, soups, Caesar salad and even a package of macaroni and cheese.

- Add leaves to your favorite sandwich, any vegetable salad, scrambled eggs or frittatas.

- Perk up cooked spinach with dill and light sour cream, grated orange peel and soy sauce, or nutmeg and allspice.

- Use steamed spinach as a bed for grilled fish steaks, beef stir-fries or poached eggs.

PER SERVING
WITHOUT SHRIMP

Calories: 139	
Protein: 3 g	
Fat: 9 g	
Carbohydrate: 15 g	
Fiber: 3 g	

Excellent source:
Beta-Carotene, Vitamin C,
Folic Acid

Good source: Iron

2. If using mangoes, peel and slice into thin julienne strips. If using asparagus, gently break off and discard woody portion of stalks. Then, slice ends of stem to form a smooth cut surface. Diagonally slice asparagus into 2 or 3 pieces. Fill a saucepan with water and bring to a boil. To evenly blanch asparagus and avoid overcooking, divide stalks into 3 or 4 groups of identical widths. If using snow peas, slice off tips and divide into 3 groups. Place 1 group of asparagus in a sieve and hold in boiling water for 1 to 2 minutes. Thin stalks and snow peas will take less than 1 minute, thick stalks no more than 2 minutes. Remove sieve from saucepan and immediately run cold water over vegetables to stop cooking. Repeat with remaining asparagus. Spread out on a cookie sheet and refrigerate. When all are cold, place in a self-sealing plastic bag and refrigerate until ready to use. Vegetables can be prepared the day before using.

3. Prepare salad greens by cleaning lettuces, drying well and breaking into bite-size pieces. Combine in a large bag or bowl. Clean spinach, dry and trim off stems. Add to lettuces. Break radicchio into small pieces and add. Seed peppers and thinly slice. Cut into bite-size pieces. Add to lettuces along with bean sprouts. Slice onions once lengthwise, then diagonally, into 1-inch pieces and add. Clean coriander leaves, dry well and add.

4. Just before serving, add mangoes or asparagus to salad mixture. Shake dressing well and toss with greens until evenly coated. Divide among 8 dinner plates.

FIERY SHRIMP ADDITION: *A pound of hot freshly sautéed shrimp turns this salad into a wonderful appetizer or party luncheon dish. In a jar, combine 2 tablespoons minced fresh ginger, 2 crushed garlic cloves, 1 tablespoon each of peanut and sesame oils and 1 teaspoon hot chili garlic paste. Shake and let stand at room temperature for up to a day. To cook shrimp, place a large wok or saucepan over high heat. (If wok isn't hot enough or shrimp are frozen or wet, they will steam instead of fry.) When piping hot, add ginger-garlic mixture, then 1 lb (500 g) medium-size shrimp. Cook, stirring constantly, just until shrimp turn pink and feel firm. Immediately scatter over prepared salad and serve.*

Vibrant Veggies on the Side

FROM CANADA'S LARGE GARDEN PATCH, WE'VE
highlighted the most nutrient-rich vegetables brimming
with beta-carotene and other antioxidants. Once
you've sampled our Garlic-and-Ginger-Scented Broccoli
with Red Pepper, Winter Greens with Garlic and
Hot Chili Peppers or Fast No-Fat Ratatouille, you'll
never take vegetables for granted again. We guarantee
that a vitamin pill will never have this kind of punch.

MICROWAVE WINTER VEGGIES

Here's a chart to help you get robust vegetables into the microwave and onto the table quickly. Most of these veggies take no more time in the microwave than it will take you to sauté or grill your entrée.

Type	Prepare	Add	Cook on High	Flavor Boosters
BRUSSELS SPROUTS	Trim brown outer leaves. Cut an "X" in root end.	2 tbsp water, chicken or vegetable broth and a dab of butter.	7 to 15 minutes, covered, for 1 lb (approximately 14 brussels sprouts). Stir every 5 minutes.	Lemon juice and peel. Sherry or port. Nutmeg, anise seeds or cumin.
CABBAGE	Remove tough outer leaves. Cut into wedges or shred.	2 tbsp water, broth or white wine.	7 to 15 minutes, covered, for 1 small head (1 lb). Stir partway through.	Dill and sour cream. Vinegar and sugar. Allspice, paprika or cumin.
CARROTS	Peel. Cut into chunks or slice.	2 tbsp orange juice or water and a dab of butter.	8 to 10 minutes, covered, for about 5 carrots (¾ lb). Stir partway through.	Garlic and butter. Cardamom, thyme, nutmeg. Cognac. Brown sugar or honey.
CAULIFLOWER	Remove green leaves. Cut off stem. Cook whole or cut into florets.	2 to 3 tbsp water.	4 to 9 minutes, covered, for 1 lb. Stir halfway through.	Cheddar or Parmesan cheese. Sour cream and paprika. Cumin, coriander, ginger and cayenne pepper.
SQUASH OR PUMPKIN	Pierce skin with a knife to allow steam to escape. Cook whole.		10 to 15 minutes, uncovered, for 1 whole squash or small pumpkin (2 lbs).	Cinnamon, allspice, nutmeg, ginger. Orange juice and peel. Curry and butter.
BROCCOLI	Cut into florets. Arrange with stems near edge of dish.	2 to 3 tbsp water.	2 to 3 minutes, covered, for 1 lb.	Fresh ginger and garlic. Balsamic vinegar and butter. Parmesan cheese. Sesame oil.
SWEET POTATOES	Cut large potatoes in half, lengthwise. Do not peel. Arrange with large ends toward edges of dish.		6 to 8 minutes, uncovered, for 2 large potatoes (1 lb).	Mash with maple syrup and butter. Rub lightly with olive oil and rosemary, or sesame oil and soy sauce.

Beautiful Brussels Sprouts with Red and Green Onions

One shouldn't fool around with sprouts. They're best simply steamed and tossed with butter. But here's a delicious way to dress them up for company.

PREPARATION TIME: 5 MINUTES / COOKING TIME: 15 MINUTES

MAKES: 4 SERVINGS

1½ pounds (750 g) brussels sprouts,
   about 20 sprouts
1 red onion
3 green onions
1 tbsp butter
¼ tsp each of salt and dried leaf thyme

1. Slice off dried section of sprouts' roots and peel off tough leaves. Make a small "X" on bottom of each. Either steam in a vegetable steamer or cook, uncovered, in a pot of boiling water until almost tender, about 8 to 10 minutes.

2. Meanwhile, finely chop red onion. Thinly slice green onions. While sprouts are cooking, melt butter in a large wide frying pan set over low heat. Add onions and sprinkle with seasonings. Sauté, uncovered, stirring often, for 5 minutes.

3. Increase heat to medium. Add hot drained sprouts and stir-fry until piping hot.

SPROUT CORSAGES

Brussels sprouts grow like vertical corsages on a single stalk and usually tower over other garden vegetables — as do their nutritional benefits. Four sprouts contain less than 40 calories and healthy amounts of vitamin A, potassium, folic acid and vitamin C.

MAPLE SPROUTS

Steam sprouts for 8 minutes. Meanwhile, combine 2 tablespoons maple syrup, 1 teaspoon butter and generous pinches of salt, dried leaf thyme and savory in a large saucepan. Stir over high heat until very bubbly, about 2 minutes. Immediately add cooked, drained sprouts. Stir over high heat until glazed, about 2 minutes. Squeeze lemon juice over top. *Serves 4.*

PER SERVING

Calories: 132	
Protein: 6 g	
Fat: 4 g	
Carbohydrate: 24 g	
Fiber: 9 g	
Excellent source: Vitamin C, Folic Acid	
Good source: Beta-Carotene, Iron	

Garlic-and-Ginger-Scented Broccoli with Red Pepper

You'll go a long way to find a better broccoli dish than this beta-carotene-rich partnership.

PREPARATION TIME: 10 MINUTES / COOKING TIME: 10 MINUTES

MAKES: 3 TO 4 SERVINGS

1 large head broccoli

1 red pepper, seeded

1 tsp sesame oil

1 tsp olive oil

2 crushed garlic cloves

1 inch fresh ginger

1 hot banana pepper, seeded and finely chopped

PER SERVING

Calories: 75

Protein: 5 g

Fat: 3 g

Carbohydrate: 11 g

Fiber: 4 g

Excellent source:
Beta-Carotene, Vitamin C,
Folic Acid

1. Cut most of stalk from broccoli florets, leaving just enough to hold florets together. Then, peel away any tough portions on stalk and slice stalk into ½-inch rounds. Divide florets into bite-size pieces. Slice red pepper into thin julienne strips, then cut into 1-inch pieces.

BROCCOLI EXPRESS

SHALLOTS AND MUSHROOMS

Sauté ¼ cup finely chopped shallots and 1 cup sliced mushrooms in 1 tablespoon butter. Toss with 4 cups cooked broccoli. Serve as a side dish or toss with cooked pasta and olive oil. *Serves 4.*

QUICK CITRUS BROCCOLI

Cut 1 large head broccoli into bite-size florets. Peel stalk and thinly slice. Place in a saucepan with 1 inch of water. Cover and bring to a boil. Add florets. Sprinkle with freshly grated peel of 1 orange, a good squeeze of orange juice, salt and pepper. Cover tightly. Cook for 2 minutes or until done as you like. Drain and toss with a little butter. *Serves 4.*

GREEN AND GRAINS

In a medium-size saucepan, bring 1 cup water to a full rolling boil. Add 2 cups small broccoli florets, generous pinches of celery salt and black pepper and ½ cup bulgur. Cook until broccoli is tender, about 2 minutes. Then, cover pan and remove from heat. Let stand for 5 minutes. Toss and serve. *Serves 3 to 4.*

COUSCOUS WITH BROCCOLI

Bring 1¼ cups water to a boil. Stir in 1 tablespoon olive oil, 1 cup chopped broccoli, ¼ teaspoon celery salt, a pinch of cayenne pepper and 1 large garlic clove. Boil 1 minute. Stir in ¾ cup couscous. Remove from heat. Cover and let stand 5 minutes. *Makes 3 cups.*

2. Place oils and garlic in a large wide saucepan. Peel ginger and coarsely chop. Then, place some ginger in a garlic press and crush into pan. Discard pulp. Repeat until all ginger is used. Or grind ginger in a mini chopper.

3. Add ½ cup water to pan. Set pan over medium heat and cook, uncovered, stirring often, until half of liquid has evaporated, about 3 to 4 minutes. This step develops garlic-ginger taste without using a lot of oil.

4. Add banana pepper and broccoli stalks and continue cooking, stirring often, until most of liquid has evaporated and stalks are almost tender, about 3 minutes. Toss in broccoli florets and red pepper. Increase heat to high and stir-fry until florets are bright green and done as you like, about 2 to 3 minutes. Add salt and pepper, if needed. Serve immediately.

BRAVO BROCCOLI

Broccoli is a nutritional powerhouse. One cup supplies about a quarter of your daily requirement of vitamin A, more vitamin C than a glass of orange juice, 6% of your calcium and 9% of your iron. It also has 5 g of protein, provides about 15% of your daily fiber needs and contains 43 calories.

American researchers have identified a chemical in broccoli — sulforaphane — that boosts the body's natural enzyme defenses against cancer-causing chemicals.

ENTERTAINING BROCCOLI

Heat juice of 1 orange, ½ teaspoon dried dillweed and 1 teaspoon butter in a large frying pan. Add 1 large head broccoli, broken into florets. Stir-fry until tender-crisp. *Serves 4.*

RICE AND BROCCOLI

In a medium-size saucepan, bring 1½ cups chicken bouillon, 2 tablespoons frozen orange juice concentrate and ¼ teaspoon salt to a boil. Stir in 1 cup long-grain rice. Cover and simmer over low heat for 15 minutes. Stir in 2 to 3 cups broccoli florets. Continue simmering, covered, for 10 more minutes. *Serves 4.*

HEALTHY MAC AND CHEESE

In a large frying pan, sauté 1 crushed garlic clove in 1 tablespoon olive oil over medium heat for 2 minutes. Stir in 3 cups bite-size broccoli florets, 2 tablespoons water, ½ teaspoon salt and a pinch of cayenne pepper. Cook, stirring often, until broccoli is tender. Pour over 3 cups hot cooked penne along with 1 cup grated cheddar cheese. Toss until pasta is coated and cheese is slightly melted. *Serves 4.*

Sweet 'n' Sour Red Cabbage with Balsamic Vinegar

This is a wonderful colorful companion to roast pork, chops and turkey. And it's great cold the next day.

PREPARATION TIME: 8 MINUTES / COOKING TIME: 25 MINUTES

MAKES: 6 TO 8 SERVINGS

PER SERVING

Calories: 28

Protein: 1 g

Fat: trace

Carbohydrate: 6 g

Fiber: 1 g

Good source: Vitamin C

½ head red cabbage

½ cup chicken broth or bouillon

¼ cup balsamic vinegar or fruit vinegar, such as raspberry or black currant

2 tbsp brown sugar

½ tsp caraway seeds

Pinch of salt

VERSATILE CABBAGE

Versatile cabbage, besides being low in calories, high in vitamin C and a source of fiber, is a member of the cruciferous family. Eating more cruciferous vegetables is recommended by health organizations as a way to lower cancer risk. *All these recipes serve 4.*

WARM DIJON CABBAGE

In a microwave-safe dish, cook 4 cups shredded cabbage, covered, on high for 4 minutes. Whisk 1 tablespoon vegetable oil with 1 tablespoon cider or white vinegar, 1 teaspoon Dijon mustard, ¼ teaspoon sugar and a pinch of salt. Toss with hot cabbage until evenly mixed.

HOT PEPPER CABBAGE

In a microwave-safe dish, stir 4 cups shredded cabbage with 2 chopped jalapeño peppers or 2 tablespoons chopped canned jalapeños, 1 teaspoon butter and ½ teaspoon ground cumin. Cover and cook on high for 4 to 5 minutes, stirring partway through.

FRAGRANT CURRIED CABBAGE

Melt 1 tablespoon butter in a large saucepan over medium heat. Add 2 crushed garlic cloves and 1½ teaspoons curry powder. Sauté, stirring often, until fragrant, about 1 minute. Stir in a 7½-oz (213-mL) can tomato sauce and ¼ teaspoon salt. Lay 1 small head shredded cabbage on top. Cook, stirring often, just until tender-crisp, about 10 minutes.

HERBED CABBAGE

Place ½ head shredded cabbage, ½ thinly sliced red or white onion and 1 cup water in a large frying pan. Cover and cook over medium heat, stirring occasionally, for 15 to 20 minutes. Drain well. Stir in 2 tablespoons white vinegar, 2 tablespoons sugar and ½ teaspoon dried leaf thyme until evenly mixed.

1. Remove tough outer leaves from cabbage. Using a large sharp knife, slice cabbage in half and thinly shred. Or slice cabbage into pieces small enough to fit into a food processor feed tube. Slice using the shredding blade.

2. Measure out about 10 cups shredded cabbage. Place in a large saucepan with all remaining ingredients. Cover, bring to a boil over medium-high heat, then reduce heat to medium-low and simmer gently, stirring often, until tender, about 20 minutes.

Oriental Glazed Carrots

Inspired by a recipe from Madhur Jaffrey, this is an easy way to dress carrots for serving with chicken, pork or fish.

PREPARATION TIME: 5 MINUTES / COOKING TIME: 7 MINUTES

MAKES: 4 TO 6 SERVINGS

8 carrots
1 tsp sesame oil
2 tbsp granulated sugar
1 tbsp each of soy sauce and sherry
Pinch of salt
Finely chopped fresh coriander, parsley
   or green onion (optional)

1. Peel carrots and thinly slice, or cut into thin julienne strips. Place oil and ¼ cup water in a large wide frying pan. Add carrots and cook, uncovered, stirring often, over medium-high heat until liquid has disappeared or carrots are almost done as you like, about 5 minutes. Add remaining ingredients and stir constantly until carrots are coated. Sprinkle with chopped coriander and serve.

SUPERIOR SWISS CHARD

As greens go, Swiss chard is so chock-full of beta-carotene and such a reliable winter green, that you should consider adding it to your winter soups, stews and lasagnas. You can even use it in place of cabbage for cabbage rolls. Or remove stems and simply shred and sauté. A whole cup of steamed sliced chard, either the green- or red-leafed variety, has only 36 calories, and lots of beta-carotene.

PER SERVING

Calories: 71	
Protein: 1 g	
Fat: 1 g	
Carbohydrate: 15 g	
Fiber: 3 g	
Excellent source: Beta-Carotene	

Colorful Cauliflower Curry

When you have a yen for curry, try this swanky low-fat mix of everyday vegetables. Then indulge. It takes no time to make and it's sky-high in nutrients. It's wonderful with roasted chicken or grilled fish, or as a main course with steamed rice and a cucumber raita.

PREPARATION TIME: 15 MINUTES / COOKING TIME: 25 MINUTES

MAKES: 7 ONE-CUP SERVINGS

PER SERVING

Calories: 175

Protein: 5 g

Fat: 3 g

Carbohydrate: 36 g

Fiber: 4 g

Excellent source: Vitamin C, Folic Acid

1 tbsp vegetable oil
1 onion, chopped
2 crushed garlic cloves
2 tbsp curry powder
2 tbsp all-purpose flour
2 cups apple juice or water

FAST-FIX CARROTS

ORANGE SAUTÉ

Sauté 2 cups grated carrots in 1 tablespoon butter, 1 tablespoon brown sugar, ½ cup orange juice and ¼ cup golden raisins until most of liquid has evaporated. *Serves 4.*

HERBED CARROT TOSS

Place 4 thinly sliced carrots in a microwave-safe bowl along with ¼ teaspoon crushed dried rosemary and 1 tablespoon water. Microwave, covered, on high for 4 to 5 minutes. Stir partway through. Drain and toss with a dab of butter, spritz of sesame oil or generous sprinkling of Parmesan, salt and pepper. *Serves 2.*

BBQ CARROTS AND HOT PEPPERS

Thinly slice 4 slim carrots. Place on 2 large pieces of heavy foil. Sprinkle each with 1 teaspoon finely chopped hot pepper, ¼ teaspoon sugar, salt and pepper. Dab with 1 teaspoon butter. Seal carrots tightly in foil. Place on barbecue and grill for 20 to 25 minutes. Turn often. *Serves 2.*

MAPLE AND RUM CARROTS

Cook 3 cups sliced carrots. Heat 2 tablespoons maple syrup, 2 tablespoons butter and 1 tablespoon rum in a pan until it comes to a boil. Toss with hot carrots. *Serves 4.*

LEMON AND HONEY CARROTS

Julienne 8 carrots. Cook in boiling water until tender, about 10 minutes. Meanwhile, stir 2 tablespoons lemon juice with 2 tablespoons honey. When carrots are cooked, drain well. Return to pan with lemon mixture. Stir over medium heat until glazed, about 2 minutes. *Serves 4.*

1 large cauliflower, trimmed
3 large potatoes, peeled
2 large ripe tomatoes, unpeeled
1 cup frozen peas
2 tbsp freshly squeezed lemon juice
¼ to ½ tsp salt

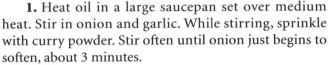

1. Heat oil in a large saucepan set over medium heat. Stir in onion and garlic. While stirring, sprinkle with curry powder. Stir often until onion just begins to soften, about 3 minutes.

2. Stirring constantly, sprinkle onion mixture with flour. Continue stirring until flour is evenly absorbed. Stir in juice or water. (Apple juice will add a pleasant natural sweetness.) Continue cooking, stirring often, until mixture begins to thicken, about 2 minutes.

3. Meanwhile, cut cauliflower into bite-size pieces and potatoes into 1-inch cubes. They should each measure about 4 cups. Stir into curry mixture. Cover and bring to a boil over medium-high heat. Then, reduce heat to low and simmer, stirring often, for 15 minutes.

4. Cut tomatoes into large chunks. After curry has simmered for 15 minutes, stir in tomatoes, peas, lemon juice and salt. Continue simmering, stirring often, until peas are hot, about 3 more minutes.

SMART BRASSICAS

Cauliflower belongs to a class of vegetables called Brassica, also known as cruciferous vegetables since their flowers are cross-shaped. Other brassicas include broccoli, cabbage, kale, broccoflower ® (a newcomer that looks like green cauliflower) and brussels sprouts. Studies show that people who eat lots of cruciferous vegetables have a reduced risk of disease. This may be due to the antioxidants, to the naturally occurring phytochemicals or to other elements in them — or all of these working together.

CLASSY WAYS WITH CAULIFLOWER

MAKE-AHEAD DILLED VEGGIES

Cut 1 large cauliflower and 2 bunches of broccoli into florets. Cook in boiling water until tender-crisp, about 3 minutes. Rinse with cold water. Refrigerate in sealed plastic bag for up to 1 day. Before serving, toss with a dressing of ¼ cup olive oil with 2 tablespoons vinegar, 2 teaspoons Dijon mustard, 2 teaspoons sugar, 1 teaspoon dried dillweed, ½ teaspoon curry powder and ½ teaspoon salt. *Serves 6 to 8.*

CURRIED PARTY VEGGIES

Cut 1 cauliflower into florets. Add to a pot of boiling water along with 2 cups baby carrots or 4 thinly sliced carrots. Boil until tender-crisp, about 4 minutes. Add 1 cup snow peas and boil for 1 minute. Drain and toss with 1 cup sour cream blended with 2 tablespoons chutney, 1 teaspoon curry powder and a pinch of salt. Serve immediately. *Serves 6.*

Winter Greens with Garlic and Hot Chili Peppers

Greens are loaded with beta-carotene and easy to cook. Remember that a big bunch cooks down to a serving for 2. Colorful peppers add panache.

PREPARATION TIME: 5 MINUTES / COOKING TIME: 10 MINUTES

MAKES: 4 TO 6 SERVINGS

3 big bunches Swiss chard, kale or spinach,
or a mixture of all three

1 large sweet red pepper

½ cup water

1 tbsp olive oil

4 large garlic cloves, minced or crushed

1 to 2 tbsp finely chopped hot pepper, or
½ tsp hot red pepper flakes

½ tsp granulated sugar

¼ tsp salt

Chopped fresh coriander or basil (optional)

1. Wash greens. Remove and discard any tough stems. Slice greens into 1- or 1½-inch-wide strips. Seed and slice sweet pepper into thin julienne strips.

2. Just before serving, combine water and remaining ingredients in a very large saucepan or wok. To develop flavors, boil gently over medium-high heat until most of liquid has evaporated, about 5 minutes. Increase heat to high. Add as much of greens to pan as it will comfortably hold, then stir in remainder as soon as there is room. Continue cooking, stirring often, just until greens are tender-crisp, about 5 minutes. Drain well, if necessary, and serve immediately. Great sprinkled with chopped fresh coriander or basil.

GUTSY GREENS

Kale, collard and mustard greens have to be some of the gutsiest greens going. Bursting with nutrients, kale and its cousins provide an excellent source of vitamins A and C, and a source of calcium and iron. In the vegetable family, kale is outstanding because of its high level of available calcium per serving. Doctors and dietitians recommend it as a source of calcium for people who don't eat dairy products. As if all this isn't enough, kale is also high in beta-carotene and has only 42 calories per cup.

PER SERVING

Calories: 56

Protein: 3 g

Fat: 2 g

Carbohydrate: 8 g

Fiber: 3 g

Excellent source:
Beta-Carotene, Vitamin C

Good source: Iron

Wilted Greens

Be sure to include Swiss chard in your vegetable repertoire. It's an excellent source of beta-carotene and takes little time to cook. This recipe also works well with kale, beet greens or collards.

PREPARATION TIME: 5 MINUTES / COOKING TIME: 5 MINUTES

MAKES: 4 SERVINGS

2 large bunches Swiss chard
1 tsp sesame oil
1 tsp soy sauce

1. Trim and discard any tough stems from Swiss chard. Roughly slice leaves into ½-inch pieces. Bring ½ cup water to a boil in a large, wide deep frying pan or saucepan set over medium-high heat. Add greens and cook, stirring often until tender, about 5 minutes. Drain off all water. Sprinkle with sesame oil and soy sauce. Stir until evenly mixed. Serve immediately.

PER SERVING

Calories: 34

Protein: 2 g

Fat: 1 g

Carbohydrate: 5 g

Fiber: 2 g

Excellent source:
Beta-Carotene

Good source: Vitamin C, Iron

Peppers with a Roast

Besides the usual potatoes and onions around the Sunday roast, why not add peppers for color and beta-carotene.

PREPARATION TIME: 5 MINUTES / ROASTING TIME: 30 MINUTES

MAKES: 8 SERVINGS

4 large peppers, preferably different colors
Olive or vegetable oil
Freshly ground black pepper

1. Cut peppers into quarters, then core and seed. Brush with oil. Place on a baking sheet, cut-side down. Place in the oven during final 30 minutes of roast's cooking time, preferably at 375°F, until peppers are softened and lightly browned. Stir at least once. Sprinkle with pepper before serving. If there is room, peppers can be cooked in roasting pan along with meat.

PER SERVING

Calories: 37

Protein: 1 g

Fat: 2 g

Carbohydrate: 5 g

Fiber: 2 g

Excellent source: Vitamin C

Good source: Beta-Carotene

Modern Mashed Potatoes

Our friend Philip Greey makes the best butter-laden mashed potatoes we've ever had. Here's our cheater version — made with buttermilk, an amazingly low-fat yet buttery-tasting substitute. Don't skimp on the garlic.

PREPARATION TIME: 15 MINUTES / COOKING TIME: 40 MINUTES

MAKES: 4 SERVINGS

4 large potatoes
4 large, whole unpeeled garlic cloves
½ to ⅔ cup buttermilk or light sour cream
Salt and ground white pepper

1. Cut unpeeled potatoes in half. Place in a saucepan with garlic and about ½ teaspoon salt. Generously cover with warm water and bring to a boil. Then, adjust heat and boil gently until potatoes are very soft, about 30 to 40 minutes. Drain potatoes and garlic. Peel and place in a mixing bowl. (Don't do this in a food processor or you'll make glue.) Peel whole garlic cloves and add. Mash garlic with a fork. Then, mash potatoes with a potato masher. Using a spoon or electric mixer, gradually whip in ¼ cup buttermilk. Then, continue adding the milk, 1 to 2 tablespoons at a time, just until light and creamy. Add salt and white pepper as needed. Serve immediately.

CURLY KALE

These frilly green leaves, often purple tipped, have a pleasant, cabbagey taste and are a rich source of beta-carotene, calcium and iron. Buy just what you can use — even stored in the refrigerator, kale develops a bite as it sits. Wash, and remove tough center ribs, then simmer in soups and stews, sauté in butter and garlic and mix with potatoes, or toss with a warm bacon dressing.

PER SERVING

Calories: 172

Protein: 5 g

Fat: trace

Carbohydrate: 38 g

Fiber: 3 g

Good source: Vitamin C

BEAUTIFUL BUTTERMILK

Buttermilk deserves a better name for these fat-conscious times. You might assume that it's thick with heavy butterfat but that's not the case. Actually, the reverse is true — buttermilk often contains less fat and calories than 2% milk. Originally, it was the natural liquid formed when butter was churned out of whole milk. The high-fat milk solids ended up in the butter and the slightly sour liquid that separated off was called buttermilk.

Most of the buttermilk sold today, however, is made by adding a bacterial culture to skim or partially skimmed milk, producing a wonderfully thick and surprisingly rich-tasting "cultured buttermilk".

If you're counting calories or fat, an 8-oz glass of buttermilk seems refreshingly colder and certainly more filling than regular thinner skim milk. Yet, it contains only 99 calories and 2 g of fat.

Creamy Sweet Potatoes

Sweet potatoes pair up eloquently with orange and a hint of ginger. A fitting companion to any special entrée.

PREPARATION TIME: 5 MINUTES / BAKING TIME: 1½ HOURS

MAKES: 6 HALF-CUP SERVINGS

4 large sweet potatoes, about 2 lbs (1 kg)
½ cup light sour cream
2 tbsp frozen orange juice concentrate
Pinches of ginger, salt and white pepper

1. Preheat oven to 400°F. Pierce unpeeled sweet potatoes with a fork and place in a shallow baking pan. Bake until very tender, about 1 hour. When cool enough to handle, peel and cut into 1-inch pieces.

2. Purée sweet potatoes in a food processor, or mash in a bowl using a potato masher or fork. Then, mix in sour cream, orange juice concentrate and seasonings. If using a food processor, whirl, using an on-and-off motion, until mixture is smooth. Scrape down sides of processor often to ensure a smooth purée.

3. If warm enough, serve right away or transfer to a baking dish. Cover and bake at 350°F until piping hot, about 20 minutes, or warm in the microwave on medium, stirring occasionally. If making ahead, cover and refrigerate for up to a day. Reheat, covered, in a 350°F oven or in the microwave.

SPRUCE UP SWEET POTATOES

- Bake, remove from skins and mash. Spice with cinnamon and nutmeg. Return to skins.
- Mash, and perk up with frozen orange juice concentrate, sesame oil, rum, mace or cumin.
- Swirl with white mashed potatoes.
- Thinly slice and bake in orange juice.
- Thickly slice, oil, sprinkle with rosemary and bake.

PER SERVING

Calories: 124	
Protein: 3 g	
Fat: 1 g	
Carbohydrate: 26 g	
Fiber: 3 g	
Excellent source: Beta-Carotene	
Good source: Vitamin C	

SWEET POTATOES OR YAMS

Sweet potatoes aren't potatoes at all — they're tubers related to morning glories. There are two kinds, reddish-brown-skinned ones with deep-orange, sweet flesh (often mislabeled "yams") and lighter-skinned yellow-flesh ones with much less flavor. Both are rich in beta-carotene. The true yam is a white, starchy, much less nutritious root not grown in North America but sold in some Caribbean markets. Sweet potatoes don't keep well, so buy only what you can use within a few days. Store at room temperature. Boil, unpeeled, for 35 to 45 minutes, or bake at 400°F for about 45 minutes.

FRUIT AND VEGGIE GRILL CHART

Grilling vegetables right along with your entrée is one of the smartest and most delicious health moves you can make. Note: When foil wrapping, make packages fairly flat and no more than 1½ inches thick.

Type	Preparation	How to Grill	Great with
CARROTS	Thinly slice, dot with butter and drizzle with maple syrup, orange juice concentrate or orange liqueur. Foil wrap.	Grill for 15 to 25 minutes. Turn packages often.	Grilled chicken, steak or sausages.
CORN	Use plain butter or mix with hot red pepper flakes, chopped chives or basil. Spread over corn and foil wrap. Or precook, brush with oil or butter and heat directly on grill.	Grill foil-wrapped corn for 20 to 25 minutes. Turn often. Remove from foil and place directly on grill for 5 minutes.	Grilled steak, burgers and roasts.
EGGPLANT	Slice lengthwise into ½-inch-thick slices. Sprinkle with salt and brush with olive oil.	Baste with herbed or garlic oil. Grill, covered, for 15 to 18 minutes. Turn often.	Chicken and lamb. Chop and mix with diced tomatoes, chopped fresh basil and garlic.
PEACHES	Peel and remove stone. Slice into wedges and foil wrap.	Add butter, brown sugar, cinnamon or rum to package. Grill for 10 to 15 minutes. Turn often.	Pork and chicken. Wonderful with cheese, yogurt, light sour cream or ice cream.
PEPPERS	Slice into thirds, lengthwise. Remove seeds. Brush with oil.	Baste with oil. Grill until slightly charred, about 5 to 10 minutes. If you want to peel, seal in a bag for 10 minutes, then peel. Or foil wrap and grill for 15 to 20 minutes. Turn often.	Steak, pork or burgers, or add to a salad. Peel and purée for an elegant sauce for chicken or fish.
POTATOES	Partially precook whole, then cut lengthwise into ½-inch pieces. Brush with oil and reheat on grill.	Baste with olive oil, or Italian dressing. Sprinkle with black pepper, rosemary or cayenne pepper. Grill for 8 to 12 minutes. Turn often.	Chops, steak or sausages.
TOMATOES	Slice in half and brush with olive oil.	Baste with garlic and oil, Caesar or creamy cucumber-style dressing. Grill for 5 to 6 minutes per side. After turning cut-side-up, sprinkle with basil or feta.	Steak or chops. Toss in salads or over burgers.

Our Favorite Roast Vegetables

We love roasted vegetables, and here's the easiest way to achieve a gorgeous caramelized flavor. They're great with a roast lamb or capon, or for a comfort dinner after a weekend visit to the market.

PREPARATION TIME: 15 MINUTES / BAKING TIME: 30 MINUTES

MAKES: 6 TO 8 SERVINGS

3 large green peppers
2 large red onions
3 sweet potatoes
1 small butternut squash
2 tbsp olive oil
2 tbsp brown sugar
1 tsp dried basil
¾ tsp salt

1. Preheat oven to 400°F. Seed peppers and cut into 2-inch (5-cm) pieces. Peel onions and slice each into 8 wedges. Peel potatoes and squash. Cut squash in half and remove seeds. Cut potatoes and squash into 2- to 2 ½-inch cubes. It's important to keep vegetables about the same size. Remember, they will shrink in cooking.

2. In a large bowl, toss vegetables with oil. Sprinkle with remaining ingredients and stir until evenly distributed. (Don't scrimp on sugar or salt.) Lightly oil the largest oven dish you have, such as a broiler pan or 2 (9x13-inch/3-L) pans. Spread vegetables out in pan. Don't crowd. Roast in preheated oven until tender and browned, about 30 to 45 minutes. Stir every 10 minutes.

VEGETABLE VARIATIONS: *White baking potatoes work beautifully in the roast mixture and there's no need to peel them. Red-skinned potatoes will add color. Consider regular onions or pumpkin, as well as a mix of sweet peppers to add a blast of color. Besides basil, a teaspoon each of dried leaf thyme and crushed rosemary are very good, especially if you're serving veggies with roast pork.*

SATISFYING WAYS WITH PURÉED SQUASH

Puréed squash is beta-carotene and fiber rich. A half cup has 40 calories. Perk up a package of frozen, cooked puréed squash by stirring in:

- Finely grated peel of half an orange and a couple tablespoons of sour cream

- A drizzle of maple syrup, a dab of butter and a pinch of nutmeg

- Pinches of cinnamon, allspice and brown sugar

- A sprinkle of curry powder, ground cumin and a dab of sour cream

PER SERVING

Calories: 173

Protein: 3 g

Fat: 4 g

Carbohydrate: 35 g

Fiber: 6 g

Excellent source:
Beta-Carotene, Vitamin C

Good source: Folic Acid

Fast No-Fat Ratatouille

Ratatouille is the essence of French country cooking — a cornucopia of harvest vegetables and fresh herbs simmered in olive oil. The choice of vegetables, depth of seasonings, and whether it's served hot, cold or at room temperature, depends solely on the whim of the cook. Here's the fastest version imaginable. It's overflowing with vitamins and makes a healthy topper for pasta.

PREPARATION TIME: 10 MINUTES

MICROWAVING TIME: 15 MINUTES / MAKES: 3 TO 4 SERVINGS

2 cups cubed peeled eggplant

2 large coarsely chopped tomatoes, including juice

1 small onion, finely chopped

3 crushed garlic cloves

1 tbsp chopped capers

¼ cup chopped fresh basil, or ½ tsp dried basil

½ tsp dried leaf oregano

¼ tsp salt

1 large green pepper, seeded and diced

1. Stir together all ingredients, except green pepper, in a 9-inch (1-L) pie plate. Microwave, uncovered, on high for 5 minutes. Stir in green pepper and continue cooking, uncovered, on high for 10 more minutes, stirring partway through. Toss with about 4 cups hot cooked pasta and generously sprinkle with grated Parmesan cheese. Ratatouille is also wonderful with chicken or steak, on top of scrambled eggs or heaped on a goat's cheese or sliced roast beef sandwich. We love it hot or cold.

MICROWAVE SQUASH SAVVY

When a whole squash is microwaved, steam forms inside. So always pierce skin several times with a small sharp knife to let it escape. If you forget, squash may explode. Microwave pierced whole or half squash on high, uncovered. An acorn squash will need 8 to 12 minutes. Two squashes will take 12 to 16 minutes. A spaghetti squash needs about 15 minutes. Turn once halfway through. Let stand for 5 to 10 minutes to allow heat to penetrate to center.

PER SERVING

Calories:	51
Protein:	2 g
Fat:	trace
Carbohydrate:	12 g
Fiber:	3 g
Excellent source:	Vitamin C

Kid Pleasers

*F*AST CHILI FAJITAS, FRECKLE MEAT LOAF AND
*Adam's Awesome Chocolate Cake have more appeal
than raw carrots or cooked broccoli — no matter what
your age. These nutrient-rich recipes loaded with hidden
veggies will have your kids craving foods that are good
for them without even knowing it.*

Freckle Meat Loaf

You'll find this old-fashioned no-fuss meat loaf one of the juiciest and most flavorful you've ever made. The secret — chopped veggies, Italian-flavored sauce and healthy oatmeal baked right into the loaf.

PREPARATION TIME: 10 MINUTES / MICROWAVING TIME: 6 MINUTES

BAKING TIME: 1 HOUR / MAKES: 8 SLICES

CRUNCH AND MUNCH

Young children sometimes prefer vegetables raw. Leave theirs out of the cooking when making a family meal. Some children even like frozen peas as a snack.

PER SLICE

Calories: 219	
Protein: 19 g	
Fat: 11 g	
Carbohydrate: 10 g	
Fiber: 2 g	
Excellent source: Beta-Carotene	
Good source: Iron	

1 cup spaghetti sauce or Italian tomato sauce, or a 7 ½-oz (213-mL) can tomato sauce

½ onion, finely chopped or grated

3 small carrots, coarsely grated or very finely chopped

¾ cup old-fashioned or quick-cooking oatmeal

2 eggs

1 ½ lbs (750 g) lean ground beef

1 ½ tsp Italian seasoning, or 1 tsp dried basil and ½ tsp dried leaf oregano

½ tsp salt

¼ tsp freshly ground black pepper

¼ cup finely chopped parsley, or 2 thinly sliced green onions

BETA-CAROTENE MORNINGS

Pumpkin is a wonderful, rich source of beta-carotene. Here are delicious ways to add it to your children's favorite breakfast foods.

JACK O'LANTERN PANCAKES

When making pancakes, add ½ cup canned pumpkin and ½ teaspoon sugar for each cup of milk used in your recipe. After plopping batter in pan, arrange raisins on top side in a "happy face" pattern.

HARVEST BRAN MUFFINS

Make up a bran muffin mix, reducing water called for by ¼ cup and stirring in ½ cup canned pumpkin and ½ teaspoon cinnamon. *Makes 12 muffins.*

BREAKFAST SANDWICHES

Make up the Harvest Pumpkin Bread on page 118. For some extra protein, stir in ½ cup chopped nuts. Thickly slice and spread with peanut butter or cream cheese.

1. Preheat oven to 350°F. Stir ⅔ cup sauce with onion and carrots in a microwave-safe dish. Save remaining sauce to glaze meat loaf. Cover and microwave on high for 6 minutes, stirring twice, until vegetables have softened. Stir in oatmeal. Or cook in a small saucepan set over medium heat, stirring often, until vegetables have softened, about 10 minutes. Remove from heat and stir in oatmeal.

2. Meanwhile, whisk eggs in a large mixing bowl. Add beef, seasonings and parsley. Using your hands, mix until blended. Then, stir in tomato-oatmeal mixture.

3. Turn into a lightly greased 9x5-inch (1.5-L) loaf pan and pat down. Or shape into a 1½-inch-thick loaf on a greased baking sheet with shallow sides. Bake in preheated oven for 45 minutes. Pour off juices. Spoon remaining sauce over top. Continue baking until top has browned, about 20 to 25 more minutes. For an easy oven dinner, bake potatoes in the oven at the same time and add a salad or cooked vegetables. Meat loaf will keep well in the refrigerator for up to 3 days. Thinly sliced cold meat loaf makes a great sandwich.

MAKE-A-FACE-LUNCH

Spread English muffins, toast rounds, pitas or tortillas with cream cheese, cheese spread or peanut butter. Let kids add a face. Grated carrots, alfalfa sprouts and celery leaves make great hair. Carrot coins, dried apricots, raisins or banana slices add eyes. Cashews, dates, pineapple tidbits, sliced celery or carrot tips create stick-out noses. Full mouths can be cut from red-skinned apples, beets, dill pickles, canned apricots or peaches.

HOT DOGS AND VEGGIES

Hot dogs have universal kid-appeal but remember, even if you choose chicken or veal, they're still high in fat. Here are some easy ways to sneak some extra nutrition into your child's favorite dinner. These recipes work equally well with a can of tuna, leftover chicken, ham or even cut-up fish sticks.

SWEET'N'SOUR DINNER

In a frying pan, stir 2 tablespoons sugar with 3 tablespoons cornstarch. Stir in juice from a 14-oz (398-mL) can pineapple chunks. Cook over medium heat, stirring frequently, for 3 minutes. Add pineapple, 6 sliced wieners, 2 tablespoons vinegar, 2 tablespoons soy sauce and 1 chopped green pepper. Continue cooking, stirring often, until wieners are hot, about 5 more minutes. Great over rice. *Serves 4.*

SKILLET SPANISH RICE

In a wide frying pan, bring a 28-oz (796-mL) can tomatoes, with juice, to a boil. Break up tomatoes. Stir in 4 sliced wieners, 1 cup uncooked rice, 1 chopped zucchini, ½ teaspoon salt or garlic salt and ½ teaspoon dried leaf thyme. Cover and simmer for 20 minutes. *Serves 2 to 4.*

SUPPER SPAGHETTI TOSS

In a saucepan, combine 4 thinly sliced wieners, 1 cup spaghetti sauce and 1 cup frozen mixed vegetables or peas. Cover and cook over medium heat, stirring often, until hot. Or heat in the microwave, covered, on high for 5 minutes, stirring halfway through. Toss with cooked spaghetti. *Makes 2 cups sauce.*

Fast Chili Fajitas

Fajitas are fun food that kids can build themselves. Set out baskets of warm flour tortillas and lots of small dishes filled with toppings. If your children don't like spices, add just a sprinkle of chili powder.

PREPARATION TIME: 10 MINUTES / COOKING TIME: 5 MINUTES

MAKES: 8 TO 10 FAJITAS

1 large onion

2 peppers, preferably 1 red and 1 green

¾ lb (375 g) sirloin steak, or 3 chicken breasts, skinned and boned

2 tsp vegetable oil

2 large crushed garlic cloves

1 tbsp chili powder

2 tsp ground cumin

1 tsp dried leaf oregano

¼ tsp each of salt and freshly ground black pepper

⅓ cup salsa or spaghetti sauce

2 large ripe tomatoes, chopped

Pinch of cayenne pepper (optional)

10 tortillas

Shredded lettuce (optional)

Chopped avocado (optional)

Light sour cream (optional)

1. Slice onion and peppers into ¼-inch strips. Slice meat or chicken into thin narrow strips.

2. Heat oil in a large frying pan set over medium-high heat. Add steak or chicken and cook, stirring often, until meat is lightly browned or chicken loses its pink color, about 2 to 3 minutes. Push to edges of frying pan.

3. Reduce heat to medium. Add onion, peppers, garlic, chili powder, cumin and oregano. Sauté for 2 minutes, stirring often, or until onion is soft. Stir in salt, pepper, salsa, tomatoes and cayenne.

COWBOY CHILI AND SHERIFF TOAST

Cowboys used to add whatever they had on the range to their chili. So, start with a can of chili and let kids choose from whatever vegetables you have on hand — tomatoes, corn niblets, mixed veggies, chopped peppers — and add to their own bowl of chili. Heat in the microwave. Serve with a sheriff's badge (stars cut from toast). Write their name on the toast with a squeeze bottle of ketchup.

FILL AND SPILL TACOS

For make-your-own dinners, let the kids fill tacos with shredded cheese, lettuce and carrots; chopped tomatoes, peppers, and green onions; and spaghetti or salsa sauce.

PER FAJITA

Calories: 212	
Protein: 12 g	
Fat: 5 g	
Carbohydrate: 30 g	
Fiber: 2 g	
Excellent source: Vitamin C	
Good Source: Iron	

4. When mixture is hot, spoon into warm tortillas. Top with shredded lettuce, chopped avocado and light sour cream, if you wish. Roll up and serve immediately.

VEGETARIAN MIX: *Omit meat and double vegetables. Top with lots of grated cheddar or crumbled feta cheese.*

Video Night Pizza

Pizza is synonymous with chill-out evenings and fast food — especially when you follow our way to heap a lot of well-cooked vegetables on a store-bought crust without making it soggy. Buon appetito!

PREPARATION TIME: 10 MINUTES / COOKING TIME: 7 MINUTES
BAKING TIME: 15 MINUTES / MAKES: 6 TO 8 WEDGES

1 tbsp olive oil

1 crushed garlic clove

3 cups thinly sliced vegetables, such as onions, peppers, baby corn, mushrooms, carrots, cauliflower and broccoli

7 ½-oz (213-mL) can tomato sauce

¾ tsp dried leaf oregano

½ tsp dried basil

½ tsp hot red pepper flakes, or ¼ tsp cayenne pepper (optional)

12-inch store-bought pizza crust

Sliced cooked meat, such as chicken, ham or pepperoni (optional)

2 cups grated mozzarella cheese

1. Preheat oven to 425°F. Heat oil in a large nonstick frying pan set over medium-high heat. Add garlic and vegetables to pan. Sauté, stirring often, until vegetables have softened, about 5 minutes. Add tomato sauce and seasonings. Cook, stirring frequently, until sauce is thick and vegetables are well cooked, about 2 to 3 more minutes. Spread over pizza crust. Scatter meat over top and sprinkle with cheese. Bake in center of preheated oven until cheese is golden, about 15 to 20 minutes.

PRONTO PIZZA CRUSTS

For cheater "homemade" pizza crusts, place 1 loaf of store-bought, frozen bread dough in a microwave-safe bowl. Cover with lightly greased waxed paper. Microwave on defrost for 5 minutes, turning dough once. Let stand, covered, for 5 minutes. Roll out dough firmly and place on a greased 14-inch pizza pan. Add toppings. Bake in a 400°F oven for about 18 minutes.

BABY PIZZAS

Spread tomato sauce on half an English muffin or bagel. Let your kids pick their favorite vegetables or fruit to add on top — peppers, mushrooms, onions and pineapple. Sprinkle with grated mozzarella cheese and bake at 375°F until cheese is melted. Or make on a pita and heat in the microwave.

PER WEDGE WITHOUT MEAT

Calories: 220	
Protein: 10 g	
Fat: 10 g	
Carbohydrate: 22 g	
Fiber: 2 g	
Good source: Beta-Carotene, Calcium	

One-Pot Mac and Cheese with Trees and Twigs

Canada's ultimate comfort dinner — homemade macaroni and cheese — in just a little more time than it takes to open a package. Add whatever veggies your kids like best. (Chop carrots small enough and no one will know they're there!)

PREPARATION TIME: 10 MINUTES / COOKING TIME: 18 MINUTES

MAKES: 4 TO 6 SERVINGS

PER SERVING

Calories: 323

Protein: 16 g

Fat: 13 g

Carbohydrate: 36 g

Fiber: 3 g

Excellent source:
Beta-Carotene, Calcium

Good source: Vitamin C,
Folic Acid

2 cups elbow macaroni

2 carrots

7-oz (200-g) bag shredded cheddar cheese,
 or 2 cups grated cheddar

2 tbsp cornstarch

½ tsp salt

1½ cups milk

2 cups small broccoli florets

QUICK WAYS WITH MAC AND CHEESE

Just because it's fast and kid-friendly doesn't mean Mac and Cheese made from a package is a nutritional cop-out. A quarter of a box (what nutritionists call a serving) is an excellent source of iron, riboflavin and thiamine. It contains 289 calories, 9.2 g protein, 10.9 g fat, 109 mg calcium. To beef up its good-for-you profile with vitamins and minerals, check out our fast additions. *Each serves 3 or 4.*

HAM 'N' PEAS

Add 1 cup frozen peas to macaroni for last 3 minutes of cooking. Stir in remaining ingredients along with 1 tablespoon regular mustard and 1 cup chopped ham, chicken or tuna.

ANY VEGGIE

Add chopped fresh, frozen or canned vegetables to boiling macaroni for last 2 or 3 minutes of cooking.

CREAMY ALFREDO

Reduce butter to 3 tablespoons and stir in ½ cup sour cream along with fresh shredded spinach, cooked broccoli or peas.

MEXICAN OLÉ

Reduce butter to 3 tablespoons and stir in ½ cup salsa. Chopped peppers and ripe tomatoes are nice additions.

TOMATO AND MAC AND CHEESE

Stir in 3 chopped tomatoes. Sprinkle with sliced green onions.

1. Bring a large pot of water to a rolling boil. Add macaroni. Peel and slice carrots into thin, julienne "twig" strips. Add to macaroni and boil rapidly, uncovered, stirring occasionally, over high heat, for 10 minutes.

2. Meanwhile, stir cheese, cornstarch and salt together. Drain cooked macaroni and carrots. Return to saucepan. Place over high heat. Add milk and broccoli and stir occasionally.

3. As soon as milk starts to boil, add cheese mixture. Reduce heat to medium. Cook, stirring gently and constantly, until sauce is thickened and smooth, about 3 to 5 minutes.

SHORT-CUT PASTA SUPPER

For a one-pot dinner, Lorraine Greey adds cut-up fresh or frozen vegetables to boiling pasta for the last few minutes of cooking. After draining, she adds tomato sauce or lots of grated cheese. She then surrounds the dish with cherry tomato halves.

BURIED TREASURES

Try putting a small bed of spinach under pasta, then hide it with sauce. Add a few extra vegetables like carrots, peas or zucchini into your regular spaghetti sauce.

CHICKEN FINGERS AND POTATO THUMBS

Kids of all ages love chicken fingers. Here's a way to make your own and cook potatoes at the same time.

Cut boneless, skinless chicken into 3x1-inch strips. Cut potatoes into thumb-size pieces. Toss chicken and potatoes with your favorite salad dressing — creamy Caesar, Italian, Ranch, etc. Place fine dry bread crumbs in a shallow dish. Add a piece of chicken and press crumbs all over. Place on a rack in a shallow pan. Repeat with all chicken and potatoes. Bake, uncovered, at 375°F. Chicken will need 15 to 20 minutes and potatoes 20 to 30 minutes.

TUNA TERRIFIC

Add 1 cup frozen mixed veggies or peas to macaroni for last 3 minutes of cooking. Then, add a 6½-oz (184-g) can tuna, pinches of dried dillweed or nutmeg, then a little sour cream, if you like.

GROWN-UP TOMATOES AND ROQUEFORT

Stir in chopped tomatoes and a crumbling of Roquefort cheese.

PIZZA TONIGHT

In place of butter, stir in ½ cup warmed pizza or spaghetti sauce. Add chopped tomatoes, peppers, sliced mushrooms or whatever you like on pizza.

Easy Mexican Lasagna

Tortillas replace lasagna noodles in this easy-to-make Southwestern-style lasagna. If your children don't like spicy foods, substitute spaghetti sauce for salsa.

PREPARATION TIME: 30 MINUTES / COOKING TIME: 15 MINUTES
BAKING TIME: 35 MINUTES / MAKES: 4 TO 6 SERVINGS

1½ cups salsa and 1 cup spaghetti sauce,
  or 2½ cups spaghetti sauce

¼ tsp hot red pepper flakes (optional)

1 egg

14-oz (475-g) container light or regular
  ricotta cheese

9 tortillas, about 7 inches across

1 green pepper, finely chopped

2 cups grated mozzarella cheese, or a 7-oz
  (200-g) bag shredded mozzarella

1. Stir salsa with spaghetti sauce and red pepper flakes, if using. In another bowl, whisk egg with ricotta.

2. Spread a thin layer of sauce in bottom of a 9-inch microwave-safe dish that will hold 10 cups (2.5 L).

3. Cut tortillas in half. Lay 6 halves over sauce, overlapping as needed. Spread with half of ricotta mixture and sprinkle with half of green pepper. Drizzle with ½ cup sauce and sprinkle with ½ cup cheese. Repeat layers, ending with tortillas. Then, cover with remaining sauce. Cover with waxed paper.

4. Microwave on medium for 30 minutes or until center is hot. If your microwave does not have a turntable, rotate dish a quarter turn every 10 minutes. Remove covering. Sprinkle with remaining cheese and microwave, uncovered, until cheese is melted, about 1½ minutes.

REGULAR OVEN: *Prepare lasagna in a baking dish that will hold at least 10 cups (2.5 L). Sprinkle top with remaining cup cheese. Bake, uncovered, in middle of a preheated 350°F oven until a knife inserted into center of lasagna feels hot, about 35 to 45 minutes.*

PIZZA STEAKS

Place 4 (6-oz/180-g) fish steaks in a lightly oiled baking dish. Spread about 1 tablespoon spaghetti sauce or mild salsa on top of each steak. Then, generously sprinkle with grated Parmesan or mozzarella cheese. Bake, uncovered, at 450°F for 13 to 18 minutes or until a knife inserted into the centers of steaks feels warm.

GET-THE-MOST

Kids like to help themselves from a central serving bowl. Fill with sliced fruit or vegetables. A lack of fondness for the vegetables is sometimes overcome by their need to get their share.

PER SERVING

Calories: 449

Protein: 24 g

Fat: 19 g

Carbohydrate: 46 g

Fiber: 3 g

Excellent source: Vitamin C, Calcium

Good source: Beta-Carotene, Iron

10-Minute Cheeseburger Pie

While shepherd's pie can take hours to make, this shortcut version uses leftover or instant potatoes.

PREPARATION TIME: 10 MINUTES
MICROWAVING TIME: 10 MINUTES / MAKES: 4 SERVINGS

1 onion, finely chopped
1 crushed garlic clove
1 lb (500 g) lean ground beef
¾ tsp Italian seasoning or a mix of dried basil
  and leaf oregano
½ tsp salt
19-oz (540-mL) can whole tomatoes, or 1 cup
  frozen peas or mixed vegetables
½ to 1 cup grated cheddar cheese
3 cups cooked mashed potatoes

FAST MASHED POTATOES
Microwave 4 potatoes until very soft, about 12 to 14 minutes. Peel and mash with a potato masher or fork. Stir in butter, salt and pepper to taste.

1. Place onion and garlic in a 9-inch (1-L) pie plate. Cover and microwave on high for 1 minute. Crumble beef over onion mixture. Sprinkle with seasonings. Cover and microwave on high, for 5 minutes. Drain off liquid. Use a fork to crumble meat. Drain tomatoes well and cut into bite-size pieces. Stir tomatoes or frozen peas into beef. Stir cheddar and generous pinches of salt into potatoes. Spread over beef mixture. Microwave, uncovered, on high until hot, about 4 minutes. Let stand for 3 minutes.

PER SERVING

Calories: 427	
Protein: 28 g	
Fat: 18 g	
Carbohydrate: 39 g	
Fiber: 4 g	

Good source: Vitamin C, Folic Acid, Iron, Calcium

CANDIED SQUASH

A little sugar helps the squash go down!

Make a slit in the skins of 2 small squashes. Place in the microwave and cook on high for 8 minutes. Cut in half and scoop out seeds. Place squash, cut-side down, on a pie plate and microwave until soft, about 8 more minutes. Meanwhile, drain a 14-oz (398-mL) can pineapple tidbits or crushed pineapple. Mix 1 tablespoon each of brown sugar and butter with pineapple and pinches of cinnamon and salt. Spoon into centers of squashes. Sprinkle halves with 1 tablespoon sugar. Then, place squash about 4 inches from a preheated broiler and cook until slightly golden, about 7 minutes. *Serves 4.*

Adam's Awesome Chocolate Cake

After one bite, our teenage tester Adam Dean aptly named this cake.

PREPARATION TIME: 20 MINUTES / BAKING TIME: 35 MINUTES

MAKES: 12 PIECES

8 medium-size carrots, about 1 lb (500 g)
2 ½ cups all-purpose flour
1 ½ tsp baking powder
½ tsp baking soda
1 tsp each of salt and cinnamon
¼ tsp nutmeg
4 (1-oz/28-g) squares semisweet chocolate
1 cup granulated sugar
4 eggs
⅓ cup vegetable oil
1 ½ tsp vanilla
¾ cup milk
½ cup chopped nuts (optional)
1 cup raisins (optional)

1. Preheat oven to 350°F. Grease a 9x13-inch (3-L) baking dish. Peel carrots. Grate, using medium grating disk of a food processor or a hand grater. You should have 4 cups. Measure flour, baking powder, soda, salt, cinnamon and nutmeg into bowl. Stir with a fork. Melt chocolate in top of a double boiler set over simmering water. Or microwave, uncovered, on medium for 2 to 3 minutes, stirring after 2 minutes. Then, stir until smooth.

2. Place sugar, eggs and oil in a large mixing bowl. Beat with an electric mixer for 2 minutes. Reduce speed to low and beat in melted chocolate, then vanilla. Beat one-third of dry ingredients into egg mixture, followed by half of milk. Repeat process, beating only briefly after each addition. End with the flour mixture. Stir in carrots, nuts and raisins.

SMART STOCK

Keep the fridge stocked with cut-up vegetable sticks and fruit for snacks. That way, they're always ready and can be the first thing your hungry kids reach for. Frozen fruit (strawberries, blueberries) is handy to have to add to milkshakes or to sprinkle over yogurt or ice cream. Canned fruit cocktail or pineapple spears, or canned or dried apricots all make handy after-school snacks.

PER PIECE

Calories: 311	
Protein: 6 g	
Fat: 12 g	
Carbohydrate: 47 g	
Fiber: 2 g	
Excellent source: Beta-Carotene	

3. Pour into prepared pan and bake in center of pre-heated oven until cake starts to come away from sides of pan, about 35 to 40 minutes. Cool on a rack. Refrigerate or freeze.

Maple Sweet Potato Muffins

If your children love pancakes with maple syrup, these easy-make muffins will be a sure winner.

PREPARATION TIME: 15 MINUTES / BAKING TIME: 20 MINUTES
MAKES: 12 MUFFINS

1⅔ cups all-purpose flour
1 cup oat bran
½ cup brown sugar
3 tsp baking powder
½ tsp baking soda
2 ½ tsp cinnamon
¼ tsp allspice or cloves
¾ tsp each of freshly ground nutmeg and salt
2 eggs
1⅓ cups milk
1½ cups cooked mashed sweet potato or
   canned pumpkin
⅓ cup maple syrup
⅓ cup melted butter or vegetable oil
1 cup pecans, chopped (optional)

1. Preheat oven to 400°F. Grease 12 muffin cups. Using a fork, stir flour with oat bran, sugar, baking powder, soda, spices and salt in a large mixing bowl. In a medium-size bowl, whisk eggs and stir in milk. Then, stir in sweet potato, maple syrup and butter. Stir egg mixture into flour mixture just until combined. Stir in pecans. Spoon into muffin cups. Bake in center of pre-heated oven until a skewer inserted into muffin comes out clean, about 20 to 25 minutes. Cool in cups for 5 minutes, then turn out onto a rack.

POLKA-DOT MUFFINS

Make up your favorite cornmeal muffin batter and stir in cooked, mixed frozen carrots and peas before baking.

MAGIC MIDDLE MUFFINS

Make up banana muffins and fill muffin tins halfway. Spoon a teaspoon of peanut butter into centers. Top with remaining batter and bake. Or add cubes of apple, banana or cheddar to center of bran muffins, or jam or whole berries to centers of oatmeal muffins.

GO FOR BLUE

Add frozen blueberries to your cake, pancake, muffin or cookie batter before mixing and baking. Your kids can be the only ones with yucky blue cookies in their lunch.

PER MUFFIN

Calories: 238
Protein: 6 g
Fat: 7 g
Carbohydrate: 41 g
Fiber: 3 g
Excellent source:
Beta-Carotene

Berry Cobbler with Chocolate Chip Cookie Topping

A giant chocolate chip cookie bakes on top of a pool of berries.

MUMBLE JUMBLE COOKIES

Using a fork, mix 1¾ cups all-purpose flour with 1 cup brown sugar and ½ teaspoon each of baking soda, salt, cinnamon and ground ginger. Whisk ⅓ cup melted butter with ½ cup milk and 1 egg. Stir into flour mixture. Fold in 2 peeled coarsely chopped apples and 1 cup each of raisins and chopped nuts. Drop by heaping tablespoonfuls, about 2 inches apart, on a greased baking sheet. Bake in a preheated 375°F oven until golden, about 12 to 14 minutes. *Makes 60 cookies.*

PREPARATION TIME: 20 MINUTES / BAKING TIME: 45 MINUTES

MAKES: 12 SERVINGS

5 cups mixed berries, such as strawberries, blueberries, raspberries and blackberries, fresh, or frozen and thawed

½ cup granulated sugar

½ cup unsalted butter, at room temperature

1 egg, well beaten

1 tsp vanilla

¼ tsp cinnamon

Pinch of nutmeg

¾ cup all-purpose flour

½ tsp baking powder

⅛ tsp salt

2 tbsp chocolate chips, or ¼ cup chopped chocolate (optional)

1. Place berries in an 8-inch baking dish that will hold at least 6 cups (1.5 L). While gently stirring, sprinkle with 2 tablespoons sugar. Stir until mixed.

2. Preheat oven to 350°F. Place remaining ⅓ cup sugar and butter in a mixing bowl. Beat by hand, or with an electric mixer, just until blended. Do not whip mixture. Beat in egg, vanilla, cinnamon and nutmeg.

3. Using a fork, blend flour with baking powder and salt in a small bowl. Stir into butter mixture until well-blended. Stir in chocolate chips.

4. Using a tablespoon, drop mixture over berries. Do not cover berries completely. Do not smooth top. Bake in center of preheated oven until top is golden and berry sauce bubbles around edges, about 45 minutes.

PER SERVING

Calories: 163

Protein: 2 g

Fat: 8 g

Carbohydrate: 21 g

Fiber: 2 g

Happy Endings

NOWADAYS, WE'RE MORE LIKELY TO SERVE FRESH
fruit at the end of a great meal than fat-heavy
cheesecake. But if a rich-tasting dessert is your cup of
tea, consider our Guilt-Free Chocolate Brownies, Magic
Lemon Meringue Pie or Elegant Easy-As-Apple Pie,
where fruit instead of fat adds the moisture. There's even
an Island Crisp with ripe warm mangoes and berries
crowned with a heavenly coconut meringue instead of a
heavy butter-oatmeal crumble — so the true fruit flavor
rings through loud and clear.

Berry and Mango Island Crisp

BUYING MANGOES

Choose mangoes by feel and smell, not skin color. Ripe mangoes have a sweet tropical aroma and flesh under tough skin feels slightly soft and yields to gentle pressure. To ripen, seal in a paper bag at room temperature. When there's a great buy on mangoes, purée pulp and freeze.

Mangoes are a great source of vitamins A and C.

PEELING AND EATING MANGOES

Mango eating is marvellously messy because of their juiciness and a large oval clingstone. Use tip of a long-bladed knife to find stone, then slice each "cheek", lengthwise, off both sides of stone. Score halves into cubes or strips, leaving skin intact. Flip skin inside out and slice fruit off skin or eat it right off skin.

Warm fragrant mangoes and luscious fresh berries bathed in rum and crowned with an amazing light coconut meringue is better than candy and has much less fat than the traditional, heavy butter-oatmeal topping.

PREPARATION TIME: 15 MINUTES / BAKING TIME: 50 MINUTES

MAKES: 6 TO 8 SERVINGS

4 large ripe mangoes

1 quart (1 L) strawberries or mix of berries

3 tbsp brown sugar

3 tbsp cornstarch

¼ cup rum, or 3 tbsp orange liqueur (optional)

1 cup unsweetened shredded coconut

¼ cup all-purpose flour

¼ tsp salt

4 egg whites, at room temperature

½ cup granulated sugar

1 tsp vanilla

1. Preheat oven to 350°F. Peel mangoes with a sharp knife and cut pulp away from pit. Slice pulp into ½-inch strips and place in a bowl. Wash berries, hull and slice in half. Add berries to mangoes. Combined fruit should measure about 6 cups.

2. Stir brown sugar with cornstarch. Stir into fruit until evenly coated. Turn into a 10-inch (1.5-L) pie plate or shallow baking dish about 9 inches wide. Pour rum or liqueur over top.

3. Place coconut, flour and salt in a medium-size bowl. Stir until mixed. Place egg whites in a medium-size mixing bowl. Using an electric mixer, beat egg whites until soft peaks form when beaters are lifted. Then, while beating, slowly add sugar until stiff shiny peaks form when beaters are lifted. Beat in vanilla. Immediately add to coconut mixture.

PER SERVING

Calories: 277

Protein: 4 g

Fat: 8 g

Carbohydrate: 52 g

Fiber: 4 g

Excellent source:
Beta-Carotene, Vitamin C

4. Using a wide spatula, fold together just until mixed. Turn onto fruit and gently spread meringue, without pressing down, until it completely covers fruit right to edges of dish. Bake in center of preheated oven until meringue is golden and fruit bubbles around pan edge, about 50 to 60 minutes.

MAKE AHEAD: *Prepare recipe up to point of beating egg whites. Fruit can be covered and left at room temperature for up to 1 day. Then, proceed as above.*

Light Easy Crisp

Better and easier than a fruit pie and a fraction of the calories.

PREPARATION TIME: 10 MINUTES / BAKING TIME: 1¼ HOURS

MAKES: 6 TO 8 SERVINGS

3 cups sliced, peeled fresh or canned peaches,
   or 8 apples
½ tsp cinnamon
1 cup fresh or frozen blueberries (if using peaches)
½ cup all-purpose flour
¾ cup rolled oats
½ cup brown sugar
¼ cup butter, melted

1. Preheat oven to 350°F. Peel and core apples, if using. Cut peaches or apples into ½-inch wedges and place in a bowl. Sprinkle with cinnamon and toss until evenly coated. If using peaches, mix in berries. (Blueberries will turn the apples gray.) Press down firmly in a 9-inch (1-L) pie plate.

2. In a medium-size bowl, stir flour with rolled oats and brown sugar. Slowly add butter, working in with a fork. Carefully mound on top of fruit and gently press into surface. Bake in center of preheated oven for 60 to 70 minutes or until fruit is tender when pierced with a skewer. This crisp is wonderful served warm with ice cream or Yogurt Cheese (page 15).

MELON AND MANGO DESSERT

Peel and pit 2 large mangoes, and peel and seed 1 large honeydew melon. Dice into ½-inch chunks and place in a large bowl. Finely grate peel from 1 lime and squeeze out juice. Stir juice and peel with 2 tablespoons liquid honey and ¼ cup orange liqueur. Add to fruit and stir well. This nutrient-rich, calorie-light salad can be served right away or covered and refrigerated for up to 2 days. *Serves 4.*

FRUIT CREPES

Stir diced pears, peaches or mangoes and a little chopped candied ginger with yogurt. Spoon over store-bought crêpes. Wrap, then drizzle with yogurt and sprinkle with toasted almonds.

PER SERVING	
Calories: 197	
Protein: 3 g	
Fat: 6 g	
Carbohydrate: 34 g	
Fiber: 2 g	

Magic Lemon Meringue Pie

This is the easiest and healthiest lemon meringue pie you'll ever make. The only thing missing is the high-calorie crust. Simply swirl the meringue in a pie plate, then spoon the tangy filling into the baked meringue. Serve with a cascade of beautiful berries over each wedge.

PREPARATION TIME: 15 MINUTES / BAKING TIME: 2 HOURS
COOKING TIME: 10 MINUTES / REFRIGERATION TIME: 1 HOUR
MAKES: 8 TO 10 SERVINGS

SHELL
5 egg whites
½ tsp cream of tartar
¼ tsp salt
⅔ cup granulated sugar
½ tsp vanilla

FILLING
4 large lemons
1 cup granulated sugar
6 tbsp cornstarch
¼ tsp salt
½ cup cold water
5 egg yolks
1½ cups boiling water
2 tbsp butter
Icing sugar (optional)
Mint (optional)
5 cups mixed berries

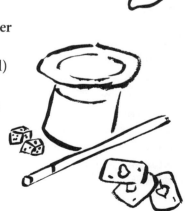

GENEROUS JUICE AND EVER-READY PEEL

To get the most juice out of your lemons, oranges or grapefruit, store them at room temperature. Before juicing, grate peel and freeze it, then use it as you would fresh grated peel. An empty citrus shell can also be frozen to be used as a party container for ice cream, salads and sauces.

EASY JUICING

When you want to juice a lemon, lime or orange, pop the fruit into the microwave and cook on high for 10 to 20 seconds. You'll be amazed how much more juice you can then squeeze from the fruit.

PER SERVING
Calories: 239
Protein: 4 g
Fat: 6 g
Carbohydrate: 45 g
Fiber: 2 g
Excellent source: Vitamin C

1. Preheat oven to 250°F. Lightly butter a deep 10-inch (1.5-L) pie plate. To prepare shell, place egg whites, cream of tartar and salt in a large mixing bowl. Beat, using high speed on an electric mixer, just until soft peaks form when beaters are lifted. Reduce mixer speed to medium. Continue beating, gradually adding sugar, about 1 tablespoon at a time. Add vanilla. Then, beat at high speed until stiff glossy peaks form when beaters are lifted, about 2 more minutes.

2. Immediately turn mixture into buttered pie plate. Using back of a large spoon, gently spread meringue out so it covers bottom and sides of plate, forming a crust with thick high sides. Then, dab bottom of crust to create small rough peaks to hold pie filling in place. Do not press meringue down firmly. You want to maintain as much volume as possible. Bake in center of preheated oven for 2 hours.

3. Meanwhile, prepare filling by grating peel from 2 lemons. Squeeze juice from all 4 lemons and measure out ¾ cup. Place sugar, cornstarch and salt in a large saucepan. Stir with a fork until well blended.

4. Gradually stir in ¾ cup lemon juice and ½ cup cold water, stirring until smooth. Whisk in egg yolks. Whisking constantly, gradually add 1½ cups boiling water. Stir in butter.

5. Place saucepan over medium-high heat. Bring mixture to a full rolling boil, stirring frequently. Then, reduce heat to low and cook, stirring slowly, until thick enough to coat a metal spoon, about 5 more minutes. Remove saucepan from heat and stir in grated peel. Turn mixture into a bowl. Press a piece of clear wrap onto surface. Refrigerate until mixture cools to room temperature, about 1 hour. Then, pour into cooled meringue shell.

6. If not serving right away, refrigerate pie, uncovered. Pie is best served the same day it is made as meringue may "bead" or soften as it sits. Sprinkle with icing sugar and use mint to garnish, if you like. Cut pie into wedges and use a wide flat spoon to carefully transfer to plates. Then, add berries to each serving.

INSTANT OLD-FASHIONED PUMPKIN PIE

Whisk 2 eggs with ¾ cup milk. Whisk in ⅔ cup brown sugar, ½ teaspoon cinnamon, ¼ teaspoon ginger and ¼ teaspoon salt. Stir in 1 cup canned pure pumpkin. Pour into a store-bought frozen pie shell and smooth top. Bake on bottom rack of a 375°F oven until center is set when pie is jiggled, about 40 minutes. For a creamy topping, stir 2 tablespoons granulated sugar with 1 cup sour cream. Spread over hot pumpkin pie. Return to oven for 5 minutes. Cool on a rack. *Serves 8.*

Elegant Easy-As-Apple Pie

Start with a package of frozen puff pastry, sold in most supermarkets, and 8 juicy apples, and we guarantee you'll wind up with a French patisserie-style apple pie — even if you've never made a pie before.

PREPARATION TIME: 15 MINUTES / BAKING TIME: 45 MINUTES

MAKES: 12 WEDGES

½ (411-g) pkg frozen puff pastry dough, thawed
6 to 8 apples
1 cup dried apricots
½ to ¾ cup granulated sugar
1 tsp ground cinnamon
2 tbsp cornstarch
1 tbsp milk
1 tbsp granulated sugar

1. Preheat oven to 475°F. Sprinkle counter with flour and lay pastry on top. Dust rolling pin with flour. Roll pastry into a thin circle, at least 14 to 16 inches across. Don't worry if edges are very uneven. Fold pastry in half and lift into a 9-inch (1-L) pie plate. Unfold pastry. It will hang over sides of dish and onto counter. Using your fingers, gently press pastry against bottom edges of pie plate.

2. Peel, core and very thinly slice apples, about ⅛ inch thick. You should have about 8 cups. Slice apricots into thin strips. Place apples and apricots in a bowl. If apples taste sweet, use ½ cup sugar; if apples are tart, use ¾ cup sugar. Stir sugar with cinnamon and cornstarch until evenly blended. Sprinkle over fruit and gently mix until evenly coated.

3. Turn fruit into pie plate and pour any juices over top. Gently press down and smooth top. Fold pastry over apples, overlapping edges as needed. Center of pie will not be covered with pastry and edges will be uneven.

ALL-SEASON SUMMER PIES

When freezing fruit for pies, line a pie plate with waxed paper. Add pie filling made according to your favorite recipe as if you're filling a pastry crust. Instead of baking, place in the freezer. As soon as it is frozen firm, remove and peel off waxed paper. Overwrap with foil and return to freezer. Then, when you're ready to bake a pie, slip frozen filling into a pie crust. Add top crust and simply increase baking time.

PER WEDGE

Calories: 176

Protein: 2 g

Fat: 5 g

Carbohydrate: 33 g

Fiber: 3 g

Excellent source: Beta-Carotene

4. Brush top of pastry with milk, then sprinkle with 1 tablespoon sugar. Place pie on lowest rack of preheated 475°F oven. Immediately turn temperature down to 350°F and bake until apples are tender when pierced with tines of a fork and pastry is golden, about 45 to 55 minutes.

5. Place hot pie on a rack and let cool until lukewarm before cutting. If you cut pie while hot, it may be too runny. Serve with a wedge of old cheddar cheese, or a scoop of vanilla ice cream sprinkled with chopped candied ginger.

Guilt-Free Chocolate Brownies

Unbelievably, these wicked-tasting squares are about half the fat of most — and the apricots pack an extra beta-carotene punch.

PREPARATION TIME: 10 MINUTES / BAKING TIME: 18 MINUTES
MAKES: 16 TWO-INCH SQUARES

¼ cup each of corn syrup and melted butter
2 eggs
1 tsp vanilla
½ cup each of all-purpose flour and
   granulated sugar
⅓ cup cocoa
½ tsp each of baking powder and salt
½ cup finely chopped dried apricots

1. Preheat oven to 350°F. Coat an 8-inch (1.5-L) square baking pan or 9-inch (1-L) pie plate with non-stick cooking spray. Whisk corn syrup with butter, eggs and vanilla just until mixed. In a larger bowl, stir together remaining ingredients except apricots. Stir in egg mixture until all ingredients are moist. Stir in apricots. Turn into prepared pan and bang pan on counter several times to get rid of any air bubbles. Bake in center of preheated oven for 18 to 20 minutes or until edges start to come away from sides of pan.

HEALTHY CARROT-SPICE SQUARES

An easy batter to stir together when it's your turn to send snacks to school.

Whisk 2 eggs with ¼ cup oil and ¾ cup unsweetened applesauce. Using a fork, stir 2 cups all-purpose flour with ½ cup brown sugar, 1 teaspoon each of baking soda, cinnamon and nutmeg and ½ teaspoon each of allspice and salt. Add egg mixture and stir until mixed. Batter will be very thick. Stir in 1½ cups grated carrots and ½ cup chopped dried apricots or raisins until evenly mixed. Turn into a greased 9-inch (2.5-L) square baking dish or 9-inch (1-L) pie plate. Push batter to edges and smooth top. Bake in center of preheated 350°F oven until a cake tester inserted into center comes out fairly clean, about 35 to 40 minutes.

PER SQUARE

Calories: 105

Protein: 2 g

Fat: 4 g

Carbohydrate: 17 g

Fiber: 1 g

Harvest Pumpkin Bread with Golden Raisins

A bowl and a fork are all you need to produce this moist quick bread. It has all the aromatic spices but calls for a mere fraction of the work and fat needed to produce a Thanksgiving pie.

JACK-O-LANTERN MUFFINS

Prepare batter for Harvest Pumpkin Bread as directed and fill 12 greased muffin cups. Bake in center of a preheated 400°F oven until a cake tester inserted in center of a muffin comes out clean, about 25 to 28 minutes.

PREPARATION TIME: 10 MINUTES / BAKING TIME: 1¼ HOURS

MAKES: 12 SLICES

1 cup all-purpose flour

1 cup whole wheat flour

2 tsp baking powder

1 tsp baking soda

2 tsp cinnamon

½ tsp each of allspice, ground ginger and salt

¾ cup brown sugar

1 egg

¼ cup vegetable oil

⅔ cup buttermilk, or ½ cup sour milk (1 tsp vinegar stirred into ½ cup milk)

1½ cups canned pure pumpkin

½ cup golden raisins (optional)

1. Preheat oven to 350°F. Oil a 9x5x3-inch (1.5-L) loaf pan. Measure all dry ingredients, in order given, into a large mixing bowl. Stir with a fork until evenly blended. Make a well in center. In a smaller bowl, whisk egg. Whisk in oil and milk. Stir in pumpkin. Pour into center of dry ingredients. Add raisins and stir just until evenly blended. Batter will be very thick.

2. Turn into loaf pan and smooth top. Bake in center of oven until a cake tester inserted into center comes out clean, about 70 minutes to 1¼ hours. Turn out of pan and cool on a rack. Wrap and refrigerate for up to 1 week or freeze.

PER SLICE

Calories: 188

Protein: 4 g

Fat: 5 g

Carbohydrate: 32 g

Fiber: 2 g

Good source: Beta-Carotene

Warm Fruit Salad with Maple and Orange Sauce

This is the answer when you want an exotic fruit salad to round out a grand dinner or brunch buffet.

PREPARATION TIME: 10 MINUTES / COOKING TIME: 6 MINUTES
MAKES: 4 SERVINGS

1 large papaya, or 2 ripe mangoes
1 pint (500 mL) fresh strawberries
1 to 2 kiwi fruit
Finely grated peel of 1 orange or 1 lime
½ cup orange juice
¼ cup maple syrup
3 tbsp orange liqueur or brandy

1. Cut peel from papaya or mangoes. Scoop and discard seeds from papaya. Cut pulp from mangoes. Cut into 1-inch cubes and place in a bowl. Hull berries and if large cut in half. Add to papaya. Peel kiwi, slice and set aside.

2. Place orange peel, juice and maple syrup in a wide frying pan or saucepan. Place over high heat and boil, stirring occasionally, until reduced to ¼ cup, about 3 minutes. Immediately add papaya and berries and stir constantly until warm, about 3 minutes. Stir in liqueur and kiwi and serve immediately. Wonderful with biscotti, over French vanilla ice cream or pancakes.

EVER-READY WINTER FRUIT COMPOTE

Fruit simmered in fragrant spiced juice is a welcome finish to a holiday dinner or brunch. In an 8-cup (2-L) microwave-safe dish, stir together 1½ cups apple juice, 1 cup each of dried apricots and prunes, ¼ cup brown sugar, ¼ cup dark rum, 1 teaspoon vanilla and a 1-inch piece of fresh ginger, thinly sliced. Cover and cook on high for 15 minutes, stirring every 5 minutes. Let stand for 5 minutes. *Makes 3 cups.*

PER SERVING

Calories: 190	
Protein: 2 g	
Fat: 1 g	
Carbohydrate: 41 g	
Fiber: 5 g	
Excellent source: Vitamin C	

FRUIT ON TOP

SHERRIED FRUIT
Stir a mix of fresh fruit, such as sliced apples, pears and berries with sherry and a dash of almond flavoring. Spoon over angel food cake or store-bought cheesecake.

BLENDER BERRY SAUCE
Whirl ripe, hulled strawberries with a few squirts of lime juice in a food processor until smooth. This is an excellent way to use those overripe berries at the bottom of the box.

Serve over melon slices, ice cream or cake. Raspberries also work well but need to be strained.

VERY BERRY
Crush 1 cup strawberries, raspberries or blueberries. Stir in 1 cup yogurt and 3 tablespoons granulated sugar. Taste and add more sugar, if you wish. Serve over crêpes, pancakes, ice cream, and even waffles. *Makes 1⅔ cups.*

HOW TO SELECT AND STORE PRODUCE

Type	Select	Store
APRICOTS	Golden-orange, firm and plump fruit.	Ripen at room temperature, then refrigerate, uncovered, for up to 1 week.
BERRIES	Firm ripe berries. Don't ripen once picked.	Refrigerate, unwashed, on paper towel in a shallow pan, loosely covered, for up to 2 days.
BROCCOLI	Compact green clusters with firm stalks.	Covered, but not airtight, in the refrigerator crisper for up to 5 days.
BRUSSELS SPROUTS	Small, firm, compact light-green heads.	Same as broccoli.
CABBAGE	Firm, heavy head with fresh outer leaves.	In the refrigerator crisper for up to 3 weeks.
CANTALOUPE	Firm plump melons. Blossom end should have a pleasant aroma.	Room temperature until ripe. Then, covered, in the refrigerator for up to 3 days, away from other produce.
CARROTS	Bright, orange, firm carrots.	Remove green leafy tops. In the refrigerator crisper, covered, for up to 2 weeks.
CAULIFLOWER	Creamy white firm heads with bright green leaves.	In the refrigerator crisper, covered, for up to 1 week.
GREENS	Fresh-looking leaves free from brown spots and decay.	Wash leafy greens, drain and wrap in paper or cloth towel. Store in a tightly sealed container in the refrigerator for 2 to 4 days. If bought in airtight packaging, store as is.
KIWI	Buy evenly ripe fruit that is slightly soft to the touch.	Ripen firm fruit at room temperature, uncovered, out of direct sunlight. Refrigerate ripe fruit, covered, for up to 2 weeks.

Type	Select	Store
MANGOES	Plump, firm, free of blemishes and wrinkles, with a pleasant aroma.	Uncovered, at room temperature, until ripe. Then, covered and refrigerated for up to 3 days.
ORANGES	Heavy firm fruit with smooth skin.	Refrigerate for up to 3 weeks.
PAPAYA	Smooth unblemished skin, light-yellow speckling is a sign of ripeness.	In a paper bag at room temperature until ripe. Then, covered and refrigerated for up to 3 days.
PEPPERS	Bright-coloured, smooth-skinned and firm.	Unwashed in the refrigerator away from fruit. Store hot peppers in a paper bag.
POTATOES	Firm, smooth well-washed potatoes free from blemishes.	Store new potatoes in a paper bag in the refrigerator for up to 1 week. Mature potatoes in a cool, dry dark place for up to 2 months, not in the refrigerator.
PUMPKIN	Choose thick-shelled pumpkin and squash that are heavy for their size.	In a cool, dry dark and ventilated place for up to 2 months. When cut, cover and refrigerate for up to 5 days.
SPINACH	Fresh, crisp bright-green leaves with a light earthy aroma.	Discard yellow or damaged leaves. Store in a crisper for 2 to 4 days. If bought in plastic packaging, store as is.
SQUASH	See Pumpkin	See Pumpkin
SWEET POTATOES	Firm, well-shaped tubers with bright coloring and skins free of cracks.	Room temperature, for up to 1 week. Or, uncovered in a cool, dry, dark place for up to 2 months.
TOMATOES	Uniform-colored firm and heavy for their size.	Uncovered, at room temperature, for up to 4 days. Only refrigerate if very ripe.

A NUTRITIONAL COMPARISON*

Type	Calories	Protein (g)	Fat (g)	Carbohydrate (g)
APRICOTS (dried, 10 halves)	83	1	0	22
BROCCOLI (1 cup, cooked)	43	5	1	8
BRUSSELS SPROUTS (1 cup, cooked)	61	4	1	14
CABBAGE (1 cup shredded, raw)	17	1	0	4
CANTALOUPE (½ raw)	93	2	1	22
CARROTS (1 medium, raw)	35	1	0	8
CAULIFLOWER (1 cup, raw)	24	2	0	5
KIWI (1 raw)	46	1	0	11
MANGOES (1 medium, raw)	135	1	1	35
ORANGES (1 medium)	62	1	0	15
PAPAYAS (1 medium)	122	2	0	31
PEPPERS, GREEN (1 raw)	32	1	0	8
PEPPERS, RED (1 raw)	32	1	0	8
POTATOES (6 oz/180 g, cooked and peeled)	119	3	0	28
PUMPKIN (1 cup, cooked)	83	3	1	20
RASPBERRIES (1 cup, raw)	60	1	1	14
SPINACH (1 cup, raw)	12	2	0	2
SQUASH (1 cup, cooked)	88	2	0	23
STRAWBERRIES (1 cup, raw)	45	1	1	10
SWEET POTATOES (6 oz/180 g, cooked and peeled)	134	2	0	31
TOMATOES (1 medium, raw)	26	1	0	6

* For nutritional values of greens, see "Comparing Raw Greens" chart on page 36.

Fiber (g)	Beta-carotene (RE)	Vitamin C (mg)	Folic Acid (mcg)	Iron (mg)	Calcium (mg)
3	1024	1	4	1.6	16
4	181	116	78	1.3	71
7	114	97	94	1.9	56
1	9	33	40	.4	33
2	1334	113	45	.6	29
2	1063	8	11	.4	22
2	1	72	66	.6	29
3	5	57	**	.3	20
4	450	57	6	.3	21
2	9	70	40	.1	52
5	53	193	3	.3	75
2	45	107	26	.5	11
2	438	227	26	.5	11
2	0	18	14	.4	7
4	1262	9	24	3.4	63
6	1	31	32	.7	27
1	384	16	109	1.5	56
5	631	16	29	1.4	70
3	3	85	26	.6	21
4	2374	32	29	.6	36
1	107	23	18	.6	6

** Data not available.

Index

SOCIETY FOR EXPERIMENTAL BIOLOGY
SEMINAR SERIES · 11

EFFECTS OF DISEASE ON THE PHYSIOLOGY OF
THE GROWING PLANT

EFFECTS OF DISEASE
ON THE PHYSIOLOGY OF
THE GROWING PLANT

Edited by

P.G.AYRES

Lecturer in Plant Physiology, University of Lancaster

CAMBRIDGE UNIVERSITY PRESS

Cambridge

London   New York   New Rochelle

Melbourne   Sydney

Published by the Press Syndicate of the University of Cambridge
The Pitt Building, Trumpington Street, Cambridge CB2 1RP
32 East 57th Street, New York, NY 10022, USA
296 Beaconsfield Parade, Middle Park, Melbourne 3206, Australia

First published 1981

Printed in the United States of America

British Library Cataloguing in Publication Data

Effects of disease on the physiology of growing
plants. – (Society for Experimental Biology
seminar series; 11)

1. Plant diseases – Congresses
I. Ayres, P. G.   II. Series
581.1'04   SB731   80-42175

ISBN 0 521 23306 2 hard covers
ISBN 0 521 29898 9 paperback

CONTENTS

CONTRIBUTORS

Ayres, P. G.
Department of Biological Sciences, University of Lancaster, Lancaster LA1 4YQ, UK.
Buchanan, B. B.
Department of Cell Physiology, University of California, Berkeley, California 94720, USA.
Fitt, B. D. L.
Plant Pathology Department, Rothamsted Experimental Station, Harpenden, Herts. AL5 2JQ, UK.
Friend, J.
Department of Plant Biology, University of Hull, Hull HU6 7RX, UK.
Gay, J. L.
Department of Botany, Imperial College of Science and Technology, Prince Consort Road, London SW7 2BB, UK.
Hornby, D.
Plant Pathology Department, Rothamsted Experimental Station, Harpenden, Herts. AL5 2JQ, UK.
Hutcheson, S. W.
Department of Cell Physiology, University of California, Berkeley, California 94720, USA.
Kimpel, J. A.
Department of Plant Pathology, University of California, Davis, California 95616, USA.
Kosuge, T.
Department of Plant Pathology, University of California, Davis, California 95616, USA.
Lewis, D. H.
Department of Botany, University of Sheffield, Sheffield S10 2TN, UK.
Magyarosy, A. C.
Department of Cell Physiology, University of California, Berkeley, California 94720, USA.
Manners, J. M.
Department of Botany, Imperial College of Science and Technology, Prince Consort Road, London SW7 2BB, UK.
(Present address: Department of Biochemistry, University of Queensland, Queensland 5067, Australia.)
Montalbini, P.
Plant Pathology Institute, University of Perugia, Perugia, Italy.

Pegg, G. F.
Department of Plant Sciences, Wye College (University of London), Wye, near Ashford, Kent TN25 5AH, UK.
(Present address: Department of Agriculture and Horticulture, University of Reading, Earley Gate, Reading RG6 2AT, UK.)

Rabbinge, R.
Department of Theoretical Production Ecology, Agricultural University, Bornsesteeg 65, 6708 PD, Wageningen, The Netherlands.

Rijsdijk, F. H.
Department of Phytopathology, 9 Binnenhaven, 6709 PD, Wageningen, The Netherlands.

Russell, G. F.
Department of Agricultural Biology, The University, Newcastle upon Tyne NE1 7RU, UK.

Whipps, J. M.
Department of Botany, University of Sheffield, Sheffield S10 2TN, UK.

PREFACE

Despite the skills and endeavours of plant breeders and agricultural chemists it seems that plant diseases, like the poor (John 12, verse 8), are always with us – at least for the foreseeable future, crop losses due to disease will be a regular feature of agriculture. Thus, until such time as we can fully understand and can *manipulate* natural mechanisms of disease resistance, it is extremely important that we should understand the relationship between the occurrence and severity of disease, and the yield loss that results. The importance of this relationship is emphasized as the cost of prophylaxis increases, and as plant breeders, epidemiologists and agriculturalists increasingly urge us to explore the possibilities of cultivar mixtures, multiline varieties and the greater use of race non-specific (minor gene) resistance, i.e. the cultivation of plant populations which may be expected to carry low levels of disease. Somewhat surprisingly, the potential that plants have to tolerate disease, in the sense of minimizing yield loss in the face of infection, is a topic which has been largely overlooked by physiologists.

It was the object of this SEB Seminar, held at Imperial College, London, 24–26 March 1980, to explore the problems of relating yield loss to physiological phenomena and, also, to provide some explanation of the physiological basis of yield loss by examining the production and utilization of metabolites in diseased plants. This brief volume can only serve as an introduction to the subject but, hopefully, it will stimulate further research into this underdeveloped branch of botany where the disciplines of physiology and pathology overlap. Any doubts about the practical importance of such studies will be immediately dispelled by reading Professor Russell's chapter in this volume.

I offer my sincere thanks to Simon Archer (Imperial College) and David Lewis (University of Sheffield) who spent so much of their valuable time helping me to formulate the ideas and plans for this seminar.

Peter Ayres
University of Lancaster

July 1980

G.E.RUSSELL

Disease and crop yield: the problems and prospects for agriculture

Economic importance of diseases

Diseases of crop plants have caused damage since the beginning of agriculture and they are, therefore, not a direct consequence of modern crop husbandry. However, modern agriculture has exacerbated the disease problem so that diseases generally are probably more damaging now than they have ever been. In particular, certain agricultural practices designed to maximize short-term profitability have increased pest and disease damage. Such practices include the use of genetically uniform crop varieties over wide geographic areas and the increased use of fertilizers and irrigation (Carlson & Main, 1976). In addition, some modern, high-yielding crop varieties have proved to be very susceptible to diseases which were previously unimportant but which quickly became widespread and damaging once these varieties were grown on a large scale. For example, some virus-tolerant sugar beet varieties were badly damaged by powdery mildew (*Erysiphe betae*) and bacterial root rot (*Erwinia* spp.) in California, where these diseases had caused little damage on the original varieties.

Rust diseases of cereals have been a problem since at least Roman times, when crop damage was attributed to the wrath of the gods. In such circumstances, farmers felt that attempts to reduce rust damage were not worthwhile and would probably have only increased the divine anger! It was not until comparatively recently, when it was recognized that most diseases are caused by pathogenic microorganisms, that any serious attempts have been made to reduce disease losses by consciously carrying out control measures. Nevertheless, farmers often achieved some degree of control, without recognizing this fact, by producing seed for succeeding crops from only the 'best' plants. In each generation such plants were usually those which had either escaped disease or which were little damaged by infection. In this way, farmers over the centuries had been selecting for inherited tendencies to escape disease, or for other kinds of disease resistance. It is not surprising therefore, that many 'land races' (or local varieties) escaped catastrophic damage from diseases which had been present for many centuries.

During the past 150 years there have been many disease epidemics which have had serious economic consequences (Klinkowski, 1970; Russell, 1978a). For example, outbreaks of potato late blight, caused by the fungus *Phytophthora infestans,* resulted in disastrous famines in Western Europe, particularly in Ireland, in 1845 and 1846 and changed the course of history. In 1845 the disease caused more than 40% of the tubers to rot; in the following year, an even earlier attack of potato blight wiped out almost the entire potato crop. As potatoes were the staple diet of most of the Irish population, widespread famine followed the blight epidemics and many thousands of people starved to death. The decline in the population of Ireland from 8.2 to 6.2 million between 1841 and 1851, chiefly because of emigration to Britain and North America, was directly attributable to the famine.

Other very damaging plant diseases caused by fungi include rust diseases of cereals (*Puccinia* spp.), Dutch elm disease (*Ceratocystis ulmi*), downy mildew of hops (*Pseudoperonospora humuli*), blue mould of tobacco (*Peronospora tabacina*), coffee rust (*Hemileia vastatrix*) and brown spot of rice (*Helminthosporium oryzae*). Epidemics of virus diseases, including curly top of sugar beet, cocoa swollen shoot and sugar cane mosaic, and of bacterial diseases, including bacterial blights of cotton and rice, have also been very damaging.

The economic losses due to diseases of crop plants are very difficult to assess accurately. Table 1 shows estimated percentage crop losses caused by insects, diseases and weeds in several of the world's most important arable crops (Cramer, 1967). For comparison, estimates of losses in four important crops in the UK, based mainly on assessments by Cramer (1967), are given in Table 2. These figures probably greatly underestimate the actual losses because they do not include post-harvest losses or damage by nematodes, molluscs and several other groups of invertebrate or vertebrate pests. Bird pests, for example weaver birds (*Quelea quelea*) and the red-winged blackbird (*Agelaius phoeniceus*), can cause very significant losses of grain in many parts of the world (Russell, 1978a).

Table 1. *Estimated percentage annual world crop losses (after Cramer, 1967)*

Crop	Insect pests	Diseases	Weeds	Total loss
Wheat, oats, barley, rye	4.9	8.5	9.5	22.9
Rice, millet, sorghum, maize	20.7	9.2	12.2	42.1
Sugar beet	8.3	10.4	5.8	24.5
Potatoes	6.5	21.8	4.0	32.3
Cotton	16.1	12.0	5.8	33.9
All crops	13.8	11.6	9.5	34.9

These estimates suggest that between one-third and one-half of the world's potential crop production is lost because of the activities of pests and diseases *in spite of present control measures*. More precise and accurate methods of assessing crop losses are urgently needed, but it is clear that much more effective control methods are desirable.

Crop loss assessment methods

There has recently been increased interest in the assessment of losses because of the need to develop more sophisticated pest and disease management schemes, which must justify and rationalize the use of pesticides, both in economic and environmental terms (James, 1974).

The term 'economic threshold' was first used to describe the critical level of damage which called for crop protection measures; it has often since been used in a rather different sense to mean the level of pest or disease attack at which the costs of reducing crop losses equal the increase in crop returns which is gained by control. Such costs include the obvious ones, such as those of buying and applying crop protection chemicals, and also several hidden costs including any phytotoxic effects of the chemicals, higher cost of disease-free seed or propagating material, and damage to beneficial organisms. It is easier to estimate the costs of control than to calculate the benefits.

Methods have been developed for assessing losses caused by individual diseases in all the world's major crops (Food and Agricultural Organisation of the United Nations, 1971), but these are based on too many variable factors to be very accurate. For example, losses due to sugar beet virus yellows have been predicted by means of a formula based on the percentage of virus-infected plants in selected fields at the end of June, July, August and September (Hull, 1968; Heathcote, Russell & Van Steyvoort, 1973). However, the accuracy of this prediction varies with the type of virus or virus strains which are present. Russell (1964) showed that infection with some strains of beet yellows virus causes little damage, even to susceptible sugar beet varieties; other, more 'virulent' virus strains can seriously decrease yields in these varieties. These virulent virus strains cause more severe symptoms in *all* varieties than do avirulent strains and

Table 2. *Estimated percentage annual crop yield losses in the UK (after Cramer, 1967)*

Crop	Insect pests	Diseases	Weeds	Total loss
Barley	2.0	4.0	7.0	13.0
Wheat	3.0	2.0	10.0	15.0
Potatoes	3.0	15.0	4.0	22.0
Sugar beet	3.7	10.3	7.4	21.4

there is, therefore, no adaptation of virus strains to particular sugar beet varieties. For this reason, predictions based on observed losses with virulent virus strains would seriously overestimate disease damage; conversely, predictions based on field data involving avirulent virus strains would usually be underestimates. Even with diseases such as virus yellows of sugar beet, where much experimental information is available about disease losses, it is not possible to predict disease damage in any situation with any degree of accuracy unless information is available about the incidence and virulence of the virus strains involved.

Work on variants of fungal pathogens has centred on those which interact with specific host plant genotypes, and particularly on resistance-breaking variants. The possibility that some fungal variants may cause more damage on *all* susceptible hosts than others, does not seem to have been examined in detail. However, such fungal variants would be analogous to 'severe' or 'virulent' virus strains, and could seriously affect the accuracy of crop loss assessments.

Plants which are attacked to the same degree as other plants, but which suffer less damage in terms of yield or quality as a result of that attack, are said to be tolerant. Varietal tolerance can also reduce the accuracy of crop loss assessment, as can more complex specific interactions between variety, fertilizer status and disease. Yield losses are largely dependent on the stage of plant development at which infection occurs and on the subsequent duration and severity of infection (Scott & Griffiths, 1980). Therefore, no single estimate of disease made at any one growth stage of a host plant is likely to be a reliable guide to the extent of yield loss. These, and many other factors, make it very difficult and expensive to obtain the necessary information for accurate disease loss assessment. The problem is further complicated by the fact that disease incidence and disease effects are not necessarily related (Hirst, 1975). The harm caused by disease may not be proportional to the extent and duration of attack but may depend on the capabilities of the surviving parts of the crop plants involved.

Biochemical and physiological causes of disease loss

The symptoms which are observed on diseased plants by the pathologist or farmer in the field are external manifestations of many effects of disease on the host plant's metabolism. A greater understanding of these effects may increase the accuracy of disease loss assessments and may help in the development of more effective control methods.

Infected plants usually grow more slowly than corresponding healthy plants and the internodes of infected plants are generally shorter. Pathogens can reduce the rate of photosynthesis by affecting either the chloroplasts or chlorophyll content directly, or the enzymes which are concerned with photosynthesis. Such effects are usually manifested as chlorosis of the leaves and often as altered starch metabolism. Plants infected by fungi, bacteria or viruses usually have an increased respiration rate, particularly where hypersensitive host reactions to infection are involved.

Pathogenesis can be associated with cell wall degradation by enzymes produced by fungi or bacteria; such degradation can cause, directly or indirectly, the death of host cells. Disease can also profoundly alter the normal nitrogen metabolism of host cells, which can be damaged as a result of a diversion of nitrogenous compounds to the pathogen to form new protein. This can cause symptoms of nitrogen deficiency, including stunted growth and chlorosis of green tissues. Many diseases involve necrosis of host plant tissues and this is usually related to enhanced polyphenoloxidase activity associated with hypersensitivity. Where necrosis is extensive, the growth and yielding capacity of the host plant are invariably reduced.

The balance of growth regulators is generally upset in diseased plants. For example, many fungal and bacterial diseases cause increased auxin levels, either by increased auxin production or by suppressed activity of auxin-degrading enzymes. These disease-induced effects on growth regulators can contribute to symptoms which are associated with yield loss.

Diseases of the root and vascular system can seriously impede the uptake and distribution of water and salts throughout the host plant, and most vascular diseases, therefore, result in wilting or desiccation of the host tissues. One consequence of this can be stomatal closure, which can reduce the rate of photosynthesis, and another is the accumulation of some compounds which can adversely affect growth.

Because diseases can affect the biochemistry and physiology of host plants in so many different ways, as described in more detail in the following chapters of this book, it is not surprising that the external symptoms of disease are so varied.

External symptoms of disease

The severity of a particular disease on a host plant depends on a number of factors, including the stage of growth at which it is attacked, the degree of inherited resistance expressed against that pathogen, the nutrition of the host plant, and many other environmental factors.

A plant which becomes infected with damping-off pathogens soon after germination may not even emerge above ground level; even if it does emerge, it is unlikely that such a plant would grow normally thereafter and yield would probably be reduced. With most diseases, infected plants are smaller and less vigorous than healthy plants because of the deleterious effects of infection on their metabolism. The development of leaves is usually delayed and the size of the leaves and root systems is generally reduced. In cereals, for example, the usual result of diseases attacking the host at an early growth stage is a stunted plant with few effective tillers and a reduced number of grains per ear (Varley, 1977).

Scott & Griffiths (1980) have found that powdery mildew, caused by *Erysiphe graminis*, reduces the grain yield of barley in several ways: these include a reduction in the number of fertile tillers, either by suppressing the development of new tillers, or by killing existing ones; a smaller root system; and a decrease in the number of grains per tiller and the size and weight of individual grains. They have emphasized, however, that as yield loss caused by powdery mildew depends to a large extent on the stage of development of the host plant at which infection occurs, no single estimate of disease is likely to give a reliable guide to yield loss.

Doodson, Manners & Myers (1964) previously found that yellow rust, caused by *Puccinia striiformis*, affects several components of grain yield in spring wheat. Early infections, in particular, reduce plant height, dry weight of root, number of tillers per plant, ear length, number of florets and grains per ear, and individual grain weight. Infection at the flag leaf stage has considerably less effect on total grain yield than earlier infections but reduces the average weight of individual grains.

These two examples illustrate the complexity of assessing the economic and other impacts of diseases on agricultural crops. The effects of even a single disease on a host plant can be so many and varied, and can be influenced by numerous independent factors. These include the genotypes of the host plant and pathogen involved, the growth stage of the host at infection, and environmental factors including the presence of other diseases. Additional knowledge about the interactions between pathogens and their host plants may eventually help to provide more reliable control and assessment methods.

The reduction of crop losses from disease

It is convenient to group control methods into three main categories: avoidance of disease, direct control measures and biological control.

Avoidance of disease

The spread of many important diseases has been prevented or delayed by the strict enforcement of quarantine regulations and other legislation. For example, a 'Wart Disease Order', which controls the planting in England of potato varieties that are very susceptible to the fungus *Synchytrium endobioticum*, has greatly reduced damage from wart disease for more than 50 years. The control of fireblight disease of apples and pears, caused by *Erwinia amylovora*, has been improved in England through enforcement of a similar 'Fireblight Disease Order' which was first introduced in 1958. Such measures, together with quarantine regulations to prevent the introduction of diseased plant material into areas where a disease is absent, are a valuable first line of defence against diseases.

Other methods of disease avoidance include suitable crop rotation of susceptible and immune crops and the manipulation of sowing dates, which can reduce damage from certain diseases. It is also important to grow crops from disease-free seed or propagating material and to remove as many potential sources of infection as possible. Such sanitation or hygiene can contribute greatly to the reduction of disease damage. Soil sterilization and the control of vectors can also be important in avoiding disease. For example, much of the sugar beet crop in Europe, Japan and the USA is sprayed each year with insecticides to control the insect vectors of viruses such as curly top virus and those which cause virus yellows.

A particularly important recent development in disease avoidance concerns the use of prophylactic chemicals. Several fungicides can be applied to crops to reduce the risks of subsequent disease. Examples include the application of copper or organic fungicides to the potato crop when weather conditions favour the spread of the potato blight fungus *Phytophthora infestans,* and the use of seed dressings in many crops, including barley and sugar beet. Recent studies by Russell (1978*b*) have shown that the application of potassium or sodium chloride to the soil can prevent serious outbreaks of yellow rust (*Puccinia striiformis*) in winter wheat.

Direct control measures

These are measures which are taken to control the spread or effects of disease, either by killing the pathogens directly or by stimulating the host plant to produce compounds which do so, or by counteracting some of the effects of disease.

Until the 1940s, chemical control of diseases was almost entirely restricted to simple inorganic non-systemic compounds such as copper, sulphur and mercury. Although these compounds are still used today, they have largely been replaced by more complex non-systemic compounds, including the dithiocarbamates, or by systemic fungicides, many of which are related to methylpyrimidine or benzimidazole. Antibiotics produced by some microorganisms, including penicillin and streptomycin, have been used to control some bacterial diseases.

Control by chemicals can be expensive, partly because these substances are very costly to produce and partly because their application usually requires extra labour and machinery. In addition, many crop protection chemicals are very toxic to mammals, including man, and can disturb the ecological balance of non-target organisms in treated environments. Some chemicals have had unforeseen effects on non-target organisms, but not all of these are detrimental either to the farmer or the environment. For example, although benzimidazole fungicides are lethal to earthworms, they can help to reduce the spread of insect-transmitted virus diseases because they also adversely affect the fecundity and feeding behaviour of aphid vectors (Russell, 1978*c*). It is no longer economic to produce very specific pesticides and it is probable that only chemicals with a broad spectrum of biological activity will be developed and marketed in the future. Some pesticides are phytotoxic to certain varieties of crop plants under certain environmental conditions; others can promote plant growth and yield by delaying senescence of leaves.

Among the potential disadvantages of chemical control is the fact that pathogens can become adapted to resist or tolerate certain chemicals. This has happened with several pathogens, for example *Cercospora beticola* and *Botrytis cinerea* to benomyl, *Helminthosporium* to mercury and *Erysiphe graminis* to ethirimol. However, in spite of many such drawbacks, chemical control has on the whole been very successful and diseases would be much more damaging if chemicals were not used. Nevertheless, pesticides should generally be applied only when there is no satisfactory alternative, or to supplement other control methods.

One of the most interesting recent developments in crop protection has been the discovery that some chemicals can control certain plant virus diseases. For example, work at Rothamsted Experimental Station has shown that tobacco mosaic can be prevented or cured by applying polyacrylic acid to the roots of tobacco plants (Kassanis & White, 1977); subsequent investigations have shown that solutions of aspirin (acetyl salicylic acid) have similar effects (White, 1979). Polyacrylic acid and aspirin apparently stimulate the production, by the host plant, of antiviral proteins. Tomlinson (1977) has demonstrated that the chlorotic leaf symptoms of beet western yellows virus in lettuce can be cured or masked by spraying the infected leaves with benomyl; this compound apparently preserves the chloroplasts so that infected leaves remain green.

Biological control

Biological control in its widest sense includes the use of resistant crop varieties and the natural enemies (parasites, predators and competitors) of the pathogens concerned. The use of natural enemies in crop protection has been confined mainly to the control of arthropod crop pests, but biological control has been used to control a few plant diseases. For example, inoculation of the cut surfaces of tree trunks with *Peniophora gigantea* (a saprophytic fungus) can protect the trunks against the pathogenic rot fungus *Fomes annosus* (Rishbeth, 1963). The implantation of wooden plugs inoculated with appropriate isolates of *Trichoderma viride* into fruit trees can protect the trees against severe attacks of silver leaf disease, caused by the fungal pathogen *Stereum purpureum* (Hirst, 1975). Soil microbes which are antagonistic to *Gaeumannomyces graminis* probably help to control take-all disease in continuous cereal-cropping systems. Biological control of insect vectors by natural insect enemies and parasitic fungi can play an important part in the control of insect-transmitted virus diseases.

Although such forms of biological control can help to reduce damage caused by some diseases and pests, the use of resistant varieties is probably the cheapest and most effective method (Russell, 1978*a*). It is as cheap for a farmer to grow a resistant variety as one which is susceptible, provided that the resistant and susceptible varieties are equal in terms of yield and quality when healthy. There have been many successes in breeding resistant varieties, and plant breeders have usually found sources of disease resistance in all crops whenever they have searched with determination. Resistant varieties have been developed against all the major groups of parasites which attack crop plants, including fungi, bacteria, mycoplasmas, viruses, invertebrate and vertebrate animal pests and parasitic flowering plants (Russell, 1978*a*). Many varieties with multiple resistance to several pests and diseases have been produced, and there is also great potential for the breeding of varieties resistant to post-harvest pests and diseases.

The advantages of many disease-resistant varieties have been short-lived because new variants of the causal pathogen, which are able to attack previously resistant variants, have soon become widespread. Although such varieties have not lost their resistance to the original variants of the pathogen, this situation is often referred to as a 'breakdown' of resistance. The importance of such 'breakdowns' has probably been exaggerated and resistance to most diseases has been long-lasting or durable. Russell (1978*a*) cites numerous examples of durable resistance to pests and diseases, many of which involve types of resistance which are simply inherited and therefore easy to use in breeding programmes; several of these examples are listed in Table 3.

Different types of resistance confer different levels of disease control and dur-

Table 3. *Some examples of durable major-gene resistance to disease (after Russell, 1978a)*

Type of pathogen	Disease and pathogen		Host crop
Fungi	Leaf rust	(*Puccinia hordei*)	Barley
	Root rot	(*Periconia circinata*)	Sorghum
	Leaf spot	(*Cercospora* spp.)	Cucumber
	Botrytis	(*Botrytis cinerea*)	Raspberry
	Scab	(*Venturia inaequalis*)	Apple
	Wart	(*Synchytrium endobioticum*)	Potato
	Fusarium	(*Fusarium oxysporum*)	Cabbage, tomatoes, peas
Bacteria	Bacterial blight	(*Xanthomonas malvacearum*)	Cotton
	Bacterial blight	(*Xanthomonas oryzae*)	Rice
	Wildfire, Angular leafspot	(*Pseudomonas* spp.)	Tobacco
Viruses	Leaf curl virus		Cotton
	Potato viruses X and Y		Potato
	Tobacco mosaic virus		Tobacco

ability. Disease-escape mechanisms have generally been both effective and durable, whereas hypersensitivity has often proved to be highly race-specific, as has resistance controlled by major genes (Russell, 1978a). However, there are good reasons for continuing to use major resistance genes because polygenically controlled resistance is more difficult to exploit by the plant breeder. Nevertheless, the presence of minor resistance genes, which might help to increase durability of resistance, can be masked by the presence of major genes. It is, therefore, desirable to study the resistance mechanisms which are controlled by different genetic systems so that plant breeders can identify and use them even when they are present in the same plant. To obtain such information it will be necessary to study a wide range of resistance mechanisms and to avoid too much concentration of effort on the elucidation of just one or two mechanisms, such as hypersensitivity.

Conclusions

Although it is impossible to assess accurately the losses of crop yields caused by disease, it is generally agreed that these losses are very great and that more effective control measures are urgently needed. It already costs many millions of dollars to develop and market a new fungicide; resistant varieties can usually be produced more cheaply and almost as quickly. It seems, therefore, that resistant varieties will play an even greater part in the control of pests and diseases in the future. However, it is unwise to rely exclusively on any one control method, and integrated control systems, involving combinations of all available methods, will probably give the most effective control of crop diseases. Plant pathologists, in collaboration with biochemists and physiologists, can provide information which may improve the accuracy of disease loss assessments, the efficiency of breeding for disease resistance and the development of new and more effective control methods.

References

Carlson, G. A. & Main, C. E. (1976). Economics of disease-loss management. *Annual Review of Phytopathology*, **14**, 381–403.

Cramer, H. H. (1967). *Plant protection and world crop production*. Leverkusen: Bayer Pflanzenschutz.

Doodson, J. K., Manners, J. G. & Myers, A. (1964). Some effects of yellow rust (*Puccinia striiformis*) on the growth and yield of a spring wheat. *Annals of Botany*, N.S., **28**, 459–72.

Food and Agricultural Organisation of the United Nations (1971). Crop loss assessment methods. In *FAO manual on the evaluation and prevention of losses by pests, diseases and weeds*. Rome: FAO.

Heathcote, G. D., Russell, G. E. & Van Steyvoort, L. (1973). Beet yellows, beet mild yellowing and beet western yellows viruses. In *FAO manual on the evaluation and prevention of losses by pests, diseases and weeds*, No. 99. Rome: FAO.

Hirst, J. M. (1975). The role of plant pathology. In *Proceedings of the Eighth British Insecticide and Fungicide Conference (1975)*, pp. 721–9. London: British Crop Protection Council.

Hull, R. (1968). The spray warning scheme for control of sugar beet yellows in England. Summary of results between 1959–66. *Plant Pathology*, **17**, 1–10.

James, W. C. (1974). Assessment of plant diseases and losses. *Annual Review of Phytopathology*, **12**, 27–48.

Kassanis, B. & White, R. (1977). Possible control of plant viruses by poly-acrylic acid. In *Proceedings of the 1977 British Crop Protection Conference – Pests and Diseases*, **3**, pp. 801–6. London: British Crop Protection Council.

Klinkowski, M. L. (1970). Catastrophic plant diseases. *Annual Review of Phytopathology*, **8**, 37–53.

Rishbeth, J. (1963). Stump protection against *Fomes annosus*. III. Inoculation with *Peniophora gigantea*. *Annals of Applied Biology*, **52**, 63–77.

Russell, G. E. (1964). Breeding for tolerance to beet yellows virus and beet mild yellowing virus in sugar beet. II. The response of breeding material to infection with different virus strains. *Annals of Applied Biology*, **53**, 377–88.

Russell, G. E. (1978a). *Plant Breeding for Pest and Disease Resistance*. London: Butterworths.

Russell, G. E. (1978b). Some effects of applied sodium and potassium chloride on yellow rust in winter wheat. *Annals of Applied Biology*, **90**, 163–8.

Russell, G. E. (1978c). Some effects of benzimidazole compounds on the transmission of beet yellows virus by *Myzus persicae*. In *Proceedings of the 1977 British Crop Protection Conference – Pests and Diseases*, **3**, pp. 831–4. London: British Crop Protection Council.

Scott, S. W. & Griffiths, Ellis (1980). Effects of controlled epidemics of powdery mildew on grain yield of spring barley. *Annals of Applied Biology*, **94**, 19–31.

Tomlinson, J. A. (1977). Chemotherapy of plant virus diseases. In *Proceedings of the 1977 British Crop Protection Conference – Pests and Diseases*, **3**, pp. 807–13. London: British Crop Protection Council.

Varley, J. E. (1977). The reaction of the cereal plant to disease. In *The Yield of Cereals*. National Agricultural Centre, Kenilworth, Warwickshire: Cereal Demonstrations and Information Unit.

White, R. (1979). Induction of resistance to tobacco mosaic virus (TMV) in tobacco by acetyl salicylic acid. *Rothamsted Experimental Station Report for 1978*, pp. 207–8.

B.B.BUCHANAN, S.W.HUTCHESON,
A.C.MAGYAROSY & P.MONTALBINI

Photosynthesis in healthy and diseased plants

General background

Life on our planet obtains its substance and energy through the process of photosynthesis – a grand device by which green plants use the electromagnetic energy of sunlight to synthesize carbohydrates (CH_2O) and other organic compounds from carbon dioxide and water (eqn 1).

$$CO_2 + 2H_2O \xrightarrow{\text{light}} (CH_2O) + O_2 + H_2O \qquad \text{(eqn 1)}$$

The carbohydrates formed by photosynthesis, and the other organic compounds into which they are transformed, provide the cellular constituents of the food for the vast numbers of living forms on our planet, from the simplest bacteria to the most highly developed animals, including man. Man's dependence on photosynthesis exceeds that of other life forms for he uses its non-edible products, such as wood and fibre, for shelter and warmth and his industrial civilization is powered by coal, oil, and natural gas – the fossilized products of photosynthesis which occurred millions of years ago.

In higher plants, the process of photosynthesis, as the name suggests, may be broadly divided into two phases: (i) a light phase in which the electromagnetic energy of sunlight is trapped and converted into biologically useful chemical energy (assimilatory power) and (ii) a synthetic (or carbon reduction) phase in which the assimilatory power generated by the light phase is used to synthesize carbohydrates and other organic compounds from carbon dioxide in a series of enzymatic reactions some of which, as noted below, are accelerated by light.

The discovery of 3-phosphoglyceric acid and other early intermediate products of carbon dioxide assimilation led to the formulation of the photosynthetic carbon cycle, according to which the conversion of one mole of carbon dioxide to the level of carbohydrate requires three moles of adenosine-5'-triphosphate (ATP) and two moles of NADPH (Bassham & Calvin, 1957; Fig. 1).

ATP is the substance that is often characterized as the universal energy currency of all living cells, be they plants, animals, or bacteria. One of the functions of ATP is to provide the activation energy needed for the myriad of cellular biosynthetic reactions, including those of photosynthesis. NADPH or NADPH$_2$ represents the reduced form of nicotinamide adenine dinucleotide phosphate. NADPH is a strong reductant in biosynthetic reactions; its great reducing power enables it to force electrons (accompanied by protons) on other molecules. In carbon dioxide assimilation, NADPH is the carrier of the electrons and protons (i.e. the hydrogen atoms) required for the conversion of phosphorylated intermediates (i.e. intermediates activated by ATP) to carbohydrates and other organic compounds.

The requirement for ATP and NADPH (or its analogue, NADH) for the conversion of carbon dioxide into carbohydrates is not peculiar to photosynthesis. The same two compounds are required when carbohydrates are formed from carbon dioxide by non-photosynthetic, autotrophic cells. What distinguishes carbon dioxide assimilation by photosynthetic cells from that by non-photosynthetic cells is the source of energy for the generation of ATP and NADPH. Photosyn-

Fig. 1. ATP and NADPH$_2$ requirements per mole of carbon dioxide assimilated in higher plants.

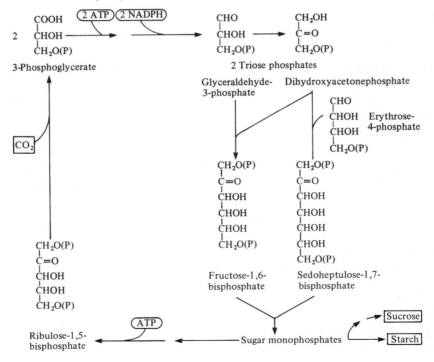

thetic cells, as may be seen below, generate these two compounds at the expense of the electromagnetic energy of sunlight, whereas nonphotosynthetic cells generate them at the expense of some external source of chemical energy.

Photophosphorylation and electron transport

The photosynthetic conversion of radiant energy into chemical energy involves two photochemical reactions, cyclic and non-cyclic photophosphorylation (Arnon, 1969, 1971, 1977). In photosynthetic eukaryotic organisms both of these reactions take place in chloroplasts – the organelles that house the photosynthetic apparatus and its associated enzyme components that catalyse the complete photosynthetic process.

In *cyclic* photophosphorylation, radiant energy is converted into the pyrophosphate bonds of ATP in the absence of a chemical substrate, as shown in eqn 2, in which Pi represents inorganic phosphate.

$$ADP + P_i \xrightarrow{\text{light}} ATP \qquad \text{(eqn 2)}$$

Cyclic photophosphorylation in isolated chloroplasts requires an added catalyst. The physiological catalyst of cyclic photophosphorylation is ferredoxin, a soluble iron–sulphur protein indigenous to chloroplasts. Artificial electron carriers, such as phenazine methosulfate, are effective substitutes for ferredoxin.

In *non-cyclic* photophosphorylation, the formation of ATP is coupled to an oxidation–reduction reaction in which electrons from water are transferred photochemically to ferredoxin (Fd), with a concomitant evolution of molecular oxygen (eqn 3).

$$4Fd_{\text{oxidized}} + 2ADP + 2Pi + 2H_2O \xrightarrow{\text{light}} 4Fd_{\text{reduced}} + 2ATP + O_2 + 4H^+ \qquad \text{(eqn 3)}$$

The ferredoxin so reduced can be used in turn to reduce NADP in a reaction that is catalysed by a flavoprotein enzyme independently of light (eqn 4).

$$2Fd_{\text{reduced}} + NADP \xrightarrow[\text{reductase}]{\text{Fd-NADP}} NADPH_2 + 2Fd_{\text{oxidized}} \qquad \text{(eqn 4)}$$

Acceptors such as ferricyanide (FeCN) act as non-physiological substitutes for ferredoxin or NADP in non-cyclic photophosphorylation (eqn 5).

$$4FeCN_{\text{oxidized}} + 2ADP + 2Pi + 2H_2O \xrightarrow{\text{light}} 4FeCN_{\text{reduced}} + 2ATP + O_2 + 4H^+ \qquad \text{(eqn 5)}$$

Non-cyclic electron transport is inhibited specifically by 3-(3,4-dichlorophenyl)-1,1-dimethyl urea (DCMU), a herbicide, and by *o*-phenanthroline, a metal-chelating agent.

The mechanism by which cyclic and non-cyclic photophosphorylation are considered to be effected in chloroplasts is shown in Fig. 2. The heart of the system is a light-driven transport of electrons from chlorophyll to each of two acceptors. In non-cyclic photophosphorylation, electrons flow through two photochemical reactions from water to ferredoxin and then to NADP; in cyclic photophosphorylation, electrons flow through a single photochemical reaction and cycle in a closed system without net oxidation or reduction. It is to be noted that the light-driven transport of electrons in both cyclic and non-cyclic photophosphorylation is accompanied by a transport of protons that results in the formation of a proton gradient across chloroplast membranes. The discharge of this ion gradient releases energy that is used for the synthesis of ATP from ADP and Pi (Trebst, 1974; Malkin & Bearden, 1978).

Assimilation of carbon dioxide

For many years it was assumed that the sole requirement for light in photosynthesis was to provide the reductant (reduced ferredoxin or $NADPH_2$) and ATP needed as substrates to drive carbon dioxide assimilation via the pathway responsible for that process (the reductive pentose phosphate cycle). Results

Fig. 2. Mechanisms of non-cyclic and cyclic photophosphorylation in chloroplasts. Non-standard abbreviations: P680, reaction centre chlorophyll of photosystem II; A_{II}, primary electron acceptor of photosystem II; PQ, plastoquinone; cyt. f, cytochrome f; PC, plastocyanin; P700, reaction centre chlorophyll of photosystem I; A_I, primary electron acceptor of photosystem I; Fd, ferredoxin; Fp, flavoprotein (ferredoxin–NADP reductase); cyt. b_6, cytochrome b_6.

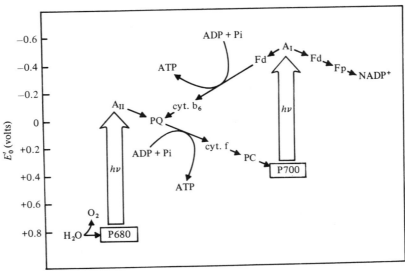

obtained during the past 15 years have caused a revision in that concept (Buchanan, Wolosiuk & Schürmann, 1979; Buchanan, 1980). It is now apparent that, in addition to its substrate function in supplying ATP and $NADPH_2$, light is required catalytically in chloroplasts for the regulation of enzymes involved with the synthesis, as well as with the degradation, of energy-rich compounds. The regulatory function of light encompasses both enzyme activation (whereby the reductive pentose phosphate cycle (Fig. 3) and related biosynthetic pathways are accelerated) and enzyme inhibition (whereby starch degradation, glycolysis, and the oxidative pentose phosphate pathway are impeded). It is because of this dual regulatory function of light that the degradative and synthetic pathways, which share a number of enzymes, can coexist and operate within the confines of the chloroplast (Fig. 4).

In fulfilling its regulatory role, light acts through several different mechanisms, which, in each case, are linked to the photosynthetic apparatus (Fig. 5). The light absorbed by chlorophyll induces changes in components associated with electron transport and thereby conveys a signal to enzymes of metabolic processes that, according to some lines of evidence, need not be restricted to chloroplasts. The light-linked changes used to elicit an alteration of enzyme activity include (i) shifts in the concentration of ions, especially H^+ and Mg^{2+}, (ii) increases in the concentration of metabolites that alter enzyme activity (enzyme effectors), such as ATP and $NADPH_2$, and (iii) changes in the oxidation–reduction state of specific regulatory proteins, such as thioredoxins. These three types of mechanisms appear to act in concert for the regulation of

Fig. 3. Role of light in the activation of enzymes of the reductive pentose phosphate cycle of carbon dioxide assimilation in higher plants.

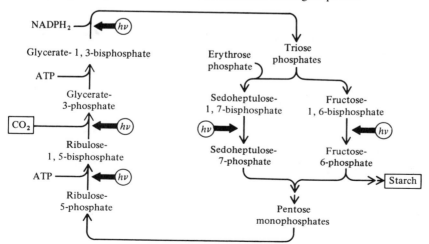

specific chloroplast enzymes during photosynthesis. Each of the changes effected by light must be reversed under conditions prevailing in the dark. It is of possible importance that the enzymes found to undergo activation by light include, among others, those catalysing apparently rate-limiting steps in photosynthesis, at least in some plants.

Fig. 4. Effect of light on regulatory enzymes of carbon pathways. Fru-P$_2$ase, fructose-1,6-bisphosphatase; Sed-P$_2$ase, sedoheptulose-1,7-bisphosphatase; NADP–GAPD, NADP–glyceraldehyde-3-phosphate dehydrogenase; RBP–Case, ribulose-1,5-bisphosphate carboxylase–oxygenase; NADP–MDH, NADP–malate dehydrogenase; Pyr., Pi dikinase, pyruvate, Pi dikinase; PFK, phosphofructokinase; G6PD, glucose-6-phosphate dehydrogenase; PGA, phosphoglycerate.

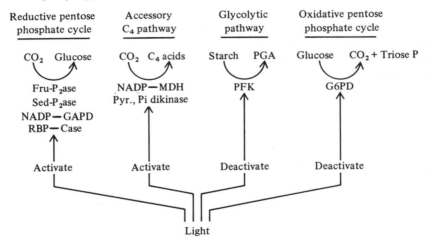

Fig. 5. Light-dependent mechanisms of enzyme activation in chloroplasts. GSSG, oxidized glutathione; LEM, light-effect mediator.

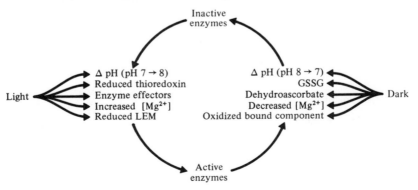

The question might be asked, why does light have a regulatory role, in addition to a well-documented energetic role, in producing the ATP and $NADPH_2$ ('assimilatory power') required for photosynthesis? It appears that the chloroplast uses the light-linked changes to enhance the activity of enzymes of photosynthetic pathways and to suppress the activity of enzymes of degradation. In this manner, the plant is assured that each pathway is fully active only during the time of greatest need. Thus, the photosynthetic and related biosynthetic enzymes are active during the day, and the degradative enzymes are active during the night when the plant must extract its energy from the breakdown of energy-rich compounds that were synthesized during the day. If the plants were unable to link the activity of the indicated enzymes to light, the light energy converted and stored in energy-rich compounds would be spent uselessly in concomitant degradative reactions.

Effect of plant pathogens on photosynthesis

Although there is extensive information on the physiological and biochemical changes induced in plants by pathogenic agents, little is known about the effect of disease-causing organisms on photosynthesis at the biochemical level. Studies with each of the three major types of etiological agents (viruses, fungi and bacteria) have revealed that the rate of photosynthesis in infected plants may be unchanged, suppressed, or, in some cases, increased. Infection can alter the products of photosynthesis, in some cases quite appreciably, irrespective of effects on the rate of photosynthesis. The mechanism by which the alteration is effected is known only in a few instances. We summarize below the effect on photosynthesis of representatives of each of the major types of etiological agents. The discussion is restricted to photosynthetic events *per se* and does not deal with the effects of pathogens on such related processes as stomatal behaviour which, however, could have important consequences for photosynthesis by the complete plant (Hall & Loomis, 1972; Ayres, 1981).

Viruses

After the discovery of viruses by Ivanovski in 1894 and later, independently, by Beijerinck (1898, 1899*a*) (who became aware of Ivanovski's work only after his own work had been published (1899*b*)), two views emerged to explain the primary effect of virus infection on leaves: (i) the view of Beijerinck, and Konig (1899), that virus infection is primarily a disease of chloroplasts and manifests itself by chloroplast damage and ultimate disintegration (Matz, 1922; Eckerson, 1926; Nelson, 1932); and (ii) the view of Woods (1902) and Ivanovski (1903) that the primary effect of virus infection does not involve chloroplasts. According to the second view, virus infection may lead to a reduction in the number of chloroplasts but it does not initially cause major changes in their photosynthetic activity. Although chloroplast activity may be altered in the later stages of disease, such changes would be a result rather than a primary cause of the diseased condition.

More recent investigations of a biochemical character have provided evidence that systemic virus infection decreases the rate of photosynthesis by leaves and of photophosphorylation by isolated chloroplasts (see Magyarosy, Buchanan & Schürman, 1973; Platt, Henriques & Rand, 1979). However, those investigations provide no evidence as to whether the lower rates reflect a primary change in chloroplasts caused by the virus, or whether the reduction in rates results from a general decline in the metabolic activities of the infected leaf. Furthermore, it is not known whether the increased synthesis of free amino acids and organic acids reported for different types of virus-infected leaves reflects changes in reactions that occur within chloroplasts.

Work from our laboratory has confirmed and extended the conclusions made at the turn of the century by Woods and Ivanovski. Leaves from squash plants (*Cucurbita pepo*) systemically infected with squash mosaic virus showed a shift in products from sugars to amino acids (in particular, alanine), an increase in cytoplasmic ribosomes and fewer chloroplasts (Magyarosy et al., 1973). There was no difference between healthy and diseased chloroplasts with respect to the other parameters tested (sensitivity of carbon dioxide assimilation to DCMU and antimycin A, an inhibitor of ferredoxin-catalysed cyclic photosphosphorylation; rate of cyclic and non-cyclic photophosphorylation; ultracentrifugation profile; products of photosynthetic $^{14}CO_2$ assimilation; activity of the enzymes ribulose, 1,5-bisphosphate carboxylase and phosphoenolpyruvate carboxylase; chloroplast ultrastructure). We found a slight increase in the rate of $^{14}CO_2$ assimilation in the infected plants similar to that observed by Owen (1957) and by others (Zaitlin & Hesketch, 1965; Smith & Neales, 1977). It is possible that the inability of plants infected with certain viruses to produce a full complement of chloroplasts is related to a reported reduction in their capacity to synthesize chloroplastic RNAs and proteins (Hirai & Wildman, 1969; Randles & Coleman, 1970; Oxelfelt, 1971; Mohamed & Randles, 1972).

Results similar to the findings with squash mosaic virus were recently reported by Platt et al. (1979) with virus-infected *Tolmiea menziesii* (piggyback plant). These investigators found, in addition, that infected leaves had an increased ratio of chlorophyll $a:b$ and a decreased content of the light-harvesting chlorophyll $a+b$ protein. They concluded that the infected leaves have a significantly lower amount of antenna chlorophyll, but no less reaction centre chlorophyll, than their healthy counterparts. The infected leaves showed an enhanced formation of glycine and a diminished formation of sucrose.

In separate studies, the research groups of Bové (Goffeau & Bové, 1965) and of Matthews (Bedbrook & Matthews, 1972, 1973) investigated the effect of turnip yellow mosaic virus on photosynthesis. Both groups used *Brassica pekinensis* (Chinese cabbage) in their studies and concluded that the chloroplasts were structurally and biochemically affected by infection. Bovë's group reported an increase of both cyclic and non-cyclic photophosphorylation in chloroplasts from infected plants; Matthews' group observed that infection causes a shift in photosynthetic products from sugars to organic acids and amino acids, a shift that was also reported by other investigators examining different virus diseases (see Platt *et al.*, 1979). Accompanying this shift in products was an increase in the activity of phosphoenolpyruvate carboxylase and aspartate aminotransferase, and a decrease in the activity of ribulose-1,5-bisphosphate carboxylase. In the case of turnip yellow mosaic virus it is noteworthy that the viral nucleic acid is formed in the vesicles of the chloroplast envelope, and the virus is thus considered to be a parasite of the chloroplast (Matthews, 1973).

It may be concluded that the photosynthetic process can be altered by virus infection in two ways. As exemplified by squash plants (infected with squash mosaic virus) and by piggyback plants (doubly infected with tomato bushy stunt and cucumber virus), virus infection may reduce the number of chloroplasts but it has little effect on photosynthesis or on chloroplast ultrastructure. In these plants, the virus influences mainly the reactions of the leaf cytoplasm (Fig. 6). As exemplified by Chinese cabbage plants (infected with turnip yellow mosaic

Fig. 6. Effect of a systemic virus infection on photosynthesis, e.g. squash mosaic virus on squash plants.

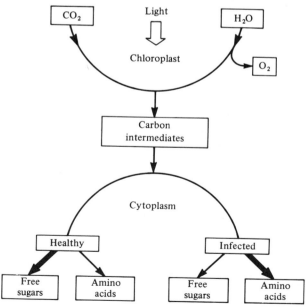

virus), virus infection alters the partial reactions of photosynthesis (e.g. photo-phosphorylation) and thereby impedes plant growth. It appears that the interaction between the host plant and a specific virus determines the course of changes in photosynthesis and in other processes of plants.

Fungi

A change in the rate of photosynthesis by whole plants or by intact leaves has been reported to be induced by mildew and rust infections (see references cited by Magyarosy, Schürmann & Buchanan, 1976; Mignucci & Boyer, 1979; Mitchell, 1979) and by leaf spot and scab diseases (see Spotts & Ferree, 1979). However, investigations of effects of different types of fungal infection on the partial reactions of photosynthesis are limited. Our laboratory has investigated the effect of infection by obligate parasites (rusts, powdery mildews) on reactions of photosynthesis. We found that powdery mildew on sugar beet (*Beta vulgaris*) and rust on broad bean (*Vicia faba*) effected a preferential inhibition of non-cyclic photophosphorylation in isolated chloroplasts (Montalbini & Buchanan, 1974; Magyarosy et al., 1976). With both of these agents, inhibition stemmed from a diminution of electron flow from water to NADP and, with powdery mildew, led to an inhibition of photosynthetic carbon dioxide assimilation and a shift in products from sucrose to amino acids (alanine, glutamate, aspartate). These observations provide an explanation for the report that sugar beet plants infected with powdery mildew have a reduced capability to form sucrose. In both rust and powdery mildew infections, chloroplasts undergo aberrations in ultrastructure (Coffee, Palevitz & Allen, 1972; Heath, 1974; Mlodzianowski & Siwecki, 1975; Magyarosy et al., 1976). In addition, there is a reduction in the activity of enzymes that lead to the production of organic acids (malate dehydrogenase, phosphoenolpyruvate carboxylase) (Magyarosy et al., 1976).

In separate studies, rust infection decreased the activity of ribulose-1,5-bisphosphate carboxylase in wheat leaves (Wrigley & Webster, 1966) but had little or no effect on photophosphorylation in oat plants (Wynn, 1963).

Infection with obligate parasites in most cases seems to cause a reduction in the rate of photosynthesis by leaves (Fig. 7). There is now solid evidence that this decrease is due, at least in part, to a parasite-induced block in the non-cyclic electron transport chain (Montalbini & Buchanan, 1974; Magyarosy et al., 1976). The chloroplasts isolated from infected leaves showed a substantial (up to 45%) decrease in the rate of non-cyclic electron transport (water as electron donor, NADP or ferricyanide as electron acceptor) and attendant phosphorylation. Infection had no effect on the coupling of phosphorylation to photosynthetic electron transport (i.e. photophosphorylation) as determined by the ratio of ATP formed to NADP reduced (P:2e). Therefore, it appears that the invading parasite causes a block in the non-cyclic electron transport chain.

At first, the nature of this parasite-induced block was a mystery. We expressed the idea that the fungal parasite effects the formation of a compound that is functionally similar to DCMU (Montalbini & Buchanan, 1974). However, this possibility now seems unlikely since subsequent experiments have revealed that extensively washed chloroplast membranes from rust-infected plants show no relief from parasite-induced inhibition when compared to their unwashed counterparts (Montalbini, Buchanan & Hutcheson, 1980). These new results indicate that parasitic infection results in an alteration of components of the non-cyclic electron transport chain.

Recent evidence confirms that this may be the case (Magyarosy & Malkin, 1978). The cytochrome content of the electron transport chain was decreased by about one-third in chloroplasts from powdery mildew-infected sugar beet plants (i.e. cytochromes f, b_{559HP}, b_6 and b_{559LP}). The photosystem I and photosystem II reaction centres and the bound iron–sulphur proteins were unaffected by infection. These results suggest that infection by obligate parasites specifically alters the content of certain carriers involved in the electron transport chain and, thereby, reduces the rate of non-cyclic electron transport. It is possible that the decrease in the cytochrome content of these electron carriers is related to the pathogen-induced reduction of ribosomes and rRNA in the chloroplasts (Plumb, Manners & Myers, 1968; Bennett & Scott, 1971; Dyer & Scott, 1972; Callow, 1973).

Fig. 7. Effect of powdery mildew infection on the rate of photosynthetic $^{14}CO_2$ assimilation by sugar beet (*Beta vulgaris*) leaf disks. Healthy leaves, O—O; infected leaves, ●—●; dark control (healthy or infected) △—△.

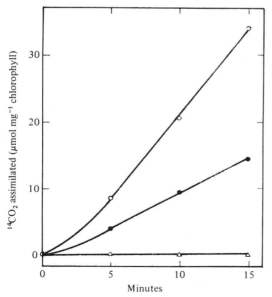

Finally, it should be remembered that changes in the rate of photosynthesis in fungus-infected plants stem basically from the diverse effects of mycelial growth during the course of the infection. Depending on the stage of infection, one can also observe differential effects on the biochemical reactions associated with photosynthesis – e.g. photophosphorylation. Results are further complicated by the different responses that pathogens elicit in susceptible and resistant plants. We believe, therefore, that caution should be exercised in making generalizations concerning the effect of fungal infection on photosynthesis and related processes.

Bacteria

Bacteria are important disease-causing agents that are responsible for extensive crop losses throughout the world. Despite the economic importance of these organisms, very little is known about their effect on photosynthesis. In those crops that have been examined, the organisms caused a continued decrease in the rate of photosynthesis (Beckman, Brun & Buddenhagen, 1962; Magyarosy & Buchanan, 1975) that was accompanied by extensive structural damage to chloroplasts (Braun, 1955; Goodman & Plulard, 1971; Sigee & Epton, 1976).

Saprophytic bacteria differ from their pathogenic counterparts, when infil-

Fig. 8. Effect of bacterial infiltration on the rate of photosynthetic $^{14}CO_2$ assimilation by bean (*Phaseolus vulgaris*) leaf disks. Saprophyte, △—△; pathogen ○----○.

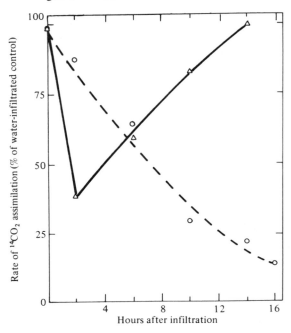

trated into leaves, in that, although they cause an initial decrease in the rate of photosynthesis, this is only transient (Fig. 8), and they induce no alterations in chloroplast ultrastructure. The photosynthetic products formed in the pathogen- and saprophyte-infiltrated plants are similar to each other and to those from water-infiltrated controls (Magyarosy & Buchanan, 1975). Although further studies are needed in this area, it is believed that the inhibition of photosynthesis and the accompanying ultrastructural changes induced by the pathogen are ow- ing, in part, to the effect of toxins formed (Mitchell, 1978) and released by the invading organisms.

Closing comments

In the decade just ended, great strides were made in our understanding of photosynthesis in healthy plants. Among other developments, new compo- nents of the photosynthetic electron transport chain were identified, and a role for light in enzyme regulation was established. During the same period, our knowledge of the effect of plant pathogens on photosynthesis also increased, but less extensively. Consequently, our understanding of the alterations of photosyn- thesis in diseased plants is far from complete.

The basic foundations have been established for the effects of some types of infections on photosynthesis, but relatively little is known about the mechanisms involved. That is, with the possible exceptions of obligate parasites and certain viruses, we know little of how a particular pathogen alters photosyn- thesis. Furthermore, the number of different types of pathogenic agents that have been examined thoroughly for causing changes in photosynthesis is limited. This situation applies to viruses, fungi, and, especially, to bacteria – the group that has been most neglected in studies of infection. The relation of different types of etiological agents to photosynthesis thus emerges as a fertile area for future stud- ies.

Acknowledgements

This work was supported in part by the US – Italy Cooperative Science Program through grants to BBB (from the US National Science Foundation) and to PM (from the Italian Consiglio Nazionale delle Ricerche).

References

Arnon, D. I. (1969). Role of ferredoxin in photosynthesis. *Naturwissenschaf- ten,* **56,** 295–305.

Arnon, D. I. (1971). The light reactions of photosynthesis. *Proceedings of the National Academy of Sciences, U.S.A.,* **68,** 2883–92.

Arnon, D. I. (1977). Photosynthesis 1950–75. Changing concepts and per- spectives. In *Encyclopedia of Plant Physiology,* New Series, vol. 5, *Photo- synthesis I, Photosynthetic Electron Transport and Photophosphorylation,* ed. A. Trebst & M. Avron, pp. 7–56. Heidelberg: Springer-Verlag.

Ayres, P. G. (1981). Responses of stomata to pathogenic microorganisms. In *Stomatal Physiology,* ed. P. G. Jarvis & T. A. Mansfield, pp. 205–21. Cambridge: Cambridge University Press.

Bassham, J. A. & Calvin, M. (1957). *The Path of Carbon in Photosynthesis.* Engelwood Cliffs, N.J.: Prentice-Hall.

Beckman, C. H., Brun, W. A. & Buddenhagen, I. W. (1962). Water relations in banana plants infected with *Pseudomonas solanacearum. Phytopathology,* **52,** 1144–8.

Bedbrook, J. R. & Matthews, R. E. F. (1972). Changes in the proportions of the early products of photosynthetic carbon fixation by TYMV infection. *Virology,* **48,** 255–8.

Bedbrook, J. R. & Matthews, R. E. F. (1973). Changes in the flow of early products of photosynthetic carbon fixation associated with the replication of TYMV. *Virology,* **53,** 84–91.

Beijerinck, M. W. (1898). Ueber ein contagium vivum Fluidum als Ursache der Fleckenkrankheit der Tabaksblätter. *Verhandelinger der Koninklyke academic van Wettenschappen te Amsterdam,* Part VI, No. 3, 3 (1898). Article is translated by J. Johnson, *Phytopathological Classics,* No. 7 (1942). American Phytopathological Society.

Beijerinck, M. W. (1899*a*). Over een Contagium vivum fluidum als oorzaak van de Vlekziekte der Tabaksbladen. *Verhandelinger der Koniklyke academic van Wettenschappen te Amsterdam,* Part VII, pp. 229–35. (Paper submitted 26 November 1898.)

Beijerinck, M. W. (1899*b*). Bemerkung zu dem Aufsatz von Herrn Iwanowsky über die Mosaikkrankheit der Tabakspflanze. *Zentralblatt für Bakteriologie und Parasitenkunde,* **5,** 310–11.

Bennett, J. & Scott, K. J. (1971). Ribosome metabolism in mildew-infected barley leaves. *Federation of European Biochemical Societies Letters,* **16,** 93–5.

Braun, A. C. (1955). A study on the mode of action of the wildfire toxin. *Phytopathology,* **45,** 659–64.

Buchanan, B. B. (1980). Role of light in the regulation of chloroplast enzymes. *Annual Review of Plant Physiology,* **31,** 341–74.

Buchanan, B. B., Wolosiuk, R. A. & Schürmann, P. (1979). Thioredoxin and enzyme regulation. *Trends in Biochemical Sciences,* **4,** 93–6.

Callow, J. A. (1973). Ribosomal RNA metabolism in cucumber leaves infected by *Erysiphe cichoracearum. Physiological Plant Pathology,* **3,** 249–57.

Coffee, M. D., Palevitz, B. A. & Allen, P. J. (1972). Ultrastructural changes in rust-infected tissues of flax and sunflower. *Canadian Journal of Botany,* **50,** 1485–92.

Dyer, T. A. & Scott, K. J. (1972). Decrease in chloroplast polysome content of barley leaves infected with powdery mildew. *Nature,* **236,** 237–8.

Eckerson, S. H. (1926). An organism of tomato mosaic. *Botanical Gazette,* **81,** 204–8.

Goffeau, A. & Bovë, J. M. (1965). Virus infection and photosynthesis. *Virology,* **27,** 243–52.

Goodman, R. N. & Plulard, S. B. (1971). Ultrastructural changes in tobacco undergoing the hypersensitive reaction caused by plant pathogenic bacteria. *Physiological Plant Pathology,* **1,** 11–15.

Hall, A. E. & Loomis, R. S. (1972). An explanation for the difference in photosynthetic capabilities of healthy and beet yellow virus-infected sugar beets (*Beta vulgaris* L.). *Plant Physiology,* **50,** 576–80.

Heath, M. C. (1974). Chloroplast ultrastructure and ethylene production of se-
nescing and rust-infected cowpea leaves. *Canadian Journal of Botany*, **52**,
2591–7.

Hirai, T. & Wildman, S. G. (1969). Effect of TMV multiplication on RNA
and protein synthesis in tobacco chloroplasts. *Virology*, **38**, 73–82.

Ivanovski, D. (1894). *Über die Mossaikkrankheit der Tabakspflanze, Belletin*
No. 3. St Petersbourgh: Imperial Academy of Sciences.

Ivanovski, D. (1903). Über die Mossikkrankheit der Tabakspflanze. *Zeitschrift
für Pflanzenkrankheiten*, **13**, 1–41.

Konig, C. J. (1899). Die Flecken-Oder für Mosaikkrankheit des Hollan-
dischen Tobaks. *Zeitschrift Pflanzenkrankheiten*, **9**, 65–80.

Magyarosy, A. C. & Buchanan, B. B. (1975). Effect of bacterial infiltration
on photosynthesis of bean leaves. *Phytopathology*, **65**, 777–80.

Magyarosy, A. C., Buchanan, B. B. & Schürmann, P. (1973). Effect of a
systemic virus infection on chloroplast function and structure. *Virology*, **55**,
426–38.

Magyarosy, A. C. & Malkin, R. (1978). Effect of powdery mildew infection
of sugar beet on the content of electron carriers in chloroplasts. *Physiological Plant Pathology*, **13**, 183–8.

Magyarosy, A. C., Schürmann, P. & Buchanan, B. B. (1976). Effect of powdery mildew infection on photosynthesis by leaves and chloroplasts of sugar
beets. *Plant Physiology*, **57**, 486–9.

Malkin, R. & Bearden, A. J. (1978). Membrane-bound iron-sulfur centers in
photosynthetic systems. *Biochimica et Biophysica Acta*, **505**, 147–81.

Matthews, R. E. F. (1973). Induction of disease by viruses. *Annual Review of
Phytopathology*, **11**, 147–70.

Matz, J. (1922). Recent developments in the study of the nature of mosaic
disease of sugar cane and other plants. *Journal of Department of Agriculture, Puerto Rico*, **6**, 22–7.

Mignucci, J. S. & Boyer, J. S. (1979). Inhibition of photosynthesis and transpiration in soybean infected by *Microsphaera diffusa*. *Phytopathology*, **69**,
227–30.

Mitchell, D. T. (1979). Carbon dioxide exchange by infected first leaf tissues
susceptible to wheat stem rust. *Transactions of the British Mycological Society*, **72**, 63–8.

Mitchell, R. E. (1978). Halo blight of beans: toxin production by several
Pseudomonas phaseolicola isolates. *Physiological Plant Pathology*, **13**,
37–49.

Mlodzianowski, F. & Siwecki, R. (1975). Ultrastructural changes in chloroplasts of *Populus tremula* L. leaves affected by the fungus *Melampsora pin-
torqua*, Braun. Rostr. *Physiological Plant Pathology*, **6**, 1–3.

Mohamed, N. A. & Randles, J. W. (1972). Effect of tomato spotted wilt virus on ribosomes, ribonucleic acids and Fraction I protein in *Nicotina tabacum* leaves. *Physiological Plant Pathology*, **2**, 235–45.

Montalbini, P. & Buchanan, B. B. (1974). Effect of a rust infection on photophosphorylation by isolated chloroplasts. *Physiological Plant Pathology*, **4**,
191–6.

Montalbini, P., Buchanan, B. B. & Hutcheson, S. W. (1981). Effect of rust
infection on rates of photochemical polyphenol oxidation and latent polyphenol oxidase activity of *Vicia faba* chloroplast membranes. *Physiological
Plant Pathology*, **18**, 51–7.

Nelson, R. (1932). *Investigations in the mosaic disease of bean. Michigan Agriculture Experiment Station Section Botany, Technical Bulletin*, No. 118.

Owen, P. C. (1957). The effects of infection with tobacco mosaic virus on the photosynthesis of tobacco leaves. *Annals of Applied Biology*, **45**, 456–61.

Oxelfelt, P. (1971). Development of systemic TMV infection. II. RNA metabolism in systemically infected leaves. *Phytopathologische Zeitschrift*, **71**, 247–56.

Platt, S. G., Henriques, F. & Rand, L. (1979). Effects of virus infection on the chlorophyll content, photosynthetic rate and carbon metabolism of *Tolmiea menziesii*. *Physiological Plant Pathology*, **15**, 351–65.

Plumb, R. T., Manners, J. G. & Myers, A. (1968). Behaviour of nucleic acids in mildew-infected wheat. *Transactions of the British Mycological Society*, **51**, 563–73.

Randles, J. W. & Coleman, D. F. (1970). Loss of ribosomes in *N. glutinosa* L. infected with lettuce necrotic yellows virus. *Virology*, **41**, 459–64.

Sigee, D. C. & Epton, H. A. (1976). Ultrastructural changes in resistant and susceptible varieties of *Phaseolus vulgaris*. *Physiological Plant Pathology*, **9**, 1–8.

Smith, P. R. & Neales, T. F. (1977). Analysis of the effects of virus infection on the photosynthetic properties of peach leaves. *Australian Journal of Plant Physiology*, **4**, 723–32.

Spotts, R. A. & Ferree, D. C. (1979). Photosynthesis, transpiration, and water potential of apple leaves infected by *Venturia inaequalis*. *Phytopathology*, **69**, 717–19.

Trebst, A. (1974). Energy conservation in photosynthetic electron transport of chloroplasts. *Annual Review of Plant Physiology*, **25**, 423–58.

Woods, A. F. (1902). *Observations on the mosaic disease of tobacco. U.S. Department of Agriculture Bureau of Plant Industry, Bulletin* No. 18. Washington, D.C.: Government Printing Office.

Wrigley, C. W. & Webster, H. L. (1966). The effect of stem rust infection on the soluble proteins of wheat. *Australian Journal of Biological Science*, **19**, 895–901.

Wynn, W. K. (1963). Photosynthetic phosphorylation by chloroplasts isolated from rust-affected oats. *Phytopathology*, **53**, 1376–7.

Zaitlin, M. & Hesketch, J. D. (1965). The short term effects of infection by tobacco mosaic virus on apparent photosynthesis of tobacco leaves. *Annals of Applied Biology*, **55**, 239–63.

T. KOSUGE & J. A. KIMPEL

Energy use and metabolic regulation in plant–pathogen interactions

Introduction

The ultimate goal of research on bioenergetics in plant–pathogen interactions is to understand fully in a quantitative sense how disease affects energy utilization by the plant. First, it will be useful to discuss certain concepts of energy generation and metabolic regulation in the healthy plant. As shown in Fig. 1, the capture of the sun's energy and the photoassimilation of carbon dioxide by the photosynthetic machinery initiates the flow of energy in the plant's metabolic machinery. Photoassimilates are converted to starch in the chloroplast for temporary energy storage or transported to sinks where they are used as sources of energy, converted to cellular constituents or converted to storage forms. The energy-generating machinery of dark respiration serves as a 'back-up' system to the photosynthetic machinery in the leaves and is the source of energy generation in roots and other non-chlorophyllous tissues. Furthermore, energy production by both oxidative phosphorylation and photophosphorylation is coupled to biosynthesis by ATP/ADP interconversions and reducing power interconversions (NADPH/NADP) as detailed in the previous chapter. Consumption of carbon by dark respiration and photorespiration, of course, works in opposition to photoassimilation and detracts from yield.

According to the schematic diagram (Fig. 1) the net amount of energy stored in the biosynthetic products of the plant determines its yield, which is the ultimate product of light energy capture and photoassimilation. In the healthy plant a relatively small proportion of biosynthesis is directed to maintenance and replacement of cellular structures undergoing turnover. Maintenance respiration detracts less than 20% from the total amount of carbon assimilated by the plant since most of the intermediates released by turnover would be recycled into the main stream of metabolism. Disease tends to interfere with the 'flow' of energy in the plant, being disruptive of one or more of the processes shown in the diagram, which weakens the capacity of the plant cells to respond to ingress by pathogens. However, such disruption may be minimized by rapid, efficient mobilization of energy and metabolites through 'maintenance' biosynthesis concerned with defence reactions of the plant.

Let us consider in greater detail the individual processes in plants responding to infection.

Response of plants to infection

General reactions

Without exception, infection of plant tissues by pathogens causes increases in respiration of host cells, apart from any direct contribution by the pathogen (Scott & Smillie, 1966; Daly, 1976; Fig. 2). However, increased respiratory activity may not be deleterious to the plant cell, but may be associated with the creation of a metabolic sink, the accompanying mobilization of energy sources and nutrients, production of energy and enhanced biosynthetic activity, all of which enable the plant to respond more effectively to infection and permit expression of resistance. On the other hand, increased respiration, creation of a metabolic sink (Livne & Daly, 1966), and the accompanying increased flow of nutrients to the site of infection, may be advantageous to any pathogen which relies on the host for nutrients necessary for its multiplication and reproduction. Thus, the outcome of the plant–pathogen interaction, resistance or susceptibility of host tissue, may be determined by the efficiency of the host metabolic machinery to provide the necessary constituents conferring resistance against the pathogen.

Allen (1959) was among the first to suggest that the plant's response to infec-

Fig. 1. Energy generating and consuming systems in plants. The role of ATP and NADPH in coupling energy-yielding and energy-requiring processes is emphasized. A certain percentage of respiration is associated with 'maintenance', which involves replacement of cell constituents undergoing normal turnover.

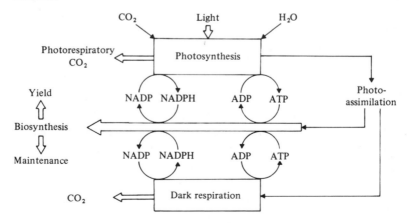

tion is a general reaction of repair of injury. Work in recent years generally supports Allen's hypothesis. Indeed, the 'wound' responses of slices of potato tuber and carrot root often mimic those observed in plant cells responding to infection (Adams & Rowan, 1970). However, metabolic responses to infection tend to be more intense and more specific in the types of metabolites produced. This discussion will emphasize responses of plants to microbial ingress in which the host's energy is efficiently utilized for the production of secondary metabolites.

Coupling respiration with biosynthesis

In incompatible plant–pathogen interactions, rapidly respiring cells surrounding the point of ingress show *intense* biosynthetic activity, increased flux of carbon through the Embden–Meyerhof and pentose phosphate pathways, increased diversion of primary metabolites into secondary metabolism, and accumulation of high concentrations of secondary metabolites such as isoflavonoids and lignin. Such results suggest that respiration is tightly coupled to biosynthesis. Even more intriguing is the evidence that these processes are initiated after the plant 'senses' the presence of the potential pathogen; the plant's response can be initiated by chemical constituents (elicitors) that occur in cell walls of fungi (Ayers, Ebel, Valent, & Albersheim, 1976).

Characteristically, the accumulation of a particular secondary metabolite such as the pterocarpan glyceollin, in response to inoculation or elicitor treatment,

Fig. 2. Respiration in healthy and infected plants. An idealized representation of the stimulatory effect of infection on the host plant's rate of respiration. (Adapted from Scott & Smillie, 1966.)

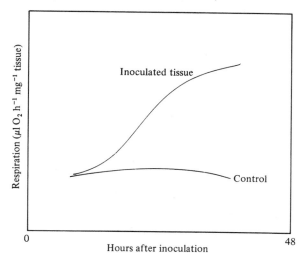

Respiration (μl O_2 h^{-1} mg^{-1} tissue)

Inoculated tissue

Control

0

48

Hours after inoculation

becomes rapid after an initial lag period of several hours (Fig. 3). If a claim is made that a compound such as glyceollin functions as a phytoalexin and is important in disease resistance, significance is attached to the steepness of the curve since it indicates the rapidity of synthesis and the intensity of the response. From the standpoint of intermediary metabolism, curves of this type raise other interesting points which will be discussed below.

Energy costs

What are the energy costs involved in sustaining the rapid rate of biosynthesis of compounds produced in response to infection? In common with the reactions concerned with the synthesis of isoflavonoids, acetyl CoA and phenylalanine are the precursors contributing carbons for the structure of glyceollin (Fig. 4). Both ATP and NADPH are needed in the conversion of these compounds to glyceollin. Although several of the reactions in glyceollin synthesis remain uncharacterized, we can roughly estimate that 5 μmol of ATP and 5 μmol of NADPH are needed for each μmol of glyceollin synthesized. Further, we can estimate from the data of Yoshikawa, Yamauchi & Masago (1978), which are corrected for glyceollin turnover, that peak rates of synthesis can be as much as 6 μmol 12 h^{-1} g^{-1} fresh weight of plant tissue. Although it is unlikely

Fig. 3. Production of a secondary metabolite by plants in response to infection. After a lag period, there is a rapid rise in the amount of the secondary compound (e.g. a phytoalexin) which accumulates in the host tissue. The rapidity of the response reflects a need for diversion of significant amounts of carbon and biosynthetic energy to attain such levels of accumulation. (Adapted from Keen, 1971.)

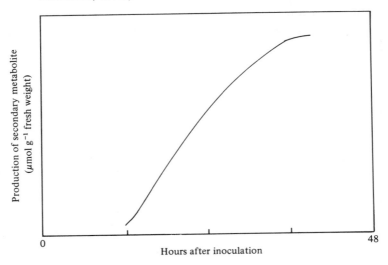

that such rates of synthesis would be maintained for prolonged periods, they do permit us to calculate that the highest demands for energy would be 30 μmol NADPH and 30 μmol of ATP 12 h^{-1} g^{-1} fresh weight of plant tissue. Reports in the literature reveal that dark respiration in plant tissues is stimulated in response to infection in an amount equivalent to yield 15 μmol ATP and 5 μmol NADPH h^{-1} g^{-1} fresh weight, which will be well in excess of the amount needed to meet the demand for secondary metabolite production. Since there is insufficient information on the intracellular location of enzymes concerned with glyceollin synthesis, it is not yet possible to identify the immediate sources of ATP and NADPH needed for glyceollin production. Nevertheless, similar calculations can also be made for lignin, which is synthesized in response to infection and restricts ingress of a pathogen into plant tissue (Ride, 1975).

Design of systems for efficient response to infection

There are several characteristics of the plant's metabolic response to infection which suggest that it is mediated by a well-designed system, and that it is involved as a mechanism of resistance to ingress by pathogens.

Fig. 4. Pathway for biosynthesis of glyceollin. Glyceollin is formed from isopentenyl pyrophosphate (IPP), acetyl CoA (ACoA), and phenylalanine (PA) by the reactions shown. Points of regulation include reactions of: phenylalanine ammonia lyase (PAL) (reaction 1) which is activated by reduction, deactivated by oxidation, and feedback-inhibited by cinnamate and hydroxylated aromatic compounds; cinnamate-4-hydroxylase (reaction 2) which requires NADPH and also is sensitive to control by the NADPH mole fraction.

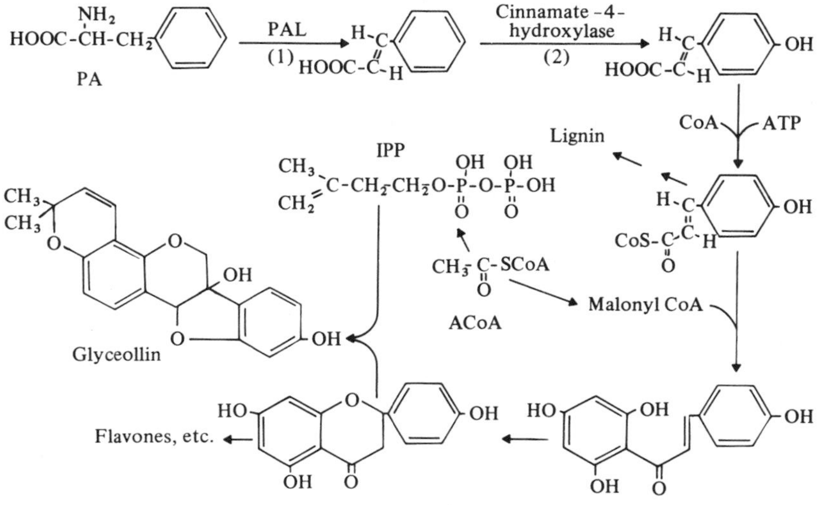

Response to infection is mediated through a combination of existing pathways and pathways responsive to stresses imposed on plants

It is significant that the precursors for glyceollin synthesis are the primary metabolites phenylalanine and acetyl CoA. Because of their primary roles in normal plant metabolism, systems for their production would be actively functioning in plant cells at the time of infection; thus, precursors for glyceollin synthesis are available in the plant prior to ingress by the potential pathogen.

To supply the carbons of glyceollin, approximately 36 μmol of acetyl CoA and 6 μmol of phenylalanine would be needed every 12 h per g fresh weight. Estimates from published information reveal that the phenylalanine content of plant cells could be as much as 1.0 μmol g^{-1} fresh weight (Widholm, 1974). This quantity would fulfill less than 15% of the amount needed for 12 h of glyceollin synthesis. Clearly, phenylalanine at the site of glyceollin synthesis must be replenished at the rate of 0.5 μmol h^{-1} g^{-1} fresh weight. Estimates of acetyl CoA content will undoubtedly reveal a similar need for enhanced production of acetyl CoA.

To provide for rapid production of phenylalanine, which occurs through the

Fig. 5. The shikimate pathway for synthesis of the aromatic amino acids. Coupling of the pathway to energy-generating sequences occurs at steps catalysed by (1) dehydroshikimate reductase, which requires NADPH, and (2) shikimate kinase which requires ATP (DAHP: 3-deoxy-arabinoheptulosonate-7-phosphate).

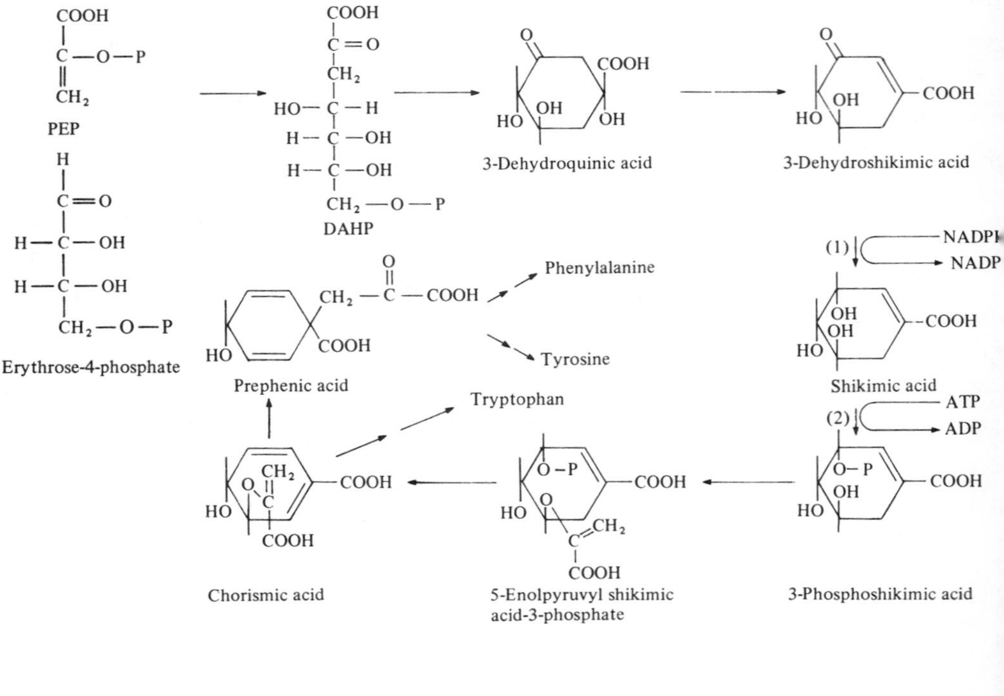

shikimate pathway (Fig. 5), there must be facilitated production of its precursors, phosphoenolpyruvate and erythrose-4-phosphate. Reports of specific activities of enzymes of the Embden–Meyerhof and pentose phosphate pathways indicate that plant tissues contain sufficient amounts to account for the increased flux of carbon through the two pathways, which not only help generate energy for glyceollin production, but also produce the precursors phosphoenolpyruvate, acetyl CoA, and erythrose-4-phosphate. Unfortunately, space does not permit discussion here of mechanisms that control flux of carbon through the two pathways. The reader is referred to publications elsewhere for discussions on control of carbohydrate metabolism (Adams & Rowan, 1970; Anderson, Ng & Park, 1974; Kachru & Anderson, 1975; Schnarrenberger, Tetour & Herbert, 1975; Heldt *et al.*, 1977; Huber, 1979).

The diversion of phenylalanine and acetyl CoA into secondary metabolism is initiated by enzymes which are induced or derepressed by factors signalling the onset of biological stress. In the case of glyceollin synthesis, cell wall fragments of the fungus *Phytophthora megasperma* var. *sojae,* or contact with the organism itself 'switches on' the synthesis of phenylalanine ammonia lyase and other enzymes concerned with the production of the secondary metabolite (Partridge & Keen, 1977). Once synthesized, phenylalanine ammonia lyase is further regulated by mechanisms that will be discussed in the following sections.

Most of the enzymes participating in the response to infection exist in plant tissues before infection; they are associated with primary metabolism but serve important roles in responses to infection by providing precursors and energy for the production of the secondary metabolites. The specific nature of the type of secondary compound produced in response to infection is governed by the type of reaction sequences activated or produced in response to infection.

Machinery for production of chemicals in response to infection is controlled mainly by major energy-generating sequences and is sensitive to the energy status of the cell

All biosynthetic sequences are coupled to and are controlled by energy-generating reactions. However, pathways for the production of secondary metabolites, activated in plants in response to infection, have certain unique features related to their regulation by energy-generating reactions.

The utilization of phosphoenolpyruvate and erythrose-4-phosphate for the production of phenylalanine will be responsive to the energy status of the cells since operation of the shikimic acid pathway is dependent upon NADPH for shikimate dehydrogenase and on ATP for shikimate kinase (Fig. 5). Furthermore, shikimate kinase is inhibited by ADP; in the presence of different ATP mole fractions, the enzyme yields a plot that is convex upward with increasing energy charge (Bowen & Kosuge, 1979; Fig. 6). Thus, the enzyme does not show a response to energy charge that is typical of an enzyme utilizing ATP which, according to Atkinson (1971), would yield a curve concave upward with increasing energy charge. Thus, it is likely that, in tissues responding to infection in incompatible interactions, energy charge will be in the range favorable for full activity of the enzyme.

In other reactions of the shikimate pathway, the plant 3-deoxy-arabinoheptulosonate-7-phosphate synthase does not appear to be feedback-inhibited by intermediates or products of the pathway in a manner demonstrated for the microbial enzyme (Huisman & Kosuge, 1974). However, feedback inhibition occurs at the reaction catalysed by chorismate mutase which exists in as many as three multiple forms, each having one of two functions (Woodin & Nishioka, 1973). One, exemplified by the CM-1 form from mung bean, is sensitive to feedback inhibition by phenylalanine and tyrosine, and is activated by tryptophan (see Fig. 7). Anthranilate synthase (reaction 1) diverts chorismate into tryptophan synthesis; control of flux through the reaction is provided by feedback inhibition (I) of anthranilate synthase by tryptophan. Chorismate mutase CM-1 (reaction 2) controls flux of carbon into phenylalanine and tyrosine synthesis; feedback inhibition of the enzyme by phenylalanine and tyrosine controls flux of carbon into aromatic amino acid synthesis. Tryptophan activates (A)

Fig. 6. Response of shikimate kinase to ATP mole fractions. +ADP, relative enzyme activity in mixtures prepared with varying proportions of ADP and ATP, with a fixed, final concentration of the adenylates to provide the appropriate mole fractions; −ADP, relative enzyme activity in mixtures with ATP alone; EC response, curve expected of an ATP-utilizing enzyme displaying a typical response to energy charge.

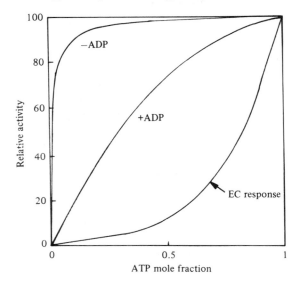

chorismate mutase CM-1 and also relieves phenylalanine and tyrosine inhibition thereby providing cross-pathway regulation of the flow of carbon into phenylalanine and tyrosine synthesis.

The CM-1 form of chorismate mutase appears to be associated with protein synthesis (Gilchrist & Kosuge, 1974). The CM-2 isozyme from mung bean is typical of the other form which is insensitive to feedback inhibition by aromatic amino acids; it may be associated with the synthesis of secondary metabolites including lignin and flavonoids such as glyceollin (Gilchrist & Kosuge, 1975; Fig. 8). The occurrence of the CM-2 isozyme, and the absence of demonstrable feedback inhibition by aromatic amino acids at other reactions of the shikimic acid pathway, indicate that this mode of metabolic control is less important in controlling the flow of carbon through the shikimate pathway into glyceollin synthesis.

Major control of phenylalanine synthesis occurs by coupling the phenylpyruvate–phenylalanine conversion to ammonia assimilation and energy-generating sequences. Wallsgrove, Lea & Miflin (1979) showed that conversion of keto acids to amino acids can be tightly coupled to ammonia assimilation by sequences shown in Fig. 9. Moreover, the flow of carbon through the 'switch point' into glyceollin synthesis can be coupled to the successive insertion (via glutamate–phenylpyruvate aminotransferase, reaction 1, Fig. 9) and removal of amino nitrogen (via phenylalanine ammonia lyase, reaction 2, Fig. 9) into and from the phenylpropane unit. The ammonia freed by phenylalanine ammonia lyase would be reassimilated into glutamate via glutamine synthetase and glutamate synthase (Wallsgrove *et al.*, 1979). The driving force for the complete system will be reactions providing ATP, and reducing power that would be generated by the increased respiratory activity accompanying the response to infection or by photophosphorylation. The system would effectively recycle the amino nitrogen and would make the flow of carbon into secondary metabolism independent of external sources of ammonia. Control through availability of NH_4^+ would be abolished – a necessary step if the system is to be catalytically

Fig. 7. Cross pathway regulation of chorismate metabolism. Details in text.

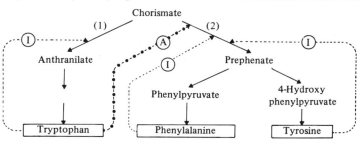

facilitated for diversion of phenylalanine into glyceollin synthesis. Although coupling glyceollin synthesis to ammonia assimilation is an energy-consuming process, it provides an important energy-linked control of glyceollin synthesis. This coupling occurs at the metabolic cost of only one equivalent of reducing power (for glutamate synthase) (reaction 4) and 1 mol of ATP (for glutamine synthetase) (reaction 3) per mole of glyceollin produced.

In addition to being coupled to ammonia assimilation, an interesting feature of glyceollin and lignin production is the requirement for NADPH and ATP in successive reactions leading to glyceollin synthesis, including shikimate dehydrogenase to shikimate kinase, cinnamate-4-hydroxylase to *p*-coumaroyl CoA ligase, and reactions providing glutamate as a substrate for the amino-transferase reaction (Fig. 9). Furthermore, the system would be controlled by feedback inhibition of phenylalanine ammonia lyase, cinnamate-4-hydroxylase, and choris-

Fig. 8. Postulated roles of chorismate mutase isozymes in the synthesis of phenylpropane compounds. Key to enzymes: 1, DAHP synthase; 2, dehydroshikimate reductase; 3, shikimate kinase; 4, chorismate mutase CM-1; 5, chorismate mutase CM-2; 6, 6', prephenate dehydratase; 7, 7', aminotransferase; 8, phenylalanine ammonia lyase (PAL); 9, cinnamate-4-hydroxylase; 10, *p*-coumaroyl CoA ligase. The diversion of carbon into secondary metabolism may begin at the step catalysed by chorismate mutase CM-2 (Reaction 5). Both branches will be coupled to ammonia assimilating systems (I, I') which are detailed in Fig. 9. The pathway for protein synthesis requires a continuous input of ammonia whereas the pathway for secondary metabolite production requires only catalytic amounts since ammonia is 'recycled' by the systems shown in Fig. 9. Once PAL is synthesized, light may either directly or indirectly modulate activity of the enzyme via reductant mediated activation.

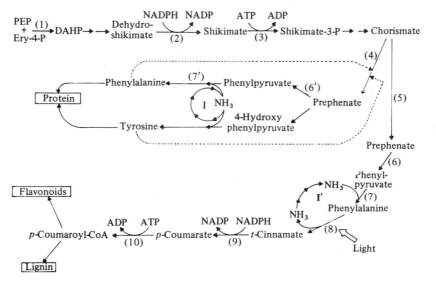

mate mutase CM-2 by various phenylpropane compounds (Fig. 8). It would be finely tuned to the energy status of the plant through reductant-activation, oxidant-inactivation of phenylalanine ammonia lyase (Nishizawa, Wolosuik, & Buchanan, 1979), and by control of cinnamate-4-hydroxylase activity by the NADPH mole fraction (Benveniste, Salaun & Durst, 1977). It is unique and undoubtedly significant that coupling to energy-yielding sequences occurs precisely at the reactions which produce phenylalanine and divert it into secondary metabolism.

Thus, the flux of carbon through the shikimate pathway may be channelled into secondary metabolism at the reaction catalysed by chorismate mutase CM-1; and through sequences that are sensitive to the availability of NADPH and ATP, and less subject to the type of feedback controls found in microorganisms.

If organized in coupled systems, as shown in Fig. 9, there will be effective synchrony of the machinery needed for the plant's rapid response to infection.

Fig. 9. Proposed scheme of catalytic facilitation of phenylalanine metabolism. Enzymes involved are: 1, amino transferase; 2, phenylalanine ammonia lyase; 3, glutamine synthetase; 4, glutamate synthase; and 5, cinnamate-4-hydroxylase. The steps requiring reducing power (reactions 4 and 5), and ATP (reaction 3) can serve as control points, since the enzymes concerned will be responsive to the energy status of the cell. Flow of carbon through this scheme could be catalytically facilitated by aggregation of enzymes 1, 2 and 5 into a complex. Coordination of the activity of such a complex with the activity of the reassimilatory pathway for ammonia (enzymes 1, 3 and 4) will further enhance the catalytic facilitation. Dithiothreitol (DTT) activation of phenylalanine ammonia lyase has been demonstrated, suggesting that in-vivo reductant activation may be a physiologically important means of controlling the enzyme. The system as shown would reside outside the chloroplast, since the NADP-linked glutamate synthase and cinnamate-4-hydroxylase have not been found in the chloroplast.

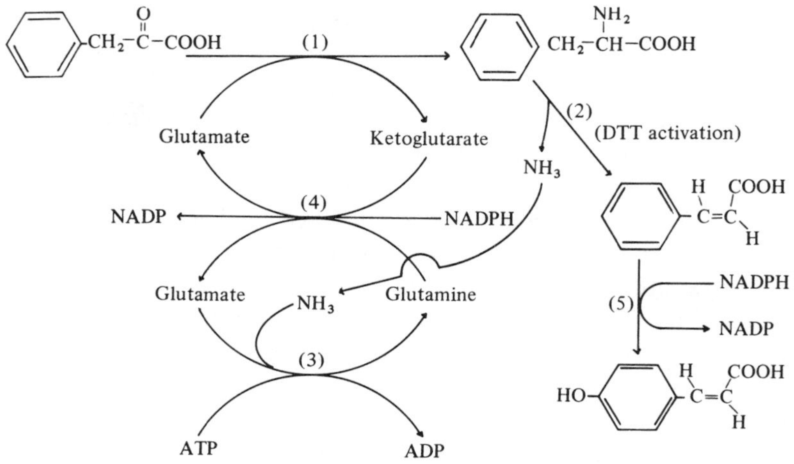

Synthesis of chemicals associated with incompatible interactions is catalytically facilitated

A system such as the one described in Fig. 9 would be maximally efficient if it were organized into a catalytic unit – perhaps an aggregate composed of two or more of the enzymes of the sequence. The concept of multienzyme complexes capable of catalytic facilitation, while well studied in microorganisms, has only recently gained recognition as a regulatory control in higher plants.

The existence of such complexes in plants is now being studied in connection with greening phenomena and aromatic metabolism including deposition of lignin and synthesis of flavonoid compounds. Both events represent a response of the plant to its environment through signals such as light, hormones and developmental stage (Ranjeva, Boudet, Harada, & Marigo, 1975; Lamb, 1979). In the case of lignin formation the occurrence of an enzyme aggregate would effectively divert large amounts of carbon preferentially into lignin precursors (Kuboi & Yamada, 1978). Hahlbrock *et al.* (1976) have shown that there is a light-triggered coordinate induction of more than 10 enzymes concerned with the formation of flavone and flavonol glycosides in parsley cell suspension cultures. Catalytic facilitation would occur here also if two or more of these enzymes were organized into a catalytic subunit.

If the system shown in Fig. 9 were organized into a multienzyme complex involving at least the aminotransferase, phenylalanine ammonia lyase and cinnamate-4-hydroxylase, and if coupled to the ammonia assimilating system, it would provide greatly facilitated production of glyceollin. It is not meant to imply that this complex is organized only in response to the need to produce glyceollin as a resistance mechanism to infection by a pathogen. Quite likely the opposite occurs. Much of the 'machinery' probably already exists in higher plant cells to be activated for later lignin synthesis – a fortuitous situation or a well-designed system, which can also be 'switched on' by pathogen invasion.

Chemicals produced in response to incompatible interactions are composed of oxygen, carbon, and hydrogen – those elements most abundantly available to the plant

Since production of secondary compounds involved in disease resistance must be rapid, their synthesis should not be limited by elements that might not be readily available to the plant or might be in short supply during certain stages of the plant development. It may be significant that all phytoalexins thus far described consist of those three elements (carbon, hydrogen and oxygen) that are most readily available to the plant, while preformed compounds believed to be involved in disease resistance include those with sulphur and/or nitrogen (Table 1). As noted earlier, in cases where nitrogenous compounds serve as precursors for phytoalexins, for example phenylalanine, amino nitrogen is required in only catalytic amounts (Fig. 9) and is eliminated in the steps leading to glyceollin synthesis.

Further, it is interesting to note from the work of Tomiyama *et al.* (1968) and Kuć, Henfling, Garas & Doke (1979) that potato tubers responding to mechanical injury and environmental stress produce increased quantities of the nitrogen-containing steroidal glycoalkaloids, which already exist in the plant cells. On the other hand, inoculation of potato tubers with *Phytophthora infestans* results in the preferential synthesis of the nitrogen-free sesquiterpene phytoalexin, rishitin, at the expense of steroidal glycoalkaloid synthesis (Kuć *et al.*, 1979). These results imply that infection rather than environmental stress elicits the more specific response in secondary metabolism.

Wasteful dissipation of host energy

In interactions involving either biotrophs or necrotrophs (perthotrophs) it is possible the plant's stored energy could be dissipated uselessly through processes initiated by loss of metabolic compartmentation. Such events would occur early in diseases caused by necrotrophic fungi but only in advanced stages of disease involving biotrophic fungi. Substrates and enzymes normally separated by compartmentation in intact tissue would come together in disrupted tissue and degradation of substrates would occur. Energy-dissipating reactions may act in opposition to energy-generating reactions, resulting in a net loss of energy. Such reactions, called futile cycles, may occur in plant cells as a result of loss of

Table 1. *Elemental composition of phytoalexins and preformed toxins*

Compound	Number of atoms				
	Carbon	Hydrogen	Oxygen	Nitrogen	Sulphur
Phytoalexins					
Rishitin	15	22	3	—	—
Glyceollin	20	17	5	—	—
Safynol	10	12	2	—	—
Wyerone	15	14	4	—	—
Casbene	20	32	—	—	—
Preformed toxins					
Avenacin	55	83	21	1	—
α-Tomatine	50	81	21	1	—
Catechol	6	6	2	—	—
Linamarin	10	17	6	1	—
Phenylisothiocyanate	7	5	—	1	1

compartmentation. Two possible futile cycles are shown in Fig. 10. Futile cycles would be detrimental to host metabolism, interfere with host development, and decrease the plant's capacity to respond to infection. If coupled to energy-generating sequences through reduced pyridine nucleotides, futile cycles can account for the increased rate of respiration in susceptible plant tissue.

Useless dissipation of potential energy could also occur by uncoupling of oxidative phosphorylation. For example, the host-specific toxin of *Helminthosporium maydis* rapidly reduced steady-state ATP concentrations in protoplasts of the Texas male-sterile maize but had no effect on ATP levels in protoplasts of the resistant male-fertile (N) maize (Walton, Earle, Yoder & Spanswick, 1979). The toxin may depolarize the mitochondrial membrane potential thus interfering with production of ATP. The toxin produces similar reductions in ATP concentrations in susceptible maize roots but not in roots of the resistant maize (Bednarski, Scheffer & Izawa, 1977). By producing a toxin which interferes with energy

Fig. 10. Examples of possible futile cycles in infected plants. (1) Quinones generated by reaction of polyphenol oxidase on polyphenols such as chlorogenic acid can be reduced to the original substrate by NADPH-linked quinone reductase. NADP produced by the reaction can be reduced by glucose-6-phosphate dehydrogenase thereby completing the cycle. The reversible phenol–quinone conversions result in the net reaction $H^+ + NADPH + \frac{1}{2} O_2 \rightleftharpoons NADP + H_2O$, a useless loss of reducing power. (2) Ascorbate oxidase, if coupled to the reactions shown, undergoes reversible ascorbate–dehydroascorbate conversions which result in the same dissipation of reducing power shown in reaction sequence 1.

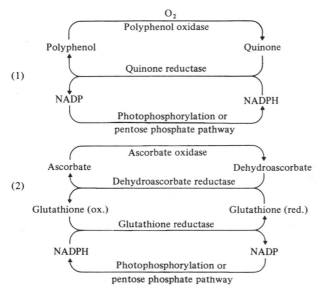

production, the pathogen effectively reduces the capacity of the host to respond to infection.

In many cases, however, reports on the uncoupling of oxidative phosphorylation in infected plant tissue may need re-examination in view of recent reports on the properties of cyanide-resistant respiration in plant tissue (Theologis & Laties, 1978). Interpretation of results with uncouplers without measurements of adenylate concentrations may lead to erroneous conclusions because tissues possessing a functional cyanide-resistant pathway do not always produce an increase in oxygen uptake when treated with uncouplers. Exogenously supplied uncouplers divert electron flow from the cytochrome system into the less efficient cyanide-resistant pathway which results in the production of only one ATP per atom of oxygen consumed in contrast to the yield of three ATP from the cytochrome system. This further complicates interpretation of earlier results since lowered phosphorus:oxygen ratios may signify functioning of cyanide-resistant pathway rather than uncoupling of oxidative phosphorylation. Cyanide-resistant respiration can be demonstated in injured plant tissue but its role in plant–pathogen interaction remains unknown and therefore deserves study.

Summary

We have considered mechanisms that would provide for rapid synthesis of secondary metabolites such as glyceollin, and have discussed the desirable features of a system that must divert primary metabolites into rapid synthesis of secondary metabolites.

Some of what is discussed is speculative and much information is extrapolated from related plant systems.

We have pieced together a framework of information which, hopefully, will be strengthened in the future by evidence provided by careful investigations.

References

Adams, P. B. & Rowan, K. S. (1970). Glycolytic control of respiration during aging of carrot root tissue. *Plant Physiology,* **45,** 490–4.

Allen, P. J. (1959). Physiology and biochemistry of defense. In *Plant Pathology,* vol. 1, ed. J. G. Horsfall & A. E. Dimond, pp. 435–67. New York: Academic Press.

Anderson, L. E., Ng, T. C. M. & Park, K. E. Y. (1974). Inactivation of pea leaf chloroplastic and cytoplasmic glucose-6-phosphate dehydrogenase by light and dithiothreitol. *Plant Physiology,* **53,** 835–9.

Atkinson, D. E. (1971). Adenine nucleotides as stoichiometric coupling agents in metabolism and as regulatory modifiers: the adenylate energy charge. In *Metabolic Pathways,* vol. 5, ed. H. J. Vogel, pp. 1–21. New York: Academic Press.

Ayers, A. R., Ebel, J., Valent, B. & Albersheim, P. (1976). Host–pathogen interactions: fractionation and biological activity of an elicitor isolated from the mycelial walls of *Phytophthora megasperma* var. *sojae*. *Plant Physiology*, **57**, 760–5.

Bednarski, M. A., Scheffer, R. P. & Izawa, S. (1977). Effects of toxin from *Helminthosporium maydis* T on respiration and associated activities in maize tissue. *Physiological Plant Pathology*, **11**, 129–41.

Benveniste, I., Salaun, J. P. & Durst, F. (1977). Wounding-induced cinnamic acid hydroxylase in Jerusalem artichoke tubers. *Phytochemistry*, **16**, 69–73.

Bowen, J. R. & Kosuge, T. (1979). *In vivo* activity, purification, and characterization of shikimate kinase from sorghum. *Plant Physiology*, **64**, 382–6.

Daly, J. M. (1976). The carbon balance of diseased plants: changes in respiration, photosynthesis and translocation. In *Encyclopedia of Plant Physiology*, New Series, vol. 4, *Physiological Plant Pathology*, ed. R. Heitefuss & P. H. Williams, pp. 450–79. Berlin: Springer-Verlag.

Gilchrist, D. G. & Kosuge, T. (1974). Regulation of aromatic amino acid biosynthesis in higher plants. Properties of an aromatic amino-acid-sensitive chorismate mutase (CM-1) from mung bean. *Archives of Biochemistry and Biophysics*, **164**, 95–105.

Gilchrist, D. G. & Kosuge, T. (1975). Regulation of aromatic amino acid biosynthesis in higher plants. Properties of an aromatic amino-acid-insensitive chorismate mutase (CM-2) from mung bean. *Archives of Biochemistry and Biophysics*, **171**, 36–42.

Hahlbrock, K., Knoblock, K. H., Kreuzaler, F., Potts, J. R. M. & Wellman, E. (1976). Coordinated induction and subsequent activity changes of two groups of metabolically interrelated enzymes. *European Journal of Biochemistry*, **61**, 199–206.

Heldt, H. W., Chon, C. J., Maronde, D., Herold, A., Stankovic, Z. S., Walker, D. A., Kraminer, A., Kirk, M. R. & Heber, U. (1977). Role of orthophosphate and other factors in the regulation of starch formation in leaves and isolated chloroplasts. *Plant Physiology*, **59**, 1146–55.

Huber, S. C. (1979). Orthophosphate control of glucose-6-phosphate dehydrogenase light modulation in relation to the induction phase of chloroplast photosynthesis. *Plant Physiology*, **64**, 846–51.

Huisman, O. C. & Kosuge, T. (1974). Regulation of aromatic amino acid biosynthesis in higher plants. II. 3-deoxy-arabino-heptulosonic acid 7-phosphate synthetase from cauliflower. *Journal of Biological Chemistry*, **249**, 6842–8.

Kachru, R. B. & Anderson, L. E. (1975). Inactivation of pea leaf phosphofructokinase by light and dithiothreitol. *Plant Physiology*, **55**, 199–202.

Keen, N. T. (1971). Hydroxyphaseollin production by soybeans resistant and susceptible to *Phytophthora megasperma* var. *sojae*. *Physiological Plant Pathology*, **1**, 265–75.

Kuboi, T. & Yamada, Y. (1978). Regulation of the enzyme activities related to lignin synthesis in cell aggregates of tobacco cell cultures. *Biochimica et Biophysica Acta*, **542**, 181–90.

Kuć, J., Henfling, J., Garas, N. & Doke, N. (1979). Control of terpenoid metabolism in the potato–*Phytophthora infestans* interaction. *Journal of Food Protection*, **52**, 508–11.

Lamb, C. J. (1979). Regulation of enzyme levels in phenylpropanoid biosynthesis: characterization of the modulation by light and pathway intermediates. *Archives of Biochemistry and Biophysics*, **192**, 311–17.

Livne, A. & Daly, J. M. (1966). Translocation in healthy and rust-affected beans. *Phytopathology*, **56**, 170–5.

Nishizawa, A. N., Wolosuik, R. A. & Buchanan, B. B. (1979). Chloroplast phenylalanine ammonia-lyase from spinach leaves. Evidence for light-mediated regulation via the ferredoxin thioredoxin system. *Planta,* **145,** 7–12.

Partridge, J. E. & Keen, N. T. (1977). Soybean phytoalexins: rates of synthesis are not regulated by activation of initial enzymes in flavonoid biosynthesis. *Phytopathology,* **67,** 50–5.

Ranjeva, R., Boudet, A. M., Harada, H. & Marigo, G. (1975). Phenolic metabolism in petunia tissues. I. Characteristic responses of enzymes involved in different steps of polyphenol synthesis to different hormonal influences. *Biochimica et Biophysica Acta,* **399,** 23–30.

Ride, J. P. (1975). Lignification in wounded wheat leaves in response to fungi and its possible role in resistance. *Physiological Plant Pathology,* **5,** 125–34.

Schnarrenberger, C., Tetour, M. & Herbert, M. (1975). Development and intracellular distribution of enzymes of the oxidative pentose phosphate cycle in radish cotyledons. *Plant Physiology,* **56,** 836–40.

Scott, K. T. & Smillie, R. M. (1966). Metabolic regulation in diseased leaves. I. The respiratory rise in barley leaves infected with powdery mildew. *Plant Physiology,* **41,** 289–97.

Theologis, A. & Laties, G. G. (1978). Relative contribution of cytochrome-mediated and cyanide-resistant electron transport in fresh and aged potato slices. *Plant Physiology,* **62,** 232–7.

Tomiyama, K., Ishizaka, N., Sato, N., Masamune, T. & Katsui, N. (1968). 'Rishitin', a phytoalexin-like substance. Its role in the defense reaction of potato tubers to infection. In *Biochemical Regulation in Diseased Plants or Injury,* ed. T. Hirai, pp. 287–92. Tokyo: Kyoritsui Printing Co.

Wallsgrove, R. M., Lea, P. J. & Miflin, B. J. (1979). Distribution of the enzymes of nitrogen assimilation within the pea leaf cell. *Plant Physiology,* **63,** 232–6.

Walton, J. D., Earle, E. D., Yoder, O. C. & Spanswick, R. M. (1979). Reduction of adenosine triphosphate levels in susceptible maize mesophyll protoplasts by *Helminthosporium maydis* Race T toxin. *Plant Physiology,* **63,** 806–10.

Widholm, J. M. (1974). Control of aromatic amino acid biosynthesis in cultured plant tissues: effect of intermediates and aromatic amino acids on free levels. *Physiologia Plantarum,* **30,** 13–18.

Woodin, T. S. & Nishioka, L. (1973). Evidence for three isozymes of chorismate mutase in alfalfa. *Biochimica et Biophysica Acta,* **309,** 211–23.

Yoshikawa, M., Yamauchi, K. & Masago, H. (1978). Glyceollin: its role in restricting fungal growth in resistant soybean hypocotyls infected with *Phytophthora megasperma* var. *sajae. Physiological Plant Pathology,* **12,** 73–82.

J.M.WHIPPS & D.H.LEWIS

Patterns of translocation, storage and interconversion of carbohydrates

Introduction

Russell (this volume) has discussed the drastic effects of various infections on the growth and yield of crop plants. By inference, the same patterns are likely to obtain in natural vegetation. Several features contribute to the decreases in yield following infection, and these, which have been examined in detail over the past 30 years, fall into three main areas – decreased photosynthesis, increased respiration and altered patterns of translocation (Manners, 1971). Buchanan *et al.* and Kosuge & Kimpel (this volume) have stressed the importance of alterations in the first two processes and this chapter, with special reference to fungi, illustrates the deleterious effects that many pathogens have on the normal distribution and metabolism of carbohydrates in their hosts.

Transport and metabolism of carbohydrates in healthy plants

Traditionally, exporting leaves have been considered as the sources of translocated sugars and consuming parts of the plants as the sinks. Herold (1980) has modified this traditional conceptual framework in an important way by stressing that the source should be regarded not as the leaf itself but as its chloroplasts. These are separated from the primary sink, the cytoplasm which houses them, by their envelopes, membranes which exert considerable control over the interchange of metabolites between the chloroplastic stroma and the cytoplasm (Herold & Walker, 1979). Herold refers to traditional sinks, i.e. vegetative and flowering meristems, developing seeds, fruits, storage organs, etc., as secondary sinks.

The most important mobile carbohydrates between source and primary sink, and between primary and secondary sinks, are different. In vascular plants, those moving from chloroplast to cytoplasm in the photosynthesizing leaf are triose phosphates (TP), principally dihydroxyacetone phosphate (see Fig. 1 of Buchanan *et al.*, this volume). This transfer involves an obligatory exchange with inorganic orthophosphate (Pi) via the so-called phosphate translocator situated in the inner of the two chloroplast membranes (Heldt & Rapley, 1970*a, b*; Herold & Walker, 1979). Sucrose (S) is synthesized in the cytoplasm (Bird, Cornelius, Keys & Whittingham, 1974; Herold & Walker, 1979) and is the main form in which carbon is transported to the distant secondary sinks (Arnold, 1968). This transport is now thought to be initially symplastic, i.e. it occurs between cells entirely within the cytoplasm via plasmodesmata, but before sucrose is loaded into the main transport system (the sieve tubes of the phloem) much may move through the outer cell membrane, the plasmalemma, into the cell wall (i.e. transport temporarily becomes apoplastic (Fig. 1). This probably occurs in the phloem parenchyma and subsequent reloading into the sieve tubes is an energy-dependent process (Giaquinta, 1976; Geiger, 1979). It should be stressed that, although the reducing sugars, glucose (G) and fructose (F), are never translocated, other non-reducing sugars are mobile in the phloem of some species.

As indicated in Fig. 1, temporary storage of fixed carbon can occur in the chloroplast as starch and, possibly, after transfer through their tonoplasts, as sucrose in the vacuoles of cells *en route* to the phloem. Also, invertase bound to the cell wall can hydrolyse sucrose in the apoplast. The 'activity' of distant secondary sinks, i.e. their metabolic processes associated with sustaining life, growth and development (Herold, 1980), can act as an internal regulator of the rates of both photosynthesis and translocation. These feedback mechanisms are discussed extensively by Neales & Incoll (1968), Geiger (1976) and Herold (1980). At least two 'messengers' relaying the controlling influence have been postulated – plant hormones and Pi. These aspects are discussed below in relation to the control of transport in the infected plant.

For considerations of various schemes to explain mechanisms of long-distance transport of sugars in the phloem, the reader should consult recent reviews, e.g. Wardlaw & Passioura (1976) or Baker (1978).

Fig. 2 summarizes the metabolic pathways concerned with the synthesis of starch and sucrose in leaves (N.B. the scheme only concerns the synthesis of α 1–4 glucan (amylose) and omits the branching enzymes necessary for the formation of amylopectin, which is often the major component of starch grains). Various metabolites, TP and Pi in particular, can exert important regulatory roles. Within the chloroplast, the primary photosynthetic product, TP, has three principal fates. Some feeds into the Calvin Cycle as an integral part of the regeneration of the carbon dioxide acceptor, ribulose bisphosphate (RBP). Some is the precursor of starch, the synthesis of which involves formation of adenosine diphosphate glucose (ADPG). This penultimate step before polymerization of glucose to starch is catalysed by ADPG pyrophosphorylase, an enzyme stimulated

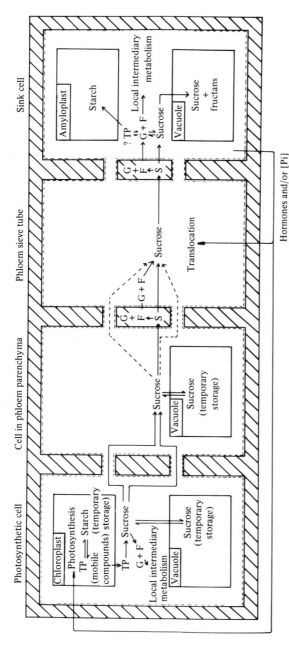

Fig. 1. Outline of physical pathways and metabolism involved in the synthesis and transport of sucrose in healthy plants. Sinks can influence rates of photosynthesis and of translocation from sources. Control mechanisms are not fully understood but hormones and [Pi] have been implicated (see text). Although the diagram features transport of sucrose only, other non-reducing carbohydrates may also be translocated. In different plants these include sucrosyl galactans, e.g. raffinose (galactosyl-sucrose) and stachyose (galactosyl-raffinose), and acylic sugar alcohols, e.g. mannitol and glucitol (sorbitol).

In addition to starch and fructans, other storage polymers include, in different plants, mannans, galactomannans and glucomannans.

'? TP': although there is good evidence that TP moves from chloroplast to cytoplasm in photosynthetic cells, it is not known whether TP is the mobile compound between cytoplasm and amyloplast in the cells of sinks which synthesize starch.

by TP, especially phosphoglycerate (PGA), and inhibited by Pi (Preiss & Levi, 1979). The PGA:Pi ratio is particularly important. Since the chloroplastic concentration of Pi ([Pi]) in the light might be expected to be maintained at a low level by photophosphorylation and TP is continually being produced by the dark reactions of photosynthesis, conditions in the light favour synthesis of starch. The third fate of TP is export to the cytoplasm via exchange for Pi controlled by the phosphate translocator (see above).

In the cytoplasm, a parallel series of reactions to those in the chloroplast leads to the synthesis of uridine diphosphate glucose (UDPG), one precursor of sucrose phosphate (SP). Again [Pi] can exert a controlling influence by its stimulatory action on phosphofructokinase, the enzyme which catalyses the synthesis

Fig. 2. Metabolic pathways involved in the synthesis of starch in chloroplasts and sucrose in the cytoplasm of photosynthetic cells, showing important points of metabolic control including the phosphate translocator which governs flux of carbon and phosphorus across the chloroplast envelope. Enzyme and metabolic sequences involved: 1, RBP carboxylase; 2, enzymes of Calvin Cycle including ATP-dependent R5P kinase; 3, aldolase; 4, fructose bisphosphatase (stimulated by FBP); 5, phosphofructokinase (inhibited by Pi); 6, phosphohexoisomerase; 7, phosphoglucomutase; 8, ADPG pyrophosphorylase (stimulated by PGA; inhibited by Pi; PGA:Pi ratio important); 9, starch synthetase; 10, pyrophosphatase; 11, UDPG pyrophosphorylase; 12, sucrose phosphate synthetase (inhibited by UTP and sucrose); 13, sucrose phosphate phosphatase (inhibited by sucrose); 14, photophosphorylation. RBP = ribulose bisphosphate; FBP = fructose bisphosphate; F6P = fructose-6-phosphate; G6P = glucose-6-phosphate; G1P = glucose-1-phosphate; ADPG = adenosine diphosphate glucose; UDPG = uridine diphosphate glucose; SP = sucrose phosphate; PGA = phosphoglycerate; TP = triose phosphate.

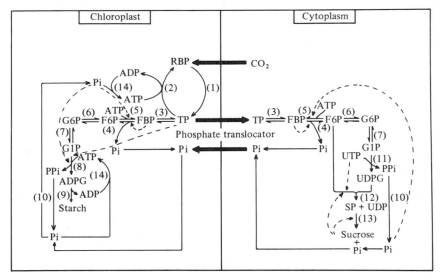

of fructose bisphosphate (FBP) from fructose-6-phosphate (F6P). Sucrose itself, via its inhibitory action on both sucrose phosphate synthetase and sucrose phosphate phosphatase, can regulate its own synthesis.

In the dark, chloroplastic starch is degraded, eventually to TP which is exported to the cytoplasmic primary sinks. In addition to the debranching enzymes necessary to hydrolyse the α 1–6 linkages of amylopectin, most degradation of the α 1–4 linked polymers may be catalysed by starch phosphorylase, a reaction for which Pi is a substrate, resulting in the formation of glucose 1-phosphate (G1P).

$$G_n + Pi \rightleftharpoons G_{n-1} + G1P$$

Although hydrolytic degradation to glucose by amylase and maltase is also possible, amylases appear to be absent from the chloroplasts of at least some species (Levi & Preiss, 1978; Stitt, Bulpin & ap Rees, 1978).

As already noted, sucrose can be degraded by invertase to glucose and fructose, an irreversible hydrolysis. Both soluble and cell-wall-bound invertases exist in leaves (see detailed references, pp. 65–70). Sucrose can also be degraded by the reversible reaction catalysed by the mis-named 'sucrose synthetase'.

$$S + UDP \rightleftharpoons UDPG + F$$

However, the activity of this enzyme is low in photosynthetic relative to non-photosynthetic tissue (Delmer & Albersheim, 1970) and its status in diseased leaves has apparently never been assessed although it has been assayed in infected non-photosynthetic tissue (see p. 66).

Although polymers of fructose do not normally occur in leaves of vascular plants to any great extent, they do accumulate in diseased tissue (see pp. 62–63). For this reason, it is appropriate to mention here a little of their chemistry and of the mechanism by which they appear to be synthesized. They always have a sucrosyl end group (i.e. they contain one terminal molecule of glucose) and are mainly found in what are considered to be the evolutionarily most advanced families of both dicotyledonous and monocotyledonous angiosperms, e.g. Compositae and Gramineae respectively. Most metabolic studies have involved the former where linkage between fructosyl residues is β 2–1 resulting in a linear polymer. Their synthesis in tubers of the Jerusalem artichoke probably involves cytoplasmic synthesis of the trisaccharide sucrosyl fructose, and a tonoplastic location for the transferase which catalyses increase in chain length (Fig. 3). The fructans of the Compositae, the inulin series, achieve a degree of polymerization (DP) of about 35. In the grasses, β 2–6 linkages as well as β 2–1 linkages occur, the chains are branched and their DP can be several hundred. Few details of their mechanism of synthesis are available. Degradation of fructans in general occurs via hydrolytic enzymes which cleave off single fructose units eventually leaving the sucrosyl end group as free sucrose (Edelman & Jefford, 1968; Smith, 1972; Manners, 1973).

For further details on transport and metabolism of carbohydrates in vascular plants, the reader is referred to a companion SEB Seminar Series publication (Lewis, 1982).

Alteration of translocation patterns in plants infected by fungi

Changes in movement of assimilates in plants induced by fungal diseases have been known for many years and have been reviewed numerous times, most recently by Daly (1976) and Bushnell & Gay (1978). However, in most

Fig. 3. Scheme for the polymerization of sucrose to fructans (after Edelman & Jefford, 1968). In the cytoplasm, sucrose is the substrate for enzyme 1, sucrose-sucrose 1-fructosyltransferase, which catalyses the synthesis of the tri saccharide, 1'-fructosylsucrose. Some sucrose also passes through the tonoplast into the vacuole. This sucrose and the trisaccharide are substrates for enzyme 2, $\beta(2 \rightarrow 1')$ fructan: $\beta(2 \rightarrow 1')$ fructan 1-fructosyltransferase, postulated to be located in the tonoplast. Successive transfers of fructosyl units by enzyme 2 increase the degree of polymerization of fructans in the vacuole. The glucose released in the cytoplasm by the action of enzyme 1 is converted to sucrose by the enzymes of sequence 3 (see Fig. 2).

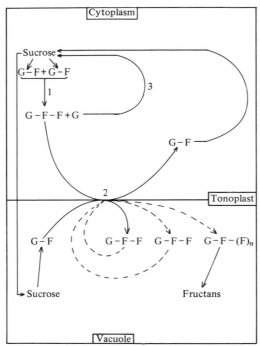

articles consideration of the mode of nutrition of the fungi involved has been lacking. We conclude from a review of research on the effects of fungal pathogens on patterns of translocation that there are two broad patterns and that these correlate with the classification of infecting organisms into biotrophs and necrotrophs (Thrower, 1966; Lewis, 1973, 1974). Biotrophs are organisms which derive their nutrients from the living cells of their hosts and must, therefore, utilize current assimilates (or recently mobilized past assimilates). Necrotrophs infect living tissues, but principally derive their nutrients from tissue killed in advance of colonization. This dichotomy is an oversimplification since the nutritional modes of fungi lie somewhere along the continuum biotrophy–necrotrophy–saprotrophy, the distinction between the last two being that, in saprotrophic nutrition, the tissues of the substrate are dead at the time of initial colonization. Many fungi, typified by leaf spots, are termed hemibiotrophs (Luttrell, 1974) since they initially have a biotrophic mode but eventually pass through necrotrophy and, when the leaf falls, to saprotrophy. Thus, biotrophy may be completely superseded by necrotrophy, or biotrophy and necrotrophy may be simultaneously operative within a site of infection but with spatial separation (see Cooke & Whipps, 1980).

Table 1 illustrates the two main ways by which patterns of translocation are altered in intact plants infected by fungal pathogens. Fungi are divided into two broad nutritional groups, biotroph–hemibiotroph and hemibiotroph–necrotroph, based upon their predominant nutritional behaviour when the experiments were conducted. This division recognizes that many hemibiotrophs are characterized by either a long biotrophic phase or a long necrotrophic one (see Cooke & Whipps, 1980). Fungi of both nutritional groups can cause a decrease in export of photosynthates from infected leaves, but in diseases where increased import of photosynthetic products to infected tissues has been demonstrated the causative fungi all belong to the biotroph–hemibiotroph nutritional grouping.

More detailed consideration of a few diseases will emphasize certain important points. When first-formed unifoliate leaves of French bean were infected by the rust *Uromyces appendiculatus,* the amount of recently fixed carbon exported in 5.5 h dropped from 50% to 2% whereas import from the next (trifoliate) leaf increased from <1% to 32% (Livne & Daly, 1966). With reference to the normal sinks, in the former case, diversion to the fungus was particularly at the expense of the roots; in the latter, the younger emerging leaf suffered most. When single leaves of wheat were infected by the rust *Puccinia striiformis* they could not attract assimilates from other leaves (Doodson, Manners & Myers, 1965). However, later experiments by Siddiqui & Manners (1971), using completely infected plants, showed that the proportion of ^{14}C-assimilate moving to the leaves was increased and that to the roots was decreased. In this way, the pattern of translocation in the whole plant was altered. Thrower & Thrower

Table 1. *Translocation of photosynthetic products in plants infected by fungi of different taxonomic groups. Numbers refer to original publications reporting altered patterns of translocation which are listed in Appendix 1 at the end of the chapter*

Fungus	Disease	Host	Export of photosynthate from infected leaf decreased	Import of photosynthate to infected tissue increased
1 Biotroph–hemibiotroph[1]				
Myxomycota				
Plasmodiophora brassicae	Club root of crucifers	*Brassica oleracea*		42, 54
Eumycota				
Mastigomycotina				
Synchytrium endobioticum	Wart disease of potato	*Solanum tuberosum*		2
Phytophthora infestans	Late blight of potato	*S. tuberosum*	21, 22, 27	
Albugo candida	White blister of crucifers	*Rhaphanus sativus*	67	
A. tragopogonis	White rust of Oxford ragwort	*Senecio squalidus*	95	
Ascomycotina (including imperfect species)				
Erysiphe graminis	Powdery mildew of barley	*Hordeum vulgare*	19, 24	
E. graminis	Powdery mildew of wheat	*Triticum* sp.[2]	47	
Microsphaera alphitoides	Powdery mildew of oak	*Quercus robur*	32	32
Claviceps purpurea	Ergot	*Secale cereale*	13	13
		Triticum sp.[2]		15, 16
		Lolium multiflorum }		57, 58
		Secale cereale		57, 58
Sphacelia sorghi	Ergot	*Setaria macrostachya*		57, 58
Epichloe typhina	Choke of grasses	*Agrostis stolonifera*	87	87
Venturia inaequalis	Scab of apple	*Malus* sp.	33	33

Basidiomycotina

Ustilago maydis	Common smut of maize	*Zea mays*	5	5
U. nuda	Loose smut of wheat	*Triticum* sp.[2]		28
Melampsora lini	Rust of flax	*Linum usitatissimum*	11	11
Puccinia graminis	Black stem rust of wheat	*Triticum* sp.[2]		62, 63
P. lagenophorae	Rust of Oxford ragwort	*Senecio squalidus*	95	
P. poarum	Rust of coltsfoot	*Tussilago farfara*	35	35
P. striiformis	Stripe rust of wheat	*Triticum* sp.[3]	17, 18, 73	
Uromyces appendiculatus	Rust of beans	*Phaseolus vulgaris*	22, 44, 101, 102	44, 62, 63, 100
		Vigna sesquipedalis	76	
U. fabae	Rust of broad bean	*Vicia faba*		88

2 Hemibiotroph–nectrotroph[1]
Eumycota
Ascomycotina (including imperfect species)

Ceratocystis ulmi	Dutch elm disease (vascular wilt)	*Ulmus americana*	64	
Septoria nodorum	Wheat glume blotch	*Triticum* sp.[2]	91	
Alternaria solani	Leaf blight of tomato	*Lycopersicum esculentum*	12	
Helminthosporium teres	Net blotch of barley	*Hordeum vulgare*	66	

[1] See text for rationale of divisions into groups 1 and 2.
[2] *Triticum aestivum* – subsp. unknown. (After Kuckuck, 1970.)
[3] *Triticum aestivum* – subsp. *vulgare*; hexaploid wheat. (After Kuckuck, 1970.)

(1966) also demonstrated that infection of broad bean by the rust *Uromyces fabae* prolonged import into infected leaves and so decreased transport of assimilate to other parts of the plant. These pioneering studies with rusts have been amply confirmed and extended to other biotrophs as the number of entries in Table 1 testifies. It should, nevertheless, be noted that these effects are only clearly seen in fully susceptible reactions. When hosts are resistant or are only lightly infected, the consequences of infection on translocation are less marked (Holligan, Chen, McGee & Lewis, 1974*a;* Parberry, 1978; Clancy, 1979). Indeed, for both susceptible and resistant reactions, it may be concluded that effects are quantitatively related to intensity of infection as well as to virulence of pathogen.

Some necrotrophic fungi can also modify translocation patterns by causing retention at infection sites (Table 1). In addition, several species have been shown to distort carbohydrate movements by inducing changes in permeability (see p. 65), by causing water stress, or by direct interference with transpiration and translocation processes, but these fungi do not necessarily depend upon such changes for their carbon assimilation (see also Ayres, this volume). For instance, accumulation of nutrients occurs around infected areas of *Rhynchosporium secalis* – infected barley and *Phytophthora infestans* – infected potato leaves where water loss is high (Garraway & Pelletier, 1966; Farrell, Preece & Wren, 1969; Farrell, 1971; Ayres & Jones, 1975), in leaves of American elm when *Ceratocystis ulmi* (Dutch elm disease) blocks transport of water in the xylem (Roberts & Stevens, 1968) and adjacent to infection sites of *Gaeumannomyces graminis* (take-all) in seminal roots of wheat, owing to water stress induced by infection (Asher, 1972). Interestingly, in cankers caused by *Hypoxylon mammatum* on aspen and *Fusarium solani* on yellow poplar where part of the phloem is destroyed, accumulation of sugar does not occur in the phloem around either lesion. Accumulation does occur in the xylem above and below the lesion in aspen (Schipper & Anderson, 1971). Translocation of photosynthate in the residual phloem is unimpaired by the canker in yellow poplar (Jensen & Roberts, 1973). At infection sites of sporulating biotrophs, carbon movement is likely to be affected by increased transpiration owing to epidermal rupture and changed permeability of host cells (see also p. 65).

Practical aspects that should be observed when carrying out studies of translocation include sampling at different stages of growth of the infected host, particularly if the pathogen can infect many plant parts such as leaves, stems and flowers, and using more than one analytical technique. For instance, in a study of rates of photosynthesis and respiration, using gas analysis, of wheat tillers infected by *Septoria nodorum* (wheat glume blotch), retention of assimilates by infected flag leaves was initially suggested to contribute to loss in yield (Scharen & Taylor, 1968). Subsequently, when only flag leaves were infected and fed ^{14}C-glucose, no hindrance to translocation from the flag leaf was found but yield was still decreased (Scharen, Schaeffer, Krupinsky & Sharpe, 1975). However, in the vegetative stage of growth, infection of the leaves below the flag leaf did cause a marked decrease in export from infected leaves and increased export from uninfected leaves on the same plant. During the reproductive phase of growth of the host, infection had no effect on export from the lower leaves (Wafford & Whitbread, 1976). These studies emphasize that, in order to understand effects of infection fully, infected plants should be considered as a whole and, where possible, in the conditions of environment and infection found in the field. Moreover, care should be taken in interpreting experiments which involve long feeding times using sealed systems where the carbon dioxide concentration must rapidly fall, often from abnormally high concentrations to the compensation point. Nevertheless, the value of $^{14}CO_2$ and other labelled compounds in studying movement of metabolites is immense and without them our understanding of host–parasite physiology would be poor.

Accumulation of carbohydrates at infection sites

Decreased export from and increased import into an infected organ can only be conclusively demonstrated by using intact plants. However, these effects, particularly the former, can be inferred from a number of approaches different from those used in the studies listed in Table 1. Firstly, accumulation of carbon compounds at sites of infection can readily be demonstrated by supply of $^{14}CO_2$ in the light or ^{14}C-sugars to detached leaves, leaf segments or disks (categories A and B in Table 2). Although it is evident from Table 2 that these effects have been most often shown for biotrophs, at least two hemibiotrophs which rapidly become necrotrophic, *Helminthosporium* sp. and *Colletotrichum lindemuthianum*, do induce some accumulation of ^{14}C (Shaw & Samborski, 1956; Wong & Thrower, 1978). In the former, this occurs around older lesions and, in the latter, in the very young infected regions. Altered patterns of translocation can also be inferred from quantitative determinations of abnormal accumulation in host tissue of their storage carbohydrates, hexoses, sucrose, starch and fructans (category C in Table 2). Similarly, for biotrophs which do not significantly degrade host tissue, accumulation of specifically fungal carbohydrates also indicates a drain on current assimilates (category D in Table 2). Such an inference is not possible for necrotrophs where accumulation of fungal carbohydrates may be at the expense of past assimilates, e.g. those already incorporated into host cell walls at the time of infection. It must be stressed in passing that other fungal compounds of a storage nature, particularly various lipids, also accumulate at sites of biotrophic infections and may constitute effective 'sinks' (see pp. 63–64) in the fungi for photosynthetic products (Lösel & Lewis, 1974; Brennan & Lösel, 1978; Lösel, 1978).

Pathogenic fungi often induce malformations of the tissues they infect and

Table 2. Examples of diseases where accumulation of carbohydrates at infection sites has been indicated at some stage of fungal development. Reference numbers refer to original publications which are listed in Appendix 1 at the end of chapter

Fungus	Disease	Host	Technique	Reference
1 Biotroph–hemibiotroph[1]				
Myxomycota				
Plasmodiophora brassicae	Club root of crucifers	Brassica oleracea	C	41, 97
		B. oleracea	C, D	42, 52
		B. napus	C	43
Eumycota				
Mastigomycotina				
Synchytrium endobioticum	Wart disease of potato	Solanum tuberosum	C	31
			A, B, C, D	2
Phytophthora infestans	Late blight of potato	S. tuberosum	A	21
Pseudoperonospora cubensis	Downy mildew of cucumber	Cucumis sativus	A	37, 38, 60
Albugo candida	White blister of crucifers	Raphanus sativus	A, C	98
			C	67
A. tragopogonis	White rust of Oxford ragwort	Senecio squalidus	A, C, D	45
		S. squalidus	A, B	94, 95
Ascomycotina				
Erysiphe graminis	Powdery mildew of wheat	Triticum sp.[3]	C	3
		Triticum sp.[3]	A, B	71
		Triticum sp.[5]	A, B	72
E. graminis	Powdery mildew of barley	Hordeum vulgare	A, B	71
		H. vulgare	C	6, 23
		H. vulgare	A	19, 20
Microsphaera alphitoides	Powdery mildew of oak	Quercus robur	D	32

Claviceps spp. } Sphacelia spp. }	Ergot	Many spp.	A, C, D	15, 56, 57, 58
Venturia inaequalis	Scab of apple	Malus sp.	C	33
Basidiomycotina				
Ustilago maydis	Common smut of maize	Zea mays	C, D	7, 8
		Z. mays	A	5
U. nuda	Loose smut of wheat	Triticum sp.[2]	A	29
U. esculenta	Gau sun	Zizania caduciflora	C, D	9
Melampsora aecidiodes	Rust of poplar	Populus canescens	D	65
M. larici-populina	Rust of poplar	P. deltoides ×	C, D	79
		P. nigra caudina		
M. lini	Rust of flax	Linum usitatissimum	A, D	11
Puccinia arachadis	Rust of peanut	Arachis hypogaea	C	78
P. carthami	Rust of safflower	Carthamus tinctorius	A	14
P. coronata	Crown rust of oat	Avena sativa	C, D	30, 53
P. graminis	Black stem rust of wheat	Triticum sp.[2,5,6]	A, B, C	68, 71, 72
		Triticum sp.[3,5]	A	40
		Triticum sp.[5]	A, B	92
		Triticum sp.[5]	B	70
		Triticum sp.[5]	A, C	83
		Triticum sp.[5,6]	A	81, 82
		Triticum sp.[4]	B	61
		Triticum sp.[5]	D	53
P. helianthi	Rust of sunflower	Helianthus annuus	A, B	70, 71, 72
P. hordei	Brown rust of barley	Hordeum vulgare	A, C, D	96
P. lagenophorae	Rust of Oxford ragwort	Senecio squalidus	A, C	94, 95
P. malvacearum	Rust of hollyhock	Althaea rosea	D	55
P. pelargonii-zonalis	Rust of pelargonium	Pelargonium inquinans	C, D	55
P. poarum	Rust of coltsfoot	Tussilago farfara	A, C, D	34, 35, 36

Table 2. (cont.)

Fungus	Disease	Host	Technique	Reference
P. recondita	Leaf rust	Arrhenatherum elatius	C	34
P. sorghi	Rust of maize	Zea mays	C	80
P. striiformis	Stripe (yellow) rust of wheat	Triticum sp.[4]	A, B, C	48, 49
Ravelenia breyniae	Rust	Melanthesa rhamnoides	C	74
Uromycladium notabile	Acacia gall	Acacia obliquinervia	A, C	59
Uromyces appendiculatus	Rust of bean	Phaseolus vulgaris	A, C	14, 39, 93
		P. vulgaris	C	26, 50, 51, 69, 89
		P. vulgaris	D	103
		Vigna sesquipedalis	A, C	76, 77
U. trifolii	Rust of clover	Trifolium subterranean	A, C	85, 86
Ustilago nuda	Loose smut	Triticum sp.[4]	D	29
2 Hemibiotroph–necrotroph[1]				
Ascomycotina (including imperfect species)				
Cercospora sojina	Frog eye leaf spot of soybean	Glycine max	C	25
Cochliobolus miyabeanus[7]	Brown spot of rice	Oryza sativa	C	1, 84
Helminthosporium oryzae[7]	Brown spot of rice	O. sativa	C	10
Colletotrichum lindemuthianum	Anthracnose of bean	Vigna sesquipedalis	A	99
Helminthosporium tetramera	Leaf spot of finger millet	Eleusine coracana	C	90
Helminthosporium sp.	Leaf spot of grasses	Bromus sp.	B	72
		Triticum sp.[6]	B	

Accumulation of carbohydrates at infection sites have been indicated by one of the following techniques:

A, ^{14}C-compounds accumulating at the infection site after exposure of the infected plant to [14]CO_2 in the light.

B, ^{14}C-compounds accumulating at the infection site after feeding the infected plant with ^{14}C-sugars.

C, Increase in concentration of one or several host storage carbohydrates at the infection site, e.g. glucose, fructose, sucrose, starch, fructans.

D, Detection of one or several fungal storage carbohydrates at the infection site, e.g. polyols (erythritol, arabitol, mannitol), trehalose, glycogen.

[1] See text for rationale of divisions into groups 1 and 2.

[2] *Triticum aestivum* – subsp. unknown.

[3] *Triticum* – species unknown.

[4] *Triticum aestivum* – subsp. *vulgare;* hexaploid wheat.

[5] *Triticum aestivum* – subsp. *compactum;* hexaploid wheat, often var. Little Club – rust susceptible.

[6] *Triticum dicoccum;* tetraploid wheat, often var. Khapli – rust resistant.

[7] Perfect and imperfect forms of same fungus.

Footnotes 2 to 6 after Kuckuck (1970).

such tissues may contain abnormal concentrations of carbohydrates. Surgeon-Major Barclay, travelling in the Himalayas in 1885, commented on such distortions of leaves caused by the aecial stage of the rust *Puccinia caricina* on the nettle *Urtica parviflora:* 'These extraordinarily hypertrophied parts contain an abundance of nutritive starchy material, which the hill natives eat with relish, selecting them before the aecidia ripen' (Barclay, 1887). Similarly, the shoots of the grass *Zizania caduciflora,* swollen in response to the smut *Ustilago esculenta,* but before ripening of teliospores, is the Chinese vegetable *gau sun* (Chan & Thrower, 1980*a*). Soluble carbohydrates, particularly hexoses, rather than starch accumulate here (Chan & Thrower, 1980*b*). Similar accumulations often occur when there is no gross distortion of the tissues (category C, Table 2) although their fresh and dry weights may increase in response to infection (Yarwood, 1977). These much-studied effects have been reviewed many times (e.g. Smith, Muscatine & Lewis, 1969; Scott, 1972; Daly, 1976).

The magnitude of carbohydrate changes in response to biotrophic fungal disease depends on a number of factors, important among which are susceptibility to, intensity of, and time after infection. Light or benign infections or partial resistance cause less change than fully susceptible reactions and the responses observed can vary considerably depending upon the developmental stage that the fungal disease has reached (e.g. see Table 2, also Inman, 1962; Mitchell, Fung & Lewis, 1978; Roberts & Mitchell, 1979). Starch, in particular, is one of the most common carbohydrates to change in amount after infection. In some dis-

Table 3. *Changes in concentration of soluble carbohydrates at infection sites on leaves of* Tussilago farfara *and* Poa pratensis *infected by the rust* Puccinia poarum. (*Values as the ratio, diseased:healthy*)

Stage of disease	Fructose	Glucose	Sucrose	Fructans
On *Tussilago farfara**				
Pycnial	2.1	7.0	0.6	1.2
Aecial with aecia visible but not dehisced	2.0	9.5	1.4	2.7
Aecial with < 50% aecia dehisced	3.4	9.5	1.1	2.8
Aecial with > 50% aecia dehisced	3.7	14.0	1.6	4.0
On *Poa pratensis*†				
Uredinial	7.4	7.6	2.1	15.0

*Data from Holligan, Chen & Lewis (1973).
†Data from Fung (1975).

eases, it initially decreases then increases and, finally, decreases accompanying sporulation of the fungus (e.g. Keen & Williams, 1969; MacDonald & Strobel, 1969, 1970). Factors responsible for these changes are discussed below. The concentration of sucrose often varies and is commonly influenced by the activity of invertases (see below also). In the angiospermous families of the Compositae and Gramineae, the synthesis of fructans is at least as important as that of starch, and the macrocyclic, heteroecious rust *Puccinia poarum,* which has hosts in both families, induces alterations in levels of these compounds after infection (Table 3). On its grass host (*Poa pratensis*) infection only results in a five-fold increase in α-glucan compared with a fifteen-fold increase in fructan. Furthermore, some of the α-glucan may be glycogen of fungal origin. However, this has only been clearly demonstrated for the composite host coltsfoot (*Tussilago farfara*), where total glucan does not change markedly in response to infection (Table 4a). (In extracts, glycogen may be partially distinguished from starch by its greater solubility in water.) In the centre of the large (to *c.* 1 cm diameter), aecial pustules on this host, most α-glucan is water soluble and does not exhibit a diurnal change, whereas in the surrounding healthy tissue, most α-glucan is insoluble and does decline in the dark (Table 4a). That most of the water-soluble fraction is glycogen was confirmed by an experiment in which $^{14}CO_2$ was supplied to leaf disks for 3 h in the light, or 3 h in the light and 20 h in the dark, before they were dissected. Immediately after fixation, little ^{14}C accumulated in the soluble glucan but ^{14}C in this fraction increased during the subsequent dark period.

Table 4. *Amounts of, and* ^{14}C-*incorporated into, soluble and insoluble* α-*glucans in the centre of pustules of* Puccinia poarum *on leaves of coltsfoot* (Tussilago farfara), *and in healthy tissues surrounding pustules, after leaf disks had been exposed to* $^{14}CO_2$ *in the light for 3 h* (L), *or 3 h in the light followed by 20 h in the dark* (LD)

	Centre of pustules		Surrounding healthy tissue	
	L	LD	L	LD
(a) Amounts of glucan (values as $\mu g\ cm^{-2}$)				
Soluble	123	114	51	9
Insoluble	31	5	104	16
Total	154	119	155	25
(b) Incorporation of ^{14}C (values as counts per minute $\times 10^{-2}\ cm^{-2}$)				
Soluble	2.5	14.5	17.5	3.5
Insoluble	5.0	5.5	24.0	4.5
Total	7.5	20.0	41.5	8.0

Starch in the healthy tissue around the pustules behaved in an opposite mannner (Table 4b; Holligan, McGee & Lewis 1974b).

In addition to glycogen, all groups of fungal pathogens contain variable amounts of the disaccharide trehalose and, for ascomycetes and basidiomycetes in particular, of the acyclic sugar alcohols, mannitol, arabitol and erythritol. One or more of these compounds accumulate at sites of infection and, when $^{14}CO_2$ or ^{14}C-sugars have been supplied via the host, become labelled with the tracer (category D, Table 2). These metabolites are not readily utilized by host tissues and, in this way, their synthesis from host sugars absorbed by the fungi maintains a chemical concentration gradient which may promote further uptake of the substrates (Smith et al., 1969). This concept can be extended to include fungal lipids, cell wall material and other metabolites which are rapidly synthesized but are not freely available to the host.

In addition to the stage and intensity of infection (see pp. 56–57), the precise concentrations of individual storage carbohydrates of the host in infected tissues also depend on a number of other factors, not all of which have been properly assessed. Among these are rate of photosynthesis in infected tissues (see Buchanan et al., this volume), partitioning of photosynthate between chloroplast and cytoplasm, rate of import of carbohydrate (principally sucrose) from other parts of the plant (see pp. 47–52) and the activity and accessibility of the relevant synthetic and degradative enzymes, several of which are subject to allosteric control (i.e. they are activated or inhibited by metabolites which are not substrates – Fig. 2). Loss of soluble carbohydrates from host cells and absorption and metabolism of them by the fungi will also be important factors influencing their concentration at sites of infection. Some of these features are considered below in relation to the overall mechanisms responsible for the observed changes in patterns of translocation and accumulation of carbohydrates described above.

Processes involved with altered translocation patterns and metabolism of carbohydrates in infected plants

Changes in concentration and distribution of hormones

Considerable experimental evidence exists which implicates all classes of plant hormones in control of rates of either or both photosynthesis and translocation (Herold, 1980). In particular, applied gibberellins, cytokinins and auxins can all induce changes in patterns of translocation under some circumstances (e.g. Shindy & Weaver, 1967; Kriedemann, 1968; Patrick, 1979). However, as noted by Herold (1980), 'there is still an urgent need to link directly production of hormone in the sink, translocation to the source and ensuing response of source'. In other words, the mechanisms involved remain obscure.

With respect to diseased tissue, changes in concentration of hormones are common and often, but not always, involve an increase (see Pegg, this volume). It follows that infection by fungi can modify patterns of translocation in the same currently unknown manner as exogenously applied hormones. As discussed by Pegg, cytokinins have been especially implicated in this connection because, like many biotrophic fungi, they can induce localized retention of chlorophyll ('green islands') in otherwise yellowing tissue. The minimal tissue damage of biotrophic diseases (including the biotrophic phase of hemibiotrophs) would permit transport of hormone(s) from the site of infection to the rest of the plant as well as allowing them to act on host cells in the diseased area. In necrotrophic diseases, however, any alteration to concentrations of hormones could be localized since the rapid death of host cells would often prevent movement of hormones from the site of infection and any subsequent physiological response at a distance (Lewis, 1973). These possible differences between biotrophs and necrotrophs could contribute to explaining the scarcity of necrotrophic fungi in Tables 1 and 2.

The morphological distortions which characterize many diseases, and which involve hormonally stimulated increases in cell division and elongation in the host, represent new sinks for the utilization of photosynthetic products. In this way, alterations in the hormone balance at sites of infection may have both direct and secondary effects on patterns of translocation.

Altered permeability

The loading of sugars into the phloem is clearly an important and orderly phase of the translocatory process, despite the probability that an apoplastic phase is involved (see Fig. 1). Both necrotrophic and biotrophic pathogens often increase the permeability of the cells they infect; necrotrophs also affect cells nearby (Jones & Ayres, 1972; Hoppe & Heitefuss, 1974; Wheeler, 1978). With regard to the ordered nature of the apoplastic phase of the translocation of sugars in uninfected plants, such changes will bring about a premature and disorganized leakage to the apoplast with consequent disruption of the controlled process of transport.

Activity of invertases

Only non-reducing di- or oligosaccharides or polyols are mobile in the phloem (Fig. 1). With reference to sucrose in healthy, mature leaves, the enzymes responsible for its degradation (invertases and sucrose synthetase) have low activity and much sucrose synthesized is moved from the leaf to the secondary sinks, where these enzymes have greater activity (ap Rees, 1974). It follows that any induction of increased activity of these enzymes by infecting fungi, particularly when accompanied by disruption of normal cellular compartmentation brought about by altered permeability, will lead to a degradation of sucrose to its constituent non-mobile reducing sugars and an enhanced movement of sucrose to the infection site.

Increases, sometimes more than ten-fold, in the activity of acid invertases (i.e. with a pH optimum near 5) have been documented for several pathogens (Table 5) but not for two infections by members of the Plasmodiophorales, club root, *Plasmodiophora brassicae,* on cabbage (Mitchell & Cooke, 1976) and 'rizomania', *Polymyxa betae* (? + virus), on beet (Macrì & Vianello, 1976). In these diseases, acid invertase expressed on a dry weight basis was lower in infected roots and hypocotyls of cabbage and, on a fresh weight basis, was not different from controls in beet. In the latter infection, however, neutral invertase was lower in infected tissue for three months after inoculation. Interestingly, either no increase (club root) (Keen & Williams, 1969) or a decrease (rizomania) (Macrì & Vianello, 1976) in activity of sucrose synthetase has also been reported. One problem in comparing these data with those in the papers cited in Table 5 is that,

Table 5. *Association between biotrophic pathogens and vascular plants in which activity of acid invertases increases on infection. Reference numbers refer to original publications which are listed in Appendix 1 at the end of the chapter*

Fungus	Disease	Host	Reference
Eumycota			
Mastigomycotina			
Albugo tragopogonis	White rust of Oxford ragwort	*Senecio squalidus*	47
Sclerospora graminicola	Green-ear of Bajra	*Pennisetum typhoides*	76
Ascomycotina			
Cochliobolus miyabeanus	Brown spot of rice	*Oryza sativa*	85
Basidiomycotina			
Ustilago maydis	Common smut of maize	*Zea mays*	4, 8
Melampsora lini	Rust of flax	*Linum usitatissimum*	11
Puccinia coronata	Crown rust of oat	*Avena sativa*	30, 54
P. graminis	Stem rust of wheat	*Triticum* sp.[1]	54
P. poarum	Rust of coltsfoot	*Tussilago farfara*	47
	Rust of meadow grass	*Poa pratensis*	47

[1]*Triticum aestivum* subsp. *compactum* var. 'Little club'.

in addition to this table being concerned entirely with leaf tissue, the proliferation of host tissue in the plasmodiophoralean infections distorts the comparison of healthy and infected systems. Invertase has been assayed in only a few necrotrophic infections (Heale & Stringer-Calvert, 1975). The maceration of carrot callus by *Sclerotinia sclerotiorum* is correlated with high activity of insoluble invertase but infection of the same tissue by *Verticillium albo-atrum,* which only produced mild symptoms, did not result in such marked increases. Also, for biotrophic infections, the degree of enhanced invertase depends on the nature of the interaction between the partners – a resistant reaction results in a less pronounced response (Clancy, 1979; D. T. Mitchell, personal communication). No increase was recorded by Hewitt & Ayres (1976) for infections of oak by the powdery mildew *Microsphaera alphitoides,* although this may reflect the different transport properties of powdery mildew infections (see below).

There is considerable controversy and uncertainty concerning the source and site of the increased activity of invertase in infected leaves. Wounding itself induces enhanced synthesis of this enzyme in healthy tissue (e.g. Matsushita & Uritani, 1974) so that physical damage by pathogens might be expected to raise the levels of host enzymes. However, many fungi, including pathogens in culture, e.g. *Claviceps purpurea* (Dickerson, 1972) and *Ustilago maydis* (Callow, Long & Lithgow, 1980), commonly possess extracellular or surface-bound invertases, so that a contribution from the fungus must be expected too. The activity of invertases in uninfected tissues (mostly storage tissues) also responds to exogenous hormones, particularly gibberellins (Edelman & Hall, 1964, Gayler & Glasziou, 1969, 1972; Kaufman *et al.,* 1973), and since some pathogens produce these in culture (see Pegg, this volume), hormones may well also influence the overall activity of invertase found in diseased plants.

The matter is further complicated not only by the possession, by host and pathogen, of both soluble and insoluble forms of the enzyme but also by the differing techniques which have been used to extract and analyse the enzyme. The simplest assay consists of measuring reducing sugars released from sucrose added to whole tissue (slices, segments, disks, etc.) which has been pre-treated with ethyl acetate to render membranes permeable, and washed with water (Bacon, MacDonald & Knight, 1965). Although total activity may not be assessed by this method, there are good correlations between activity of invertase measured this way and intensity and degree of infection (see Table 5 and Heale & Stringer-Calvert, 1975). Table 6 records the activity, measured by this technique, in the centres of the large aecial pustules of *Puccinia poarum* on *Tussilago farfara* and in concentric rings around these, and during the uredinial stage on *Poa pratensis.*

Studies using *extracted* enzymes indicate some further features of the activity and distribution of the enzyme in healthy and diseased leaves of some grasses.

Emerging leaves initially import carbohydrate and have a high activity of acid invertase. As leaves mature, this activity declines (Billett, Billett & Burnett, 1977; Pollock & Lloyd, 1977; Greenland, 1979). Insoluble activity is commonly about 10% of the soluble but precise figures depend on techniques of extraction. During the decline in activity in blades of the third leaf of oat, the complement of soluble isoenzymes separated by gel filtration on Sephadex G 150 changes. An isoenzyme of molecular weight 85 000 is dominant in tissue when it is still within the sheath of the next oldest leaf. After emergence, its activity falls so that another isoenzyme (molecular weight 143 000), the activity of which has remained constant, becomes the principal component in mature tissues (Fig. 4). During development of the rust *Puccinia coronata* both soluble and insoluble invertases become more active, the former to the greater extent. This is correlated with the appearance of a third isoenzyme (molecular weight 218 000) which, within eight days of inoculation, becomes the most active isoenzyme (Fig. 4).

A similar situation occurs in smutted maize (Callow *et al.*, 1980), where the invertases of leaf sheaths were investigated. Healthy tissue contains a single isoenzyme (molecular weight 100 000) but, in smutted sheaths, the major activity is due to another isoenzyme (molecular weight 145 000) which is identical to one present in extracts of cultured haploid cells of the smut (N.B. infective hyphae are dikaryotic). However, a second major isoenzyme of these cells (molecular weight 300 000) is not present in infected tissue. A third minor component of molecular weight *c.* 47 500 is present in fungus and infected tissue. Callow's group concludes that most increased activity is due to a fungal enzyme but that

Table 6. *Activity of acid invertase, at near optimal pH values, in healthy and rusted leaf tissue of both hosts of* Puccinia poarum (*data from Long* et al., *1975*)

Tissue	Invertase activity (μg reducing sugar mg^{-1} dry weight h^{-1})
Poa pratensis	
(a) Healthy segments (1 cm)	133
(b) Segments with uredinial pustules (1 cm)	329
Tussilago farfara	
(a) Healthy disks (5 mm diam.)	44
(b) Centre of aecial pustule (5 mm diam.)	495
(c) Annulus around (b) (5–9 mm diam.)	138
(d) Annulus around (c) (9–14 mm diam.)	59

Fig. 4. Activities of isoenzymes of invertase (I, II, III) from leaves of oat seedlings during development and after infection by the rust *Puccinia coronata* (Greenland, 1979). (Isoenzymes separated by gel filtration on Sephadex G 150; open symbols = healthy tissue, closed symbols = rusted tissue.) (*a*) Non-emerged tissue within sheath of next oldest leaf; (*b*) young emerged tissue 4 days after emergence of leaf tip; (*c*) whole leaf blades at ligule emergence (11 days after emergence of leaf tip); (*d*) mature leaf blades (c. 18 days after emergence of leaf tip); (*e*) mature leaf blades 5 days after inoculation (flecking stage); (*f*) mature leaf blades 7 days after inoculation; (*g*) mature leaf blades 10 days after inoculation (sporulating stage).

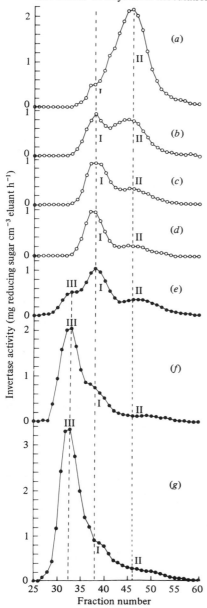

stimulation of host invertase makes some contribution to the overall increase in activity although Billett *et al.* (1977) attribute the increase entirely to a host enzyme. From electrophoretic studies, however, Callow and his colleagues showed that the extra isoenzyme of infected tissue was distinct from that produced by the fungus in pure culture. Although Greenland (1979) did not use electrophoresis, he showed that separations by ion-exchange chromatography on DEAE-cellulose gave three peaks of activity for healthy and rusted oat tissues. Even though the soluble enzymes of cultured rusts have not been examined, Greenland's data support the overall conclusions of Callow's group despite the differences in molecular weights noted above. It should also be stressed that hybrid molecules of both host and fungus cannot be excluded at present.

The sites of the increased activity of invertases have not yet been resolved. Sucrose may be hydrolysed by isoenzymes in the cell wall (insoluble), periplasmic space (soluble) or cytoplasm (soluble) of the host. Alternatively, it may be hydrolysed later as it crosses the extrahaustorial matrix and enters the haustorium or as it crosses the walls of intercellular hyphae (Greenland, 1979). For precise location, probes such as fluorescent antibodies will need to be used. (The structure of the host–parasite interface is described in detail by Manners & Gay, this volume, who argue that, in powdery mildews, sucrose is not hydrolysed until after it enters the haustorium.)

Activity of amylase

Several comparisons between amounts of starch in healthy and diseased leaves have revealed an initial loss following infection before a subsequent enhanced synthesis (Shaw, 1963; Mirocha & Zaki, 1966; Schipper & Mirocha, 1969*a,b;* MacDonald & Strobel, 1969, 1970). This loss in leaves of bean following infection by the rust *Uromyces appendiculatus* has been attributed to an activator of β-amylase produced by the fungus (Schipper & Mirocha, 1969*b*). A very similar heat-stable, uncharged and dialysable activator was also extractable from spores of several other biotrophic fungi (four other species of rust, one smut and one powdery mildew) but not from those of two necrotrophs or the smut *Ustilago maydis*. These activators have not been further characterized. An increase in β-amylase activity and a corresponding loss in starch also occurs in the leaf spots caused by two hemibiotrophs, *Alternaria helianthi* on sunflower and *Cercospora cruenta* on mung bean (*Phaseolus aureus*) (Vidhyasekaran & Kandasamy, 1972; Bhaskaran & Kandaswamy, 1977). By contrast, Tanaka & Akai (1960) have suggested that *increased* starch content in leaves of rice formed in response to *Cochliobolus miyabeanus*, a hemibiotroph, was due to a *decrease* in the activity of β-amylase.

Unresolved problems here concern the location of this enzyme and the normal mechanism of degradation of assimilatory starch in leaves. The site of such starch is within chloroplasts and its degradation here may be phosphorolytic and not amylolytic (see p. 51). At least some chloroplasts appear to be devoid of amylase but what function any non-chloroplastic amylase in leaves would have is obscure. Certainly, more work on the mechanism of degradation of starch in healthy leaves is necessary before any conclusions about mechanisms in diseased leaves can be made.

'Sugar-feeding'

Increased activity of invertase in diseased leaves when accompanied by massive import of sucrose to sites of infection essentially means that the cells of the host are exposed to abnormally high concentrations of hexose (Long *et al.*, 1975). This situation can be simulated by supplying hexoses to healthy leaves, and such 'sugar-feeding' to many plants results in the synthesis of starch within chloroplasts. In addition to starch, Chandorkar & Collins (1972, 1974*a,b*) and Collins & Chandorkar (1973) have demonstrated that, in leaves of species of the Compositae, *de novo* synthesis of fructans occurs from exogenous sugars. Much of the synthesis of starch and fructans in response to biotrophs noted above may be due to this 'sugar-feeding' effect induced by pathogens. In the case of starch, glycolytic degradation of hexose to TP is first necessary to permit rapid entry of substrates into chloroplasts (see Fig. 2). Synthesis of fructans in response to infection of the grass *Poa pratensis* and the composite *Tussilago farfara* by the rust *Puccinia poarum* (Table 3) may indeed be stimulated by supply of glucose or sucrose to leaf segments and disks, respectively (Table 7). Furthermore, the spectrum of molecular weights of fructan synthesized by both tissues in response

Table 7. *Changes in concentration of fructan (including free fructose and sucrose) following supply of glucose or sucrose to leaf disks of* Tussilago farfara *and leaf segments of* Poa pratensis *in the dark. (Unpublished data of E. E. M. McGee and D. H. Lewis) (values as µg per disk or segment) (original values before feeding of sugar: for* T. *farfara, 34 µg per disk; for* P. *pratensis, 51 µg per segment)*

	Tussilago			Poa		
Time of feeding (h)	24	48	72	24	48	72
Buffer only	20	18	22	38	21	20
0.5% glucose	42	78	118	87	83	78
5.0% glucose	68	132	180	121	165	151
0.5% sucrose	56	93	136	39	57	62
5.0% sucrose	177	250	468	99	130	140

to infection appears to be the same so that the enzymes responsible for their synthesis are likely to be those shown in Fig. 3. However, participation of fungal enzymes cannot be excluded and Dickerson (1972) has demonstrated a transferase in the ascomycetous biotroph *Claviceps purpurea* (ergot of grasses) that can produce fructo-oligosaccharides and glucose from sucrose.

Effects attributable to changes in concentration of orthophosphate

Although an explanation based on 'sugar-feeding' may be sufficient to account for the enhanced synthesis of fructans in leaves in response to biotrophs, provided activities of the transferase enzymes are adequate, changes in local [Pi] induced by these pathogens may also contribute significantly to the observed changes in starch. As discussed earlier (p. 48–51), synthesis of this polymer is controlled in at least three ways by [Pi]; in all three cases, low [Pi] will favour enhanced synthesis and limited breakdown of starch. A question that must therefore be asked is, 'Do biotrophs locally lower [Pi] in host cells so that these effects on accumulation of starch can operate?'. The available data are conflicting and, at present, inadequate to answer this. Those of MacDonald & Strobel (1970) show an inverse correlation between concentrations of Pi and of starch 10–12 days after inoculation of wheat by *Puccinia striiformis* at the time of most rapid accumulation of starch, but at other times the fit is not so good. They assayed the activity of ADPG pyrophosphorylase, extracted from healthy and diseased leaves, in the presence of concentrations of sugar phosphates and Pi found in these tissues at different times. The observed activities correlated well with the differences in the starch contents of healthy and diseased leaves. Their conclusions have been criticized by Daly (1976) on the grounds that analyses were made for whole leaves and not chloroplasts, and that the fluctuations they observed in concentrations of Pi and organic phosphates have not been recorded by others. There is also no information on the distribution of these metabolites between host and fungus and between parts of leaves. This is important since the enhanced synthesis of starch is limited to cells near fungal pustules. However, the fact that polyphosphates accumulate in hyphae of rusts (Bennett & Scott, 1971) may indicate a depletion of Pi from adjacent cells (Scott, 1972) and [Pi] in the cytoplasm and chloroplast do equilibrate (see Heldt *et al.*, 1977).

That depletion of cytoplasmic phosphate in healthy tissues can result in an accumulation of starch has been conclusively shown by the use of analogues of glucose about carbon atom 2 (mannose, glucosamine and 2-deoxyglucose). These are substrates for hexokinase and, although phosphorylated after absorption by plant tissues, they are, in many species, not metabolized further. Hence, phosphorus becomes sequestered as organic phosphates and [Pi] drops (Herold & Lewis, 1977). In this way, these analogues simulate the suggestion made for fungal polyphosphates above. Thus, both mannose and the rust *Puccinia poarum* stimulate accumulation of starch in *Poa pratensis*. (Mannose is not a direct substrate for synthesis of starch (Chen-She, Lewis & Walker, 1975).) Data on rates of photosynthesis and partitioning of photosynthate between chloroplast and cytoplasm are available for other species. Mannose and its analogues lower rates of photosynthesis and induce a retention of metabolites within chloroplasts (Herold & Lewis, 1977; Herold, McGee & Lewis, 1980). Fungal sequestration of phosphate during biotrophic infection may therefore contribute to the lowered rate of photosynthesis in infected tissue (Buchanan *et al.*, this volume). In relation to the effects of biotrophs on permeability discussed earlier, it is also interesting that mannose induces loss of metabolites from tissues in which it sequesters phosphate (Herold, 1978), probably by interference with the metabolic turnover and integrity of phospholipids in membranes.

In conclusion, it seems highly probable that sequestration of phosphate by pathogens contributes to the observed reduction in rates of photosynthesis, increased permeability of cells of the host and enhanced synthesis of starch caused by biotrophs. Critical analyses and experiments need to be devised and executed to confirm this.

A final point concerning [Pi] and effects of biotrophs relates to patterns of translocation and rates of photosynthesis in non-infected parts of plants. Fig. 1 indicated that Pi could be a messenger between 'sinks' and 'sources'. This suggestion (Herold, 1980) is based not only on considerations of the control exerted by Pi on apportioning of photosynthate between chloroplast and primary sinks as discussed on pp. 48–50 but also on an indication that activity of secondary sinks may cause redistribution of Pi throughout the plant. In this way, maximum import of Pi by leaves occurs during maximum export of sugar (Hopkinson, 1964; Thorne & Koller, 1974). If this hypothesis is correct, sequestration of phosphate could not only contribute to the lowered rate of photosynthesis and diminished export of photosynthate from exporting leaves but could also influence rates of photosynthesis in other parts of the plant. Thus, it may be relevant that infection of the lower leaves of pea by the powdery mildew *Erysiphe pisi* stimulates photosynthesis in upper, uninfected leaves (Ayres, 1981). Evidence that other biotrophic infections can initially stimulate photosynthesis in infected leaves and in other parts of the plant has been discussed by Yarwood (1967), Scott (1972) and Daly (1976).

Comparisons with infections of higher plants by other organisms

From the preceding sections which have exclusively concerned fungal infections, it is clear that, as far as patterns of translocation and synthesis of carbohydrates in the hosts are concerned, biotrophs have more profound effects than necrotrophs. Biotrophic fungi exert their influences by various combinations and permutations of the six processes discussed in the previous section and, probably, of others. These same factors are implicated in infections of plants by other pathogenic organisms.

Tomatoes infected with curly top virus retain photosynthetic assimilates in their leaves (Panopoulos, Faccioli & Gold, 1975), and, following supply of $^{14}CO_2$ in the light to leaves of tobacco and thornapple infected by tobacco mosaic virus, radioactivity accumulates at infection sites (Thrower, 1965). Starch also accumulates at sites of virus infection (Watson & Watson, 1951; Watson & Mulligan, 1960; Orlob & Arny, 1961; Jensen 1968, 1969; Cohen & Loebenstein, 1975). Although, for the first example, damage to phloem may be responsible, the other effects may be consequences of sequestration of phosphate (as nucleic acid) by the viruses. 'Green islands' are also induced by some viruses (Yarwood, 1967), implicating hormone changes in the host.

Mycoplasma-like organisms and bacteria can induce accumulation of sugars, as well as retention of photosynthate in infected tissue but, in no infection, has increased import to infected tissues been yet clearly demonstrated (Hale & Whitbread, 1973; Catlin, Olsson & Beutel, 1975; Whitbread & Bhatti, 1976; Braun & Sinclair, 1978). This may be due to lack of attention to these aspects of diseases caused by the few biotrophic bacterial pathogens, e.g. *Agrobacterium tumefaciens, Pseudomonas savastanoi* and *Corynebacterium fascians*. However, since these produce starch-containing galls on their hosts and hormones in culture (Thimann & Sachs, 1966; Wood, 1967), their effects do fall within the overall biotrophic syndrome. Furthermore, since one or more of the following, altered patterns of translocation, accumulation of starch, induction of 'green islands', synthesis of polyphosphates and altered hormone levels, have also been recorded for infections of vascular plants by biotrophic angiospermous parasites, insects and nematodes, the mechanisms of biotrophy appear to be universal.

Acknowledgments

We wish to thank Dr A. J. Greenland and Dr A. Herold for helpful discussion and for permission to quote unpublished information. We are grateful to the Agricultural Research Council for financial support.

References

ap Rees, T. (1974). Pathways of carbohydrate breakdown in higher plants. In *M.T.P. International Review of Science*, Biochemistry Series I, vol. II, *Plant Biochemistry*, ed. D. H. Northcote, pp. 89–127. London: Butterworths.

Arnold, W. N. (1968). The selection of sucrose as the translocate of higher plants. *Journal of Theoretical Biology*, **21**, 13–20.

Asher, M. J. C. (1972). Effect of *Ophiobolus graminis* infection on the growth of wheat and barley. *Annals of Applied Biology*, **70**, 215–23.

Ayres, P. G. (1981). Powdery mildew stimulates photosynthesis in uninfected leaves of pea plants. *Phytopathologische Zeitschrift*, **100**, 312–8.

Ayres, P. G. & Jones, P. (1975). Increased transpiration and the accumulation of root absorbed ^{86}Rb in barley leaves infected by *Rhynchosporium secalis* (leaf blotch). *Physiological Plant Pathology*, **7**, 49–58.

Bacon, J. S. D., MacDonald, I. R. & Knight, A. H. (1965). The development of invertase activity in slices of the root *Beta vulgaris* L. washed under aseptic conditions. *Biochemical Journal*, **94**, 175–82.

Baker, D. A. (1978). *Transport Phenomena in Plants*. London: Chapman & Hall.

Barclay, A. (1887). *Aecidium urticae*, Schum., var. *Himalayense*. *Scientific Memoirs by Medical Officers of the Army of India*, **2**, 29–38.

Bennett, J. & Scott, K. J. (1971). Inorganic polyphosphates in the wheat stem rust fungus and in rust-infected wheat leaves. *Physiological Plant Pathology*, **1**, 185–98.

Bhaskaran, R. & Kandaswamy, T. K. (1977). Carbohydrate metabolism of sunflower leaves infected by *Alternaria helianthi*. *Phytopathologia Mediterranea*, **16**, 103–8.

Billett, E. E., Billett, M. A. & Burnett, J. H. (1977). Stimulation of maize invertase following infection by *Ustilago maydis*. *Phytochemistry*, **16**, 1163–6.

Bird, I. F., Cornelius, M. J., Keys, A. L. & Whittingham, C. P. (1974). Intracellular site of sucrose synthesis in leaves. *Phytochemistry*, **13**, 59–64.

Braun, E. J. & Sinclair, W. A. (1978). Translocation in phloem necrosis-diseased American elm seedlings. *Phytopathology*, **68**, 1733–7.

Brennan, K. M. & Lösel, D. M. (1978). Physiology of fungal lipids: selected topics. *Advances in Microbial Physiology*, **17**, 47–179.

Bushnell, W. R. & Gay, J. (1978). Accumulation of solutes in relation to the structure and function of haustoria in powdery mildews. In *The Powdery Mildews*, ed. D. M. Spencer, pp. 183–235. London: Academic Press.

Callow, J. A., Long, D. E. & Lithgow, E. D. (1980). Multiple molecular forms of invertase in maize smut infections. *Physiological Plant Pathology*, **16**, 93–107.

Catlin, P. B., Olsson, E. A. & Beutol, J. A. (1975). Reduced translocation of carbon and nitrogen from leaves with symptoms of peach curl. *Journal of the American Society for Horticultural Science*, **100**, 184–7.

Chan, Y.-S. & Thrower, L. B. (1980a). The host–parasite relationship between *Zizania caduciflora* Turcz. and *Ustilago esculenta* P. Henn. I. Structure and development of the host and host–parasite combination. *New Phytologist*, **85**, 201–8.

Chan, Y.-S. & Thrower, L. B. (1980b). The host–parasite relationship between *Zizania caduciflora* Turcz. and *Ustilago esculenta* P. Henn. III. Carbohydrate metabolism of *U. esculenta* and the host–parasite combination. *New Phytologist*, **85**, 217–24.

Chandorkar, K. R. & Collins, F. W. (1972). *De novo* synthesis of fructo-oligosaccharides in leaf discs of certain Asteraceae. *Canadian Journal of Botany*, **50**, 295–303.

Chandorkar, K. R. & Collins, F. W. (1974a). The mechanism of *de novo* synthesis of fructo-oligosaccharides in leaf discs of certain Asteraceae. III. *Canadian Journal of Botany*, **52**, 181–8.

Chandorkar, K. R. & Collins, F. W. (1974b). Enzymological aspects of *de novo* synthesis of fructo-oligosaccharides in leaf discs of certain Asteraceae. IV. The activity of sucrose-sucrose-fructosyl transferase. *Canadian Journal of Botany*, **52**, 1369–77.

Chen-She, S.-H., Lewis, D. H. & Walker, D. A. (1975). Stimulation of photosynthetic starch formation by sequestration of cytoplasmic orthophosphate. *New Phytologist*, **74**, 383–92.

Clancy, F. G. (1979). Comparative carbohydrate physiology of susceptible and resistant flax in response to inoculation with the flax rust. PhD thesis, University of Dublin.

Cohen, J. & Loebenstein, G. (1975). An electron microscope study of starch lesions in cucumber cotyledons infected with tobacco mosaic virus. *Phytopathology*, **65**, 32–9.

Collins, F. W. & Chandorkar, K. R. (1973). *De novo* synthesis of fructo-oligosaccharides in leaf discs of certain Asteraceae. II. Certain physiological and biochemical changes accompanying fructo-oligosaccharides formation. *Canadian Journal of Botany*, **51**, 1931–7.

Cooke, R. C. & Whipps, J. M. (1980). The evolution of modes of nutrition in terrestrial plant parasitic fungi. *Biological Reviews*, **55**, 341–62.

Daly, J. M. (1976). The carbon balance of diseased plants: changes in respiration, photosynthesis and translocation. In *Encyclopedia of Plant Physiology*, New Series, vol. 4, *Physiological Plant Pathology*, ed. R. Heitefuss & P. H. Williams, pp. 450–79. Berlin: Springer-Verlag.

Delmer, D. P. & Albersheim, P. (1970). The biosynthesis of sucrose and nucleoside diphosphate glucoses in *Phaseolus aureus*. *Plant Physiology*, **45**, 782–6.

Dickerson, A. G. (1972). A β-D-fructofuranosidase from *Claviceps purpurea*. *Biochemical Journal*, **129**, 263–72.

Doodson, J. K., Manners, J. G. & Myers, A. (1965). Some effects of yellow rust (*Puccinia striiformis*) on [14]carbon assimilation and translocation in wheat. *Journal of Experimental Botany*, **16**, 304–17.

Edelman, J. S. & Hall, M. A. (1964). Effect of growth hormones on development of invertase associated with cell walls. *Nature*, **201**, 296–7.

Edelman, J. S. & Jefford, T. G. (1968). The mechanism of fructosan metabolism in higher plants as exemplified in *Helianthus tuberosus*. *New Phytologist*, **67**, 517–31.

Farrell, G. M. (1971). Localization of photosynthetic products in potato leaves infected by *Phytophthora infestans*. *Physiological Plant Pathology*, **1**, 457–68.

Farrell, G. M., Preece, T. F. & Wren, M. J. (1969). Effects of infection by *Phytophthora infestans* (Mont.) De Bary on the stomata of potato leaves. *Annals of Applied Biology*, **63**, 265–75.

Fung, A. K. (1975). Carbohydrate metabolism of rust-infected plants. PhD thesis, University of Sheffield.

Garraway, M. O. & Pelletier, R. L. (1966). Distribution of ^{14}C in the potato plant in relation to leaf infection by *Phytophthora infestans*. *Phytopathology*, **56**, 1184–9.

Gayler, K. R. & Glasziou, K. T. (1969). Plant enzyme synthesis. Hormonal regulation of invertase and peroxidase synthesis in sugar cane. *Planta*, **84**, 185–94.

Gayler, K. R. & Glasziou, K. T. (1972). Physiological function of acid and neutral invertases in growth and sugar storage in sugar cane. *Physiologia Plantarum*, **27**, 25–31.

Geiger, D. R. (1976). Effects of translocation and assimilate demand on photosynthesis. *Canadian Journal of Botany*, **54**, 2337–45.

Geiger, D. R. (1979). Control of partitioning and export of carbon in leaves of higher plants. *Botanical Gazette*, **140**, 241–8.

Giaquinta, R. (1976). Evidence for phloem loading from the apoplast. Chemical modification of membrane sulphydryl groups. *Plant Physiology*, **57**, 872–5.

Greenland, A. J. (1979). Invertases of healthy and rusted leaves of oat. PhD thesis, University of Sheffield.

Hale, C. N. & Whitbread, R. (1973). The translocation of ^{14}C-labelled assimilates by dwarf bean plants infected with *Pseudomonas phaseolicola* (Burk.) Dows. *Annals of Botany*, N.S., **37**, 473–80.

Heale, J. B. & Stringer-Calvert, A. (1975). Invertase levels and induced resistance in tissue cultures of *Daucus carota* L. invaded by fungi. *Cytobios*, **10**, 167–80.

Heldt, H. W., Chon, C. J., Maronde, D., Herold, A., Stankovic, Z. S., Walker, D. A., Kraminer, A., Kirk, M. R. & Heber, U. (1977). Role of orthophosphate and other factors in the regulation of starch formation in leaves and isolated chloroplasts. *Plant Physiology*, **59**, 1146–55.

Heldt, H. W. & Rapley, L. (1970a). Unspecific permeation and specific uptake of substances in spinach chloroplasts. *FEBS Letters*, **7**, 139–46.

Heldt, H. W. & Rapley, L. (1970b). Specific transport of inorganic phosphate, 3-phosphoglycerate and dihydroxyacetone phosphate, and of dicarboxylates across the inner membrane of spinach chloroplasts. *FEBS Letters*, **10**, 143–8.

Herold, A. (1978). Induction of wilting by mannose in spinach beet leaves. *New Phytologist*, **81**, 299–305.

Herold, A. (1980). Regulation of photosynthesis by sink activity – the missing link. *New Phytologist*, **86**, 131–44.

Herold, A. & Lewis, D. H. (1977). Mannose and green plants: occurrence, physiology and metabolism, and use as a tool to study the role of orthophosphate. *New Phytologist*, **79**, 1–40.

Herold, A., McGee, E. E. M. & Lewis, D. H. (1980). The effect of orthophosphate concentration and exogenously supplied sugars on the distribution of newly fixed carbon in sugar beet leaf discs. *New Phytologist*, **85**, 1–13.

Herold, A. & Walker, D. A. (1979). Transport across chloroplast envelopes – the role of phosphate. In *Handbook on Transport Across Membranes*, ed. G. Giebisch, D. C. Tosteson & H. H. Ussing, pp. 411–39. Berlin: Springer-Verlag.

Hewitt, H. G. & Ayres, P. G. (1976). Effect of infection by *Microsphaera alphitoides* (powdery mildew) on carbohydrate levels and translocation in seedlings of *Quercus robur*. *New Phytologist*, **77**, 379–90.

Holligan, P. M., Chen, C. & Lewis, D. H. (1973). Changes in the carbohydrate composition of leaves of *Tussilago farfara* during infection by *Puccinia poarum*. *New Phytologist*, **72**, 947–55.

Holligan, P. M., Chen, C., McGee, E. E.M. & Lewis, D. H. (1974a). Carbohydrate metabolism in healthy and rusted leaves of coltsfoot. *New Phytologist*, **73**, 881–8.

Holligan, P. M., McGee, E. E. M. & Lewis, D. H. (1974b). Quantitative determination of starch and glycogen and their metabolism in leaves of *Tussilago farfara* during infection by *Puccinia poarum*. *New Phytologist*, **73**, 873–9.

Hopkinson, J. M. (1964). Studies on the expansion of the leaf surface. IV. The carbon and phosphorus economy of a leaf. *Journal of Experimental Botany*, **15**, 125–37.

Hoppe, H. H. & Heitefuss, R. (1974). Permeability and membrane lipid metabolism of *Phaseolus vulgaris* infected with *Uromyces phaseoli*. III.

Changes in relative concentration of lipid bound fatty acids and phospholipase activity. *Physiological Plant Pathology*, **4**, 25–36.

Inman, R. E. (1962). Disease development, disease intensity and carbohydrate levels in rusted bean plants. *Phytopathology*, **52**, 1207–11.

Jensen, K. F. & Roberts, B. R. (1973). Effects of *Fusarium* canker on translocation in yellow-poplar seedlings. *Physiological Plant Pathology*, **3**, 359–62.

Jensen, S. G. (1968). Photosynthesis, respiration and other physiological relationships in barley infected with barley yellow dwarf virus. *Phytopathology*, **58**, 204–8.

Jensen, S. G. (1969). Composition and metabolism of barley leaves infected with barley yellow dwarf virus. *Phytopathology*, **59**, 1691–9.

Jones, P. & Ayres, P. G. (1972). The nutrition of the subcuticular mycelium of *Rhynchosporium secalis* (barley leaf blotch): permeability changes induced in the host. *Physiological Plant Pathology*, **2**, 383–92.

Kaufman, P. B., Gosheh, W. S., La Croix, J. D., Soni, S. L. & Ikuma, H. (1973). Regulation of invertase levels in *Avena* stem segments by gibberellic acid, sucrose, glucose and fructose. *Plant Physiology*, **52**, 221–8.

Keen, N. T. & Williams, P. H. (1969). Synthesis and degradation of starch and lipids following infection of cabbage by *Plasmodiophora brassicae*. *Phytopathology*, **59**, 778–85.

Kriedemann, P. E. (1968). An effect of kinetin on the translocation of ^{14}C-labelled photosynthate in citrus. *Australian Journal of Biological Sciences*, **21**, 569–72.

Kuckuck, H. (1970). Primitive wheats. In *Genetic Reserves in Plants – their Exploration and Conservation*, IBP Handbook No. 11, ed. O. H. Frankel & E. Bennett, pp. 249–66. Oxford: Blackwell.

Levi, C. & Preiss, J. (1978). Amylopectin degradation in pea chloroplast extracts, *Plant Physiology*, **61**, 218–20.

Lewis, D. H. (1973). Concepts in fungal nutrition and the origin of biotrophy. *Biological Reviews*, **48**, 261–78.

Lewis, D. H. (1974). Micro-organisms and plants: the evolution of parasitism and mutualism. *Symposia of the Society for General Microbiology*, **24**, 367–92.

Lewis, D. H. (ed.) (1982). *Storage Carbohydrates in Vascular Plants: Distribution, Physiology and Metabolism*. Cambridge: Cambridge University Press. (In press.)

Livne, A. & Daly, J. M. (1966). Translocation in healthy and rust-affected beans. *Phytopathology*, **56**, 170–5.

Long, D. E., Fung, A. K., McGee, E. E. M., Cooke, R. C. & Lewis, D. H. (1975). The activity of invertase and its relevance to the accumulation of storage polysaccharides in leaves infected by biotrophic fungi. *New Phytologist*, **74**, 173–82.

Lösel, D. M. (1978). Lipid metabolism of leaves of *Poa pratensis* during infection by *Puccinia poarum*. *New Phytologist*, **80**, 167–74.

Lösel, D. M. & Lewis, D. H. (1974). Lipid metabolism in leaves of *Tussilago farfara* during infection by *Puccinia poarum*. *New Phytologist*, **73**, 1157–69.

Luttrell, E. S. (1974). Parasitism of fungi on vascular plants. *Mycologia*, **66**, 1–15.

MacDonald, P. W. & Strobel, G. A. (1969). Starch accumulation in wheat plants infected with stripe rust. *Phytopathology*, **59**, 1039 (Abst.).

MacDonald, P. W. & Strobel, G. A. (1970). Adenosine diphosphate–glucose pyrophosphorylase control of starch accumulation in rust infected wheat leaves. *Plant Physiology*, **46**, 126–35.

Macrì, F. & Vianello, A. (1976). Sucrose synthetase and neutral invertase depression in sugar roots affected by *Rizomania*. *Phytopathologische Zeitschrift*, **86**, 327–34.

Manners, D. J. (1973). Starch and inulin. In *Phytochemistry. The Process and Products of Photosynthesis*, vol. 1., ed. L. P. Miller, pp. 176–97. London: Van Nostrand Reinhold.

Manners, J. G. (1971). Cereals: rusts and smuts. In *Diseases of Crop Plants*, ed. J. M. Western, pp. 226–53. London: Macmillan.

Matsushita, K. & Uritani, I. (1974). Change in invertase activity of sweet potato in response to wounding and purification and properties of its invertases. *Plant Physiology*, **54**, 60–6.

Mirocha, C. J. & Zaki, A. I. (1966). Fluctuation in amount of starch in host plants invaded by rust and mildew fungi. *Phytopathology*, **66**, 1220–4.

Mitchell, D. T. & Cooke, R. C. (1976). Carbohydrate composition and activity of invertase in infected cabbage root tissues during clubroot formation. *Transactions of the British Mycological Society*, **67**, 344–9.

Mitchell, D. T., Fung, A. K. & Lewis, D. H. (1978). Changes in the ethanol-soluble carbohydrate composition and acid invertase in infected first leaf tissues susceptible to crown rust of oat and wheat stem rust. *New Phytologist*, **80**, 381–92.

Neales, T. F. & Incoll, L. D. (1968). The control of leaf photosynthesis rate by the level of assimilate concentration in the leaf: a review of the hypothesis. *Botanical Review*, **34**, 107–25.

Orlob, G. B. & Arny, D. C. (1961). Some metabolic changes accompanying infection by barley yellow dwarf virus. *Phytopathology*, **51**, 768–75.

Panopoulos, N. J., Faccioli, G. & Gold, A. H. (1975). Sulfate uptake and translocation in curly top infected tomatoes. *Phytopathology*, **65**, 77–80.

Parberry, D. G. (1978). A consideration of tolerance to parasites in plants. *Annals of Applied Biology*, **89**, 373–8. (Proceedings.)

Patrick, J. W. (1979). An assessment of auxin-promoted transport in decapitated stems and whole shoots of *Phaseolus vulgaris* L. *Planta*, **146**, 107–12.

Pollock, C. J. & Lloyd, E. J. (1977). The distribution of acid invertase in developing leaves of *Lolium temulentum* L. *Planta*, **133**, 197–200.

Preiss, J. & Levi, C. (1979). Metabolism of starch in leaves. In *Encyclopedia of Plant Physiology*, New Series, vol. 6, *Photosynthesis* II, *Photosynthetic Carbon Metabolism and Related Processes*, ed. M. Gibbs & E. Latzko, pp. 282–312. Berlin: Springer-Verlag.

Roberts, B. R. & Stevens, J. M. (1968). Some effects of Dutch elm disease on the movement of ^{14}C-photosynthate in American elm. *Advancing Frontiers of Plant Science*, **21**, 127–34.

Roberts, S. M. & Mitchell, D. T. (1979). Carbohydrate composition and invertase activity in poplar leaf tissues infected by *Melampsora lini* (D.C.) Schroeter. *New Phytologist*, **83**, 499–508.

Scharen, A. L., Schaeffer, G. W., Krupinsky, J. M. & Sharpe, F. T. (1975). Effects of flag leaf axial lesions caused by *Septoria nodorum* on ^{14}C translocation and yield of wheat. *Physiological Plant Pathology*, **6**, 193–8.

Scharen, A. L. & Taylor, J. M. (1968). CO_2 assimilation and yield of Little Club wheat infected by *Septoria nodorum*. *Phytopathology*, **58**, 447–51.

Schipper, A. L. & Anderson, G. W. (1971). Alteration of sugar translocation in aspen by *Hypoxylon mammatum*. *Phytopathology*, **61**, 366–8.

Schipper, A. L. & Mirocha, C. J. (1969a). The histochemistry of starch depletion and accumulation in bean leaves at rust infection sites. *Phytopathology*, **59**, 1416–22.

Schipper, A. L. & Mirocha, C. J. (1969b). The mechanism of starch depletion in leaves of *Phaseolus vulgaris* infected with *Uromyces phaseoli*. *Phytopathology*, **59**, 1722–7.

Scott, K. J. (1972). Obligate parasitism by phytopathogenic fungi. *Biological Reviews*, **47**, 537–72.

Shaw, M. (1963). The physiology and host parasite relations of the rusts. *Annual Review of Phytopathology*, **1**, 259–94.

Shaw, M. & Samborski, D. J. (1956). The physiology of host–parasite relations. I. The accumulation of radioactive substances at infections of facultative and obligate parasites including tobacco mosaic virus. *Canadian Journal of Botany*, **34**, 387–405.

Shindy, W. & Weaver, R. J. (1967). Plant regulators alter translocation of photosynthetic products. *Nature*, **24**, 1024–5.

Siddiqui, M. Q. & Manners, J. G. (1971). Some effects of general yellow rust (*Puccinia striiformis*) infection on ^{14}carbon assimilation and growth in spring wheat. *Journal of Experimental Botany*, **22**, 792–9.

Smith, D. (1972). Carbohydrate reserves of grasses. In *The Biology and Utilization of Grasses*, ed. V. B. Younger & C. M. Mokell, pp. 318–33. New York: Academic Press.

Smith, D., Muscatine, L. & Lewis, D. (1969). Carbohydrate movement from autotrophs to heterotrophs in parasitic and mutualistic symbiosis. *Biological Reviews*, **44**, 17–90.

Stitt, M., Bulpin, P. V. & ap Rees, T. (1978). Pathway of starch breakdown in photosynthetic tissues of *Pisum sativum*. *Biochimica et Biophysica Acta*, **544**, 200–14.

Tanaka, H. & Akai, S. (1960). On the mechanism of starch accumulation in tissues surrounding spots in leaves of rice plants due to the attack of *Cochliobolus miyabeanus*. II. On the activities of β-amylase and invertase in tissues surrounding spots. *Annals of the Phytopathological Society of Japan*. **25**, 80–4.

Thimann, K. V. & Sachs, T. (1966). The role of cytokinins in the 'fasciation' disease caused by *Corynebacterium fascians*. *American Journal of Botany*, **53**, 731–9.

Thorne, J. H. & Koller, H. R. (1974). Influence of assimilate demand on photosynthesis, diffusive resistances, translocation, and carbohydrate levels of soybean leaves. *Plant Physiology*, **54**, 201–7.

Thrower, L. B. (1965). A radioautographic study of the formation of local lesions by tobacco mosaic virus. *Phytopathology*, **55**, 558–62.

Thrower, L. B. (1966). Terminology for plant parasites. *Phytopathologische Zeitschrift*, **56**, 258–9.

Thrower, L. B. & Thrower, S. L. (1966). The effect of infection with *Uromyces fabae* on translocation in broad bean. *Phytopathologische Zeitschrift*, **57**, 267–76.

Vidhyasekaran, P. & Kandasamy, D. (1972). Carbohydrate metabolism of *Phaseolus aureus* infected with obligate and facultative parasites. *Indian Phytopathology*, **25**, 48–53.

Wafford, J. D. & Whitbread, R. (1976). Effects of leaf infections by *Septoria nodorum* Berk. on the translocation of ^{14}C-labelled assimilates in spring wheat. *Annals of Botany*, N.S., **40**, 83–90.

Wardlaw, I. F. & Passioura, J. B. (1976). *Transport and Transfer Processes in Plants*. New York: Academic Press.

Watson, M. A. & Mulligan, T. E. (1960). Comparison of two barley yellow-dwarf viruses in glasshouse and field experiments. *Annals of Applied Biology*, **48**, 559–74.

Watson, M. A. & Watson, D. J. (1951). The effect of infection by beet yellows and beet mosaic viruses on the carbohydrate content of sugar beet leaves and on translocation. *Annals of Applied Biology*, **38**, 276–88.

Wheeler, H. (1978). Disease alterations in permeability and membranes. In *Plant Disease, An Advanced Treatise*, vol. III, *How Plants Suffer From Disease*, ed. J. G. Horsfall & E. B. Cowling, pp. 327–47. New York: Academic Press.

Whitbread, R. & Bhatti, M. A. R. (1976). The translocation of ^{14}C-labelled assimilates in dwarf bean plants infected with *Xanthomonas phaseoli* (E. F. Sm) Dowson. *Annals of Botany*, N.S., **40**, 499–509.

Wong, P. Y. O. & Thrower, L. B. (1978). Sugar metabolism and translocation in *Vigna sesquipedalis* infected by *Colletotrichum lindemuthianum*. *Phytopathologische Zeitschrift*, **92**, 102–12.

Wood, R. K. S. (1967). *Physiological Plant Pathology*. Oxford: Blackwell Scientific Publications.

Yarwood, C. E. (1967). Responses to parasites. *Annual Review of Plant Physiology*, **18**, 419–38.

Yarwood, C. E. (1977). Pathogens which increase plant growth. In *Current Topics in Plant Pathology*, ed. Z. Király, pp. 177–81. Budapest: Akadémiae Kiadó.

Appendix 1. Publications cited in Tables 1, 2 and 5

1. Akai, S., Tanaka, H. & Noguchi, K. (1958). *Ann. phytopath. Soc. Japan*, **23**, 111–16.

2. Allen, J. S. (1977). MSc thesis, University of Sheffield.

3. Allen, P. J. (1942). *Am. J. Bot.*, **29**, 425–35.

4. *Billett, E. E., Billett, M. A. & Burnett, J. H. (1977). *Phytochemistry*, **16**, 1163–6.

5. Billett, E. E. & Burnett, J. H. (1978). *Physiol. Pl. Pathol.*, **12**, 103–12.

6. Bushnell, W. R. & Allen, P. J. (1962). *Plant Physiol.*, **37**, 50–9.

7. Callow, J. A. & Ling, I. T. (1973). *Physiol. Pl. Pathol.*, **3**, 489–94.

8. *Callow, J. A., Long, D. E. & Lithgow, E. D. (1980). *Physiol. Pl. Pathol.*, **16**, 93–107.

9. *Chan, Y. -S. & Thrower, L. B. (1980). *New Phytol.*, **85**, 217–24.

10. Chattopadhyay, S. B. & Bera, A. K. (1977). *Curr. Sci. India*, **46**, 450.

11. *Clancy, F. G. (1979). PhD thesis, University of Dublin.

12. Coffey, M. D., Marshall, C. & Whitbread, R. (1970). *Ann. Bot.*, N.S., **34**, 605–15.

13. Corbett, K., Dickerson, A. G. & Mantle, P. G. (1974). *J. gen. Microbiol.*, **84**, 39–58.

14. Daly, J. M., Inman, R. E. & Livne, A. (1962). *Plant Physiol.*, **37**, 531–8.

15. Dickerson, A. G., Mantle, P. G. & Nisbet, L. J. (1976). *J. gen. Microbiol.*, **97**, 267–76.

16. Dickerson, A. G., Mantle, P. G., Nisbet, L. J. & Shaw, B. I. (1978). *Physiol. Pl. Pathol.*, **12**, 55–62.

17. Doodson, J. K., Manners, J. G. & Myers, A. (1964). *Ann. Bot.*, N.S., **28**, 459–72.

18. *Doodson, J. K., Manners, J. G. & Myers, A. (1965). *J. exp. Bot.*, **16**, 304–17.

19. Edwards, H. H. (1971). *Plant Physiol.*, **47**, 324–8.
20. Edwards, H. H. & Allen, P. J. (1966). *Plant Physiol.*, **41**, 683–8.
21. *Farrell, G. M. (1971). *Physiol. Pl. Pathol.*, **1**, 457–67.
22. Farrell, G. M. (1977). In *Current Topics in Plant Pathology*, ed. Z. Király, pp. 133–41. Budapest: Akadémiai Kiadó.
23. Frič, F. (1964). *Biologia, (Bratislava)*, **19**, 597–610.
24. Frič, F. (1975). *Phytopath. Z.*, **84**, 88–95.
25. Fucikovsky, C. A. (1966). *Phytopathology*, **56**, 987.
26. Galbiati, C. (1978). *Riv. Patol. Veg. Padova*, **14**, 47–57.
27. Garraway, M. O. & Pelletier, R. L. (1966). *Phytopathology*, **56**, 1184–9.
28. Gaunt, R. E. & Manners, J. G. (1971). *Ann. Bot.*, N.S., **35**, 1141–50.
29. Gaunt, R. E. & Manners, J. G. (1971). *Ann. Bot.*, N.S., **35**, 1151–62.
30. *Greenland, A. J. (1979). PhD thesis, University of Sheffield.
31. Gretchushnikov, A. I. & Yakovleva, N. N. (1951). *Compt. rend. acad. sci. URSS*, (N.S.), **76**, 303–4. (In *Rev. appl. Mycol.*,**30**, 428.)
32. *Hewitt, H. G. & Ayres, P. G. (1976). *New Phytol.*, **77**, 379–90.
33. Hignett, R. C. & Kirkham, D. S. (1967). *J. gen. Microbiol.*, **48**, 269–75.
34. Holligan, P. M., Chen, C. & Lewis, D. H. (1973). *New Phytol.*, **72**, 947–55.
35. *Holligan, P. M., Chen, C., McGee, E. E. M. & Lewis, D. H. (1974). *New Phytol.*, **73**, 881–8.
36. *Holligan, P. M., McGee, E. E. M. & Lewis, D. H. (1974). *New Phytol.*, **73**, 873–9.
37. Inaba, T. & Kajiwara, T. (1974). *Ann. phytopath. Soc. Japan*, **40**, 30–8.
38. Inaba, T. & Kajiwara, T. (1975). *Bull. natl. Agric. Sci.*, Ser. C, **29**, 65–139.
39. *Inman, R. E. (1962). *Phytopathology*, **52**, 1207–11.
40. Jain, A. C. & Pelletier, R. L. (1958). *Nature*, **182**, 882–3.
41. *Keen, N. T. & Williams, P. H. (1969). *Phytopathology*, **59**, 778–85.
42. Keen, N. T. & Williams, P. H. (1969). *Plant Physiol.*, **44**, 748–54.
43. Linss, H. (1977). *Z. Pflkrankh. Pflschutz.*, **84**, 497–508.
44. *Livne, A. & Daly, J. M. (1966). *Phytopathology*, **56**, 170–5.
45. Long, D. E. & Cooke, R. C. (1974). *New Phytol.*, **73**, 889–99.
46. *Long, D. E., Fung, A. K., McGee, E. E. M., Cooke, R. C. & Lewis, D. H. (1975). *New Phytol.*,**74**, 173–82.
47. Lupton, F. G. H. & Sutherland, J. (1973). *Ann. appl. Biol.*, **74**, 35–9.
48. *MacDonald, P. W. & Strobel, G. A. (1969). *Phytopathology*, **59**, 1039.
49. *MacDonald, P. W. & Strobel, G. A. (1970). *Plant Physiol.*, **46**, 126–35.
50. Mirocha, C. J. (1965). *Phytopathology*, **55**, 1068.
51. *Mirocha, C. J. & Zaki, A. I. (1966). *Phytopathology*, **56**, 1220–4.
52. *Mitchell, D. T. & Cooke, R. D. (1976). *Trans. Brit. mycol. Soc.*, **67**, 344–9.
53. *Mitchell, D. T., Fung, A. K. & Lewis, D. H. (1978). *New Phytol.*, **80**, 381–92.
54. Mitchell, D. T. & Rice, K. A. (1979). *Ann. appl. Biol.*, **92**, 143–52.
55. Mitchell, D. T. & Roberts, S. M. (1973). *Physiol. Pl. Pathol.*, **3**, 481–8.
56. Mower, R. L., Gray, G. R. & Ballou, C. E. (1973). *Carbohydr. Res.*, **27**, 119–34.
57. Mower, R. L. & Hancock, J. G. (1975). *Can. J. Bot.*, **53**, 2813–25.
58. Mower, R. L. & Hancock, J. G. (1975). *Can. J. Bot.*, **53**, 2826–34.
59. *Parberry, D. G. (1978). *Ann. appl. Biol.*, **89**, 373–8.
60. Perl, M., Cohen, Y. & Rotem, J. (1972). *Physiol. Pl. Pathol.*, **2**, 113–22.
61. Pfeiffer, E., Jäger, K. & Reisener, H. -J. (1969). *Planta*, **85**, 194–201.
62. Pozsár, B. I. & Király, Z. (1964). In *Host-parasite Relations in Plant Pathology*, ed. Z. Király & G. Ubrizsy, pp. 199–210. Budapest: Research Institute for Plant Protection.

63. Pozsár, B. I. & Király, Z. (1966). *Phytopath. Z.*, **56**, 297–309.
64. *Roberts, B. R. & Stevens, J. M. (1968). *Adv. Frontiers Pl. Sci.*, **21**, 127–34.
65. *Roberts, S. M. & Mitchell, D. T. (1979). *New Phytol.*, **83**, 499–508.
66. Rowe, J. & Reid, J. (1979). *Can. J. Bot.*, **57**, 208–14.
67. Saettler, A. W. & Pound, G. S. (1966). *Phytopathology*, **56**, 898.
68. Samborski, D. J. & Shaw, M. (1956). *Can. J. Bot.*, **34**, 601–19.
69. Schipper, A. L. & Mirocha, C. J. (1969). *Phytopathology*, **59**, 1416–22.
70. Shaw, M. (1961). *Can. J. Bot.*, **39**, 1393–407.
71. Shaw, M., Brown, S. A. & Rudd-Jones, D. (1954). *Nature*, **173**, 768–9.
72. *Shaw, M. & Samborski, D. J. (1956). *Can. J. Bot.*, **34**, 389–405.
73. *Siddiqui, M. Q. & Manners, J. G. (1971). *J. exp. Bot.*, **22**, 792–9.
74. Singh, V. P., Singh, J. N. & Pavgi, M. S. (1970). *Phytopath. Z.*, **68**, 361–6.
75. Sinha, A. K. (1976). *Geophytology*, **6**, 150–1.
76. So, M. L. & Thrower, L. B. (1976). *Phytopath. Z.*, **86**, 252–65.
77. So, M. L. & Thrower, L. B. (1976). *Phytopath. Z.*,**86**, 302–9.
78. Subrahmanyam, P., Gopal, G. R., Malakondaiah, N. & Reddy, M. N. (1976). *Phytopath. Z.*, **87**, 107–13.
79. Suzuki, K. (1975). *Ann. phytopath. Soc. Japan*, **41**, 378–82.
80. Syamanda, R. & Staples, R. C. (1963). *Boyce Thompson Inst. Contrib.*, **22**, 1–8.
81. Sydow, B. von (1966). *Phytopath. Z.*, **56**, 78–96.
82. Sydow, B. von (1966). *Phytopath. Z.*, **56**, 105–16.
83. Sydow, B. von & Durbin, R. D. (1962). *Phytopathology*, **52**, 169–76.
84. *Tanaka, H. & Akai, S. (1960). *Ann. phytopath. Soc. Japan*, **25**, 80–4.
85. Thrower, L. B. (1964). *Phytopath. Z.*, **51**, 425–36.
86. Thrower, L. B. (1965). *Phytopath. Z.*, **52**, 269–94.
87. Thrower, L. B. & Lewis, D. H. (1973). *New Phytol.*, **72**, 501–8.
88. *Thrower, L. B. & Thrower, S. L. (1966). *Phytopath. Z.*, **57**, 267–76.
89. Tschen, J. & Fuchs, W. H. (1970). *Phytopath. Z.*, **67**, 78–86.
90. Vidhyasekaran, P. (1974). *Physiol. Pl. Pathol.*, **4**, 457–67.
91. *Wafford, J. D. & Whitbread, R. (1976). *Ann. Bot. N.S.*, **40**, 83–90.
92. Wang, D. (1960). *Can. J. Bot.*, **38**, 635–42.
93. Wang, D. (1961). *Can. J. Bot.*, **39**, 1595–604.
94. Whipps, J. M. (1977). PhD thesis, University of Sheffield.
95. Whipps, J. M. & Cooke, R. C. (1978). *New Phytol.*, **81**, 307–19.
96. Whipps, J. M. & Lewis, D. H. (1980). Unpublished results.
97. Williams, P. H., Keen, N. T., Strandberg, J. O. & McNabola, S. S. (1968). *Phytopathology*, **58**, 921–8.
98. Williams, P. H. & Pound, G. S. (1964). *Phytopathology*, **54**, 446–51.
99. *Wong, P. Y. O. & Thrower, L. B. (1978). *Phytopath. Z.*, **92**, 102–12.
100. Yarwood, C. E. & Jacobsen, L. (1955). *Phytopathology*, **45**, 43–8.
101. Zaki, A. I. & Durbin, R. D. (1962). *Phytopathology*, **52**, 758.
102. Zaki, A. I. & Durbin, R. D. (1965). *Phytopathology*, **55**, 528–9.
103. Zimmer, D. E. (1970). *Phytopathology*, **60**, 1157–63.

*Also cited in text.

J.L.GAY & J.M. MANNERS

Transport of host assimilates to the pathogen

Pathogenic fungi which establish a biotrophic relationship with plants are extremely successful in obtaining host metabolites over prolonged periods. Of these, powdery mildews (Erysiphales) are outstanding because they establish a special functional relationship with individual host cells and, even when they produce spores to bring about new infections, they do so without disrupting host tissues. Particular representatives of the group parasitize many genera of angiosperms, and in temperate and sub-tropical regions they are important crop pathogens. Their organization in relation to the host makes them particularly amenable to experimental study of photosynthate uptake; in most genera almost the whole fungus lies on the surface of the plant so it can be easily collected and its activity assessed, and more importantly, the host–pathogen interface can be isolated. Since the interface is confined to epidermal cells with haustoria, analysis is not confused by the possible contribution of intercellular hyphae as in rust and downy mildew infections.

Although haustoria have been known for over 100 years, and studies by Smith (1900) provided detailed descriptions of their structure, their role in the transport of nutrients has until recently been based on *circumstantial* evidence. In powdery mildews in particular, it has seemed inconceivable that fungal growth external to the host could be maintained without the intervention of the haustoria. In studies of the cereal mildew *Erysiphe graminis* Hoskin (reported in Bushnell, 1971), Mount & Ellingboe (1969) and Slesinski & Ellingboe (1971) provided the first *experimental* evidence of their function. Hoskin established microcolonies on barley coleoptiles and observed an immediate cessation in the extension of connected hyphae when the haustorium was excised. Ellingboe and his colleagues supplied isotopes of sulphur and phosphorus to wheat leaves and monitored their transport into the superficial fungal structures during the course of infection. Radioactivity only accumulated when the haustoria approached maturity.

The host–parasite interface

Further advances in haustorial physiology have been made possible by extensive studies of the haustorium–host interface of pea mildew, *Erysiphe pisi,* (Gil & Gay, 1977). Electron microscopic examination of sections of infected leaves corroborated the observation established for many fungal pathogens (Bracker & Littlefield, 1973) that each haustorium is contained in an invagination of the plasmalemma of the infected cell. This region is the extrahaustorial membrane, and between it and the haustorium surface is the amorphous extrahaustorial matrix which light- and electron-microscope cytochemistry has shown to be rich in polysaccharide. During this work the method which Dekhuijzen (1966) used to isolate haustoria from powdery mildew-infected cucumber was further developed (Fig. 1). It was then recognized (Gil & Gay, 1977) that the

Fig. 1. Flow diagram for isolation of haustorial complexes from pea infected with *Erysiphe pisi*.

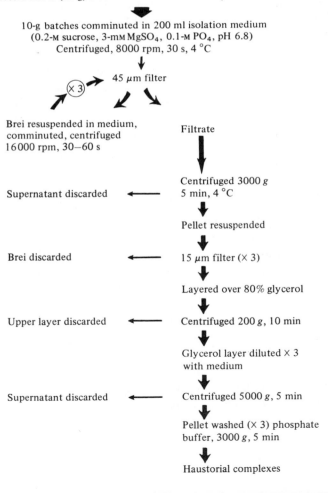

Infected leaves (30 g) brushed to remove surface mycelium and washed

10-g batches comminuted in 200 ml isolation medium
(0.2-M sucrose, 3-mM MgSO$_4$, 0.1-M PO$_4$, pH 6.8)
Centrifuged, 8000 rpm, 30 s, 4 °C

(× 3)   45 µm filter

Brei resuspended in medium, comminuted, centrifuged 16000 rpm, 30–60 s

Filtrate

Supernatant discarded ⟵ Centrifuged 3000 g 5 min, 4 °C

Pellet resuspended

Brei discarded ⟵ 15 µm filter (× 3)

Layered over 80% glycerol

Upper layer discarded ⟵ Centrifuged 200 g, 10 min

Glycerol layer diluted × 3 with medium

Supernatant discarded ⟵ Centrifuged 5000 g, 5 min

Pellet washed (× 3) phosphate buffer, 3000 g, 5 min

Haustorial complexes

invaginated portion of the host plasma membrane was isolated together with the haustorium. The extrahaustorial matrix and haustorial cytoplasm were also retained, the latter by the closure of the pore in the septum across the haustorial neck. The term 'haustorial complex' was introduced for this compound structure. Since it comprises the parasitic interface, and can be obtained in numbers sufficient for population studies *in vitro,* its isolation has provided an essential technique for studies of nutrient transport in powdery mildews.

Light microscopy of haustorial complexes immediately indicated a limitation of the potential pathway for transport into haustoria (Gil & Gay, 1977). Living haustorial complexes swelled and shrunk in water and aqueous solutions respectively. In the swollen condition the matrix was expanded but the extrahaustorial membrane remained firmly attached to the haustorial neck at a distinct dark band (B band). A second annulus (the A band; Fig. 2) was also distinguished and, for both, electron microscopy demonstrated the close association of the extrahaustorial membrane with the surface of the neck wall. From these studies it was concluded that the invaginated portion of the host cell plasmalemma was semipermeable, and that the seal to the haustorial neck was instrumental in preventing both the escape of solutes from the extrahaustorial matrix and the ingress of host metabolites along the wall of the neck. Thus, since the haustorial surface is isolated from the apoplast of the leaf, it was proposed that metabolites are directed along a pathway through the host cytoplasm. Recent observation using substances which do not pass through plasma membranes has confirmed this conclusion. When epidermes from infected pea were placed in a fluorescent stilbene (P. Spencer-Phillips, personal communication), and isolated haustorial complexes were treated with uranyl acetate and examined by electron micros-

Fig. 2. Diagrams of freshly isolated haustorial complexes from pea infected with *Erysiphe pisi* at magnification of approximately 1600. (*a*) In isolation medium containing 100-mM sucrose where the extrahaustorial membrane follows the contour of the haustorium. (*b*) Mounted in water showing the expanded extrahaustorial matrix (m) and distended extrahaustorial membrane (ehm) attached to the B neckband and the tips of the haustorial lobes (l). The significance of the lobe attachment is unclear. The transition in the structure of the host plasma membrane occurs at the A neckband. (Based on Gil & Gay, 1977.)

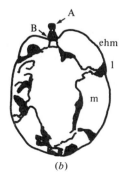

(*a*)   (*b*)

copy after precipitating the uranyl ion (Gay & Manners, 1981), neither substance passed the neckband region. The uranyl experiment also confirmed that the extrahaustorial membrane was semi-permeable; the matrix was not entered unless the membrane was damaged in preparation. The implications of these results are shown in Fig. 3.

The invaginated portion of the plasmalemma differs in many respects from the region lining the cell wall (Gil & Gay, 1977). It is over twice as thick, highly convoluted and contains polysaccharide in unusually high amounts. When swelling was induced, it distended slowly and did not rupture as plasma membranes normally do in hypotonic media. Even after detergent treatment it remained intact although its distension rate increased. However, the thickness of the membrane was reduced, and swelling rates substantially increased, when cell wall degrading enzymes were applied. The distinctive structure of the extrahaustorial

Fig. 3. Diagram to show the interfaces, and to illustrate the pathways and barriers to nutrient flux, between *Erysiphe pisi* and *Pisum sativum*. The haustorium occupies an invagination (extrahaustorial membrane, ehm) of the epidermal plasmalemma (pp). When the mycelium is removed from the surface of the leaf, or the haustorium is released from the cell during isolation, the neck (n) is broken at the host cell wall (open arrow) and the extrahaustorial membrane remains attached at the neckbands (shown here as one) so that it and the enclosed matrix (m) are retained with the haustorium as a structural unit (haustorial complex). The haustorial cytoplasm (hc) is retained by closure of the pore in the neck septum. The solid arrows indicate the postulated nutrient pathway. a, appressorium; c, cuticle; fp, fungal plasmalemma; fw, fungal cell wall: pw, plant cell wall. (From Manners & Gay, 1978a. Reproduced by permission of Academic Press Inc. (London) Ltd.)

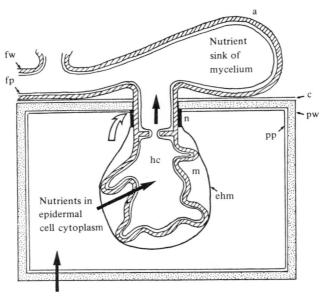

membrane was also demonstrated in freeze-fracture preparations (Gil, 1976; Bushnell & Gay, 1978). The 10-nm particles characteristic of plasma membranes occurred in the wall-lining region of the host membrane and in the fungal plasma membrane, but were absent from the extrahaustorial membrane. Clearly, infection results in a cell with a new structural aspect adjacent to the haustorium but a normal structure in regions adjacent to neighbouring cells.

Uptake of photosynthates by haustoria

The next stage of the investigation of infected pea was to attempt formal proof that haustoria take photosynthates from the host. This was achieved by extracting haustorial complexes from infected leaves photosynthesizing in the presence of $^{14}CO_2$ (Manners & Gay, 1978a). In some experiments, estimation of radioactivity was confined to components soluble in ethanol, because starch grains and other fragments of the host could be seen in haustorial complex fractions. In other experiments, fractions were washed with detergent to disrupt contaminant chloroplasts, and controls with equivalent fractions from uninfected plants were included. However, it was recognized that these controls were not entirely comparable because the ratio of soluble to insoluble metabolites in the host was increased by infection. Recent autoradiographic examination of haustorial complex fractions obtained in similar $^{14}CO_2$ feeding experiments has shown that about 85% of the label in the isolated fraction is associated with the complexes and this is probably mostly insoluble (Manners & Gay, 1980a).

An essential adjunct to the proof of uptake was the subsequent collection of $^{14}CO_2$ released by the respiration of labelled haustorial complexes incubated *in vitro*. This showed that photosynthates had entered the haustorial cytoplasm and were not confined to the extrahaustorial matrix which is devoid of cellular organelles. Furthermore, liberation of $^{14}CO_2$ lagged behind uptake of ^{14}C, indicating that the assimilate had not immediately entered the haustorium, but instead had been transported through the matrix. Similar quantities of label in haustorial complexes were found in experiments where the superficial mycelium was left in place during exposure to $^{14}CO_2$, or removed beforehand. It became clear that the haustoria were to some degree autonomous in collecting host assimilates, but their capacity was extremely small and much greater quantities moved into the mycelium when it remained attached.

Biochemical studies

Investigations were aimed specifically at elucidating three aspects of haustorial biochemistry: first, the nature of compounds which traverse the interface (translocates); second, the primary transformations associated with their assimilation by the fungus; and third, the biochemical composition and properties of the interfacial structures traversed. Progress is reported in each of these areas.

Translocates

Analysis of haustorial complexes isolated from infected leaves following 'pulse-chase' feeding of $^{14}CO_2$ has indicated that sucrose is the major compound which traverses the extrahaustorial membrane (Manners & Gay, 1978b; Manners, 1979). In these experiments mildewed pea leaves were fractionated into mycelial, haustorial complex and host fractions either immediately after a 30 min 'pulse' exposure to $^{14}CO_2$, or after a similar 'pulse' of $^{14}CO_2$ followed by a 'chase' period of 20 h without the isotope. The host fraction consisted of infected leaves cleared of mycelia but still containing the haustoria; less than 2% of the ^{14}C in these leaves is in the haustoria and, thus, their contribution is negligible. The general distribution of ^{14}C among the biochemical classes of each fraction immediately indicated the importance of ethanol-soluble carbohydrates in transport to the fungus. These compounds contained over half of the ^{14}C found in both host and mycelial fractions following the 'pulse'. Large reductions in the radioactivities in these compounds occurred with 'chase', and a concomitant increase in the labelling of high molecular weight components in the mycelium suggested their utilization for grow h.

In contrast to the host and mycelium, haustorial complexes in both 'pulse' and 'chase' experiments contained only minor proportions of their ^{14}C in soluble carbohydrates. However, significant redistribution of ^{14}C among the constituent sugars occurred. Following the 'pulse', the greatest proportions of ^{14}C were in sucrose and glycerol, and their isotope content was subsequently considerably reduced (four- and six-fold respectively) with 'chase'. Thus, these compounds are transient and likely to be translocates. Highly significant differences between the distribution of ^{14}C in the carbohydrates and other compounds of the host and haustorial complex fractions from both 'pulse' and 'chase' experiments indicated that host contaminants were not responsible for these results.

Although sucrose and glycerol contained similar quantities of radioactivity in these experiments, it is most probable that sucrose rather than glycerol is the major translocate. Analysis of the unlabelled soluble carbohydrates from haustorial complex fractions has indicated that sucrose is the major carbohydrate of the complexes (Table 1), being present in concentrations seven-fold higher than glycerol. Furthermore, sucrose is a characteristic host sugar and thus sucrose is more likely than glycerol to be derived directly from the host. Two explanations are suggested for the transience of glycerol. It may be synthesized in the haustoria as an intermediate of fungal metabolism. Alternatively, it may be derived directly from the host, in which case it is necessary to consider the possibility that it is only formed near the haustoria since it is barely detectable in leaf analyses. The rapid accumulation of lipids in haustorial complexes shown in 'pulse' and 'chase' experiments indicates that glycerol is immediately utilized in their formation. Glycerol has been shown to be transported across the biotrophic interface between zoo-xanthellae and their animal host (Muscatine, 1967; Smith, Muscatine & Lewis, 1969) and is probably an intermediate in lipid metabolism in these animal cells (Smith et al., 1969). Significantly, in that system glycerol constitutes a very small proportion of the carbohydrate in the free-living alga.

Assimilation by the fungus

Haustorial complexes are composite structures comprising two distinct compartments, viz., the haustorial cytoplasm and the extrahaustorial matrix, each bounded by semi-permeable barriers (Gay & Manners, 1981). Thus, although the data indicate that compounds, in particular sucrose, traverse the extrahaustorial membrane, absorption by the haustorium is not necessarily implied. Available evidence suggests that in other biotrophic associations sucrose is probably hydrolysed *prior* to uptake by the fungus (see Whipps & Lewis, this volume), but two lines of evidence indicate that in powdery mildews sucrose is absorbed by the haustorium and subsequently translocated to the mycelium. Edwards & Allen (1966) sampled the superficial mycelium of E. graminis after exposing infected barley leaf sections to $^{14}CO_2$. After a 15-min exposure, 57% of the isotope in the mycelium was in sucrose; the proportion later declined, indicating assimilation into fungal metabolites. Small quantities of radioactive sucrose were detected in the mycelium of E. pisi after 'pulse' exposures to $^{14}CO_2$, but only traces were detected after the 'chase'. Additional evidence has been obtained from studies of invertase in E. pisi (Manners, 1979). When mycelia and

Table 1. *Major constituents of the ethanol-soluble carbohydrates of host, haustorial complex and mycelial fractions. Haustorial complexes were isolated in ionic media. Carbohydrates were quantified by gas–liquid chromatography of their trimethylsilyl esters. Each value (mg ethanol-soluble carbohydrate 100 mg^{-1} dry weight) is the mean of at least three samples. (From Manners, 1979)*

	Fraction		
	Host	Haustorial complex	Mycelial
Sucrose	0.94	0.45	0.19
Glucose	2.16	0.16	0.63
Fructose	0.87	0.05	0.56
C_4–C_6 polyols	0.27	0.18	12.25
Glycerol	0.00	0.06	0.00

haustorial complexes were homogenized in distilled water, almost all the invertase activity of the fractions was solubilized. This suggests that the enzyme was not bound to fungal cell walls as would be expected if sucrose were hydrolysed prior to uptake. Furthermore the activity of invertase contained in the mycelium covering 1 cm^2 of leaf was 25 times greater than that in the complexes in the same leaf area. This indicates that the major site of sucrose hydrolysis (a prerequisite for its metabolism) is in the mycelium and that it is absorbed *intact*. All systems in which hydrolysis occurs prior to uptake have large areas of intercellular contact between host and pathogen. Furthermore, sucrose is transported intact across many plant cell membranes (Geiger, 1975; Giaquinta, 1977) and is commonly the mobile translocate in plants. The direct absorption by powdery mildews would thus be a valuable adaptation to biotrophy.

In the mycelium of *E. pisi* the primary sink for photosynthates is mannitol (Manners, 1979, and Table 1). It includes almost half of the ^{14}C extracted from the mycelium after the 'pulse' exposure, but within the 20-h 'chase' the proportion of radioactivity in mannitol declines, and glycogen becomes the major sink. Glycogen is a major constituent of the conidia of *E. pisi* (Martin & Gay, 1981). Other secondary sinks in the mycelium are arabitol, erythritol and high molecular weight compounds (protein, nucleic acids and constituents of cell walls). Thus, it seems likely that mannitol is the mobile compound in the mycelium.

The functional roles of fungal polyols are discussed by Whipps & Lewis (this volume) who suggest that conversion of host sugars to polyols is important in maintaining the concentration gradient from host to parasite. It is improbable that conversion provides the major driving force for solute transport at the interface in *E. pisi*, since it is likely that most of the sucrose is inverted in the mycelium. The mechanism of transport is discussed below.

During ^{14}CO$_2$ feeding experiments only a small proportion of the total quantity of isotope assimilated by the fungus resides in the haustorial complexes. However, more than 68% of the ^{14}C in the complexes in the 'pulse–chase' experiments was located in the cell-wall-type and lipid fractions. Analysis of these two fractions indicated little redistribution of ^{14}C within their constituents and, since their total radioactive content increased during this period, these represent true sinks in the complexes. Their presence in the complexes means that they may have key roles in influencing transport at the interface and thus they are discussed as interface components.

Composition of the parasitic interface

The major sink for ^{14}C photosynthates in the haustorial complexes was in the fraction corresponding to cell wall constituents. Following hydrolysis in 2-M trifluoroacetic acid and ion-exchange chromatography, approximately 50–60% of this crude fraction was recovered in neutral compounds. Analysis of this hydrolysate indicated that it contained mainly glucose (88% of ^{14}C) with small proportions of galactose (7%) and mannose (5%), and so differed significantly from the equivalent host fraction in which only glucose (54%) and galactose (45%) were detected. The cell walls of the mycelium contained glucose, galactose and mannose in the approximate ratio of $3:1:1$. Thus, qualitatively the polysaccharides of the complexes resembled those of the mycelium. However, quantitatively there was an excessive proportion of glucose, which suggests that polysaccharides, and in particular glucans other than those normally present in the fungal wall, are synthesized in the complexes. Cytochemical staining of haustorial complexes with silver methenamine and calcofluor (Gil, 1976; Gil & Gay, 1977) have both indicated that the extrahaustorial matrix and membrane are rich in polysaccharide, but absence of fluorescence in ultraviolet light with weak aniline blue makes it unlikely that this includes callose (P. Spencer-Phillips, personal communication). Significantly Spencer-Phillips and Gay (1980) have demonstrated by high-resolution autoradiography that approximately 30% of the ^{14}C photosynthates incorporated by the complexes *in vivo* is located in this interfacial region. This corresponds approximately to the proportion of the total radioactivity in the complexes which is present in the polysaccharides, and suggests that the extrahaustorial membrane and matrix are the sites of their deposition. Unfortunately, it is not yet possible to state whether it is the fungus or the host which is responsible for the synthesis of this glucan-rich polysaccharide. Manners (1979) showed that isolated complexes synthesize ethanol-insoluble glucan from UDPG and, by combining this technique with high-resolution autoradiography and further fractionation, it should be possible to elucidate fully the nature and site of synthesis of these glucans. Although it seems improbable that these matrical components are able to enter the fungus, they represent photosynthate which has left the host. In addition, they may have a functional role in parasitism. Gay & Manners (1981) have shown that horseradish peroxidase applied to isolated haustorial complexes does not enter the extrahaustorial matrix, even when the extrahaustorial membrane is broken. This indicates a restriction of the movement of large molecules across this region which would greatly affect the exchange of chemical information between pathogen and host.

The lipids of the complexes were composed of about 50% triglycerides and 40% polar lipids. The triglycerides most probably correspond to the osmophilic spherical structures observed in electron micrographs of haustoria and may function as nutrient reserves. The production of lipids removes organic compounds from the aqueous phase and thus permits their retention in a structure which is essentially organized for translocating solutes to the mycelium.

The polar lipids found in haustorial complexes are probably membrane constituents. The haustorial plasmalemma is extensive, lining the many lobes extending from the body of the haustorium, and the extrahaustorial membrane is a highly convoluted structure. Thus, these interfacial membranes constitute a large proportion of the membranes of the complexes and indeed autoradiography showed that the extrahaustorial membrane incorporated photosynthetic products almost as fast as any part of the complex (Spencer-Phillips & Gay, 1980). Further analyses of the polar lipids should provide valuable information about the special properties of the interface.

Mechanisms of transport

Solutes are transported from their sources in vascular and mesophyll tissues to the infected epidermal cells. When they have entered the haustoria they travel to the superficial hyphae where they are utilized in growth processes and in forming conidia which constitute the ultimate sinks. The source is affected by reduced photosynthesis, increased respiration and redistribution of solutes within the infected plant (see Chapters 2, 3 and 4 of this volume and the discussion in Bushnell and Gay (1978)). Intercellular transport in the plant probably occurs through plasmodesmata. In the fungus the path to the hyphal apices and conidia is not interrupted by cross walls since all the septa have open pores (Martin & Gay, in preparation). Translocation within fungal hyphae is described in detail by Jennings (1976). The present discussion is confined to transport through the epidermal cell and the entry of solutes to the haustorium.

Solutes entering haustoria are directed through the epidermal cells. In pea leaves, these contain only a few chloroplasts, and those are of abnormal structure, and therefore solutes have to be imported. Although plasmodesmata are common between leaf cells, these connections are rarely found between mesophyll and epidermal cells (M. Martin, personal communication). Thus, it is most probable that the rate of entry into epidermal cells is influenced by the concentration of photosynthates in the apoplast. Pea mildew increases the loss of electrolytes from leaf cells (Ayres, 1977), but the concentration of photosynthates in the apoplast is slightly decreased by infection (Manners, 1979). The latter is partly attributable to smaller quantities of soluble photoassimilates in the leaf, but since infection also reduces the proportion which is leached from leaf disks, a decrease in plasma membrane permeability is also likely to be a contributory factor. Infection of barley by E. graminis increases the proportion of nitrogenous compounds which leach from leaf segments (Bushnell & Gay, 1978) although this probably reflects the increased proportion of soluble nitrogenous compounds reported in infected cells by Sadler & Scott (1974).

Several lines of evidence indicate that the epidermal cytoplasm plays an essential role in transporting assimilates into powdery mildew haustoria. For example, Sullivan, Bushnell & Rowell (1974) found that microsurgical opening of a mildew-infected epidermal cell of barley caused a cessation of hyphal growth almost as immediate as that found by Hoskin (Bushnell, 1971) when haustoria were excised. Also, Gil (1976) compared detached infected pea epidermes freed from mycelia and isolated haustorial complexes in fluorescein diacetate. This compound enters living cells and is broken down by cytoplasmic esterases releasing fluorescein which, being unable to diffuse through the plasma membrane, accumulates and is detectable by its fluorescence in ultraviolet light. Haustoria fluoresced if they were still contained in epidermal cells but not if they were in the isolated complexes. Furthermore, Manners (1979, and reported in Bushnell & Gay, 1978) and Manners & Gay (1980b) found that isolated haustorial complexes could not accumulate sucrose against a concentration gradient. Glucose entered slightly faster than sucrose, but uptake was little affected by pH, detergents or 2,4 dinitro phenol, and was proportional to the ambient concentration. Even at concentrations of 0.4 M, sucrose did not affect the respiration rate of haustorial complexes *in vitro*.

Objections may be raised to all the above evidence for the role of the host cytoplasm in transport. For example, it may be pointed out that isolated haustorial complexes lack the major sink normally provided by the mycelium which when removed for experiments *in vivo* reduces transport to the fungus 500-fold (Manners & Gay, 1978a). Also, cold osmotic shock and glycerol treatments, both of which occur during the isolation of haustorial complexes, remove constituents of membranes (Rubinstein, Mahar & Tattar, 1977). Therefore, in order to obtain further evidence of the transport mechanism, Manners (1979) calculated the flux of photosynthates across the extrahaustorial membrane. The quantities of radioactive assimilates which collected in the superficial mycelium while infected leaves were exposed to $^{14}CO_2$ were related to the surface area of the extrahaustorial membranes of all the haustoria within the area of leaf. A value of 2.4 ng cm^{-2} s^{-1} was obtained for this efflux. This is several orders of magnitude greater than sucrose effluxes from plant cells down large concentration gradients (Edelman, Schoolar & Bonnar, 1971), is similar to the ATP-coupled sucrose influx for maize scutellum (Humphreys, 1978), and is within one order of magnitude of the sucrose flux in sieve-tube loading (18 ng cm^{-2} s^{-1} (Sovonick, Geiger & Fellows, 1974)), and of glucose influx calculated for *Neurospora* (16.2 ng cm^{-2} s^{-1} (Jennings, 1976)). Manners thus proposed that transport across the interface was limited by an active or facilitated process. This conclusion is supported by recent studies of the distribution of ATP-ase and β-glycerophosphatase activities at pH 5.5 and 7.2 in infected cells. The part of the plasmalemma lining the epidermal wall showed the high level of ATP-ase activity characteristic of these cells. However, the portion of the membrane invaginated around the haustorium was completely devoid of any phosphatase activity (Spencer-Phillips & Gay, 1981). The transition occurred precisely where the invagination began and coincided with the edge of the A neckband described above (Fig. 4). Thus, the two structural domains recognized in the plasmalemma by Gil & Gay (1977) are enzymatically and, therefore, *functionally* distinct. The haustorial plasma-lemma showed ATP-ase and other phosphatase activity.

This information makes it possible to propose models for the mechanism of assimilate transport at the interface. Entry into the epidermal cells is presumed to be almost exclusively by transmembrane import, and the high ATP-ase activity (similar to that of phloem transfer cells in the same leaf) shown by the wall-lining section of the plasmalemma suggests that the epidermal cells scavenge solutes from the apoplast, thereby increasing the concentration of solutes within their cytoplasms. The ATP-ase activity of the haustorial plasmalemma is assumed to deplete the solutes in the extrahaustorial matrix simultaneously and, thus, a high concentration gradient is maintained across the extrahaustorial membrane. It should be noted in addition that the two membranes with ATP-ase activity have the same polarity with regard to both their cytoplasms and the direction of transport. Therefore, Spencer-Phillips & Gay (1981) further suggested that the ionic products of the ATP-ase pumps may complement one

Fig. 4. Section through haustorium of *Erysiphe pisi* where the fungus enters the epidermal cell. ATP-ase activity is indicated by the dense deposits which occur over the fungal plasma membrane (f) and the plant plasma membrane (wd) where it lines the cell wall. No activity above control level is shown by the invaginated domain of the plant membrane (ehd, extrahaustorial membrane) and the transition is arrowed. Deposits in the region (p, papilla) confluent with the cell wall (w) represent the positions of sequestered membranes. A and B are the neckbands where the invagination of the plasmalemma is sealed to the neck wall. v = host vacuole. Magnification: × 28 500. (From Spencer-Phillips & Gay, 1981. Reproduced by permission of the trustees of the *New Phytologist*.)

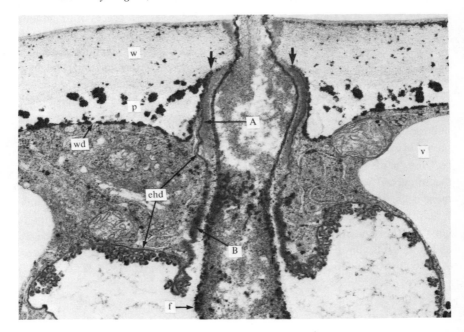

another, interacting at the intervening extrahaustorial membrane to activate the efflux of assimilates through it.

The phosphatases demonstrated by their reaction with β-glycerophosphate may also play a role in transport. In particular, activity at the fungal plasmalemma may establish a concentration gradient towards the haustorium. It should also be noted that because the powdery mildew haustorium has long, finger-like lobes, the haustorial plasmalemma is extensive and, e.g. in rose mildew, may be twice the area of the extrahaustorial membrane (Perera & Gay, 1976). Autoradiography suggests that the relative rate of assimilate absorption by the lobes is twice that of the haustorial body (Spencer-Phillips & Gay, 1980).

The essential features of these proposals arise from the observation of two unique circumstances, viz. the functional differentiation of two domains of one plasmalemma, and the interpolation of a sealed compartment between particular regions of the plasmalemmas of two cells. Active influx occurs into both cells, and thus the plant cell is presumed to *cooperate* with the fungus to maintain the flux. It seems that by means of the extreme structural and functional modification of the host plasmalemma in the region which surrounds the haustorium, the fungus controls efflux from the host to its own nutritional advantage. This is very probably a key factor in the parasitism. At present there is no evidence to indicate whether ATP-ase is absent from the invaginated region of the plasma membrane, or whether enzyme activity is inhibited. In freeze-fracture studies the absence of 10-nm particles from this region suggests that it may be the former. Whichever is true, it seems certain that, as recognized by Gil & Gay (1977), the A band maintains the distinctive characteristics of the two domains.

This transport model is probably not exclusive to carbohydrates. It seems highly likely that lipid precursors traverse the interface, and the triglyceride reserves may have a direct role in their transport. Isolated haustorial complexes accumulate long-chain fatty acids (lauric and linoleic) and other lipophilic compounds against very large concentration gradients (Manners & Gay, 1980b), and it is probable that these are partitioned into the haustorial lipids. Coupled with esterification by glycerol, which is also present in the complexes, this would maintain a steep concentration gradient of fatty acids towards the lipids in the haustorial cytoplasm. Linoleic and other fatty acids occur in superficial cells of plant tissues and are probably cuticle precursors (Kolattukudy, 1977). The possibility that their synthesis is enhanced by infection should be examined. Lipid droplets are a common feature of biotrophic fungi growing on their hosts (Brennan & Lösel, 1978) and the mechanism outlined above may be common.

Isolated haustorial complexes also accumulate organic cations. Ethanolamine and methyl pyridinium accumulated to concentrations which were 18- and 46-fold respectively above ambient (Manners & Gay, 1980b). This may be the result of an electrochemical gradient across the fungal plasmalemma. High negative potentials have been recorded for fungal cells by Slayman, Lu & Shane (1970).

However, evidence of uptake based entirely on in-vitro studies should be considered with caution until it is corroborated by biotrophic studies, especially because the membranes of some haustorial complexes are ruptured (Gay & Manners, 1980) and therefore uptake does not necessarily represent transmembrane flux.

Comparative aspects of other biotrophic pathogenic interfaces

Haustorial complexes have been isolated from a variety of powdery mildew infections (Dekhuijzen, 1966; Manners & Gay, 1977) and the distinctive structural characteristics of the invaginated domain of the host plasmalemma, and the neck bands maintaining domain limitation and plasma membrane attachment, seem to be common features. It is unfortunate that in cereal mildews (*E. graminis*) the haustoria are extremely long and narrow and the extrahaustorial domain is delicate (Manners & Gay, 1977). These features make it unlikely that haustorial complexes can be obtained in the numbers necessary for population studies where the genetic constitutions of the host varieties are well known.

The haustoria formed by fungal pathogens of other taxonomic groups are usually in mesophyll cells and the additional presence of intercellular hyphae makes it difficult to assess their absorptive function. In rust fungi the haustorial interface shares several features with that in powdery mildews. In cow pea infected by *Uromyces phaseoli* var. *vignae*, and corn infected by *Puccinia sorghi*, the invaginated region of the plasma membrane is attached to the surface of the neck and, as in *E. pisi*, apoplastic transport along the fungal wall in this region is precluded (Heath, 1976). Investigations of flax infected by *Melampsora lini* show that, from the neckband, the invaginated region lacks the staining and freeze-fracture characteristics of the wall-lining region (Littlefield & Bracker, 1972) and also, as in *E. pisi*, ATP-ase activity is absent from the invaginated domain of french bean infected by *Uromyces appendiculatus* (Spencer-Phillips & Gay, 1981). However, the ATP-ase activity of the wall-lining region is slight compared with that of the epidermal cells. This probably reflects the presence of chloroplasts and photosynthetic activity in mesophyll cells and, thus, a lower influx than occurs in epidermal cells. The similarity in the functional aspects of these polarized cells infected with different kinds of fungi indicates, however, that a general mechanism exists, and that other biotrophic associations deserve attention.

Acknowledgements

We acknowledge financial assistance from the Science and Agricultural Research Councils and Imperial Chemical Industries (Plant Protection, Jealott's Hill).

References

Ayres, P. G. (1977). Effects of powdery mildew *Erysiphe pisi* and water stress upon the water relations of pea. *Physiological Plant Pathology*, **10**, 139–45.

Bracker, C. E. & Littlefield, L. J. (1973). Structural concepts of host–pathogen interfaces. In *3rd Long Ashton Symposium 1971, Fungal Pathogenicity and the Plant's Response*, ed. R. J. W. Byrde & C. V. Cutting, pp. 159–318. London: Academic Press.

Brennan, P. J. & Lösel, D. M. (1978). Physiology of fungal lipids. *Advances in Microbial Physiology*, **17**, 47–179.

Bushnell, W. R. (1971). The haustorium of *Erysiphe graminis:* an experimental study by light microscopy. In *Morphological and Biochemical Events in Plant–Parasite Interaction*, ed. S. Akai & S. Ouchi, pp. 229–54. Tokyo: Phytopathological Society of Japan.

Bushnell, W. R. & Gay, J. L. (1978). Accumulation of solutes in relation to the structure and function of haustoria in powdery mildews. In *The Powdery Mildews*, ed. D. M. Spencer, pp. 183–235. London: Academic Press.

Dekhuijzen, H. M. (1966). The isolation of haustoria from cucumber leaves infected with powdery mildew. *Netherlands Journal of Plant Pathology*, **72**, 1–11.

Edelman, J., Schoolar, A. I. & Bonnar, W. B. (1971). Permeability of sugarcane chloroplasts to sucrose. *Journal of Experimental Botany*, **22**, 534–5.

Edwards, H. H. & Allen, P. J. (1966). Distribution of the products of photosynthesis between powdery mildew and barley. *Plant Physiology*, **41**, 683–8.

Gay, J. L. & Manners, J. M. (1981). Permeability of the parasitic interface in powdery mildews. *Physiological Plant Pathology*. (In press.)

Geiger, D. R. (1975). Phloem loading. In *Encyclopedia of Plant Physiology*, New Series, vol. 1, *Transport in Plants 1, Phloem Transport*, ed. M. H. Zimmerman & J. A. Milburn, pp. 395–431. New York: Springer-Verlag.

Giaquinta, R. (1977). Sucrose hydrolysis in relation to phloem translocation in *Beta vulgaris. Plant Physiology*, **60**, 339–43.

Gil, F. (1976). Ultrastructural and physiological properties of haustoria of powdery mildews and their host interfaces. PhD. thesis, University of London.

Gil, F. & Gay, J. L. (1977). Ultrastructural and physiological properties of the host interfacial components of haustoria of *Erysiphe pisi in vivo* and *in vitro. Physiological Plant Pathology*, **10**, 1–12.

Heath, M. C. (1976). Ultrastructural and functional similarity of the haustorial neckband of rust fungi and the Casparian Strip of vascular plants. *Canadian Journal of Botany*, **54**, 2484–9.

Humphreys, T. E. (1978). A model for sucrose transport in the maize scutellum. *Phytochemistry*, **17**, 679–84.

Jennings, D. H. (1976). Transport and translocation in filamentous fungi. In *The Filamentous Fungi*, vol. 2, ed. J. E. Smith & D. R. Berry, pp. 32–64. London: Edward Arnold.

Kolattukudy, P. E. (1977). Biosynthesis and degradation of lipid polymers. In *Lipids and Lipid Polymers in Higher Plants*, ed. M. Tevini & H. K. Lichtenthaler, pp. 271–92. New York: Springer-Verlag.

Littlefield, L. J. & Bracker, C. E. (1972). Ultrastructural specialization at the host–pathogen interface in rust-infected flax. *Protoplasma*, **74**, 271–305.

Manners, J. M. (1979). Physiology of fungal haustoria (Erysiphales). Ph.D. thesis, University of London.

Manners, J. M. & Gay, J. L. (1977). The morphology of haustorial complexes isolated from apple, barley, beet and vine infected with powdery mildews. *Physiological Plant Pathology*, **11**, 261–6.

Manners, J. M. & Gay, J. L. (1978*a*). Uptake of ^{14}C photosynthates from *Pisum sativum* by haustoria of *Erysiphi pisi*. *Physiological Plant Pathology*, **12**, 199–209.

Manners, J. M. & Gay, J. L. (1978*b*). Translocation and metabolism of photosynthates by haustoria of *Erysiphe pisi*. *Abstracts 3rd International Congress of Plant Pathology Munich*. Berlin: Paul Parey.

Manners, J. M. & Gay, J. L. (1980*a*). Autoradiography of haustoria of *Erysiphe pisi*. *Journal of General Microbiology*, **116**, 529–33.

Manners, J. M. & Gay, J. L. (1980*b*). Accumulation of systemic fungicides and other compounds by haustorial complexes isolated from *Pisum sativum* infected with *Erysiphe pisi*. *Pesticide Science*. (In press.)

Martin, M. & Gay, J. L. (1981). Ultrastructure of conidium development in *Erysiphe pisi*. *Canadian Journal of Botany*. (In preparation.)

Mount, M. S. & Ellingboe, A. H. (1969). ^{32}P and ^{35}S transfer from susceptible wheat to *Erysiphe graminis* f. sp. *tritici* during primary infection. *Phytopathology*, **59**, 235.

Muscatine, L. (1967). Glycerol excretion by symbiotic algae from corals and *Tridacna* and its control by the host. *Science*, **156**, 519.

Perera, R. & Gay, J. L. (1976). The ultrastructure of haustoria of *Sphaerotheca pannosa* (Wallroth ex Fries) Leveille and changes in infected and associated cells of rose. *Physiological Plant Pathology*, **9**, 57–65.

Rubinstein, B., Mahar, P. & Tattar, T. A. (1977). Effects of osmotic shock on some membrane regulated events of oat coleoptile cells. *Plant Physiology*, **59**, 365–8.

Sadler, R. & Scott, K. J. (1974). Nitrogen assimilation and metabolism in barley leaves infected with the powdery mildew fungus. *Physiological Plant Pathology*, **4**, 235–47.

Slayman, C. L., Lu, C. Y. H. & Shane, K. L. (1970). Correlated changes in membrane potential and ATP concentrations in Neurospora. *Nature*, **226**, 274–6.

Slesinski, R. S. & Ellingboe, A. H. (1971). Transfer of ^{35}S from wheat to the powdery mildew fungus with compatible and incompatible parasite–host genotypes. *Canadian Journal of Botany*, **49**, 303–10.

Smith, D.C., Muscatine, L. & Lewis, D. H. (1969). Carbohydrate movement from autotroph to heterotroph in parasitic and mutalistic symbiosis. *Biological Reviews*, **44**, 17–90.

Smith, G. (1900). The haustoria of the *Erysiphaceae*. *Botanical Gazette*, **29**, 153–84.

Sovonick, S. A., Geiger, D. R. & Fellows, R. J. (1974). Evidence for active phloem loading in the minor veins of sugar beet. *Plant Physiology*, **54**, 886–91.

Spencer-Phillips, P. T. N. & Gay, J. L. (1980). Electron microscope autoradiography of ^{14}C photosynthate distribution at the haustorium–host interface in powdery mildew of *Pisum sativum*. *Protoplasma*, **103**, 131–54.

Spencer-Phillips, P. T. N. & Gay, J. L. (1981). ATP-ase domains and transport in infected plant cells. *New Phytologist*. (In press.)

Sullivan, T. P., Bushnell, W. R. & Rowell, J. B. (1974). Relations between haustoria of *Erysiphe graminis* and host cytoplasm in cells opened by microsurgery. *Canadian Journal of Botany*, **52**, 987–98.

D. HORNBY & B. D. L. FITT

Effects of root-infecting fungi on structure and function of cereal roots

Introduction

Perusal of standard texts of physiological and biochemical plant pathology shows that root diseases receive relatively little attention compared to aboveground infections. Research on soil-borne plant pathogens (Schippers & Gams, 1979) has been developing strongly for many years, but without really tackling the challenging question of how they affect the physiological processes of the root. This must in part be because root diseases are fewer, less obvious and generally less easily studied and assessed than above-ground diseases, as well as being less amenable to practical and economical control by chemicals (Jones & Clifford, 1978). Also, root rots as described in the literature may seem rather prosaic to the physiological plant pathologist and in little need of further inquiry.

There are many kinds of organism associated with roots, but fungi, nematodes and insects are the most common pathogens. Because details of many host–parasite interactions initiated by these disease-causing organisms are either unknown or remain uncollated, this chapter is restricted to one area where some progress has been made, i.e. infections of temperate, small-grain cereals. Work on major root diseases and 'minor pathogens' (Salt, 1979) of cereals, and biological control of take-all disease, caused by *Gaeummanomyces graminis* (var. *tritici,* unless stated otherwise) (Wong & Southwell, 1980), illustrate some of the more general problems of studying the effects of root diseases on root structure and function, and suggest new avenues of inquiry.

Cereal root systems

Structure and anatomy

Cereal plants have two root systems: the seminal, which originates from the seed, and the crown or nodal system, which develops later at the basal nodes of the stem. Wheat develops 'thick' and 'thin' nodal roots which differ in branching, lignification and stelar development (Troughton, 1962). In natural condi-

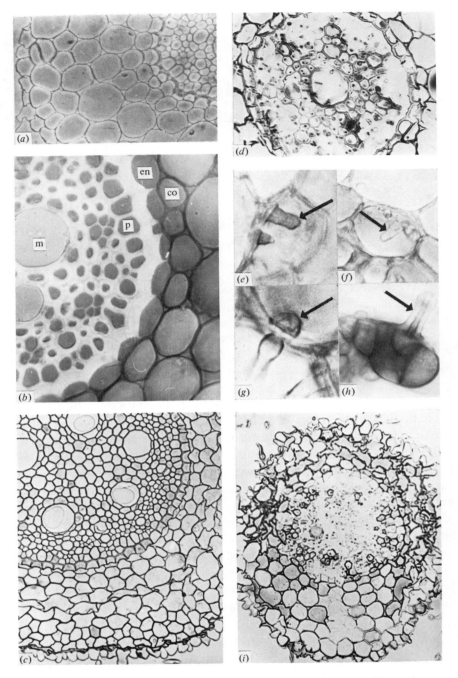

Fig. 1. Transverse sections of wheat roots. Uninfected roots, illustrating most of the features mentioned in the text. (*a*) Seminal root of a 13-day-old plant grown on agar (× 170). (*b*) seminal root of a 21-day-old plant grown in sand, showing increased thickening of the endodermis and stelar tissues (× 520; m, metaxylem; p, pericycle; en, endodermis; co, inner cell of cortex). (*c*) Crown

tions the seed and crown are usually separated by an elongated part of the stem known as the subcrown internode or rhizome.

A young root is bounded by a layer of epidermal cells which have slightly cutinized outer walls and produce delicate root hairs in the zone behind the root apex. Beneath the epidermis lie the cortex and stele (Fig. 1). The cortex consists of seven to eight cell layers in seminal roots, and a few more in crown roots. Its innermost layer, the endodermis, is a single layer of closely-fitting cells which ensheaths the stele. The stele contains the pericycle and a polyarch central cylinder of xylem vessels and phloem bundles. The pericycle, a single layer of cells which abuts directly onto the endodermis, is the tissue from which the lateral roots originate (Troughton, 1962). The walls of pericycle cells become thickened in older roots. As roots age, the endodermal cell walls thicken and root hairs, epidermis and part of the cortex die (Holden, 1975), whereas the vascular tissue remains functional throughout a plant's life (Clarkson & Robards, 1975). Cereal roots do not develop secondary thickening because their vascular bundles have no cambium, but some thick nodal roots of winter wheat develop a resistant exodermis and two to three layers of sclerotized outer cortical cells (Troughton, 1962; Burdonov, 1974*a*).

Soil temperature, moisture content, aeration, nutrient distribution, structure and microflora may all affect root morphology. Soil compaction decreases the size of root systems (Goss & Drew, 1972), and roots may be concentrated in regions with most nutrients (Drew & Saker, 1973). However, alterations in root morphology do not necessarily affect root function, and root-infecting fungi which change the morphology of the root system may not affect growth.

Function

The major function of the cereal root system is to absorb water and nutrients from the soil. Usually the surface area available for absorption is enormous; Dittmer (1937) estimated that the total length of the fibrous root system of a single winter rye plant was greater than 623 km. Roots of one plant possessed

Caption to Fig. 1 (cont.)
root of a 35-day-old plant grown in sand ($\times$ 160). Infected roots, showing lignitubers or papillae (arrowed) in endodermal cells, (*e*) caused by *Gaeumannomyces graminis* var. *tritici*, ($\times$ 1120), (*f*) caused by *Fusarium culmorum* ($\times$ 730); in cortical cells, (*g*) caused by *Cochliobolus sativus* ($\times$ 1090), (*h*) caused by *Phialophora radicicola* var. *graminicola* ($\times$ 1000). Transverse sections of disrupted tissue in infected roots: (*d*) stele and endodermis of a seminal root of a 35-day-old plant infected with *F. culmorum* – pericycle, phloem and associated parenchyma disrupted ($\times$ 200); (*i*) crown root of a 35-day-old plant infected with *G. graminis* var. *tritici*, showing disintegration of the stele and collapse of part of the cortex ($\times$ 150).

about 1.5×10^{10} root hairs, giving a total length of about 10626 km. Growing roots require a continuous supply of growth regulators (Kozlowski, 1978) and are also sites of growth regulator production (Pilet, 1974; see also Pegg, this volume). Crown roots are important as a means of anchorage for a plant. Root-infecting fungi which seriously impair these functions of absorption, transport, synthesis, regulation and anchorage will certainly affect plant growth. However, the root cortex, and especially the thick-walled endodermis, can play a role in protecting vital tissues from root-infecting fungi (Van Fleet, 1961).

The dead xylem vessels are the pathway for upward transport of water and nutrient ions from the soil to the shoot (Stout & Hoagland, 1939; Biddulph, Nakayama & Cory, 1961). This upward transport is driven by leaf transpiration which causes a difference in water potential between the soil solution and the xylem sap (see Ayres, this volume). Water movement is considered to be a function of the apoplast ('free space' in unlignified cell walls) and dead tissues can behave as 'wicks' (Talboys, 1978). Near the root tip, radial transport across roots from the soil to the xylem is via both apoplast and symplast (cell protoplasts connected via plasmodesmata) (Clarkson & Robards, 1975). Suberization blocks the apoplastic pathway and therefore stops uptake of Ca^{2+}, Mg^{2+} and Fe^{3+} (Harrison-Murray & Clarkson, 1973) which is mainly passive (Lüttge & Laties, 1967) and transpiration-dependent (Ferguson & Clarkson, 1975). Symplastic, active uptake of nitrogen, phosphorus and potassium is unaffected by suberization (Clarkson & Robards, 1975), but is decreased by metabolic inhibitors (Pitman, 1975).

Uptake of most ions is independent of transpirational flow; it is regulated by factors such as the supply of photoassimilates (Pitman, 1975), and hormones (Davies & Wareing, 1965; Pitman, Lüttge, Lauchli & Ball, 1974) and may include feedback control involving the return of excess ions, through the phloem, to sites of uptake (Bukovac & Wittwer, 1957; Biddulph & Biddulph, 1959). Phloem translocation occurs in the sieve elements (Trip & Gorham, 1967). Both the detailed structure of the phloem and the translocation mechanism are in dispute, but it is agreed that any interference with the delicate phloem structure causes dysfunction. Therefore, root-infecting fungi which invade the phloem can quickly disrupt a plant's metabolism.

Death of apparently healthy cells in the cortex has assumed considerable significance in the study of microbial invasion of cereal roots (Holden, 1976; Deacon & Henry, 1978). In laboratory studies made on the first seminal roots of wheat seedlings, death was most rapid during the 5–10 days after sowing in a sand-soil mixture. Cell death started in the outer cortex behind the root hair zone and progressed inwards, although cells in the layer next to the endodermis, near the seed, and around emerging laterals remained alive. Cortical cell death is more rapid in wheat than in barley. Under field conditions, 50% of the cortex in the upper 6 cm of the first seminal root of spring wheat was dead after 35 days but this condition did not occur in barley until day 67.

Although many fungi commonly occur in the cortex of mature roots, most rarely penetrate or even approach the endodermis. According to Van Fleet (1961), the endodermal walls are resistant to fungal cell-wall-degrading enzymes. The Casparian Strip in the radial walls is one of the plant tissues most resistant to hydrolysis. The cytoplasm, vacuole and walls of endodermal cells contain high concentrations of phenols and quinones, which inhibit the growth of fungi and bacteria and may inactivate the pathogen's enzymes. Although the endodermis ensheaths the vascular tissue, there are gaps in this defensive barrier where branching occurs and where suberization is delayed at the site of passage cells (Clarkson & Robards, 1975). These gaps may provide entry points for pathogens.

Cereal root infections

Numbers and kinds of diseases

Jones & Clifford (1978) published a compendium of cereal diseases in the UK which contained 45 caused by fungi, five by bacteria and spiroplasmas, and five by viruses. Eight (18%), one, and two of these, respectively, are named diseases of the root system, or are diseases known by their leaf symptoms although the pathogen enters through roots, (e.g. soil-borne viruses). In an earlier list (Plant Pathology Committee of the British Mycological Society, 1962), two (13%) out of fifteen diseases of wheat, and three (21%) out of fourteen diseases of barley, involved roots. Of 55 species of common parasitic fungi on grasses and cereals (Boerema & Verhoeven, 1977), we estimate that only seven (13%) are likely to be associated with root disease in cereals. Gair, Jenkins & Lester (1972) listed UK cereal diseases in five categories: seedling, root and stem base, stem and leaf, ears, grain. Those that are recognized root diseases, or involve root infection, are listed in Table 1. The percentage of diseases that are root diseases is similar in cereal and in non-cereal host plants. Out of a list of 50 000 parasitic and non-parasitic diseases in the USA, 6.7% are root diseases, and of these 64% are root rots, 9% damping-off diseases, 7% wilts, 6% seedling blights, 6% crown and foot rots, 3% root-browning diseases, 3% root-infecting fungi and 1% club roots (Kommedahl & Windels, 1979). On balance, wheat in the UK probably suffers more than the other cereals from root diseases.

Classification of disease

Classifying diseases according to hosts or organs attacked may be convenient, but it is not a natural system that recognizes the physiological nature of disease (Roberts & Boothroyd, 1972). The McNew system (Table 2) attempts to

Table 1. *Named root infections of cereals in the UK (after Gair et al., 1972)*

Host[1]	Disease	Fungus	Notes	Significance
	Seedling diseases			
W,B,O,R	Seedling blight	*Fusarium* spp.		Doubtful importance[2]
W,B,O	Browning-root rot	*Pythium* spp. (*P. arrhenomanes* and *P. graminicola*)[3]	B more susceptible than W[3]	Unknown. *P. graminicola* important in SW Ontario, Canada
W,B,O	Root rot	*Rhizoctonia solani* (perfect state: *Thanatephorus cucumeris*)	Occasionally in O	Minor
	Root and stem base diseases			
W,B,O,R	Take-all	*Gaeumannomyces graminis* var. *tritici* (main cause of take-all in W); var. *avenae* (main cause of take-all in O)	B more tolerant than W R least susceptible	One of the most important diseases of cereals
W,B,O,R	Brown foot rot	*Fusarium* spp.	Roots infected in severe cases. Fewer records on B than W.	Doubtful importance[2]
W,B	Foot rot (common root rot in Canada)	*Cochliobolus sativus* (conidial state: *Helminthosporium sativum* = *Bipolaris sorokiniana*)	Stem base rot, infects roots	Uncommon (important debilitating disease in Canada)

[1] W, wheat; B, barley; O, oats; R, rye.
[2] Colhoun & Park (1964).
[3] Waller (1979).

do this. However, it suggests the diseases listed in Table 1 should only affect a *limited* range of physiological functions, being rot roots, or foot rots, or seedling blights in which root rotting occurs. Moreover, the morphological symptom in all these diseases is necrosis of the roots (Roberts & Boothroyd, 1972). It soon becomes apparent that these categorizations are sometimes too simple and difficult to apply in practice. Thus, 'root rot' according to Roberts & Boothroyd is synonymous with cortical rot, although take-all, which is primarily a root rot, is most damaging when the pathogen invades the phloem and when it enters the xylem it may affect the conduction of water.

Classification of root-infecting fungi

Root-infecting fungi have been classified by disease symptoms, taxa, hosts, nutrition, mode of life and ecological relations (Kommedahl & Windels, 1979). Kommedahl & Windels' system, based on the interaction of fungus and host, is applied to cereal root-infecting fungi in Table 3. (In this scheme several fungi, e.g. *Gaeumannomyces graminis* and *Phialophora radicicola,* are categorized only on the basis of early literature.) Classification according to mode of life and nutrition leads to problems of definition. As necrosis and disintegration are the hallmark of root rots it is reasonable to assume that the pathogens are necrotrophic (perthophytic) rather than biotrophic fungi (see Whipps & Lewis, this volume, for further discussion of these terms). However, some cereal-root-rots pathogens may be hemibiotrophs, *sensu* Luttrell (1974), since living cells are attacked by hyphae and the point at which they die is not known.

Table 2. *The McNew system for the classification of infectious plant diseases (after Roberts & Boothroyd, 1972, and Wheeler, 1976)*

Physiological processes affected	Diseases
(1) Storage of food	Soft rots and seed decays
(2) Hydrolysis and utilization of stored food	Damping-off, seedling blights
(3) Absorption and accumulation of water and minerals	Root and foot rots
(4) Growth (meristematic activity)	Galls, cankers, leaf curls, witch's brooms, club root
(5) Conduction of water	Vascular wilt
(6) Photosynthesis	Leaf spots, mildews, rusts
(7) Translocation of elaborated food materials	Diseases caused by viruses and mycoplasma-like organisms

Effects of root disease

Synopsis of conventional view of root diseases

The conventional view of the effect of root rots on cereals has changed little since Henry (1924) described them as inhibiting root growth, destroying absorbing cells and, by attacking the vascular system, preventing transport of water and food materials, all of which contribute to poor shoot growth or death. Although piliferous and cortical regions are commonly attacked, causing loose cortex or decortication, vascular infections are usually more serious. The endo-dermis constitutes a natural barrier to invasion by many decorticating fungi and protection is increased as endodermis, pericycle and conjunctive parenchyma of the stele become sclerotized.

Methods of study

Field studies on effects of cereal root diseases have frequently tried to relate disease incidence to yield loss (e.g. Nilsson, 1969; Slope & Etheridge,

Table 3. *Classification of the cereal root-infecting fungi listed in Table 1 or elsewhere in the text according to the scheme of Kommedahl & Windels (1979)*

Categories	Fungi
Pathogen-dominant diseases	
Macerative pathogens	*Microdochium (Aureobasidium) bolleyi*[1]
	Pythium spp.
	Rhizoctonia solani
Toxicogenic pathogens	—
Host-dominant diseases	
Tissue non-specific pathogens	
Macerative	—
Toxicogenic	*Cochliobolus sativus*
Tissue specific pathogens[2]	
Vascular pathogens	*Hymenula cerealis*[1]
Cortex-specific	*Gaeumannomyces graminis*
	Fusarium avenaceum
	F. culmorum
	F. graminearum
	F. nivale
	Wojnowicia graminis
Epidermis-specific	*Phialophora radicicola*
	Polymyxa graminis

[1] Not in Kommedahl & Windels (1979).
[2] Two other categories, cambium-specific and periderm-specific, do not apply to cereal roots.

1971; Ledingham *et. al.,* 1973; MacNish & Dodman, 1973). The many interacting biological and physical factors in the complex soil environment can make it difficult to assess the incidence of major diseases, let alone minor pathogens whose effects are less obvious. Also, a single end-of-season measurement of yield loss often gives limited information on a disease. To obtain more precise information about effects of root diseases experiments have been done under more controlled conditions in glasshouses and controlled environment rooms in soil (Sivasithamparam & Parker, 1978), sand (Asher, 1972*a,b;* Fitt & Hornby, 1978) or hydroponic conditions (Clarkson, Drew, Ferguson & Sanderson, 1975).

Aerial symptoms of root diseases, such as yellowing, epinasty, chlorosis and wilting, give little indication of the extent of the disease. Therefore it is essential to excavate the root systems of diseased plants and assess the extent of diseased root several times during a growing season (Simmonds, Russell & Sallans, 1935). Slope & Etheridge (1971) and Hornby & Goring (1972) assessed disease by recording the percentages of infected plants and infected roots. However, even in this kind of assessment there is frequently no clear association between infection and effects on host growth and physiology because the severity of an infection is also dependent on position and depth of lesions. The depth of penetration has been investigated by examination of squashed and stained roots (Salt, 1974; Weste, 1975), freehand root sections (Holden, 1976; Fitt & Hornby, 1978; Speakman & Lewis, 1978), wax-embedded sections (Malalasekera, Sanderson & Colhoun, 1973) and cryostat microtome sections (Clarkson *et al.,* 1975). Other changes in roots have been examined by nuclear staining (Holden, 1975) and fluorescence microscopy (Holland & Fulcher, 1971). Information about the physiology of diseased plants is of limited value when the extent of root damage is not measured.

The effects of root diseases have been assessed by examining shoot growth and physiology. Shoot dry weight (Asher, 1972*a;* Verma, Morrall & Tinline, 1976) is a good estimate of growth. Measurements of leaf temperature (McClintic, 1980), leaf area, tiller number (Asher, 1972*a*), plant height and shoot fresh weight (Chambers, 1971), water content (Asher, 1972*a*), chlorophyll content (Fitt, 1977), mineral composition (Hornby & Goring, 1972; Fitt & Hornby, 1978) and glume silicon content (Salt & Rushforth, 1976) may also be useful.

Direct measurements of the dysfunction of transport processes have been made with tracers. Downward phloem translocation into roots has been assessed by feeding $^{14}CO_2$ to shoots (Asher, 1972*b;* Kararah, 1976; Fitt & Hornby, 1978) or by injecting ^{86}Rb into the stem (Clarkson *et al.,* 1975). To monitor ion uptake ^{32}P, ^{42}K and ^{45}Ca (or ^{85}Sr) have been fed to plant roots (Clarkson *et al.,* 1975; Fitt, 1977); ^{32}P, ^{42}K and ^{45}Ca were used together because they have different half-lives or energy spectra. Water uptake and movement has been followed using water-soluble dyes (Spalding, Bruehl & Foster, 1961; Deacon & Henry,

1978) and transpiration has been measured directly using a micropotometer (Kararah, 1976).

Structural changes

Pathogenic root-infecting fungi may affect the morphology of the root system as well as causing anatomical changes in individual roots. If a root-rotting fungus invades and destroys the vascular system, the root on the distal side of the lesion dies. This effectively prunes the root system and may stimulate the development of new roots. Such a mechanism was noted in plants attacked by the take-all fungus and has become known as 'disease escape' (Garrett, 1948). Macerative pathogens of the pathogen-dominant group of diseases (Table 3) cause discoloration and dissolution of tissues with little evidence of defensive responses by the host, and the structural changes that occur in the cell walls are degenerative. The processes of cell wall breakdown have been most studied in soft rots (Wood, 1967), but are difficult to define chemically (Kommedahl & Windels, 1979). They involve the degradation of structural components of the cell wall and cell contents, and interference with cellular functions. They seem to be initiated in the middle lamella of host cell walls by the action of pectic enzymes produced by the pathogen, but also involve cellulolytic, hemicellulolytic, proteolytic and other enzymes. In soft rots, for instance *Pythium* root rot (Waller, 1979), tissues soon lose their coherence, but in the more slowly developing dry rot diseases, which are more common on older parts of cereal roots, tissues maintain their coherence until lesions are advanced (Wood, 1967). Where there is no evidence of injurious substances diffusing from, or being translocated from, the rotting tissue, the effect on the form and function of the root system might again be likened to root pruning or amputation.

Root pathogens of the host-dominant diseases (Table 3) elicit host responses such as the formation of lignitubers or papillae around hyphae attempting to penetrate living cells (Fig. 1), plugging of xylem vessels and thickening of cell walls in advance of the fungus. Lignitubers are a common feature of cereal roots invaded by fungi of the *Gaeumannomyces–Phialophora* complex, and also occur in cortical and vascular tissues of subcrown internodes invaded by *Cochliobolus sativus* (Huang & Tinline, 1976). They are one of several forms of wall-like deposition that also occur in leaves, and which Aist (1976) refers to collectively as 'papillae' in his review of these structures. The most common chemical constituent of papillae is callose, although they do exhibit chemical heterogeneity, and lignitubers induced by *G. graminis* seem on histochemical evidence to be chiefly composed of lignin (Fellows, 1928). This accounts for Fellows' choice of name; a name that most subsequent cereal root pathologists have adopted. Papillae are generally deposited by the host protoplast and may form before, during, or after cell wall penetration. It is not known whether lignitubers caused by *G. graminis* (and those of other root-infecting fungi) perforate the host plasmalemma, or whether amorphous deposits that sometimes form in response to an attempted penetration occur between the cell wall and the plasmalemma (Holland & Fulcher, 1971). The lignitubers caused by *C. sativus* have been described as being between the host plasmalemma and cell wall (Huang & Tinline, 1976). The concept that lignitubers are a response to wounding by encroaching pathogens is a useful one according to Aist, but as he points out they are not invariably formed during the penetration of living cells. There has been speculation that they prevent damage by providing impermeable barriers to toxins or minimize the damage caused by the parasite's entry into the cell. A popular idea is that they impede the process of penetration pegs (Skou, 1975; Holden, 1976; Speakman & Lewis, 1978), and sometimes the morphology and size of lignitubers have correlated well with the failure of penetration. However, there may be biochemical resistance mechanisms unrelated to lignituber formation. Lignitubers seem to contribute little to resistance of wheat or barley to *C. sativus* because they occur in both susceptible and resistant varieties and seem not to impede the branching of infection pegs (Huang & Tinline, 1976).

To synthesize most of the above points, it is useful to examine Weste's (1972) description of the reaction of cereal seedlings to *G. graminis*, making allowance for the fact that her experimental conditions were extremely artificial (22 °C, on moist filter paper with no added nutrients, ascospore inoculum; Table 4). Weste maintained that hyphal growth and enzyme action alone explained the observed symptoms: extracellular fungal toxins were not detected and there was no evidence of inhibited root growth in the presence of any fungal extracts. *In vitro,* *G. graminis* produced extracellular polygalacturonase, pectinmethylesterase and cellulases in the presence of appropriate substrates, but extracellular peptidase seemed to be constitutive (Weste, 1970a). All these enzymes occurred in infected seedling roots (Weste, 1970b), and Weste (1972) drew attention to the fact that polygalacturonase and indoleacetic acid have been associated with root hair deformation during the invasion of legume roots by *Rhizobium*. Like Fellows (1928), she found lignitubers arose as thickenings of the tertiary layer of the cell wall. Within invaded tissue infected cells died first (Faull & Campbell (1979) found that cytoplasm in penetrated cells was almost invariably necrotic), and inter- and intracellular mycelia flourished. The cells separated along middle lamellae. Hyphae finally invaded the xylem, but not the phloem. This is contrary to the findings of Clarkson *et al.* (1975) and our own observations and suggests a need for wider experience of infections under different conditions. No lignitubers or plugged xylem occurred in oat roots invaded by *G. graminis* var. *tritici* and it was only when this variety invaded wheat that the cortex was almost completely eroded and the root system died.

Table 4. *Reactions of wheat seedlings to root invasion by* Gaeumannomyces graminis *var.* tritici *(based on Weste, 1972)*

Time after inoculation	Root					Other observations
	Hairs	Epidermis	Cortex	Stele	Whole	
(h)						
4	Collapsed at point of contact					
6	Penetration, cell wall damaged, granular diffusate					
8	Plasmolysed, bent, lignitubers					
10		Penetration				
15			First lesions, cells separated, walls torn, contents plasmolysed			
18	Shrivelled					
21			Lesions larger Lignitubers common			
(days)						
1			Lesions extended into endodermis			

Days					
1½		Heavily infected, cell contents granular, walls fractured			
2		Cell contents contracted to centre			
6		[Cell layers 4–6 of 1st seminal root penetrated]			
8		Lesions common	Dark plugs in xylem, lignitubers		
11			[Penetrated]	Lesions large and numerous	
15	Suppressed or shrivelled	Eroded away	Some entirely black. Lesions extensive. Cell contents disorganized		Stem base rotted
21			No autolysis of hyphae under gnotobiotic conditions (Faull & Campbell, 1979)		
63					Plant dying

[ ] Holden (1976): test in sand–soil mix; maize meal–sand inoculum, mean temp. 20°C.

Burdonov (1974*b*) described a similar series of events in winter wheat infected by *G. graminis* in Russia, as well as noting a brown, gum-like substance filling sclerotized cells in the infected cortex and, later, necrosis of the pericycle and adjacent parenchyma. The discoloured vessels of infected steles may have abnormal, swollen walls (Scott, 1978). Colonization of seedling steles differed proximally and distally from the point of inoculation of the root (Holden, 1976): upwards spread was mostly by dark runner hyphae *outside* the endodermis, but downwards spread was by hyaline hyphae *inside* the stele. Lignitubers were observed in the endodermis ·and pericycle, amorphous yellow plugs formed in the pericycle cells and xylem vessels in advance of hyphae, and a chocolate discoloration developed in their walls. Holden interpreted these as host resistance mechanisms that impede the spread of the pathogen and observed that they occurred mostly upwards from the point of inoculation. (Lignitubers in seedlings grown from surface-sterilized grains, inoculated with *G. graminis* and maintained under *sterile* conditions, did not seem to limit growth (Faull & Campbell, 1979).) Holden (1976) suggested the plugs arose from swelling cell wall pectin and hemicellulose, and the chocolate discoloration arose from oxidation of phenolic substances, making pectinaceous walls more resistant to rupture. Walls of healthy cortical cells have a greenish-blue autofluorescence, whereas those of vascular tissue and the endodermis autofluoresce bright blue, the colours being attributed to phenolic compounds (Holland & Fulcher, 1971). Yellow autofluorescence occurs in the zone where hyphae penetrate, or attempt to penetrate, the walls of living cells. Large areas of cell walls may autofluoresce orange in advance of hyphae, or fail to autofluoresce as wall-degrading enzymes accumulate and diffuse into the tissue. Smith & O'Brien (1979) found that culture filtrates of *G. graminis* containing esterase and many polysaccharide hydrolases removed the blue autofluorescent layer from wheat root epidermal cell walls. Such studies support the theory that *G. graminis* penetrates walls by enzymic degradation rather than by mechanical penetration. Further evidence for this was obtained from electron microscope studies (Faull & Campbell, 1979), which noted that the hole in the penetrated host cell wall was enlarged beyond the size needed for passage of the hypha. On the basis of observations of closely-associated dead, infected cells and living cells with normal cytoplasm, it has been suggested that cell death is not the result of readily diffusible toxins. Living cells adjacent to infected cells had thicker walls and distorted plasma membranes (Faull & Campbell, 1979).

Information about the diseases, other than take-all, listed in Table 1 is less detailed and more fragmentary. Table 5 summarizes information selected, and also provides some interesting variations on the progress and effects of root infection as previously illustrated by take-all. *Fusarium graminearum*, *F. culmorum* and *C. sativus* all produce polygalacturonase, pectinmethylesterase and cellulase enzymes on appropriate substrates *in vitro* (Weste, 1978).

Functional changes

Severe infections may destroy cereal root systems and cause lodging because the plants have no anchorage in the soil, but generally the effects of root-infecting fungi are more subtle. An infection which impairs root function may quickly upset the delicate balance between the interrelated physiological processes of the root and shoot. Thus an indirect indication of root dysfunction is provided by alterations in shoot physiological processes and growth. Verma, Morrall & Tinline (1976) found that increased severity of common root rot (*Cochliobolus sativus*) was associated with decreased shoot dry weight and grain yield. Take-all can decrease leaf area, tiller number, plant height and grain yield (Fig. 2). Root-infecting fungi such as *Phialophora radicicola, Pythium sclero-*

Fig. 2. Some effects of take-all on wheat. (*a*) Decreased leaf area (○, unin-oculated; ●, inoculated) (from Asher, 1972*a*); (*b*) fewer tillers (○, uninocu-lated; ●, inoculated) (from Asher, 1972*a*); (*c*) shorter plants (from Chambers, 1971); (*d*) decreased grain yield (regression line for 72 winter wheat crops at Rothamsted, Slope & Etheridge, 1971). ▲, significantly different, $P < 0.05$.

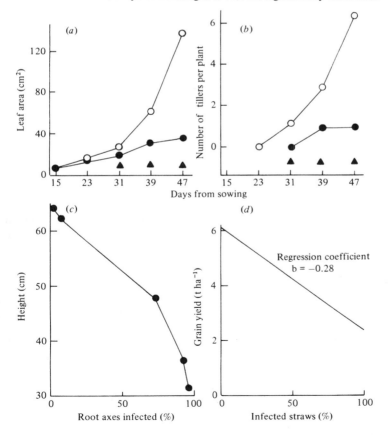

Table 5. *Invasion, invivo characteristics of the pathogen, and host responses in some cereal root infections*

Observations	Pathogens		
	Fusarium spp.	*Pythium graminicola*[6]	*Helminthosporium* spp.
Invasion			
Root			
Tips and hairs	May[1] or may not[2] be penetrated		
Epidermis	Hyphae in depressions on surface 3–4 days after inoculation[3]		
Cortex			
Colonization	5–7 days[3]	Sporangia form 4 h to 2 days, sexual bodies after 3 days	Before xylem[7]
Location	Intercellular,[3,4,5] localized[2]		In and between cells[4]
Damage			Necrosis[7]
Stele			
Colonization	10–14 days[3]	Sexual bodies numerous after 7 days	Xylem[7]
Location	In cells,[4] but not central trachea[3], between cells in grasses[5]		
Damage	Precedes cortical damage[4]		
Subcrown internode			
Colonization			Through hairs, guard cells, epidermal walls or junctions[8]
Location			In and between cells[8]
Damage			Partial or complete block-

		out walls and with erose plasmalemma	
Host responses			
Cell walls			
Infection site	Host walls split chemically and mechanically to one side of middle lamella[3]	Chemical (wall cavities, separation of wall layers) and mechanical (rim) penetration	Chemical and mechanical penetration[8]
Penetration	Slow spread lengthwise[3]	Rapid invasion	Initiates dark bodies in infected tissues[8]
Cell walls			
Infection site	Browning precedes general disintegration[4]		
Penetration	Papillae (4–5 μm) which break down[3], lignitubers and swellings[5]	Rim where hypha first contacts cell wall	Lignitubers in all tissues[8]
Cell contents			
Infection site			Nuclei move towards infection[8]
Penetration ⎫ Infected ⎭	Plasmalemma breaks down Brown contents = mycelium + disintegration products[4]		Cytoplasm becomes granular, stains differently[8] Nuclei densely stained[8]
Root			General or local browning[4]. Nodals smaller, less thickening of outer cortex, less infection than seminals[7]

[1] Colhoun & Park (1964), *F. graminearum*.
[2] Malalasekera *et al.* (1973), *F. culmorum*.
[3] McKeen (1977*a*), *Fusarium* sp. on barley and maize.
[4] Henry (1924), *F. culmorum, F. graminearum, Helminthosporium* spp.
[5] Labruyère (1979), *Fusarium* spp. on grasses.
[6] McKeen (1977*b*), for barley.
[7] Burdonov (1974*a*), *Cochliobolus sativus* on wheat.
[8] Huang & Tinline (1976), *C. sativus*.

teichum and *Wojnowicia graminis* appear to have little effect on shoot growth (Fitt & Hornby, 1978).

Root diseases which impair water uptake lead to flaccid, wilted shoots in young plants, and bleached or prematurely ripened heads in mature plants. Take-all decreased shoot water content in glasshouse experiments (Asher, 1972a) and the silicon content of glumes, which is related to the total water transpired during a growing season (Hutton & Norrish, 1974) in field-grown wheat (Salt & Rush-forth, 1976). However, decreases in shoot water content may be the result of changes in water retention rather than a dysfunction of the water uptake process. Plants infected by *Microdochium bolleyi*, *C. sativus* or *F. culmorum* had lower shoot water contents than uninoculated plants one week after sowing (Fitt & Hornby, 1978), although it was unlikely that the infected root systems were insufficient to supply water to shoots of these small seedlings. It is more likely that there was some remote-acting effect of infection which prevented stomatal closure or reduced cell turgor.

Shoot mineral composition is altered by dysfunction in the uptake of ions. Shoots of wheat plants severely infected by *G. graminis* or *F. culmorum* contained less K^+ and more Ca^{2+} than those of uninoculated plants (Fig. 3). Compensation by uninfected root axes may mask the effects of a pathogen, which explains why the mineral composition of shoots of plants with 18% of their root

Fig. 3. Changes in (*a*) shoot potassium and (*b*) shoot calcium in infected wheat plants. Bars indicate LSDs in relation to uninoculated plants ($P < 0.05$). ○, uninoculated; ● *Gaeumannomyces graminis;* □ *Fusarium culmorum.* (From Fitt & Hornby, 1978.)

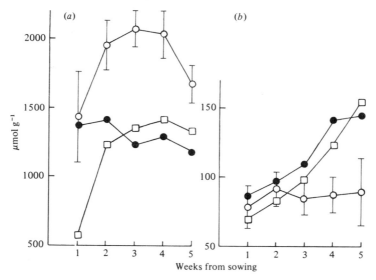

axes infected by *G. graminis* did not differ from that of controls in pot experiments (Hornby & Goring, 1972). Shoots of plants infected by *M. bolleyi, C. sativus* or *F. culmorum* contained less potassium than controls one week after sowing (Fitt & Hornby, 1978). It is probable that this was not because of a dysfunction of ion uptake processes but that it was more likely due to damage to the shoot tissue so that K^+, which is a highly mobile ion, was not retained.

A common symptom of root diseases is yellowing owing to reduced shoot chlorophyll content. This may be a more sensitive measure of a pathogen's activity than changes in shoot water content or mineral composition because chlorophyll, a product of secondary metabolism, is rapidly broken down in diseased tissue. Fitt (1977) showed that infection by *F. culmorum* or *G. graminis* reduced the shoot chlorophyll content of young wheat plants. However, shoot symptoms such as yellowing have many causes (Haspel-Horvatic & Horickova, 1974) and some root pathogens cause shoot symptoms before affecting root function (Fitt, 1977). Therefore, in order to establish the primary effects of pathogens on root function, measurements on shoots need to be complemented by direct measurements of root function.

Few such direct measurements exist for cereal root-infecting fungi, and these have been obtained mostly from wheat infected with *G. graminis*. Asher (1972*b*) studied the distribution of photosynthetic assimilates in infected plants by exposing leaves to $^{14}CO_2$. From autoradiographs he concluded that assimilates were not translocated past severe lesions, a result confirmed by Manners & Myers (1975) and Fitt & Hornby (1978). Clarkson *et al.* (1975) showed that phloem translocation of ^{86}Rb, and root elongation, ceased when 75–100% of phloem in a root axis was invaded by the fungus. Some leaf pathogens accumulate host assimilates at the site of infection (see Whipps & Lewis, this volume) but this was not the case with *G. graminis*. However, infection by *G. graminis* did stimulate accumulation of ^{14}C-labelled assimilates in undamaged crown roots, as did infection by *C. sativus* or *F. culmorum* (Table 6).

Some evidence for interference with water uptake was provided by Spalding *et al.* (1961) who showed that the cut leaves from wheat plants infected by *Hymenula cerealis*, and with decreased shoot water content, did not take up dye, and that the xylem vessels were extensively blocked by a 'gum', suggesting the pathogen had caused a vascular dysfunction. Deacon & Henry (1978) showed that *G. graminis* infection blocked uptake of the water-soluble dye eosin. Unfortunately tracers are of limited use in quantitative studies of water uptake since they may bind to walls of vessels and other cells. Kararah (1976) showed that less water was taken up by plants infected by *G. graminis*, even when leaf area, shoot dry weight and shoot water content were similar to those of healthy plants.

Experimental work on the uptake of ions by diseased roots is relatively recent. In hydroponic tests (Fitt, 1977), plants infected by *G. graminis* took up less ^{32}P,

[45]Ca and [42]K than uninoculated plants over a 24-h period. Clarkson *et al.* (1975) observed similar effects on ion uptake in their more detailed work with individual root axes. Xylem translocation of ^{32}P, [42]K and [85]Sr (a tracer for calcium) was little affected in infected roots which were still elongating, but was severely decreased if phloem translocation and elongation had ceased. In the field, severe take-all infection decreased uptake of ^{32}P by a wheat crop (Salt, Ellis & Howse, 1975).

Cereal root-infecting fungi may be divided into three categories on the basis of their effects on root function:

(1) those which do not penetrate root steles or affect root function and shoot growth;

(2) those whose effects on root function and shoot growth can be explained by stelar disruption;

(3) those which affect shoot growth before disrupting root steles and damaging root function.

Category 1 includes such fungi as *Phialophora radicicola, Pythium scleroteichum* and *Wojnowicia graminis* (Fitt & Hornby, 1978). Amongst these usually non-pathogenic inhabitants of the cortex, *Microdochium bolleyi* is very common (Waller, 1979) and has caused rotting of the seminal roots of young experimental wheat seedlings (Fitt & Hornby, 1978). *Olpidium brassicae* has caused iron deficiency in cabbage (Macfarlane, Clarkson & Sanderson, 1974) and *Polymyxa graminis* is a vector for certain virus diseases. Most of these fungi stimulate the host's physiological activities (causing papillae, lignification, thickening of cell walls, granular cytoplasm, prominent nuclei) without affecting root function (Fitt & Hornby, 1978; Talboys, 1978).

Table 6. *The effects of root-infecting fungi on distribution of ^{14}C-labelled assimilates in wheat*

	% [14]C in tissues, 24 h after exposure to [14]CO$_2$				
	One-week-old plants		Five-week-old plants		
	Shoot	Seminal roots	Shoot	Seminal roots	Crown roots
Control	77	23	77	10	13
Microdochium bolleyi	73	27	77	11	12
Cochliobolus sativus	76	24	70	12	18
Fusarium culmorum	82	18	74	6	20
Gaeumannomyces graminis	83	17	76	0	24
S.E.D. (12 d.f.)	4.6	4.6	4.9	3.2	3.8

From Fitt & Hornby (1978).

Gaeumannomyces graminis is in category 2 since the crucial stage in lesion development is disruption of the phloem (Clarkson *et al.*, 1975). When phloem bundles were disrupted, control of ion uptake broke down because phloem-translocated hormones, photosynthetic assimilates and redistributed ions (Pitman, 1975) could not reach sites of ion uptake. This explains why infection reduced shoot potassium but increased shoot calcium in pot experiments (Fitt & Hornby, 1978); potassium uptake is mainly active (Pitman, 1975), whereas calcium uptake has a large transpiration-dependent component (Sutcliffe, 1976). Also, calcium is immobile in the phloem and cannot be redistributed from senescent leaves (Richardson, 1975). Subsequently the xylem is colonized by *G. graminis* and uptake of calcium (Clarkson *et al.*, 1975; Fitt, 1977) and water (Kararah, 1976) decreased.

Remote-acting toxins may be involved in pathogenesis in plants infected by *Fusarium culmorum* and *Cochliobolus sativus* where shoot dry weight, water content and potassium content are decreased before the pathogen penetrates the stele (category 3). *Hymenula cerealis* (*Cephalosporium gramineum*) which causes *Cephalosporium* stripe disease of winter wheat (Mathre & Johnston, 1975), may also fall into category 3. The disease is recognized by its leaf symptoms, but is rarely serious in the UK. The fungus enters the plant through wounds in the roots caused by soil animals or soil 'heaving' during thaws, but, unlike other fungi treated in this chapter, it is primarily a xylem invader. It sporulates and spreads as conidia in the xylem, occasionally filling the vessels with hyphae. Brown discoloration of vascular elements where mycelium is scarce suggests that harmful metabolites are produced and translocated.

Nearly all observations on effects of cereal root pathogens on root function have been made in artificial conditions and caution is necessary in extrapolating from these results to the more complex field situation where symptoms may be different and water and nutrients are less readily available.

Cross-protection and the root cortex

Deacon (1974) observed that roots with thick cortices were often less diseased than roots with thin cortices and suggested that host resistance resides in the cortex and the endodermis. His explanation for this was that thicker cortices allowed time for secondary suberization of the endodermis in response to increased aeration following damage to the outer cortex. When the avirulent parasite *Phialophora radicicola* var. *graminicola* (*Prg*), or the weakly pathogenic *Phialophora radicicola* var. *radicicola* (*Prr*), penetrated the outer cortex of seminal roots of wheat seedlings they elicited lignification of the stele and lignification and suberization of the inner tangential walls of the endodermis, whereas the highly pathogenic *Gaeummanomyces graminis* var. *tritici* (*Ggt*) did not, and possibly even suppressed lignification (Speakman & Lewis, 1978). The 'elicitor system' moved in an almost entirely lateral direction, but did not limit spread of *Prg* or *Prr*, neither of which penetrated as far as the thickened walls: *Prg* was arrested by lignitubers in the third cortical layer and *Prr* hyphae stopped at the outer tangential wall of the endodermis, confirming earlier observations (Deacon, 1974). Prior colonization of roots by *Prg* prevented *Ggt* from spreading longitudinally in the stele, but whether the extensive lignification of the stele caused by *Prg* presented a mechanical barrier or was merely correlated with resistance is not known. Caffeic acid, a precursor of lignin, inhibits *Ggt* in culture and may accumulate in roots invaded by *Prg*, increasing their resistance to *Ggt* (Cowan, 1978). Although *Prg* was most common in fields where take-all developed slowly, Slope, Prew, Gutteridge & Etheridge (1979) stressed that there is no direct evidence for cause and effect. Introducing *Prg* on oat grains did not protect wheat in the field, whereas *Prr* or *G. graminis* var. *graminis* (*Ggg*) gave economically significant protection against slight to moderate take-all (Wong & Southwell, 1980). The work of Deverall, Wong & McLeod (1979) indicates that phytoalexins are unlikely to be important in cross-protection by *Ggg*.

Discussion

No system of classification of root pathogens is wholly satisfactory and most treat their effects much too narrowly. For example *G. graminis* var. *tritici* is most damaging when it is disrupting the phloem or blocking the xylem, which hardly accords with the classification of 'cortex-specific' (Kommedahl & Windels, 1979), and since the disease interferes with absorption and conduction of water it is both a root rot *and* a vascular wilt in the McNew system (Table 2). To produce a satisfactory classification would be extremely difficult since variable environmental factors affect the host–pathogen interaction, and it may be impossible to find effects which remain constant under all conditions. Often a pathogen can cause several different symptoms, depending on host maturity and environmental conditions. For example, both *Fusarium graminearum* and *F. culmorum* may cause seedling blight, foot rot or ear blight (Gair *et al.*, 1972). However, it might be helpful to have a scheme in which simple, quick measurements of effects of root pathogens on root structure or function can be related to yield decreases.

Such a scheme would require further research on the detailed structural changes in cereal roots invaded by root-infecting fungi. Histopathological knowledge has progressed little since work done in the 1920s and 1930s. Whilst obvious responses, such as lignitubers, have been studied and described in detail, histological changes have received far less attention. There seems to be much scope for applying existing histochemical methods as well as trying new techniques, such as enzyme cytochemistry (MacDonald & Lewis, 1978), to detect metabolically active hyphae in roots (M. E. Brown, personal communication). The need for more information about infection processes is possibly secondary to a more immediate need to collate what information we have for different pathogens. It is still to be resolved whether lignitubers and wall thickenings are significant host resistance mechanisms, how much they impede invading hyphae, and when cell death occurs if they fail. Such information for *G. graminis* might lead to a more critical consideration of its present classification as a necrotroph.

The role of extracellular enzymes in cereal root infections is often unclear and usually inferred; enzymes may be only one facet of pathogenesis, which is also determined by the pathogen's 'rapidity and aggressiveness of growth' (Weste, 1970*b*). However, Mount (1978) suggested that in some cases the composition of cell walls, and the induction or repression of specific degradative enzymes in the pathogen, determine recognition and compatibility phenomena that in turn determine host susceptibility or resistance, and pathogen virulence or avirulence. Even the extent of destruction caused by each pathogen may depend on the enzymes that host cell walls elicit and the barriers they present. Unfortunately knowledge of cereal root infections is too rudimentary to contribute much to this kind of debate. At present those who are intent on explaining virulence in terms of cell-wall-degrading enzymes are faced with problems such as explaining the equally low polygalacturonase activities in both avirulent and some virulent members of the *Gaeumannomyces—Phialophora* complex (Holden & Ashby, 1978).

All parasites in the *Gaeumannomyces—Phialophora* complex cause lignitubers in roots. The general growth pattern is a fan of hyphae spreading mostly between cells from individual entry points. Interestingly, the vesicular-arbuscular mycorrhiza *Endogone (Glomus) mossae* also develops in this way and forms large intercellular vesicles (Cox & Sanders, 1974) which may have a parallel in the vesicles of *P. radicicola* var. *radicicola*. When *E. mossae* penetrates cells of *Allium cepa* there is no extensive disruption of the host wall and a small collar of wall material is left around the hypha of the invading biotroph. This may be the remains of a papilla that forms early in the penetration process. The *Endogone* sp. in cereals (Salt, 1977) also fails to induce lignitubers, but whether this is because it does not stimulate the host response mechanism, or suppresses it, is not known. A thorough anatomical and histochemical comparison of cereal roots infected by *Endogone* or *Phialophora* may indicate the basis of these differences. Concerning similarities, Weste (1972) suggested that slow growth, intercellular mycelium and lack of extracellular toxins are necessary for a symbiotic relationship and that in the early stages of infection *G. graminis* actually exists in (commensalistic?) equilibrium with the host.

Existing information relating anatomical changes in roots to root dysfunction (Clarkson *et al.*, 1975; Kararah, 1976; Fitt & Hornby, 1978) needs to be extended to other host–pathogen systems. Many of the principles derived from research with cereal root-infecting fungi may well apply to these also. For example, cyst-nematode attack on potato roots affects the mineral composition of above-ground parts of the plant in the same way as *G. graminis* infection affects wheat; potassium and phosphorus contents are decreased while that of calcium is increased (Trudgill, Evans & Parrott, 1975). Therefore, a similar mechanism involving phloem disruption may operate. It needs to be stressed that symptoms in the field are often the result of the activities of two or more organisms, e.g. damage to grass roots by nematodes (*Pratylenchus* spp.) provides places for invasion by a *Phialophora* sp. (Labruyère, 1979), and the presence of the potato cyst-nematode increases wilting and chlorosis of potato plants infected by *Verticillium dahliae* (Corbett & Hide, 1971).

An opinion expressed occasionally over the last decade is that the effects of root disease are assessed better by measuring the uninfected parts of the root system than by assessing the portion of the root system that is infected or discoloured. This presupposes that disease renders roots inoperative without poisoning or disrupting the remainder of the plant so that the effects of disease are expressed as the interaction of active root and environment. The root diseases that do most damage to UK cereals do seem to be of this kind and are characterized by host responses that are not specific to the fungi involved, and have not been shown unequivocally to be resistance mechanisms.

Much attention is paid to fungal parasites invading the root cortex, but many of these seem not to be pathogenic. Some are regarded as potentially damaging (Waller, 1979), waiting only for conditions that favour pathogenicity, while others make it possible for true pathogens to enter the cortex (Kommedahl & Windels, 1979). The natural tendency for the cortex beyond the piliferous zone to die in cereals suggests that invasion and loss of much of the cortex through parasitism do not significantly disturb translocation and may not constitute much of a threat to the plant. However, the cortex has several roles: it increases the absorptive surface of the root, it protects the stele and it stores starch (Byrne, 1974). Damage to the epidermis and cortex near the root tip and in the piliferous zone will certainly impair the function of the root as an absorbing organ (Talboys, 1978). In view of this, it is unfortunate that field assessments of disease are quite often made on older parts of the root system where cortical cell death may be widespread, or the cortex much depleted, thereby confining the growth of parasites to the inner cortex. Although it could be argued that *any* destruction of cortex makes the plant more sensitive to stress, there is clearly a need to define the role of the cortex in different parts of the root system so that the effects of its loss or damage can be assessed more accurately and the significance of cortical invasion can be better understood.

References

Aist, J. R. (1976). Papillae and related wound plugs of plant cells. *Annual Review of Phytopathology*, **14**, 145–63.

Asher, M. J. C. (1972*a*). Effect of *Ophiobolus graminis* infection on the growth of wheat and barley. *Annals of Applied Biology*, **70**, 215–23.

Asher, M. J. C. (1972*b*). Effect of *Ophiobolus graminis* infection on the assimilation and distribution of ^{14}C in wheat. *Annals of Applied Biology*, **72**, 161–7.

Biddulph, S. & Biddulph, O. (1959). The circulating system of plants. *Scientific American*, **200**, 44–9.

Biddulph, O., Nakayama, F. S. & Cory, R. (1961). Transpiration and ascension of calcium. *Plant Physiology*, **36**, 429–36.

Boerema, G. H. & Verhoeven, A. A. (1977). Check-list for scientific names of common parasitic fungi. Series 2b: Fungi on field crops: cereals and grasses. *Netherlands Journal of Plant Pathology*, **83**, 165–204.

Bukovac, M. J. & Wittwer, S. H. (1957). Absorption and mobility of foliar applied nutrients. *Plant Physiology*, **32**, 428–35.

Burdonov, E. I. (1974*a*). [Anatomy of winter wheat roots infected by *Cochliobolus sativus.*] *Nauchnye Trudy Stavropolskii Selskokhotyaistennyi Institut*, **3**, 141–7. (In Russian.)

Burdonov, E. I. (1974*b*). [Anatomy of winter wheat roots infected by *Gaeumannomyces graminis.*] *Nauchnye Trudy Stavropolskii Selskokhotyaistennyi Institut*, **3**, 148–51. (In Russian.)

Byrne, J. M. (1974). Root Morphology. In *The Plant Root and its Environment*, ed. E. W. Carson, pp. 3–27. Charlottesville: University of Virginia Press.

Chambers, S. C. (1971). Glasshouse studies on *Ophiobolus graminis* as a cause of whiteheads in wheat. *Phytopathologische Zeitschrift*, **71**, 169–82.

Clarkson, D. T., Drew, M. C., Ferguson, I. B. & Sanderson, J. (1975). The effect of the take-all fungus, *Gaeumannomyces graminis*, on the transport of ions by wheat plants. *Physiological Plant Pathology*, **6**, 75–84.

Clarkson, D. T. & Robards, A. W. (1975). The endodermis, its structural development and physiological role. In *Development and Function of Roots*, ed. J. G. Torrey & D. T. Clarkson, pp. 415–36. London: Academic Press.

Colhoun, J. & Park, D. (1964). *Fusarium* diseases of cereals. 1. Infection of wheat plants, with particular reference to the effects of soil moisture and temperature in seedling infection. *Transactions of the British Mycological Society*, **47**, 559–72.

Corbett, D. C. M. & Hide, G. A. (1971). Interactions between *Heterodera rostochiensis* Woll. and *Verticillium dahliae* Kleb. on potatoes and the effect of CCC on both. *Annals of Applied Biology*, **68**, 71–80.

Cowan, M. C. (1978). Lignification in wheat roots parasitised by *Gaeumannomyces graminis* and *Phialophora radicicola*. *Annals of Applied Biology*, **89**, 101.

Cox, G. & Sanders, F. (1974). Ultrastructure of the host–fungus interface in a vesicular-arbuscular mycorrhiza. *New Phytologist*, **73**, 901–12.

Davies, C. R. & Wareing, P. F. (1965). Auxin-directed transport of radiophosphorus in stems. *Planta*, **65**, 139–56.

Deacon, J. W. (1974). Further studies on *Phialophora radicicola* and *Gaeumannomyces graminis* on roots and stem bases of grasses and cereals. *Transactions of the British Mycological Society*, **63**, 307–27.

Deacon, J. W. & Henry, C. M. (1978). Studies on the virulence of the take-all fungus, *Gaeumannomyces graminis*, with reference to methodology. *Annals of Applied Biology*, **89**, 401–9.

Deverall, B. J., Wong, P..T. W. & McLeod, S. (1979). Failure to implicate antifungal substances in cross-protection of wheat against take-all. *Transactions of the British Mycological Society*, **72**, 233–6.

Dittmer, H. J. (1937). A quantitative study of the roots and root hairs of a winter rye plant (*Secale cereale*). *American Journal of Botany*, **24**, 417–20.

Drew, M. C. & Saker, L. R. (1973). Effects of variation in the supply of nutrients within the rooting zone on root growth and nutrient absorption. *ARC Letcombe Report for 1972*, pp. 15–16.

Faull, J. L. & Campbell, R. (1979). Ultrastructure of the interaction between the take-all fungus and antagonistic bacteria. *Canadian Journal of Botany*, **57**, 1800–8.

Fellows, H. (1928). Some chemical and morphological phenomena attending infection of the wheat plant by *Ophiobolus graminis*. *Journal of Agricultural Research*, **37**, 647–61.

Ferguson, I. B. & Clarkson, D. T. (1975). Ion transport and endodermal suberization in the roots of *Zea mays*. *New Phytologist*, **75**, 69–79.

Fitt, B. D. L. (1977). Effects of root-infecting fungi on transport of metabolites in wheat. PhD thesis, London University.

Fitt, B. D. L. & Hornby, D. (1978). Effects of root-infecting fungi on wheat transport processes and growth. *Physiological Plant Pathology*, **13**, 335–46.

Gair, R., Jenkins, J. E. E. & Lester, E. (1972). *Cereal Pests and Diseases* Ipswich: Farming Press.

Garrett, S. D. (1948). Soil conditions and the take-all disease of wheat. IX. Interaction between host plant nutrition, disease escape and disease resistance. *Annals of Applied Biology*, **35**, 14–17.

Goss, M. J. & Drew, M. C. (1972). Effect of mechanical impedance on growth of seedlings. *ARC Letcombe Report for 1971*, pp. 35–42.

Harrison-Murray, R. S. & Clarkson, D. T. (1973). Relationships between structural development and absorption of ions by the root system of *Cucurbita pepo*. *Planta*, **114**, 1–16.

Haspel-Horvatic, E. & Horickova, B. (1974). Changes of the assimilatory pigments indicating the degree of damaging of plants. II. Chlorophyll changes as diagnostical and prognostical symptoms of damaging. *Phytopathologische Zeitschrift*, **81**, 65–71.

Henry, A. W. (1924). *Root rots of wheat. Technical Bulletin of the Minnesota Agricultural Experimental Station*, No. 22, 71 pp.

Holden, J. (1975). Use of nuclear staining to assess rates of cell death in cortices of cereal roots. *Soil Biology and Biochemistry*, **7**, 333–4.

Holden, J. (1976). Infection of wheat seminal roots by varieties of *Phialophora radicicola* and *Gaeumannomyces graminis*. *Soil Biology and Biochemistry*, **8**, 109–19.

Holden, M. & Ashby, M. (1978). Polygalacturonase production in liquid culture by isolates of *Gaeumannomyces graminis* and *Phialophora*-like fungi from cereal roots. *Transactions of the British Mycological Society*, **71**, 499–501.

Holland, A. A. & Fulcher, R. G. (1971). A study of wheat roots infected with *Ophiobolus graminis* (Sacc.) using fluorescence and electron microscopy. *Australian Journal of Biological Sciences*, **24**, 819–23.

Hornby, D. & Goring, C. A. I. (1972). Effects of ammonium and nitrate nutrition on take-all disease of wheat in pots. *Annals of Applied Biology*, **70**, 225–32.

Huang, H. C. & Tinline, R. D. (1976). Histology of *Cochliobolus sativus* infection in subcrown internodes of wheat and barley. *Canadian Journal of Botany*, **54**, 1344–54.

Hutton, J. T. & Norrish, K. (1974). Silicon content of wheat husks in relation to water transpired. *Australian Journal of Agricultural Research*, **25**, 203–12.

Jones, D. G. & Clifford, B. C. (1978). *Cereal Diseases. Their Pathology and Control*. Ipswich: BASF, United Kingdom.

Kararah, M. A. (1976). Host–parasite relationships in the take-all disease of wheat by *Gaeumannomyces graminis* v. *tritici*. PhD thesis, Southampton University.

Kommedahl, T. & Windels, C. E. (1979). Fungi: pathogen or host dominance in disease. In *Ecology of Root Pathogens*, ed. S. V. Krupa & Y. R. Dommergues, pp. 1–103. Amsterdam: Elsevier Scientific Publishing Company.

Kozlowski, T. T. (1978). How healthy plants grow. In *Plant Disease: an Advanced Treatise*, vol. III, *How Plants Suffer from Disease*, ed. J. G. Horsfall & E. B. Cowling, pp. 19–51. New York: Academic Press.

Labruyère, R. E. (1979). Resowing problems of old pastures. In *Soil-Borne Plant Pathogens*, ed. B. Schippers & W. Gams, pp. 313–26. London: Academic Press.

Ledingham, R. J., Atkinson, T. G., Horricks, I. S., Mills, J. T., Piening, L. T. & Tinline, R. D. (1973). Wheat losses due to common root rot in the prairie provinces of Canada, 1969–71. *Canadian Plant Disease Survey*, **53**, 113–22.

Lüttge, U. & Laties, G. G. (1967). Absorption and long-distance transport by isolated stele of maize roots in relation to the dual mechanism of ion absorption. *Planta*, **74**, 172–87.

Luttrell, E. S. (1974). Parasitism of fungi on vascular plants. *Mycologia*, **66**, 1–15.

MacDonald, R. M. & Lewis, M. (1978). The occurrence of some acid phosphatases and dehydrogenases in the vesicular-arbuscular mycorrhizal fungus *Glomus mosseae*. *New Phytologist*, **80**, 135–41.

Macfarlane, I., Clarkson, D. T. & Sanderson, J. (1974). *Olpidium* infection and iron deficiency in cabbage. *Rothamsted Experimental Station Report for 1973*, Part 1, p. 124.

McClintic, D. (1980). Shoot your crop to measure stress. *The Furrow*, **86**, 17.

McKeen, W. E. (1977a). *Fusarium* in barley and corn roots. *Canadian Journal of Botany*, **55**, 12–16.

McKeen, W. E. (1977b). Growth of *Pythium graminicola* in barley roots. *Canadian Journal of Botany*, **55**, 44–7.

MacNish, G. C. & Dodman, R. L. (1973). Relation between incidence of *Gaeumannomyces graminis* var. *tritici* and grain yield. *Australian Journal of Biological Sciences*, **26**, 1289–99.

Malalasekera, R. A. P., Sanderson, F. R. & Colhoun, J. (1973). *Fusarium* diseases of cereals. IX. Penetration and invasion of wheat seedlings by *Fusarium culmorum* and *Fusarium nivale*. *Transactions of the British Mycological Society*, **60**, 453–62.

Manners, J. G. & Myers, A. (1975). The effect of fungi (particularly obligate pathogens) on the physiology of higher plants. In *Symbiosis*, Society for

Experimental Biology Symposium, vol. 29, pp. 279–96. Cambridge: Cambridge University Press.

Mathre, D. E. & Johnston, R. H. (1975). *Cephalosporium* stripe of winter wheat: infection processes and host response. *Phytopathology*, **65**, 1244–9.

Mount, M. S. (1978). Tissue is disintegrated. In *Plant Disease: an Advanced Treatise*, vol. III, *How Plants Suffer from Disease*. ed. J. G. Horsfall & E. B. Cowling, pp. 279–97. New York: Academic Press.

Nilsson, H. E. (1969). Studies of root and foot rot diseases of cereals and grasses. I. On resistance to *Ophiobolus graminis* Sacc. *Lantbruks-Lögskolans Annaler*, **35**, 275–807.

Pilet, P.-E. (1974). Control by the root cap on growth and georeaction of roots. In *Proceedings of the 8th International Conference on Plant Growth Substances*, pp. 1104–10. Tokyo: Hirokawa Publishing Inc.

Pitman, M. G. (1975). Whole plants. In *Ion Transport in Plant Cells and Tissues*, ed. D. A. Baker & J. L. Hall, pp. 267–308. Amsterdam: North Holland Publishing Co.

Pitman, M. G., Lüttge, U., Lauchli, A. & Ball, E. (1974). Action of abscisic acid on ion transport as affected by root temperature and nutrient status. *Journal of Experimental Botany*, **25**, 147–55.

Plant Pathology Committee of the British Mycological Society (1962). *List of Common British Plant Diseases*. Cambridge: Cambridge University Press.

Richardson, M. (1975). *Translocation in Plants*, 2nd edn. London: Edward Arnold.

Roberts, D. A. & Boothroyd, C. W. (1972). *Fundamentals of Plant Pathology*. San Francisco: W. H. Freeman.

Salt, G. A. (1974). Chytrids and other fungi on roots of winter wheat. *Rothamsted Experimental Station Report for 1973*, p. 134.

Salt, G. A. (1977). A survey of fungi in cereal roots at Rothamsted, Woburn, and Saxmundham, 1970–1975. *Rothamsted Experimental Station Report for 1976*, pp. 153–68.

Salt, G. A. (1979). The increasing interest in 'minor pathogens'. In *Soil-borne Plant Pathogens*, ed. B. Schippers & W. Gams, pp. 289–312. London: Academic Press.

Salt, G. A., Ellis, F. & Howse, K. R. (1975). Nutrient and water uptake by healthy and diseased wheat roots. Field observations. *Rothamsted Experimental Station Report for 1974*, pp. 218–19.

Salt, G. A. & Rushforth, H. M. (1976). Silicon uptake as a measure of root damage. *Rothamsted Experimental Station Report for 1975*, pp. 249–50.

Schippers, B. & Gams, W. (eds.) (1979). *Soil-borne Plant Pathogens*. London: Academic Press.

Scott, D. B. (1978). Take-all of wheat in the Eastern Free State. *Phytophylactica*, **10**, 123–6.

Simmonds, P. M., Russell, R. C. & Sallans, B. T. (1935). A comparison of different types of root rot of wheat by means of root excavation studies. *Scientific Agriculture*, **15**, 680–700.

Sivasithamparam, K. & Parker, C. A. (1978). Effect of infection of seminal and nodal roots by the take-all fungus on tiller numbers and shoot weight of wheat. *Soil Biology and Biochemistry*, **10**, 365–8.

Skou, J. P. (1975). Studies on the take-all fungus *Gaeumannomyces graminis*. IV. Entry and growth of the fungus and significance of lignituber formation in the roots of the hosts. *Royal Veterinary and Agricultural University, Copenhagen, Denmark. 1975 Yearbook*, pp. 121–41.

Slope, D. B. & Etheridge, J. (1971). Grain yield and incidence of take-all (*Ophiobolus graminis* Sacc.) in wheat sown in different crop sequences. *Annals of Applied Biology*, **67**, 13–22.

Slope, D. B., Prew, R. D., Gutteridge, R. J. & Etheridge, J. (1979). Take-all, *Gaeumannomyces graminis* var. *tritici*, and the yield of wheat grown after ley and arable rotations in relation to the occurrence of *Phialophora radicicola* var. *graminicola. Journal of Agricultural Science, Cambridge,* **93**, 377–89.

Smith, M. M. & O'Brien, T. P. (1979). Distribution of autofluorescence and esterase and peroxidase activities in the epidermis of wheat roots. *Australian Journal of Plant Physiology*, **6**, 201–20.

Spalding, D. H., Bruehl, G. W. & Foster, R. J. (1961). Possible role of pectinolytic enzymes and polysaccharides in pathogenesis by *Cephalosporium gramineum* in wheat. *Phytopathology*, **51**, 227–35.

Speakman, J. B. & Lewis, B. G. (1978). Limitation of *Gaeumannomyces graminis* by wheat root responses to *Phialophora radicicola. New Phytologist*, **80**, 373–80.

Stout, P. R. & Hoagland, D. R. (1939). Upward and lateral movement of salt in certain plants as indicated by radioactive isotopes of potassium, sodium and phosphorus absorbed by roots. *American Journal of Botany*, **26**, 320–4.

Sutcliffe, J. F. (1976). Regulation in the whole plant. In *Transport in Plants,* vol. II, Part B, *Tissues and Organs,* ed. U. Lüttge & M. G. Pitman, pp. 394–411. Berlin: Springer-Verlag.

Talboys, P. W. (1978). Dysfunction of the water system. In *Plant Disease: an Advanced Treatise,* vol. III, *How plants suffer from disease,* ed. J. G. Horsfall & E. B. Cowling, pp. 141–62. New York: Academic Press.

Trip, P. & Gorham, P. R. (1967). Autoradiographic study of the pathway of translocation. *Canadian Journal of Botany*, **45**, 1567–73.

Troughton, A. (1962). *The roots of temperate cereals* (*wheat, barley, oats and rye*). Mimeographed Publication No. 2/1962. Farnham Royal: Commonwealth Agricultural Bureaux.

Trudgill, D. L., Evans, K. & Parrott, D. M. (1975). Effects of potato cyst nematodes on potato plants. II. Effects on haulm size, concentration of nutrients in haulm tissue and tuber yield of a nematode resistant and a nematode susceptible potato variety. *Nematologia*, **21**, 183–91.

Van Fleet, D. S. (1961). Histochemistry and function of the endodermis. *Botanical Reviews*, **27**, 165–220.

Verma, P. R., Morrall, R. A. A. & Tinline, R. D. (1976). The epidemiology of common root rot. IV. Appraisal of biomass and grain yield in naturally infected crops. *Canadian Journal of Botany*, **54**, 1656–65.

Waller, J. M. (1979). Observations on *Pythium* root rot of wheat and barley. *Plant Pathology*, **28**, 17–24.

Weste, G. (1970*a*). Extracellular enzyme production by various isolates of *Ophiobolus graminis* and *O. graminis* var. *avenae*. I. Enzymes produced in culture. *Phytopathologische Zeitschrift*, **67**, 189–204.

Weste, G. (1970*b*). Extra-cellular enzyme production by various isolates of *Ophiobolus graminis* and *O. graminis* var. *avenae*. II. Enzymes produced within the host tissue. *Phytopathologische Zeitschrift*, **67**, 327–36.

Weste, G. (1972). The process of root infection by *Ophiobolus graminis. Transactions of the British Mycological Society*, **59**, 133–47.

Weste, G. (1975). Comparative pathogenicity of root parasites to wheat seedlings. *Transactions of the British Mycological Society*, **64**, 43–53.

Weste, G. (1978). Comparative pathogenicity of six root parasites towards cereals. *Phytopathologische Zeitschrift*, **93**, 41–55.

Wheeler, B. E. J. (1976). *Diseases in Crops. The Institute of Biology Studies in Biology* No. 64. London: Edward Arnold.

Wood, R. K. S. (1967). *Physiological Plant Pathology*. Oxford: Blackwell Scientific Publications.

Wong, P. T. W. & Southwell, R. J. (1980). Field control of take-all of wheat by avirulent fungi. *Annals of Applied Biology*, **94**, 41–9.

P.G.AYRES

Effects of disease on plant water relations

It is unusual for plants growing naturally in a terrestrial environment to be free from water stress for a period of more than a few days, yet a reduction in tissue water potential from zero to -0.1 MPa (-1.0 bar) may halve the rate of cell division in apical meristems (Hsiao, Acevedo, Fereres & Henderson, 1976; Meidner & Sheriff, 1976). Cell division, involving both expansion and wall synthesis, is the physiological process which is perhaps the most sensitive to stress measured as a lowering of water potential, but other critical processes such as stomatal opening in mesophytes, and nitrate reduction, may be affected at water potential deficits of less than 1.0 MPa (see Fig. 1). Clearly, water stress is a factor commonly and regularly restricting plant growth, and any other factor which modifies that stress, such as disease, will affect plant growth.

Fig. 1. Generalized sensitivity to water stress of plant processes and parameters. Length of horizontal line represents the range of stress levels within which a process first becomes affected. ($+$) increase, ($-$) decrease in process; ψ= water potential. (Based on Hsiao *et al.*, 1976, where full references are given.)

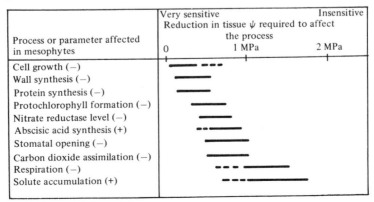

Process or parameter affected in mesophytes	Very sensitive Insensitive Reduction in tissue ψ required to affect the process		
	0	1 MPa	2 MPa
Cell growth ($-$)			
Wall synthesis ($-$)			
Protein synthesis ($-$)			
Protochlorophyll formation ($-$)			
Nitrate reductase level ($-$)			
Abscisic acid synthesis ($+$)			
Stomatal opening ($-$)			
Carbon dioxide assimilation ($-$)			
Respiration ($-$)			
Solute accumulation ($+$)			

Recent reviews of plant water relations (Kaufmann, 1976; Weatherley, 1976; Davies, 1981) have placed emphasis on the movement of water through the soil–plant–air continuum and have identified the driving forces governing water movement through the plant. This approach, which pinpoints the factors affecting the development of water stress in the plant, will be followed here, and then examples of diseases which specifically modify the various factors will be examined in detail. A more comprehensive discussion of disease types and their effects on plant water relations may be found in an earlier review (Ayres, 1978).

Sources of water stress

In a steady state, the flux of water through the plant (from the soil–root interface to the evaporating surface of the leaf cells) and through the gas phase (from the evaporating surface, through the stomata and boundary layer to the ambient air) will be equal and will theoretically follow an Ohm-type law. Thus,

$$F = \frac{\psi_s - \psi_l}{r_p} = \frac{\psi_l - \psi_a}{r_g} \qquad \text{(eqn 1)}$$

where F is the transpirational flux of water through the system, ψ_s, the water potential at the soil–root interface, ψ_l, the leaf water potential, ψ_a, the water potential of the ambient air; r_p is the sum of a number of component resistances in root, stem and leaf, and represents the total resistance to liquid flow into and through the plant, and r_g represents the resistance in the gas phase. The diffusion of water vapour away from the leaf obeys Fick's Laws, and thus the driving force is strictly a deficit of vapour pressure rather than one of water potential. The relationship between vapour pressure (p) and water potential is given by:

$$\psi = \frac{RT}{V} (\ln p - \ln p_0) \qquad \text{(eqn 2)}$$

where R is the gas constant, T, the absolute temperature, V, the partial molal volume of water and p_0 the saturation vapour pressure at T_0. Thus,

$$\psi_l - \psi_a = \frac{RT}{V} (\ln p_l - \ln p_0). \qquad \text{(eqn 3)}$$

In practice this means that the lower the vapour pressure, the steeper must be the water potential gradient to produce a given flux of water. We will see that pathogens can directly affect r_p, r_g and ψ_l.

It is generally agreed that r_g is much greater than r_p. For example, it has been calculated that in a plant with a leaf water deficit of 2 MPa, growing in saturated soil, r_g/r_p would be approximately 50 in an atmosphere of 50% relative humidity (Weatherley, 1976). Obviously stomata, being in the gas phase, are in the best possible position to control transpiration. Effects of disease on gas phase resistance are more likely to produce major changes in the water relations of the plant than are effects on liquid phase resistance.

The extent to which the healthy plant can *regulate* its internal water balance depends in the short term upon its ability to increase r_g by closing its stomata. This strategy may be unavailable to the diseased plant because, as described later, many pathogens immobilize stomata in an open condition, or lower the level of the cuticular resistance below that of the stomatal resistance, with which it is in parallel,

$$\frac{1}{r_g} = \frac{1}{r_{stomata}} + \frac{1}{r_{cuticle}} \qquad \text{(eqn 4)}$$

so that most water leaves the leaf by a non-stomatal pathway.

Even if r_g is increased, ψ_l may still fall in the diseased plant if resistances 'upstream' to the leaf, i.e. those offered by xylem elements of the roots and stem, are increased as a consequence of infection. The plant is less able to take advantage of conditions such as darkness, or periods of abundant soil water after rainfall, to restore a favourable tissue water balance.

Thus, under non-steady-state conditions the rate of evaporation may exceed or fall below the rate of flux through the plant. During this period

$$F = f_a \pm f_c \qquad \text{(eqn 5)}$$

where f_a is the rate of absorption through the roots and f_c is the adjustment of the water content of the tissues. As water is withdrawn from the tissue (f_c is positive) water stress develops until the water potential (ψ) of the cells of the tissue falls below that of the normal source of water, either soil, or apoplast (including xylem). The lowest limit to which ψ can fall is governed effectively by the solute potential of the cells since, for each cell

$$\psi = \psi_{sol} + \psi_p + \psi_m \qquad \text{(eqn 6)}$$

where ψ_{sol}, ψ_p, ψ_m are the solute, pressure and matric potentials, respectively. ψ_{sol} and ψ_p normally have opposite signs, while ψ_m is negligible in practice. In the long term, a plant may become adapted to *withstand* low soil water potential by accumulating high concentrations of solutes in its tissues, thus lowering its solute potential. As will be seen later, pathogens often reduce the capacity of cells to retain solutes to such an extent that they are unable to withstand even the mildest stress.

Changes in liquid phase resistance – the root component

The major resistance to water movement in the liquid phase is in the root (Davies, 1981) and within the root the radial resistance to flow inward from the soil to the centrally located xylem is probably greater than the axial resistance to flow upward within the xylem from the root to the stem (Newman, 1976;

Landsberg & Fowkes, 1978). The greater resistance arises because, whether radial transport across the cortex and pericycle is predominantly apoplastic or symplastic, living membranes which offer a high resistance to flow have to be crossed at least in the endodermis, where the apoplastic pathway is interrupted by hydrophobic deposits of suberin, the Casparian Strip. There is an interdependence between the transport of water and solutes in the radial pathway (Fiscus, 1977; Nulsen & Thurtell, 1978), and any disturbance of the solute relations of the tissues may reduce the osmotically driven component of water flow. Tobacco etch virus systemically introduced into the leaves of host plants induces wilting. The wilting does not occur because of any change in the resistance to movement of water in the xylem, since wilting is relieved if root tips of wilted plants are excised before the roots are placed in water. Wilting results because infection specifically causes permeability changes in the roots, as indicated by leakage of Na^+ from roots but not from leaves of infected plants, and so disrupts the normal solute relations of the root (Ghabrial & Pirone, 1967).

Water continues to flow through roots after their death; indeed, their resistance to flow is abnormally low immediately after death (Duniway, 1977). Accordingly, a rise in leaf water potential occurred at moderate transpiration rates when the root system of cotton plants, grown in water culture and with a normal root:shoot ratio, was killed by immersion in boiling water. The healthy root was able to lower its root resistance as transpiration increased, until its resistance matched that of heat-killed roots (Fig. 2). Although at moderate transpiration rates plants grown in water culture could maintain normal leaf water potentials when half the root system was excised, simply by reducing the resistance to flow in the remaining half of the root system very high transpiration rates (Fig. 2), or removal of half the root system from plants grown in soil of less than field water

Fig. 2. Effect of transpiration rate on the depression of leaf water potential, $\triangle \psi$, for living roots (—) and those killed by immersion in hot water (---). Intact (●,○), halved (▲). (From Stoker & Weatherley, 1971.)

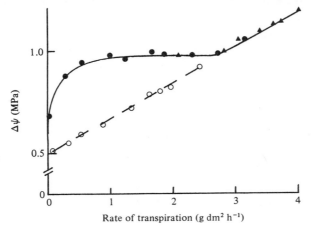

Rate of transpiration (g dm^2 h^{-1})

capacity caused an immediate fall in leaf water content and transpiration rate, and a rise in leaf water potential deficit ($\Delta\psi$).Stoker & Weatherley (1971) propose that this simple experiment demonstrates how increased influx per unit surface area can cause a critical lowering of soil water potential in the perirhizal zone.

Root death caused by pathogens can have similar effects on gradients of water potential in the perirhizal zone, masking any effects on radial resistance to flow, as is illustrated by a study of the water relations of avocado trees growing in their natural environment and suffering wilt as the result of infection of the root system by *Phytophthora cinnamomi* (Sterne, Kaufmann & Zentmeyer, 1978).

From eqn 1 a relationship may be derived (Kaufmann, 1976),

$$\psi_{leaf} = \psi_{soil} - \text{Flux} \times (r_{soil\ to\ leaf}),\qquad\qquad\text{(eqn 7)}$$

which predicts that leaf water potential is decreased by a reduction in soil water potential if neither transpiration rate nor resistance from soil to leaf changes. In avocado trees, night-time leaf water potentials of healthy plants (effectively the same as the measured xylem pressure potentials) reached −0.18 MPa while those of diseased plants and of water-stressed healthy plants reached only −0.80 and −0.70 MPa, respectively. There was a consistent relationship between leaf water potential and transpiration in healthy trees, but in infected plants and water-stressed healthy plants there was a marked hysteresis, i.e. at a given transpiration rate in the afternoon the leaf water potential was considerably lower than at the same transpiration rate in the morning (Fig. 3). Thus, well-watered

Fig. 3. Relationship between water potential and transpiration in leaves of avocado trees, unstressed (irrigated every 7–8 days), water stressed (without irrigation for 30 days) and infected by root rot, *Phytophthora cinnamomi*. Numbers indicate time of measurement, e.g. 4 = 0400 hours. Line for unstressed was fitted after regression analysis. (From Sterne, Kaufmann & Zentmeyer, 1978.)

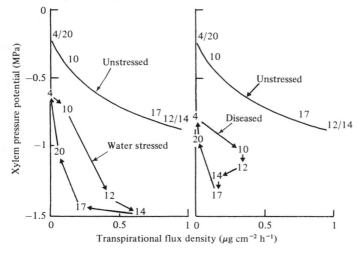

healthy plants behaved as predicted by eqn 7, but infected plants and water-stressed healthy plants, although resembling each other, deviated from the predicted behaviour. Sterne *et al.* (1978) suggested that such deviations were caused by a decrease in the hydraulic conductivity of the soil, most critically at the soil–root interface. In healthy droughted plants the roots encountered only dry soil, while in infected plants the inhibition of root growth meant that the soil water content in the perirhizal zone was reduced sharply below that in the bulk soil. Problems will increase for the diseased plant because the existing root system will become more suberized as it ages and, thus, more resistant to water movement. As Talboys (1978) has pointed out, invasion of the cortex may stimulate the process of suberization. Hornby & Fitt emphasized in the previous chapter, by reference to cereal root diseases which are not dealt with here, that the position occupied by the pathogen and its local effects on root tissue are of paramount importance in determining the abnormal physiology that results from disease.

Any lowering of resistance to flow through living cells that occurs as their death is induced by a pathogen will also be masked if there is an accompanying increase in the resistance to axial flow through non-living xylem elements. The wilt that results from *Phytophthora* root rot of safflower has been attributed to increased resistance to water movement in the root. Leaves from safflower (*Carthamus tinctorius* plants infected by *Phytophthora cryptogea* (*drechsleri*) showed a normal relationship between ψ_l and diffusive resistance and, if excised from wilted plants and supplied with water, they attained the same relative water contents as leaves excised from uninfected plants. However, if an intact infected plant was supplied with water it failed to recover from stress, indicating that infection interfered with water movement through the root (Duniway, 1975). This was confirmed when direct measurements were made of the resistance to water movement in different parts of plants grown in solution culture. Duniway (1977) applied an external pressure of 0.1 to 0.4 MPa to force water through the xylem of excised root systems, with or without intact adjoining segments of stem, to determine their resistance, and also calculated the resistance resident in leaves from measurements of steady transpiration rates at known gradients of water potential. By the time that wilting appeared on the fifth day after infection the resistance to flow in roots had increased from approximately 0.3×10^5 to 2.2×10^5 MPa s^{-1} cm^{-1}; resistance in the stem had also risen, from approximately 0.05×10^5 to 2.2×10^5 MPa s^{-1} cm^{-1}, but resistance in the leaves was unaltered by infection. Although root growth was reduced by the pathogen, Duniway did not consider this a major factor contributing to wilt.

Changes in liquid phase resistance – stem and leaf components

Many root-infecting pathogens which do not kill their host rapidly, such as *Phytophthora cryptogea*, spread through the vascular system into the stem region. Their presence in the vascular system causes further obstruction to the pathway of water movement. Similar effects are induced by a group of pathogens causing diseases known as 'Vascular Wilts', but these are generally regarded as being more specialized because their spread is typically confined within the xylem network until the phase of dispersal to a fresh host is reached. The group includes not only pathogens which enter the plant by active invasion of the root system, e.g. Fusarium and Verticillium Wilts, but also pathogens that enter wounds, e.g. the bacterium *Pseudomonas solanacearum* which causes wilt in many solanaceous plants, and those which are introduced into aerial parts of plants by vectors, e.g. the fungus *Ceratocystis ulmi* (Dutch elm disease) carried by bark-boring *Scolytus* beetles.

Flow of water through the lumen of xylem vessels is laminar and therefore obeys Poiseiulle's Law,

$$\text{Flow} = \Delta P \times \frac{\pi r^4}{8Ln} \qquad \text{(eqn 8)}$$

where ΔP is the pressure difference across the system, L and r are the length and radius of the vessel and n is the viscosity of the medium transported. This means that halving the radius of a vessel will reduce the flow by a factor of 16; or, more relevantly for diseased plants, a given obstruction will reduce flow by a proportionately greater amount when it occurs in a narrow vessel than when it occurs in a wide vessel. Furthermore, Poiseiulle's Law predicts that most flow will occur through the widest vessels, with which the stem is plentifully supplied. Not surprisingly, resistance to water flow is comparatively low in the stem of healthy plants. Vascular wilt pathogens have the greatest effect on overall r_p when they grow into petioles, and towards vein ends in leaves where vessels are narrower and fewer. Thus, in Fusarium-infected tomato plants, in which older leaves but not the experimental leaf were wilted (petiole and leaflet resistances were normal), a 500-fold increase in stem resistance only increased the *total* plant resistance by a factor of two. Wilting of experimental leaves occurred when the *petiole* resistance reached an infinitely high value (Duniway, 1971).

In chrysanthemum infected by the vascular wilt pathogen *Verticillium dahliae* a clear correlation has been demonstrated between the progress of the pathogen towards the vein ends in the lobes of the leaf and the reduction of relative water content and appearance of wilt symptoms in tips of those lobes (Table 1).

It must not be assumed that interruption of water movement is caused solely, or principally, by cells of the pathogen. The pathway may be blocked by factors of host origin, including tyloses produced by distension of the pit-closing membrane of adjacent parenchyma cells, gums secreted by parenchyma cells, and gels arising by distension of the primary wall and middle lamella of perforation plates and end walls (Van der Molen, Beckman & Rodenhorst, 1977). In addition, the pathogen may liberate enzymes which degrade host cell walls, causing wall fragments to accumulate in the sap. Each of these factors is discussed in detail by Talboys (1968) who concludes that they constitute collectively a much greater obstruction to water movement than do cells of the pathogen.

Water in xylem elements is normally under tension, so if the wall is dissolved by enzymes of the pathogen, or punctured by the stylet of a feeding insect, air may be drawn in. Since an air–water interface can penetrate a wet pore if pore diameter (in μm) × pressure difference (in MPa) > 0.3, a 1-μm puncture would allow air to pass into the xylem whenever tension exceeded 0.2 MPa (Zimmerman & McDonough, 1978). In small herbaceous plants which have the capacity to develop positive xylem pressures when well watered at night, elements may be refilled, but under conditions of stress, or in larger plants such as trees, the embolism may become permanent as the empty vessel extracts dissolved gases from wet cell walls. In the past, the occurrence of embolisms in pathogenically wilted plants has been largely ignored by pathologists, but recently Zimmerman & McDonough (1978) have argued cogently that embolisms represent the major cause of the failure of water conduction. They suggest that gels, tyloses, etc., may be formed as a *result* of a break in the water column, i.e. in order to isolate embolisms. It is difficult entirely to reconcile this last idea with certain observations, for example that gums and tyloses may occur in young hop roots before the xylem is entered by *Verticillium albo-atrum,* or may be induced in hop and apple by the presence of canker-causing pathogens in the cortex of stem or root (Talboys, 1978).

Plants at greatest risk of embolisms are those ring-porous trees such as elm which transport the bulk of their water through a few exceptionally large vessels situated just below the bark, though perennials, including elm (MacHardy & Beckman, 1973), can recover from moderate infections by producing new func-

Table 1. *Water stress develops in chrysanthemum as* Verticillium dahliae *colonizes tips of leaf lobes*

Base of lobe			Tip of lobe		
Colonies cultured from 1-cm diam. leaf disk	Relative water content (%)	Symptom	Colonies cultured from 1-cm diam. leaf disk	Relative water content (%)	Symptom
44	87	None	50	66	Wilted
19	89	None	23	79	Flaccid
12	89	None	16	87	None
0	88	Control	0	89	Control

From MacHardy, Hall & Busch (1974); MacHardy, Busch & Hall (1976).

tional wood. Furthermore, most plants are over supplied with vascular elements in the stem and so are protected against the loss of function in a certain proportion of those elements. Water will move around a blockage, passing through pit pores that are too small to allow passage of air bubbles or other obstructing agents. Differences in vascular anatomy have sometimes been correlated with different susceptibility to disease. When water was sucked under vacuum through single nodes of sugar cane, a clone that was immune to the bacterial disease 'Ratoon Stunting' allowed a flow rate of 1.4 cm^3 min^{-1}, three tolerant clones allowed rates of 2.6 to 8.4 cm^3 min^{-1}, and susceptible clones allowed rates of 13.0 to 19.6 cm^3 min^{-1} (Teakle, Smith & Steindl, 1975). The number of vessels that were continuous across nodes was smaller in resistant than in susceptible clones and this probably limited the movement of both water and the pathogen in the resistant clones.

Changes in gas phase resistance

Healthy plants protect themselves against developing water stress by closing their stomata, sensitive structures that represent the greatest *variable* resistance in the pathway of water movement through the plant. Stomatal guard cells in tissues colonized by a pathogen, and occasionally those at some distance from the pathogen, characteristically lose their mobility (Ayres, 1980). This is most damaging when the final state of stomata approximates to the normal open position, for water stress may develop unchecked. Stress may also develop if the final state of stomata approximates to the normal closed position but there is a reduction in the normally very high, fixed, cuticular resistance, as may happen when a fungus ruptures the epidermis prior to sporulation.

In both leaf blotch of barley, caused by *Rhynchosporium secalis,* and blight of potatoes, caused by *Phytophthora infestans,* infection induces stomata to open more widely than normal in the light and to fail to close in the dark (Farrell, Preece & Wren, 1969; Ayres, 1972). In barley leaf blotch, the fungus grows in a subcuticular position prior to sporulation and causes solutes to leak from epidermal cells so that there is a reduction in the back pressure (turgor) offered by epidermal cells to oppose guard cell opening. There is an increase in transpiration (Fig. 4), and a decrease in leaf relative water content (Ayres, unpublished results). However, the impact of such changes on the water balance of the whole plant is minimized because, as in potato blight, they are localized to colonized tissues, and because the fungus only spreads under cool moist conditions when the force driving transpiration ($\psi_l - \psi_a$, see eqn 1 and eqn 3) is at a minimum.

Immobilization of stomata in an open position leads to much more serious consequences in canker disease of peach and almond, caused by the fungus *Fusicoccum amygdali.* The fungus slowly colonizes the host after invasion of buds or leaf scars but it releases a phytotoxic terpenoid glucoside, fusicoccin, which is rapidly transported with the transpiration stream. The toxin stimulates stomatal opening in both light and dark in leaves up to 40 cm away from the nearest point of infection (Fig. 5). Since both hosts grow naturally in a dry Mediterranean-type environment infection is frequently associated with wilting and death of leaves (Turner & Graniti, 1976). Fusicoccin is not host-specific; it produces similar effects on disease-resistant varieties of peach and almond, and on non-host plants. Detailed studies of its mechanism of action on non-hosts reveal that fusicoccin acts by affecting ion transport across guard cell mem-

Fig. 4. Infection by leaf blotch, *Rhynchosporium secalis,* increases transpiration rate of barley in light (—) and dark (---) before sporulation commences. Healthy (○), infected (●). (From Ayres & Jones, 1975.)

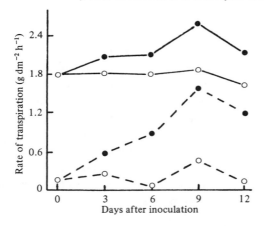

Fig. 5. Fusicoccin reduces stomatal diffusion resistance in light and dark when painted on leaves of almond. Sunrise 0630 hours, sunset 1700 hours. 10^{-5}-M fusicoccin (●), control (○), illumination (△). (From Turner & Graniti, 1976.)

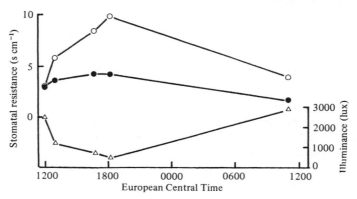

branes. It stimulates the K^+_{in}/H^+_{out} exchange that is a normal part of solute accumulation and, thereby, turgor development as guard cells open in response to illumination (Marrè, 1979). Other properties of fusicoccin, including its growth-promoting activity, are discussed later by Pegg (this volume).

Many host–parasite combinations involve the production of substances, such as enzymes and toxins (from the pathogen) and phytoalexins (from the host), which alter host membrane permeability and are therefore associated with changes in water and solute relations. For example, the water-soaked 'runners' that extend up the sugar cane leaf from 'Eyespot' lesions caused by *Helmintho-sporium sacchari* are produced by the action of helminthosporoside toxin re·leased by the fungus (Strobel, 1974). However, the *primary* site of action of such substances is not the stomatal apparatus and their effects on r_g are largely unknown.

Stomatal opening in the light is inhibited in rust, powdery mildew and some virus infections, e.g. sugar beet yellows virus (Hall, Hunt & Loomis, 1972). In rust diseases this only leads to a temporary reduction in transpiration because the sporulating structures of the fungus tear open the epidermis and protrude beyond the leaf surface. The consequent loss of control over transpiration which occurs may be seen in beans (*Phaseolus vulgaris*) infected by *Uromyces phaseoli*. When water is withheld from healthy beans the diffusive resistance of leaves increases to 50 s cm^{-1} by the time their relative water content falls to 70%, whereas the resistance of rusted leaves remains at less than 8 s cm^{-1} as relative water content falls to 50% and severe wilting occurs (Fig. 6; Duniway & Durbin, 1971).

Fig. 6. Infection of bean by rust, *Uromyces phaseoli*, prevents leaf diffusion resistance from increasing as relative water content decreases. Healthy (—); infected with 30 urediosori cm^{-2}(–––). (From Duniway & Durbin, 1971.)

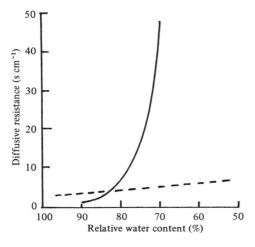

In powdery mildews a band resembling the Casparian Strip of the root endo-dermis is laid down around the narrow neck which connects the fungal hausto-rium inside the epidermal cell with the mycelium on the leaf surface (Bushnell & Gay, 1978). This probably prevents rapid transcuticular water movement via fungal cell walls, i.e. through an apoplastic pathway of potentially low resis-tance. Some water is lost from fungal surfaces, after transcuticular movement via the fungal symplast, but the net effect of infection is to reduce transpiration rates in the light to levels below those occurring in healthy plants, whether plants are compared in well-watered or moderately dry soil (Fig. 7). Under the latter conditions, uninfected leaves may benefit because there is less internal competi-tion for water, with the result that conductance and rates of photosynthesis are enhanced (Ayres, 1981). This may be one reason why mildew diseases are unu-sually tolerant of dry conditions. Under conditions of severe drought, transpira-tion rates of infected tissues exceed those of healthy tissues because stomata in diseased tissues are unable to close as completely as those in healthy tissues.

Irreversible wilting may occur in heavily infected tissues for a combination of reasons. Some powdery mildew fungi, such as *Erysiphe pisi* on pea, increase the permeability of host cells in the later stages of disease, particularly when plants are water stressed. As may be seen from eqn 6, a loss of solutes (rise in solute potential) will result in reduced turgor and tissue water content even if an unre-stricted supply of water is available. Thus, when mildewed pea leaves attached

Fig. 7. Infection of pea by powdery mildew, *Erysiphe pisi*, reduces the reg-ulatory effect of leaf water potential on transpiration rate. Healthy ($-$O$-$), infected 7 days (--●--). Each point represents an individual measurement taken 3 h after the onset of illumination. (P. G. Ayres, unpublished results.)

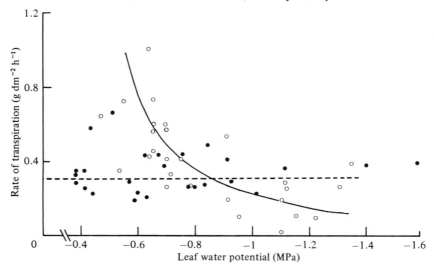

to well-watered plants were enclosed for five days in polythene bags lined with moist filter paper to prevent transpiration, they wilted nevertheless; their fresh weight was 1.14 ± 0.01 g dm^{-2}, while turgid healthy controls had a fresh weight of 1.58 ± 0.02 g dm^{-2} (Ayres, 1977*a*). Reduced root growth caused by a reduced supply of photoassimilate is a further factor that may contribute to water stress in plants suffering foliar infection.

Interactions between drought and disease

Unfortunately, studies of the water relations of diseased plants growing in the field are rare because they are subject to many difficulties besides those of maintaining some control over infection levels and the availability of soil water. Apart from effects of water on infection processes *per se* (described by Yarwood, 1978), there are interactions between plant water relations, pre- and post-inoculation host resistance, and growth of the pathogen. For example, drought reduces the resistance of cotton to root rot caused by *Macrophomina phaseolina* (Ghaffar & Erwin, 1969), and of wheat to Fusarium root rot (Papendick & Cook, 1974), but stimulates the development of adult plant resistance to powdery mildew in barley (Ayres & Woolacott, 1980) and inhibits spore production by powdery mildew of pea (Ayres, 1977*b*). Many more examples of similar phenomena are cited by Schoeneweiss (1978).

Experiments carried out in climate chambers, where some control can be exercised over environmental variables, demonstrate the complex interactions between drought and disease. When spring wheat was grown at three soil water levels, -1.0 MPa (dry), -0.4 MPa (medium) and -0.2 MPa (wet), and infected with leaf rust (*Puccinia recondita*), both dry soil and rust reduced the growth of plants but accelerated their maturation. A temporary increase in transpiration was associated with sporulation of the rust but at other times both dry soil and rust reduced transpiration per plant (Fig. 8; Van der Wal, Smeitink & Maan, 1975). Largest yield losses occurred in wet soil, where conditions favoured development of rust, and in dry soil, because rust lowered leaf water potentials (exacerbated stress) by increasing transpiration from leaves and reducing the flow of water to developing heads. This latter flow was estimated as the difference between total water loss per plant at the same leaf area before and after heading (Fig. 8), and its reduction was believed to cause abortion of grain (Cowan & Van der Wal, 1975). It will be seen that results of experiments combining the effects of drought and disease will reflect the particular levels of treatments selected and their interaction.

Some 40 years before Cowan & Van der Wal's work, the conclusion that drought and disease have additive effects was also drawn by Murphy (1935). He studied the effects of crown rust (*Puccinia coronata*) on the growth of oats in soil of 85% or 50% soil moisture content. Rust depressed yield at both water levels, but the reduction, as a percentage of control, was less in the drier soil than in the wetter soil. Similar results were obtained recently from a climate chamber study of barley grown at three soil water levels and infected at different growth stages with powdery mildew (Ayres & Zadoks, 1979). Mildew did not inhibit growth by deleteriously affecting the water relations of the plant, for infection neither induced water stress in well-watered plants nor exacerbated the stress already existing in plants in dry soil. Infection increased the shoot:root ratio in plants in wetter soils but had no effect on the ratio when the plants were in dry soil, where such an increase would have been most damaging. Water consumption per plant was reduced by infection because the transpiring area of the plant was reduced and also because stomatal opening in the light was inhibited in infected tissues. Yield of infected plants, relative to that of uninfected controls, was reduced least when plants were grown in dry soil, although this may have been due partly to the restricted development of mildew on the upper leaves of plants in dry soil.

Growth and development

Similar levels of water stress will have a broadly similar pattern of effects in both healthy and diseased plants, as described in Table 1. However,

Fig. 8. Effects of leaf rust, *Puccinia recondita,* on the relationship between transpiration per plant and turgid leaf area of wheat grown in dry soil (water potential -1.0 MPa). Healthy (O), infected (●). Heading (H), inoculation (I), increase in transpiration caused by rust (R). Numbers refer to weekly samples and show different maturation rates of healthy and rusted plants. (From Cowan & Van der Wal, 1975.)

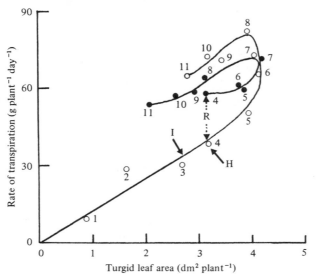

disease-induced or exacerbated stress represents a particularly serious threat to the growth and development of the plant because the progressively accumulating effects (r_p increases as more xylem elements are obstructed, r_g decreases as more lesions are formed in leaves) are not directly reversible. Only if the growth of the pathogen is stopped, by, for example, a change in environmental conditions, will the plant be able to 'grow away' from the effects of infection. The dangers of disease-induced water stress are increased because the pathogen disrupts several areas of the host's physiology, each reducing the vigour of the plant. Some of these accompanying changes may, in turn, have indirect effects on plant water relations.

In Fusarium wilt of tomato, photosynthesis is reduced not only because reduced water movement to leaves causes stomatal closure and an increase in the resistance to diffusion of carbon dioxide into the leaf (r_g CO_2), but also because there is an increase in mesophyll resistance (r_{mes}), i.e. carboxylation efficiency declines (Table 2). It is known that water stress can increase r_{mes} in healthy leaves (Boyer, 1976), but this does not provide a satisfactory explanation of events in the present case since r_{mes} in healthy tomatoes did not increase until water potentials fell below -1.2 MPa, whereas in diseased tomatoes r_{mes} was already infinitely high at leaf water potentials of -0.8 to -0.9 MPa. Thus, water stress was only one factor causing the failure of photosynthesis; other factors such as those described by Buchanan *et al.* (this volume) were probably operative.

Reduced photosynthesis means that reduced amounts of photoassimilate are

Table 2. *Decreases in rates of photosynthesis and transpiration in Fusarium-infected tomato plants are associated with increases in stomatal and mesophyll (intracellular) diffusion resistances*

	Days after inoculation	Photosynthesis (g CO_2 cm^{-2} s$^{-1} \times 10^{-9}$)	Transpiration (g H_2O cm^{-2} s$^{-1} \times 10^{-6}$)	Stomatal resistance (s cm^{-1})	Mesophyll resistance (s cm^{-1})
Healthy	12	120	16	1	3
	13	—	—	—	—
	14	115	20	1	3
	15	—	—	—	—
Infected	12	—	—	—	—
	13	95	16	1	3
	14	—	—	—	—
	15	10	2	9	20

From Duniway & Slatyer (1971).

available for translocation to shoot and root apices (transport through the phloem may be inhibited since it depends on the circulation of water through the plant). Growth fails because not only are apices deprived of the materials needed to build new cells but also they are unable to develop the low solute potentials required to maintain the turgor needed for the expansion of those newly formed cells.

References

Ayres, P. G. (1972). Abnormal behaviour of stomata in barley leaves infected with *Rhynchosporium secalis* (Oudem.) J. J. Davis. *Journal of Experimental Botany,* **23,** 683–91.

Ayres, P. G. (1977a). Effects of powdery mildew (*Erysiphe pisi*) and water stress upon the water relations of pea. *Physiological Plant Pathology,* **10,** 139–45.

Ayres, P. G. (1977b). Effects of leaf water potential on sporulation of *Erysiphe pisi* (pea mildew). *Transactions of the British Mycological Society,* **68,** 97–100.

Ayres, P. G. (1978). Water relations of diseased plants. In *Water Deficits and Plant Growth,* vol. V, ed. T. T. Kozlowski, pp. 1–60. London: Academic Press.

Ayres, P. G. (1980). Responses of stomata to pathogenic microorganisms. In *Stomatal Physiology,* ed. P. G. Jarvis & T. A. Mansfield, pp. 205–21. Cambridge: Cambridge University Press.

Ayres, P. G. (1981). Powdery mildew stimulates photosynthesis in uninfected leaves of pea plants. *Phytopathologische Zeitschrift,* **100,** 312–18.

Ayres, P. G. & Jones, P. (1975). Increased transpiration and the accumulation of root absorbed ^{86}Rb in barley leaves infected by *Rhynchosporium secalis* (leaf blotch). *Physiological Plant Pathology,* **7,** 49–58.

Ayres, P. G. & Woolacott, B. (1980). Effect of soil water level on the development of adult plant resistance to powdery mildew in barley. *Annals of Applied Biology,* **94,** 255–63.

Ayres, P. G. & Zadoks, J. C. (1979). Combined effects of powdery mildew disease and soil water level on the water relations and growth of barley. *Physiological Plant Pathology,* **14,** 347–67.

Boyer, J. S. (1976). Photosynthesis at low water potentials. *Philosophical Transactions of the Royal Society, London, B,* **273,** 501–12.

Bushnell, W. R. & Gay, J. L. (1978). Accumulation of solutes in relation to the structure and function of haustoria in powdery mildews. In *The Powdery Mildews,* ed. D. M. Spencer, pp. 183–235. London: Academic Press.

Cowan, M. C. & Van der Wal, A. F. (1975). An ecophysiological approach to crop losses, exemplified in the system wheat, leaf rust and glume blotch. IV. Water flow and leaf-water potential of uninfected wheat plants and plants infected with *Puccinia recondita* f.sp. *triticina. Netherlands Journal of Plant Pathology,* **81,** 49–57.

Davies, W. J. (1981). Transpiration and the water balance of plants. In *Plant Physiology,* vol. VII, ed. J. F. Sutcliffe & F. C. Steward. (In press.) London: Academic Press.

Duniway, J. M. (1971). Resistance to water movement in leaves of healthy and Fusarium infected tomato plants. *Nature,* **230,** 252–3.

Duniway, J. M. (1975). Water relations in safflower during wilting induced by Phytophthora root rot. *Phytopathology*, **65**, 886–91.

Duniway, J. M. (1977). Changes in resistance to water transport in safflower during development of Phytophthora root rot. *Phytopathology*, **67**, 331–7.

Duniway, J. M. & Durbin, R. D. (1971). Detrimental effect of rust infection on the water relations of bean. *Plant Physiology*, **48**, 69–72.

Duniway, J. M. & Slatyer, R. O. (1971). Gas exchange studies on the transpiration and photosynthesis of tomato leaves affected by *Fusarium oxysporum* f.sp. *lycopersici*. *Phytopathology*, **61**, 1377–81.

Farrell, G. M., Preece, T. F. & Wren, M. J. (1969). Effects of infection by *Phytophthora infestans* (Mont.) de Bary on stomata of potato leaves. *Annals of Applied Biology*, **63**, 265–75.

Fiscus, E. L. (1977). Effects of coupled solute and water flow in plant roots with special reference to Brouwer's experiment. *Journal of Experimental Botany*, **28**, 71–7.

Ghabrial, S. A. & Pirone, T. P. (1967). Physiology of tobacco etch virus-induced wilt of tabasco peppers. *Virology*, **31**, 154–62.

Ghaffar, A. & Erwin, D. C. (1969). Effect of soil water stress on root rot of cotton caused by *Macrophomina phaseolina*. *Phytopathology*, **59**, 795–7.

Hall, A. E., Hunt, W. F. & Loomis, R. S. (1972). Variations in leaf resistances, net photosynthesis and tolerance to the beet yellows virus among varieties of sugar beet (*Beta vulgaris* L.). *Crop Science*, **12**, 558–60.

Hsiao, T. C., Acevedo, E., Fereres, E. & Henderson, D. W. (1976). Water stress, growth and osmotic adjustment. *Philosophical Transactions of the Royal Society, London, B*, **273**, 479–500.

Kaufmann, M. R. (1976). Water transport through plants: current perspectives. In *Transport and Transfer Processes in Plants*, ed. I. F. Wardlaw & J. B. Passioura, pp. 313–27. London: Academic Press.

Landsberg, J. J. & Fowkes, N. D. (1978). Water movement through plant roots. *Annals of Botany*, N.S., **42**, 493–508.

MacHardy, W. E. & Beckman, C. H. (1973). Water relations in American elm infected with *Ceratocytis ulmi*. *Phytopathology*, **63**, 98–103.

MacHardy, W. E., Busch, L. V. & Hall, R. (1976). *Verticillium* wilt of chrysanthemum; quantitative relationship between increased stomatal resistance and local vascular disfunction preceding wilt. *Canadian Journal of Botany*, **54**, 1023–34.

MacHardy, W. E., Hall, R. & Busch, L. V. (1974). *Verticillium* wilt of chrysanthemum: relative water content and protein, R.N.A., and chlorophyll levels in leaves in relation to visible wilt symptoms. *Canadian Journal of Botany*, **52**, 49–54.

Marrè, E. (1979). Fusicoccin: a tool in plant physiology. *Annual Review of Plant Physiology*, **30**, 273–88.

Meidner, H. & Sheriff, D. W. (1976). *Water and Plants*. London: Blackie. [p. 148.]

Murphy, H. C. (1935). Effect of crown rust infection on yield and water requirement of oats. *Journal of Agricultural Research*, **50**, 387–401.

Newman, E. I. (1976). Water movement through root systems. *Philosophical Transactions of the Royal Society, London, B*, **273**, 463–78.

Nulsen, R. A. & Thurtell, G. W. (1978). Osmotically induced changes in the pressure-flow relationship of maize root systems. *Australian Journal of Plant Physiology*, **5**, 469–76.

Papendick, R. J. & Cook, R. J. (1974). Plant water stress and development of Fusarium root rot of wheat subjected to different cultural practices. *Phytopathology*, **64**, 358–63.

Schoeneweiss, D. F. (1978). Water stress as a predisposing factor in plant disease. In *Water Deficits and Plant Growth*, vol. V, ed. T. T. Kozlowski, pp. 61–99. London: Academic Press.

Sterne, R. E., Kaufmann, M. R. & Zentmeyer, G. A. (1978). Effect of Phytophthora root rot on water relations of avocado; interpretation with a water transport model. *Phytopathology*, **68**, 595–602.

Stoker, R. & Weatherley, P. E. (1971). The influence of the root system on the relationship between the rate of transpiration and depression of leaf water potential. *New Phytologist*, **70**, 547–54.

Strobel, G. A. (1974). Phytotoxins produced by plant parasites. *Annual Review of Plant Physiology*, **25**, 541–66.

Talboys, P. W. (1968). Water deficits in vascular disease. In *Water Deficits and Plant Growth*, vol. II, ed. T. T. Kozlowski, pp. 255–311. London: Academic Press.

Talboys, P. W. (1978). Dysfunction of the water system. In *Plant Disease*, vol. III, ed. J. G. Horsfall & E. B. Cowling, pp. 141–62. London: Academic Press.

Teakle, D. S., Smith, P. M. & Steindl, D. R. L. (1975). Ratoon stunting disease of sugarcane; possible correlation of resistance with vascular anatomy. *Phytopathology*, **65**, 138–41.

Turner, N. C. & Graniti, A. (1976). Stomatal response of two almond varieties to fusicoccin. *Physiological Plant Pathology*, **9**, 175–82.

Van der Molen, G. E., Beckman, C. H. & Rodehorst, E. (1977). Vascular gelation: a general response phenomenon following infection. *Physiological Plant Pathology*, **11**, 95–100.

Van der Wal, A. F., Smeitink, H. & Maan, G. C. (1975). An ecophysiological approach to crop losses exemplified in the system wheat, leaf rust and glume blotch. III. Effects of soil-water potential on development, growth, transpiration, symptoms and spore production of leaf rust-infected wheat. *Netherlands Journal of Plant Pathology*, **81**, 1–13.

Weatherley, P. E. (1976). Water movement through plants. *Philosophical Transactions of the Royal Society, London, B*, **273**, 435–44.

Yarwood, C. E. (1978). Water and the infection process. In *Water Deficits and Plant Growth*, vol. V, ed. T. T. Kozlowski, pp. 141–73. London: Academic Press.

Zimmerman, M. H. & McDonough, J. (1978). Dysfunction of the flow of food. In *Plant Disease*, vol. III, ed. J. G. Horsfall & E. B. Cowling, pp. 117–40. London: Academic Press.

G.F.PEGG

The involvement of growth regulators in the diseased plant

The growth and development of healthy and diseased higher plants is controlled by gradients of endogenous plant growth substances. There are five known classes of growth substance, viz., indolyl auxins, cytokinins, gibberellins, unsaturated hydrocarbon gases and inhibitors. The two latter groups are represented by ethylene and abscisic acid as dominant if not exclusive members of their respective classes. Under conditions of stress, changes occur in the concentration of some or all endogenous regulators which profoundly affect the physiology and in some cases the morphology of the plant. In this sense pathogenesis may be regarded as a chronic stress effect and it is not surprising, therefore, that many plant diseases show greatly exaggerated symptoms of growth substance activity and enhanced tissue levels of some growth regulators. Since plant pathogens (other than viruses) have been shown to produce growth substances in culture, the idea has grown up that pathogens induce many symptoms of disordered growth as a result of producing an alien growth substance or by contributing in excess the same growth substance as is found in the hosts' endogenous pool. Although there are some good examples of likely 'cause and effect' relationships between host, pathogen and tissue overgrowths, the evidence for many of the examples is conjectural and lacking firm experimental proof. Moreover it should be remembered that growth regulators may often exert powerful effects on the physiology and metabolism of plants in the absence of obvious growth effects. In discussing growth regulators one cannot exclude certain fungal toxins, several of which, notably fusicoccin from *Fusicoccum amygdali,* the diaporthins and helminthosporol from *Drechslera sorokiniana (Helminthosporium sativum),* exhibit characters similar to those of growth substances in addition to other effects.

The object of this review is to present selected examples of the occurrence of growth regulators in plant disease and consider in particular their multiple and interacting roles. It is not intended to give encyclopaedic coverage to the subject and further reference should be made to reviews by Sequeira (1973), Pegg (1976c), Daly & Knoche (1976) and Marrè (1979).

Ethylene

Ethylene (ethene, C_2H_4) is one of the most unusual of the plant hormones produced by higher plants, fungi and bacteria. Next to acetylene it is the simplest of the unsaturated hydrocarbon gases and exerts a strong regulating effect on most aspects of plant growth and development (see Abeles, 1973). Ethylene is not unique as a gaseous hydrocarbon growth regulator but it is the most powerful. Compounds showing unsaturation next to a terminal carbon atom are active, but activity decreases with increasing chain length. For example, propylene is 100 times less active than ethylene in growth assays and 60 times less active in abscission tests.

At 25 °C the absorption coefficient of ethylene is 0.108 and at a gaseous concentration of 1 vpm the molar concentration in water is 4.43×10^{-9}. This is five times the solubility of oxygen. Nothing is known of its solubility in cell sap or its affinity for lipid components of cell membranes and organelles. Most studies are based on gas evolved from stems, leaves or roots in trapping experiments over periods of time. At the site of production or action, however, the effective concentration in solution may be orders of magnitude higher than that detected. A major problem in the study of ethylene in pathogenesis is that it may be produced by the pathogen but it is also produced in response to physical wounding in the absence (Saltveit & Dilley, 1978) or in the presence of a pathogen (Imaseki, Teranishi & Uritani, 1968). Measurements made on detached leaves or excised tissue are different from those made on parts of intact plants. Most of our knowledge of ethylene metabolism, however, is based on tissue segments in which wound ethylene may be an important part of the response.

Biosynthesis of ethylene

One of the first reports of ethylene production by diseased plants was for citrus fruits infected with *Penicillium digitatum* (Miller, Winston & Fisher, 1940). Ketring, Young & Biale (1968), working on this pathogen, showed that monofluoroacetate, which inhibits interconversion of citric acid and isocitric acid in the trichloracetic acid cycle, also inhibited ethylene production and concluded that ethylene was derived from the CH_2 carbons of citrate. Chou & Yang (1973) subsequently showed that ethylene was derived from carbons 3 and 4 of 2 keto-glutarate or glutamic acid.

Early work by Mapson and his colleagues based on model systems postulated that ethylene synthesized in higher plants was derived from methionine via methional or 2 keto-4-methyl mercaptobutyric acid (KMB). In cauliflower florets, Mapson (1970) reported the requirement of a transaminase to convert methionine to KMB, a glucose oxidase to release H_2O_2 and a peroxidase to generate free radicals which react in the presence of phenolic co-factors with KMB or methional to form ethylene. Doubt has been expressed as to the existence of KMB or methional as intermediates of ethylene biosynthesis *in vivo*. In apple, methional does not stimulate ethylene production (Lieberman, Kunishi, Mapson & Wardale, 1966). Similarly, in fruit tissue ^{14}C methionine was converted twice as fast as ^{14}C KMB.

The importance of peroxide in ethylene evolution in cauliflower florets infected with *Erwinia carotovora* was demonstrated by Lund (1973). In these experiments cell wall preparation of florets supplemented with KMB generated ethylene in the presence of bacterial enzymes and in particular *endo*-pectate lyase. The postulated role of this enzyme was to release wall-bound oxidases which functioned on substrates such as glucose or amino acids to release hydrogen peroxide. In the presence of peroxidase, this hydrogen peroxide was considered to form free radicals which reacted non-enzymically with methionine *or* KMB, causing a fission to ethylene and other products.

Two pieces of evidence, however, do not support the H_2O_2–peroxidase–KMB scheme. Fowler & Morgan (1972) and Kang, Newcomb & Burg (1971), working on pea stem section and cotton, could not find the expected relationship between endogenous ethylene production and extractable peroxidase. Moreover, Yang, Ku & Pratt (1966) showed that catalase which degrades H_2O_2 had no effect on ethylene output in an FMN, light-stimulated ethylene-generating reaction.

In contrast to the foregoing, Adams & Yang (1979) proposed a new mechanism for ethylene biosynthesis in which methionine is converted to S-adenosylmethionine (SAM) by an ATP-dependent step. SAM is converted to the immediate precursor of ethylene, 1-amino-cyclopropan-1-carboxylic acid (ACC), by the action of aminocyclopropane carboxylate synthetase (Yu, Adams & Yang 1979). This enzyme is probably the key factor in the synthesis and regulation of ethylene production. Adams & Yang (1979) and Yu & Yang (1979) have shown the effect of endogenous auxin in inducing the enzyme which is also dependent on pyridoxal phosphate. In mung bean hypocotyls the conversion of methionine to SAM was unaffected by indol-3-yl-acetic acid (IAA), but the corresponding SAM to ACC conversion *only* occurred in IAA-treated tissue. The results of these workers threw much light on the long-recognised interrelationship between IAA and ethylene (Morgan & Hall, 1964) and suggest a rate-limiting role for it. The by-product of ACC synthesis, 5-methylthioadenosine, is cycled as part of the sulphur economy of the cell, ultimately combining with homoserine in new methionine synthesis (Fig. 1). The enol ether amino analogues from *Rhizobium japonicum* (rhizobitoxin) and from *Streptomyces* sp., amino ethoxyvinyl glycine (AVG), are potent inhibitors of ethylene, inhibiting ACC synthetase. ACC first isolated from apples and pears by Burroughs (1957) has been found in a number of higher plants. The production of ethylene from ACC is oxygen-dependent and presumably under enzyme control. This enzyme, however, has not been identified and is likely to be an unusual and sensitive one since ethylene evolution ceases completely in tissue homogenates. Plants treated with ACC show rapid, increased (10–20-fold) ethylene production (Cameron *et al.*, 1979), unlike those treated with methionine where the response is lacking or reduced. Current work on stress physiology strongly implicates ACC and the Adams & Yang (1979) pathway (Fig. 1). The precise role of pectolytic enzymes in ethylene formation and the possibility of an additional or alternative KMB pathway and hydrogen peroxide-dependence *in vivo* remains to be established.

Wound ethylene

Tissues which normally have a low ethylene turnover produce large quantities on wounding (see Yang & Pratt, 1978). In the extreme of tissue wounding, i.e. homogenisation, ethylene production stops but ethane (C_2H_6) production is stimulated. Ethane synthesis is associated with injury (Konze & Elstner, 1978) and with the peroxidation of linolenic acid associated with the lipid moiety of cell membranes. Lieberman & Mapson (1964) showed that ethylene and ethane could be produced from linolenate; however, the substance of

Fig. 1. Methionine metabolism and ethylene biosynthesis. (After Adams & Yang, 1979, and Yu & Yang, 1979.)

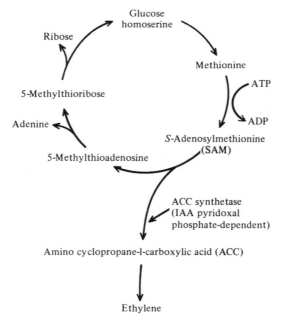

Konze & Elstner's work (1978) suggests that the period of enhanced ethane production following wounding can be used to measure the duration of the *wound* ethylene response which may contribute to increased total ethylene output resulting from several causes.

Ethylene as a phytotoxin

The phytotoxic effects of ethylene have been known from the middle of the nineteenth century. Plants exposed to an atmosphere contaminated with coal gas – containing ethylene and carbon monoxide as impurities – showed many of the symptoms associated with disease, e.g. in the short term, epinasty and foliar abscission and, over longer periods, formation of adventitious root initials, stunting, chlorosis, necrotic lesions and death. Abscission is a physiologically complex phenomenon involving ethylene, auxin, cellulase, abscisic acid (ABA), protein and nucleic acid synthesis. The ability of ethylene to induce abscission depends to a great extent on the plants' propensity to absciss and also on the endogenous foliar auxin levels. Time of exposure to ethylene is as important as concentration. Exposure of six-week-old tomato plants to 0.1 vpm ethylene for 120 h induced epinasty, chlorosis and foliar necrotic spotting. With young cotton plants, however, the major effect was abscission of all the lower leaves. Williamson (1950) attributed abscission in rose leaves infected with *Diplocarpon rosae* to ethylene. It is indicative of ethylene action in this disease that chlorosis spreading beyond the fungal stroma is usually well advanced prior to abscission although in the light of Sequeira & Steeves' (1954) work on leaf fall of coffee (see p. 158) the direct involvement of auxins in black spot abscission cannot be discounted. Wiese & DeVay (1970) showed that a strain of *Verticillium dahliae* (T 9) causing defoliation in cotton produced twice as much ethylene *in vitro* as a pathogenic non-defoliating (SS4) strain. Dimond & Waggoner (1953) were first to ascribe a role for ethylene in a vascular wilt disease (*Fusarium* wilt of tomatoes). Many symptoms of infection are those of advanced senescence, suggesting to some authorities that disease represented accelerated senescence. As senescence proceeds, ethylene evolution increases until tissue dies. However, Gentile & Matta (1975) and Pegg & Cronshaw (1976a) showed in both *Fusarium*- and *Verticillium*-infected susceptible tomato plants that ethylene was produced as a pulse commencing 7 days after infection and reaching a peak at 9–12 days. Peak ethylene production coincided with foliar chlorosis only in older leaves; in young leaves the peak preceded the appearance of symptoms by several days. Cronshaw & Pegg (1976) and G. F. Pegg & S. Austin (unpublished) have shown an interaction between ethylene and polysaccharide toxins of *Verticillium* in which pretreatment of tissue with ethylene may increase its sensitivity to the toxin; alternatively, ethylene may interact synergistically with *Verticillium* metabolites inducing symptoms. The picture in vascular wilt diseases is that ethylene plays a complex and interacting role and in certain cases may function as a primary toxin. Great caution must be exercised in the interpretation of experimental findings on detached leaves. Gentile & Matta (1975), working on detached tomato leaves, claimed that wilting was a cause of ethylene production. Pegg & Cronshaw (1976a), in ethylene trapping experiments on leaves of drought-stressed, *intact* plants, could find no such early relationship with ethylene. Similarly, in gassing experiments on intact plants polyphenol oxidase but not peroxidase or phenylalanine ammonia lyase (PAL) activity was stimulated, whereas on detached leaves Gentile & Matta (1975) reported a major increase in peroxidase.

Although most plant pathogens are capable of producing ethylene there is little evidence in the majority of diseases to indicate that the pathogen contributes measurably to the ethylene pool. In bacterial wilt of banana caused by *Pseudomonas solanacearum*, Freebairn & Buddenhagen (1964) showed that ethylene production in diseased fruit caused premature ripening. Bonn, Sequeira & Upper (1972) claimed that bacterial ethylene production was proportional to the virulence of the strain. However, Pegg & Cronshaw (1976b), working with the same strains, found no correlation between ethylene and virulence. A virulent strain (S225) produced 9.83×10^{-24} mol min^{-1} cell^{-1} and an avirulent (B1) produced 1.8×10^{-22} mol min $^{-1}$ cell^{-1} in culture on a protein hydrolysate carbon source. *In vivo*, 1 g of leaf tissue containing 34.8×10^6 cells of S225 produced ethylene at the rate of 1.275 nl h^{-1} 48 h after inoculation. The *maximum* rate for this strain in culture, however, was 0.009 nl h^{-1} produced by 6.6×10^8 bacteria. There is thus a shortfall of two orders of magnitude in the tissue bacterial cell numbers required to produce the levels of ethylene detected. In this disease it must be concluded that ethylene contributed by bacteria is negligible. Chalutz (1979) presented convincing evidence that ethylene production in *Penicillium digitatum* rot of orange and lemon fruit is largely contributed by the fungus. A non-ethylene-producing fungal isolate, however, was as pathogenic as the wild (ethylene-producing) type, suggesting no role for the gas in pathogenicity. Whereas most pathogens produce only small quantities of the gas, *Fusarium oxysporum* f. sp. *tulipae* produces up to 4000 vpm *in vitro*. In *Fusarium* disease of tulips ethylene functions directly as a gaseous toxin, stunting and distorting flowers in the soil and in packs of cut blooms (Smith, Meigh & Parker, 1964). The basis of resistance to *F. oxysporum* f. sp. *tulipae* are tuliposides A and B which are converted to methylene and hydroxymethylene butyrolactones. Beijersbergen (1973) and Beijersbergen & Lemmers (1978) have shown that the *de novo* synthesis of tuliposide A in the outer living bulb scale is inhibited when the bulb is exposed to ethylene concentrations of 2 to 20 vpm for 12 to 144 h. No effect on tuliposide degradation could be shown.

Ethylene and resistance

A role for ethylene in disease resistance is based on evidence from (i) plants treated with ethylene gas or ethrel (2-chloro-ethylphosphonic acid) which subsequently show diminished infection or symptoms, (ii) ethylene-induced changes in enzymes which are presumed to be associated with resistance, (iii) ethylene-stimulated biosynthesis of known antifungal chemicals.

Lockhart, Forsyth & Eaves (1968) showed that ethylene reduced the incidence of *Gloeosporium* rot of apple. Hislop, Archer & Hoad (1973) similarly showed a reduction in rot growth of *Sclerotinia fructigena*. Ross & Pritchard (1972) recorded a 20–30% reduction in tobacco mosaic virus lesion growth on tobacco following pre-inoculation gassing. Ethylene-treated tomato plants showed reduced symptoms and colonization when subsequently infected with *Verticillium albo-atrum* (Pegg, 1976a).

Much of the importance of ethylene is attributed to its role in enzyme synthesis. Table 1 lists some of the enzymes known to increase in quantity following ethylene treatment and which change in the diseased plant.

Table 1. *Enzymes which increase in quantity after treatment with ethylene*

Enzyme	Plant	Reference
α-Amylase	Cotton	Herrero & Hall (1960)
	Sweet potato	Stahmann, Clare & Woodbury (1966)
Catalase	Cotton	Herrero & Hall (1960)
Cellulase	Dwarf bean	Abeles (1969); Abeles & Leather (1971)
Chitinase	Dwarf bean	Abeles, Forrence & Habig (1971)
1, 3-β-Glucanase	Dwarf bean	Abeles *et al.* (1971)
	Tomato	Pegg (1976b)
Cinnamic acid-4-hydroxylase	Pea	Hyodo & Yang (1971)
Invertase	Morning Glory	Shimokawa & Kasai (1968)
Peroxidase	Sweet potato	Shannon, Uritani & Imaseki (1971); Imaseki (1970)
Phenylalanine ammonia lyase	Citrus fruit	Riov, Monselise & Kahan (1969)
	Sweet potato	Imaseki, Teranishi & Uritani (1968)
Polyphenol oxidase	Sweet potato	Stahmann *et al.* (1966)
	Tomato	Pegg (1976a)
Pectin esterase	Cotton	Herrero & Hall (1960)

Peroxidases, catalase and polyphenol oxidases have been found to increase in resistant reactions and have thus been considered important markers of a resistance mechanism (Fehrmann & Dimond, 1967; Macko, Woodbury & Stahmann, 1968; Benedict, 1972). The latter stems from their role in oxidizing host or fungal metabolites such as phenolic substances, IAA, toxins, etc. Hydrogen peroxide is extremely phytotoxic and peroxidases are envisaged as removing free (potentially damaging) H_2O_2 in host substrate oxidations, while catalase degrades it directly. Lovrekovich, Low & Stahmann (1967) found that infection of tobacco with heat-killed cells of *Pseudomonas tabaci* induced a defence reaction protecting against subsequent inoculation with live cells, while showing a substantial increase in peroxidase. Disease development was also suppressed following injection of horseradish peroxidase. Nadolny & Sequeira (1980), working on *Pseudomonas solanacearum,* confirmed the increase in peroxidase but found that cells of *Escherichia coli* and *Bacillus subtilis,* which *did not* induce protection, also caused increased peroxidase and the induction of a novel peroxidase isozyme. The conclusion drawn from this work is that increased peroxidase probably results incidentally from a wound reaction and may involve wound ethylene.

Pegg (1976*a*) found that pre-inoculation gassing of tomatoes with ethylene at 10.0 vpm substantially reduced vascular colonization by *Verticillium albo-atrum* and increased xylem differentiation. 1,3-β-Glucanase was significantly increased in leaves and reduced in stems. Chitinase activity was reduced in stems and leaves. Abeles, Forrence & Habig (1971) found intense stimulation of chitinase in ethylene-treated *Phaseolus* sections. The possibility that ethylene may function in induced resistance as a trigger for the synthesis of enzymes that lyse the pathogen is attractive and requires more work on intact plants.

Ethylene has been shown to stimulate the antifungal compound 6-methoxy-8-hydroxy 3,4-dihydroisocoumarin (MMHD) in carrot. The enhanced production of this compound was strictly proportional to the ethylene exposure time. IAA, 2,4-D and 2,4,5-T also stimulated MMHD production via endogenous ethylene production (Carlton, Peterson, Tolbert, 1961; Chalutz, DeVay & Maxie, 1969). Chalutz & Stahmann (1969) also showed that pisatin could be induced by ethylene treatment. The evidence to date suggests an important role for ethylene in disease resistance. The timing of the response, however, in relation to infection is critical. Moreover, the wounding effect produced in plant tissue or organ experiments necessitates careful techniques which simulate as closely as possible naturally-occurring events on whole plants.

Auxins

Growth substances based on the indole nucleus are referred to as auxins. The principle auxin, indol-3-yl-acetic acid, is widespread in higher plants and is produced readily from tryptophan by a wide range of fungal and bacterial pathogens and saprophytes (see Gruen, 1959). Although plants contain a number of indolyl metabolities such as indol-3-yl-acetonitrile (IAN) or indol-3-yl-ethanol (tryptophol), it is likely that the ultimate growth substance is IAA. The propensity for saprophytic bacteria to form IAA, given suitable precursors, has caused Libbert (see Libbert *et al.*, (1968) and Libbert & Silhengst (1970) for full references) to question the accuracy of cited IAA values where extraction conditions were unsterile. Hyperauxiny has been described for many diseases even where symptoms give no indication of excessive growth, for example cereals infected by rusts or mildew.

Research into auxin involvement in plant disease has for the most part been based on the following questions: (i) What is the source of IAA in the diseased host? (ii) What role does IAA play in pathogenesis and resistance?

Host involvement in IAA synthesis

Sequeira (1973) and Pegg (1973c) have listed examples of increased levels of auxins in a variety of plant diseases. The ability of the pathogen to synthesize IAA *in vitro*, however, especially on a tryptophan-containing medium, provides no evidence for a direct contribution of the pathogen to the host's IAA pool. The generally accepted pathway of IAA synthesis in higher plants and in many microorganisms is from tryptophan by decarboxylation to tryptamine, which is oxidized to indol-3-yl-acetaldehyde before conversion to IAA. Alternatively, under the activity of an amino transferase, tryptophan is deaminated to indol-3-yl-pyruvic acid, which is decarboxylated to IAA. Many bacteria use this pathway or may convert anthranilic acid either direct from the shikimic acid pathway or from tryptophan-derived kynurenine to IAA. Working with *Pseudomonas solanacearum* wilt of tobacco, Sequeira & Williams (1964) established that a virulent isolate preferentially utilized ring-labelled rather than chain-labelled UL ^{14}C-tryptophan. This was via the kynurenine–anthranilate pathway. A non-pathogenic mutant produced five times more IAA than the virulent isolate utilizing both ring and chain-labelled tryptophan. The virulent isolate was unable to synthesize IAA from tryptophan via tryptamine. When UL ^{14}C-tryptamine was fed to tobacco plants prior to inoculation, labelled IAA was produced by the host plant up to six days after inoculation. Sequeira & Williams (1964) concluded that over this period at least, the enhanced levels of IAA were of host origin. Subsequent increases in non-labelled IAA were from host precursors, for which a bacterial involvement could not be eliminated. Pegg & Sequeira (1968) showed that *de novo* synthesis of tryptophan occurred 12 h after inoculation, providing an excess of precursor at 144 h. In most other host–pathogen relationships studied the pathogen has been either obligate or has had the same IAA biosynthetic pathway as the host, thereby making a comparison of the individual contributions difficult or impossible.

Direct pathogen involvement in hyperauxiny

Pseudomonas savastanoi causes severe gall cankers on a range of host plants including ash, olive and oleanders. From the work of Beltra (1961) it was known that galling in olive was associated with growth substance production in cultures, and Magie & Wilson (1962) identified IAA. Kosuge, Heskett & Wilson (1966) showed that IAA was derived from indol-3-yl-acetamide (IAm) from oxidative decarboxylation of tryptophan and its synthesis was regulated through a feedback mechanism by IAA, IAm or tryptophan. Smidt & Kosuge (1978) obtained mutants of *P. savastanoi* which failed to produce IAA, or produced twice as much as the wild type when cultured on a medium containing α-methyl tryptophan (MT). MT induced an altered form of anthranilate synthetase in tolerant mutants which is not sensitive to MT inhibition. This enzyme was considered to be insensitive to tryptophan feedback inhibition. Thus in MT-resistant mutants, increased anthranilic acid led to increased tryptophan and increased IAA which did not repress the enzyme.

Using these mutants, Smidt & Kosuge (1978) showed that the ability to induce galling in oleander was correlated with the ability to produce IAA. Moreover, the size of galls was to a great extent proportional to the quantity of IAA synthesized *in vitro*. Non-IAA-producing mutants failed to induce galling.

Regulation of IAA by pathogen enzymes

Although stunting syndromes are frequently interpreted in terms of host or pathogen inhibitors, they may also result from a deficit in endogenous regulators. With a multiplicity of interacting systems operating such an effect is difficult to establish. Abscission, on the other hand, presents a *prima facie* case for auxin imbalance. Sequeira & Steeves (1954) claimed that leaf gall in coffee and other plants, resulting from *Omphalia flavida* (*Mycena citricola*) infection, was due to proximal IAA oxidation by a fungal extracellular IAA oxidase. The evidence for this was circumstantial, but filtrates from 12 cultures of *Omphalia* degraded IAA at up to 500 μg h^{-1}, stimulated by Mn^{2+}. Rodrigues & Arny (1966) confirmed the IAA oxidation in coffee leaves *in vivo* using ^{14}C-IAA. Kazmaier (1960) showed that culture filtrates of *Diplocarpon rosae* could also inactivate IAA. It is known, however, that ethylene is also produced in *Diplocarpon*-infected tissue and the precise role of IAA, ethylene and possibly ABA *in vivo* in diseases causing foliar abscission has yet to be demonstrated.

Regulation of IAA by host enzymes

Much work has been done on hyperauxiny in diseases caused by biotrophic pathogens and, in particular, by rusts. Most increases in IAA, or IAA equivalents, in diseased plants have been of the order of five-fold, but Shaw & Hawkins (1958) reported increases of 24-fold in the susceptible wheat cultivar Little Club infected with race 15B of *Puccinia graminis*. Unlike most diseases where IAA is increased, rust-infected cereals do not manifest abnormal cellular growth. Attempts have been made by Shaw and Daly and their colleagues to relate the decarboxylation of IAA and peroxidase activity in cereals to major gene rust resistance. This idea is based on experiments like those of Samborski & Shaw (1957) in which applications of anti-auxins such as maleic hydrazide increased susceptibility in the rust-resistant wheat cultivar Khapli and, conversely, treatment with IAA slightly increased resistance. Notwithstanding the detailed studies on decarboxylation of IAA in resistant and susceptible cereals, the position is still confusing and the real importance of IAA in rust pathogenicity, if any, is unclear. Shaw & Hawkins (1958) reported levels of IAA of 0.5 μg kg^{-1} fresh weight in healthy Little Club wheat (susceptible) and in healthy and infected Khapli (resistant), while infected Little Club had 2.4 μg kg^{-1} fresh weight. This increase in IAA in Little Club correlated with decreased carboxylation (oxidation/peroxidation) of labelled indolyl potassium acetate in feeding experiments on the susceptible host. This work showed large experimental variation and IAA levels were based on bioassay with no account taken of endogenous inhibitors which might modify the IAA coleoptile response. Subsequent work by Daly & Deverall (1963) on Little Club showed reduced decarboxylation in inoculated plants 2, 3 and 4 days after inoculation in the pre-sporulation period. At 9, 10 and 11 days, during sporulation, decarboxylation was three times greater. Some confusion has arisen in the interpretation of this and other work by a failure to distinguish (*a*) between *net* IAA production in susceptible hosts, regardless of the intensity of IAA-destroying systems, and (*b*) the degree of reduction of endogenous levels in resistant hosts. Comparisons of Little Club and Khapli were made difficult by the activity of modifier genes affecting the genes for resistance. However, when Antonelli & Daly (1966) examined near isogenic lines of Chinese spring wheat containing the temperature-sensitive *Sr6* allele for resistance (incompatibility) and the corresponding *sr6* allele for susceptibility, decarboxylation was unaltered in *sr6* plants after inoculation but a substantial increase in IAA decarboxylation occurred in *Sr6* plants 3 to 4 days after inoculation. If such findings reflected changes in IAA levels *in vivo,* the end result would appear to conflict with the findings of Samborski & Shaw (1957). Seevers & Daly (1970) found fairly good correlation between peroxidase activity and changes in IAA decarboxylation. The role of IAA and peroxidase (presumably acting as an IAA oxidase/peroxidase) in resistance is made more uncertain by the temperature reversal of *Sr6* resistance. At 25–26 °C plants with the *Sr6* allele behaved like *sr6* wheat, but there was no corresponding decrease in peroxidase activity. Treatment of susceptible and resistant wheat cultivars with ethylene (80 vpm) at 20–21 °C increased peroxidase (including new isozymes) in both. In these experiments, however, the *Sr6* allele became susceptible. These results and those of Nadolny & Sequeira (1980) suggest that changes in *total* peroxidase activity may be irrelevant to endogenous IAA levels and to major gene resistance in general (see Daly & Knoche, 1976). Some of the regulation of IAA levels in diseased plants can be attributed to the action of phenolic compounds which may act as stimulators or inhibitors of IAA oxidase systems. In general, orthodihydric phenols or polyphenols inhibit, while monohydric phenols activate or accelerate IAA oxidase. Since many of these occur as products of the shikimic acid pathway (see Kosuge & Kimpel, this volume), the induction of a specific hydroxylase may indirectly control IAA accumulation via the stimulation or inhibition of its destructive system.

It is now clear that light, phenol synthesis, lignification and auxin regulation are all intimately involved in plant pathogenesis and resistance. The details of this subject now need to be worked out by the simultaneous examination of all these aspects and their enzymic control for particular diseases under defined conditions.

Cytokinins

By definition cytokinins are substances capable of inducing cell division in callus tissue. Additionally they stimulate the growth of lateral buds, delay senescence of detached leaves and stimulate the germination of some dormant seeds. Naturally-occuring cytokinins are substituted adenine derivatives for the most part with an isoprenoid side chain. Since tRNA species, corresponding to codons with the initial base U(racil), contain 2-isopentenyladenosine (2iP) in a position adjacent to the anti-codon of the tRNA, a biological role for cytokinins has been suggested in relation to tRNA activity. The origin of 'free' cytokinins as isolated from healthy and diseased plants, and their mechanism of action in relation to RNA metabolism, are not yet clear and some research suggests that applied cytokinins are not simply bound onto tRNA and may have an independent mode of action.

It has been assumed that galling and tissue overgrowths involving hyperplasia must be associated with an imbalance of cytokinins. The evidence for this exists for a limited number of examples only.

Fasciation and shoot proliferation

Corynebacterium fascians causes leafy galls, fasciation and shoot proliferation in herbaceous plants. Thimann & Sachs (1966) discovered cytokinin activity in culture filtrates of the bacterium and by application of these to pea plants were able to reproduce some of the symptoms of natural infection. Klämbt, Thies & Skoog (1966) and Helgeson & Leonard (1966) isolated and characterized 2iP. Sachs & Thimann (1967) showed that 2iP, kinetin and the synthetic benzyl adenine all induced symptoms of *C. fascians* infection. Although superficially the results suggest a cause and effect relationship between bacterium, bacterial 2iP and host symptoms, there are several reservations. Relatively high concentrations ($0.03\mu g$) are required to cause pea bud growth, and swelling from natural infection is greater than from applied cytokinins alone. Moreover, the concentration produced *in vitro* is in the range 2 μg litre^{-1} (Rathbone & Hall, 1972) to 10 μg litre^{-1} (Klämbt *et al.*, 1966). The possibility is high in this disease as in others that the bacterium stimulates excess production of *host* cytokinins as well as other endogenous growth regulators.

Crown gall

Crown gall induced in a wide range of host plants by *Agrobacterium tumefaciens* has been the subject of intensive research over many years (see Lippincott & Lippincott, 1976). Based on the nature of the hypertrophic and hyperplastic gall tissue, various workers have suggested an hormonal imbalance as the primary cause of the symptoms based on the finding of IAA (Dye, Clarke & Wain, 1962) and cytokinins (Klämbt, 1967; Upper, Helgeson, Kemp & Schmidt, 1970) in gall tissue and the fact that IAA supplied to the stems will induce neoplasms. Romanow, Chalvignac & Pochon (1969) showed that a virulent strain of *A. tumefaciens* produced cytokinins, while an avirulent strain growing on an adenine-enriched medium did not. However, galled tissue is self-sufficient for IAA and cytokinins when grown as a continuous culture, unlike comparable healthy callus cultures. This argues strongly against a direct participation of bacterial regulators in symptom formation. The nature of the induction of neoplastic growth has led to the postulation of a tumor-inducing principle (TIP). More recently Quetier, Huguet & Guille (1969) and Schilperoort *et al.* (1973) have suggested that the TIP is extracellular bacterial DNA, or that it is very closely related to bacterial DNA. Two cytokinin-like compounds, cytokinesin I and II, have been isolated from crown gall. Cytokinesin I is a glucose-containing 3,7-dialkyl-2 alkylthio-6-purinone (Wood, 1970). Kinetin treatment of *Vinca rosea* cells induces cytokinesin I formation. This substance, like theophylline (1,3 dimethylxanthine), is a powerful inhibitor of 3^1, 5^1 cyclic AMP-phosphodiesterase (Wood, Lin & Braun, 1972) and both promote cell division of tobacco callus. This suggests that kinetin-like substances in crown gall promote cytokinesins which inhibit cyclic AMP esterases, resulting in an increase in cyclic AMP levels. The relationship between cyclic AMP and hyperplasia, however, is not clear. Other substances such as fluorene derivatives which are unrelated to cytokinesin I or cyclic AMP induce tobacco callus in the absence of exogenous cytokinins. In spite of the voluminous literature on growth hormones and crown gall, more work is needed, particularly in relation to cyclic AMP, cytokinins and unrestricted cell division.

Club root

Root galls in plants infected with *Plasmodiophora brassicae* have been shown to contain abnormally high amounts of auxins, particularly IAN and cytokinins (Matsubara & Nakahira, 1967; Dekhuijzen & Overeem, 1971; Butcher, El-Tigani & Ingram, 1974). Dekhuijzen & Overeem (1971) found total cytokinin activity of 1–10 μg kg^{-1} fresh weight clubs expressed as zeatin equivalents. These levels were 10–100 times higher than the cytokinin contents of healthy roots. When *infected* root gall is grown as a tissue culture, the cells are independent of exogenous auxins and cytokinin, although maximal growth requires supplemental auxin (Williams, Reddy & Strandberg, 1969). Reddy & Williams (1970) have shown the presence of at least three cytokinins in infected gall tissue cultures grown on a cytokinin-free medium. Unlike crown gall, however, the independency for growth regulators is lost when the gall is cultured free from the pathogen. Williams (1966) has shown large increases in DNA and nucleolar RNA in hypertrophic cells containing the pathogen. In these circumstances cell division was inhibited. Cell division and RNA synthesis appear to be critically determined by the mass of the plasmodium which, when large, stimulates reduplication of nuclear DNA with a corresponding increase in nuclear, nucleolar and cell volume. Cells not containing the pathogen show no stimulated cell division (Williams, 1966), suggesting that this process and the involvement of cytokinins is intimately related to the interaction of host cytoplasm and plasmodium.

Maize smut tumour

Ustilago maydis induces large neoplastic galls in maize in centres of meristematic activity, cobs and stem and leaf intercalary meristems. Early work by Moulton (1942) and Wolf (1952) reported increased IAA levels in tumours, and IAA production by *U. maydis*. Magro & Marciano (1974) showed that auxins were not solely responsible for neoplastic growth. Mills & Van Staden (1978), using teliospore-infected maize apices showing greatly enhanced growth, found a number of cytokinins in healthy and diseased plants. Cytokinins corresponding to zeatin, zeatin riboside and zeatin glucoside were present in both, but in somewhat greater amounts in infected plants. A unique polar cytokinin, which was also produced in *U. maydis* cultures, was found in diseased apices in amounts proportional to the growth increase.

Metabolic effects

The phenomenon of 'green islands', residual areas of chlorophyllous tissue surrounded by chlorotic tissue is associated with lesions caused by biotrophic pathogens such as rusts, powdery and downy mildews. It may also be mimicked by application of cytokinins (kinetin, benzyl adenine) to leaves, in which case chlorophyll retention is increased and chlorophyllase activity arrested. The suggestion that the green island effect is cytokinin-induced is based on a number of circumstantial observations and deductions. Thus, as described by Whipps & Lewis (this volume), biotrophs appear to redirect metabolites to the infection pustule, which acts as a nutrient sink. Earlier, Mothes & Engelbrecht (1961) had demonstrated that sites of cytokinin droplets on leaves behaved similarly. Király, El Hammady & Pozsar (1967) and Dekhuijzen & Staples (1968) showed that extracts of rust-infected bean leaves gave cytokinin responses in several bioassays, while Bushnell & Allen (1962) and Bushnell (1966) induced a green island effect with water-soluble extracts from the conidia of *Erysiphe graminis*. The contribution of cytokinins by the pathogen, however, is doubtful since Dekhuijzen, Singh & Staples (1967) showed that the cytokinins from bean-rust-infected leaves were different from tRNA hydrolysates from rust uredospores or isolated mycelium. It should be noted that green islands can be induced by fungal metabolites unrelated to cytokinins, e.g. arabitol and mannitol (Daly & Knoche, 1976) and siderochromes (Atkin & Neilands, 1972).

Gibberellins and gibberellin-like substances

Prior to 1956, when West & Phinney (1956) and Radley (1956) discovered gibberellins as naturally-occurring growth substances of higher plants, this group of compounds represented by gibberellic acid (GA_3) from *Gibberella fujikuroi* were recognized more as fungal toxins than as growth substances *per se*. Gibberellins are cyclic diterpenes and show a wide range of activity on plant growth and metabolism, viz, internode elongation, flower induction, reversal of dwarfism, sub-apical cell division, induction of parthenocarpy, stimulation of α- and β-amylase, stimulation of cellulase and stimulation or inhibition of ethylene production depending on the plant species (see Abeles, 1973). The rice pathogen *G. fujikuroi* produces a range of 20 or more gibberellins in culture of which GA_3 is one. The symptoms of 'bakanae' disease of rice, caused by the conidial stage of this pathogen (*Fusarium moniliforme*), are excessive stem internode growth and rotting of the collar region. Similar symptoms of elongation may be induced in rice and a wide range of di- and monocotyledons by the application of GA_3, or other gibberellins which also occur in culture filtrates and in certain higher plant genera. On a suitable medium, *F. moniliforme* will produce 1.0 g GA_3 litre^{-1}, whereas dwarf maize and pea plants will give growth extension log dose responses in the general range of 0.02 to 12 μg per plant (some maize mutants will respond to as little as 0.001 μg per plant). While this would seem to be good evidence for a 'cause and effect' relationship between pathogen and host, it should be remembered that GA_3 is an endogenous gibberellin of healthy rice. Muromtsev & Globus (1976) have suggested an alternative role for GA_3 in the 'bakanae' syndrome. Strains of *F. moniliforme* which were incapable of producing GA_3 in culture all produced a constitutive α-amylase. Thus GA_3 could be seen primarily as a stimulus to α-amylase synthesis for the hydrolysis of starch, providing respiratory substrate for the pathogen. Where a constitutive α-amylase was present, this role for GA_3 would be superfluous. Unfortunately no information is available on the pathogenicity or symptom pattern induced by non-gibberellin-producing isolates.

Bailiss & Wilson (1967) carried out a detailed analysis of the growth of *Cirsium arvense* infected by *Puccinia punctiformis* in relation to levels of endogenous gibberellins. *P. punctiformis* is partially systemic in thistle and infected plants grow taller than healthy plants during the early part of the season. During this period increases were found in infected plants in a single gibberellin-like substance (GLS) corresponding in chromatographic characteristics to GA_1 or GA_2. Since this was present in healthy plants, but in lower concentration, the GLS increase was interpreted as pathogen stimulation of host endogenous compounds. Subsequently, at 3–8 weeks a major peak of activity occurred corresponding to GA_3. Thereafter, when the growth of healthy and infected plants was comparable, the levels of these two GLSs were identical in both plants. To date, the work of Bailiss & Wilson is the most convincing for providing a close correlation between endogenous gibberellins and host growth.

In contrast to the foregoing, the smut infection of sea campion (*Silene vulgaris* subsp. *maritima*) by *Ustilago violacea* is characterized by stunting. Evans & Wilson (1971) found a reduction in one major GLS corresponding to GA_3. However, the pathogen produces IAN in culture and IAN levels *in vivo* rise only in the infected plant. Applications of GA_3 but not IAN reversed the stunting syndrome. Curiously, smut infection causes a change in the sex of the flowers – a phenomenon usually attributed to gibberellins.

In virus infections any changes of growth substance are host-mediated. Bailiss (1974, 1977) showed that the development of stunting in cucumber caused by cucumber mosaic virus is associated with a progressive reduction in GLSs corresponding to GA_1 and GA_3. No differences were found in levels of the endogenous growth inhibitor *cis*-abscisic acid (ABA) (see later), indicating that ABA is not involved in disease-induced stunting. Considerable difficulty is encountered in attempts to interpret stunting in terms of changes of growth regulators in view of the complex interaction of these with multiple sites of action. One explanation for stunting could be the compartmentalization of host nutrients in tissues or cells containing the pathogen, i.e. nutrient sinks, depriving growth centres in the plant of an adequate supply of essential metabolites. In this case growth hormones, especially cytokinins and gibberellins, would play a dominant role. Alternatively, a reduction in sub-apical mitosis, caused either by a pathogenic toxin at sub-lethal dose, or a reduction in cytokinins, would result in stunting regardless of other growth substance changes which superficially might not support this effect. Kuriger & Agrios (1977) found such a negative correlation between mitosis in cowpea root tips following tobacco ringspot virus infection and the levels of extractable cytokinins. Misaghi, DeVay & Kosuge (1972) showed a marked reduction in one of three cytokinins in cotton plants infected with *Verticillium dahliae*. Cotton wilt, like tomato *Verticillium* wilt in which a similar reduction in cytokinins has been shown, involves stunting (Patrick, Hall & Fletcher, 1977), but no investigations on meristem mitotic activity have been conducted in these diseases.

Inhibitors

Bentley (1958) described a range of naturally-occurring compounds in higher plants which function as growth inhibitors in bioassays. Many of these are phenolic in nature including aesculin, scopoletin, chlorogenic acid and cinnamic acid and its derivatives. Although these may increase in diseased tissue, virtually nothing is known about their growth-limiting properties in the host plant.

The sesquiterpenoid ABA is regarded as the major growth inhibitor in plants in a hormonal sense (see Pegg, 1976*f*). Attempts have been made by Pegg & Selman (1959), Van Steveninck (1959) and Steadman & Sequeira (1969) to implicate ABA (or putative ABA) in the stunting syndrome in fungus-, virus- and bacterium-infected plants. The work of Wright & Hiron (1969), Mittelheuser & Van Steveninck (1969) and Jones & Mansfield (1970) established a primary role for ABA in stomatal closure. Wilting in healthy plants is accomplished by a rapid rise in ABA level. It follows therefore that where stunting is accompanied by loss of turgor – especially in vascular wilt diseases – levels of ABA will rise as a result and not as a cause of the syndrome. When tomato seedlings are inoculated with *Verticillium albo-atrum* at the cotyledon stage, stunting and especially reduced leaf area and slow acropetal desiccation develop rather than wilting. Depending on the distribution of mycelium in the vascular bundles, single leaves may show acute reduction in area in the absence of other symptoms.

Table 2 shows the endogenous levels of *cis*-ABA in six-week-old shoots of resistant (R) and susceptible (S) tomato isolines, root-inoculated with 4×10^5 bud cells of *V. albo-atrum*. Although 18 and 25 days after inoculation leaf area of the S line was reduced by 63 and 55% respectively, no significant differences in overall ABA content could be found. When individual leaves and stems were examined, only the youngest leaves (5–7) in susceptible plants showed a marked increase over the resistant symptomless leaves (Fig. 2). Maximum levels detected were 0.28 μg *cis*-ABA g^{-1} fresh weight. Attempts were made to simulate unilateral symptoms of leaf area reduction by applying 1000 μg *cis*-ABA to leaf 3 of plants at the six-leaf stage. (ABA exists as a *cis,trans* racemic mixture in nature, but only the *cis* isomer is active.) Growth was reduced by

33% in the leaf receiving 1000 μg ABA and in the higher subtending leaf (Fig. 3), but after surface washing their endogenous level of *cis*-ABA was 2.0 μg ABA g^{-1}, 100-fold higher than the more severely stunted infected leaf. When healthy and *V. albo-atrum*-infected susceptible tomato plants were grown in sealed containers with a controlled root water supply and maintained in a water

Table 2. *Levels of* cis-*abscisic acid (ABA) in healthy and* Verticillium albo-atrum-*infected resistant and susceptible tomato plants, cultivar Craigella. (Mean values from five plants)*

	Days after inoculation	Craigella R		Craigella S	
		ABA (μg g^{-1})	Leaf area (cm^2)	ABA (μg g^{-1})	Leaf area (cm^2)
Healthy	11	0.01*	30	0.08	31
(autoclaved	18	0.07	120	0.23	115
inoculum)	25	0.22	320	0.14	335
	11	0.01	32	0.01	23
Infected	18	0.24	119	0.24	44
	25	0.24	325	0.25	147

*Data based on tissue ether extracts chromatographed on Merck F254 TLC plates with authentic *cis*-ABA. *cis*-ABA was determined by GLC using a stationary phase of 5% OV225 at an isothermal temperature of 180 °C. Experiments with added *cis*-ABA showed a recovery of 60%. For further details see Pegg (1976*f*).

Fig. 2. Levels of *cis*-abscisic acid (ABA) in leaves and stems of resistant (R) and susceptible (S) tomato plants, cultivar Craigella, following inoculation with *Verticillium albo-atrum*.

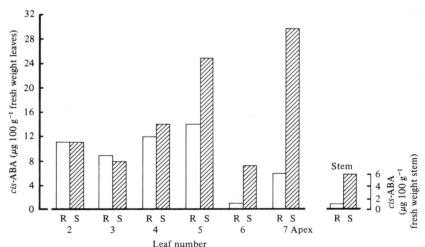

saturated atmosphere with continuous leaf surface wetness (Fig. 4), no diminution in leaf stunting occurred and infected plants were more severely affected than those maintained under normal glasshouse conditions. It is concluded that increased ABA levels found in vascular wilt stunting by different workers are

Fig. 3. Effect of 1000μg of exogenously applied *cis*-abscisic acid (ABA) on the area of treated, third leaf, and subtending leaves of Potentate tomato plants at the six-leaf stage (●–––●). (No photolysis of ABA occurred under the conditions of the experiment.) O—O, untreated controls.

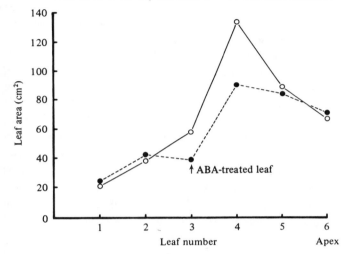

Fig. 4. The effect of continuous leaf surface wetness on leaf growth in healthy and *Verticillium*-infected tomato plants, cultivar Potentate. ●—●, healthy mist; ▲—▲, healthy non-mist; ▲–––▲, infected non-mist; ●–––●, infected mist. Bars are LSD (*P* = 0.05).

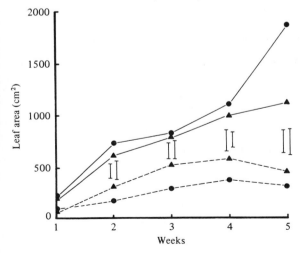

not the *direct* cause of stunting but rather they are related to the development of water deficits.

Microbial toxins with growth regulator properties

Fusicoccin

The intense interest in fusicoccin, the toxin produced by *Fusicoccum amygdali* (canker and vascular wilt of peach and almond), results from the fact that it exhibits growth-promoting properties reminiscent of auxins and also cytokinins and gibberellins. Since it is an alien molecule in the plant, research workers are able to study its mode of action in isolation from natural metabolites. Fusicoccin, in addition to opening stomata (as discussed by Ayres, this volume), promotes germination of light-requiring seeds such as lettuce and *Phacelia,* a process also stimulated by gibberellins and cytokinins (Lado, Rasi-Caldogno & Colombo 1974). Significantly, like IAA, it induces extension growth in pea stem segments and increases of fresh weight in a number of species (Marrè, Colombo, Lado & Rasi-Caldogno, 1974). Unlike IAA, fusicoccin promotes root growth in a range of species and at high concentrations (Pilet, 1976). The basic mechanism by which all these growth effects are brought about is an extrusion of protons from the cell. Since Strugger's (1934) work it has been known that acidic buffers will induce *Avena* coleoptiles to extend ('acid growth') and that IAA treatment causes a reduction in pH of the bathing solution. Fusicoccin treatment is accompanied by a negative shift in the transmembrane potential and growth of tissue is proportional to the reduction in external pH, i.e. the degree of proton extrusion. H^+ extrusion is accompanied by Na^+ extrusion and a rapid influx of K^+ with a corresponding stimulated uptake of sugars, amino acids and anions. The net

Table 3. *Cellular effects of fusicoccin*

1. Proton extrusion
2. Hyperpolarization of the membrane potential
3. Stimulated cation uptake
4. Stimulated anion uptake
5. Na^+ extrusion
6. Stimulated sugar and amino acid uptake
7. Stimulated respiration and dark carbon dioxide–malate fixation
8. Increased pyruvate and glucose-6-phosphate levels
9. Stimulated cell enlargement in stems, roots and leaves
10. Stimulated stomatal opening
11. Breaking of seed dormancy
12. Enhanced membrane water permeability

effect is an increase in osmotic potential of the cell and enhanced cellular metabolism. Several binding proteins for IAA have now been described on the plasmalemma and tonoplast in cells of different plants. The evidence for fusicoccin suggests that IAA and fusicoccin stimulate a plasmalemma K^+, Mg^{2+}-activated ATP-ase as a result of binding which provides the energy for H^+ extrusion. All treatments which suppress the intracellular ATP level similarly suppress fusicoccin-promoted H^+/K^+ exchange. Fusicoccin and ABA seem to operate at the same site but with opposing effects on K^+ transport. The effects of fusicoccin *in vivo* are summarized in Table 3.

The toxin cotylenin (Sassa, Togashi & Kitaguchi, 1975) shows structural and physiological similarities to fusicoccin. Ophiobolin, however, which is structurally similar, lacks the growth and ion transport attributes of fusicoccin. Studies on fusicoccin may be invaluable for mode-of-action studies on endogenous growth regulators since the former may act at a single specific site, e.g. H^+ extrusion, while growth regulators have a multiplicity of interactive sites which makes interpretation difficult.

Helminthosporol and derivatives

The sesquiterpenoid alcohol helminthosporol from *Helminthosporium sativum* causes necrosis and chlorosis in oat and wheat infected by this pathogen. Helminthosporol, the corresponding aldehyde and helminthosporic acid were shown by Tamura, Sakurai, Kainuma & Takai (1963) to cause elongation in rice and growth elongation in other species (Hashimoto & Tamura, 1967). In these tests helminthosporol and its derivatives seemed to be functioning like a gibberellin.

Other toxins

Victorin (*Helminthosporium sativum*) and Race-T toxin (*Helminthosporium maydis*) show auxin and cytokinin effects *in vitro* (Evans, 1973, 1974). HM-T toxin seems to function like ABA in preventing light-induced K^+ uptake, thereby closing stomata (Arntzen, Haugh & Bobick, 1973). The substituted isocoumarins – diaporthins, produced by a range of saprophytes and pathogens – function variously as toxins, phytoalexins or as growth promoters. Hadicin (n-formyl hydroxyaminoacetic acid) produced by *Penicillium frequentans* and *P. purpurescens* induces dwarfing in pea and bean in the absence of necrosis. The malformins produced by *Aspergillus wentii*, as the name implies, induce growth abnormalities in *Phaseolus vulgaris* (Curtis, 1969). These toxins may operate through an ethylene-mediating system, since ethylene and malformins induce similar effects.

References

Abeles, F. B. (1969). Abscission: role of cellulase. *Plant Physiology*, **44**, 447–52.

Abeles, F. B. (1973). *Ethylene in Plant Biology*. London: Academic Press.

Abeles, F. B., Forrence, R. P. & Habig, W. H. (1971). Preparation and purification of glucanase and chitinase from bean leaves. *Plant Physiology*, **47**, 129–34.

Abeles, F. B. & Leather, G. F. (1971). Abscission – control of cellulase secretion by ethylene. *Planta*, **97**, 89–91.

Adams, D. O. & Yang, S. F. (1979). Ethylene biosynthesis: identification of 1-aminocyclopropane-1-carboxylic acid as an intermediate in the conversion of methionine to ethylene. *Proceedings of the National Academy of Science, U.S.A.*, **76**, 170–4.

Antonelli, E. & Daly, J. M. (1966). Decarboxylation of indoleacetic acid by near isogenic lines of wheat resistant or susceptible to *Puccinia graminis tritici*. *Phytopathology*, **56**, 610–18.

Arntzen, F. J., Haugh, M. F. & Bobick, S. (1973). Induction of stomatal closure by *Helminthosporium maydis* pathotoxin. *Plant Physiology*, **52**, 569–74.

Atkin, C. L. & Neilands, J. B. (1972). Leaf infections: siderochromes (natural polyhydroxamates) mimic the 'green island' effect. *Science*, **176**, 300–2.

Bailiss, K. W. (1974). The relationship of gibberellin content to cucumber mosaic virus infection of cucumber. *Physiological Plant Pathology*, **4**, 73–80.

Bailiss, K. W. (1977). Gibberellins, abscisic acid and virus-induced stunting. In *Current Topics in Plant Pathology*, ed. Z. Király, pp. 361–73. Budapest: Akadémiae Kiadó.

Bailiss, K. W. & Wilson, I. M. (1967). Growth hormones and the creeping thistle rust. *Annals of Botany*, N. S., **31**, 195–211.

Beijersbergen, J. C. M. (1973). Reported in *Fungal Pathogenicity and the Plant's Response*, ed. R. J. W. Byrde & C. V. Cutting, p. 114. London: Academic Press.

Beijersbergen, J. C. M. & Lemmers, C. B. G. (1978). Influence of ethylene produced by *Fusarium oxysporum* on the postulated mechanism underlying the resistance of *Tulipa* sp. tissues to this fungus. *Proceedings of the 3rd International Congress of Plant Pathology, Munchen*, 1978, p. 229.

Beltra, R. (1961). Efecto morfoginetico observado en los extractos hormonales de los tumores del olivo. *Microbiologia Espanola*, **14**, 177–87.

Benedict, W. G. (1972). Influence of light on peroxidase activity associated with resistance of tomato cultivars to *Septoria lycopersici*. *Canadian Journal of Botany*, **50**, 1931–6.

Bentley, J. A. (1958). The naturally-occurring auxins and inhibitors. *Annual Review of Plant Physiology*, **9**, 47–80.

Bonn, W. G., Sequeira, L. & Upper, C. D. (1972). *Determination of the rate of ethylene production by* Pseudomonas solanacearum. *Proceedings of the Canadian Phytopathological Society*, No. 39.

Burroughs, L. F. (1957). 1, Aminocyclopropane-1-carboxylic acid: a new amino acid in Perry pears and cider apples. *Nature*, **179**, 360–1.

Bushnell, W. R. (1966). Delay of senescence in wheat leaves by cytokinins, nickel and other substances. *Canadian Journal of Botany*, **44**, 1485–93.

Bushnell, W. R. & Allen, P. J. (1962). Induction of disease symptoms in barley by powdery mildew. *Plant Physiology*, **37**, 50–9.

Butcher, D. N., El-Tigani, S. & Ingram, D. S. (1974). The role of indole glucosinolates in the club root disease in the *Cruciferae*. *Physiological Plant Pathology*, **4**, 127–41.

Cameron, A. C., Fenton, C. A. L., Yu, Y., Adams, D. O. & Yang, S. F. (1979). Increased production of ethylene by plant tissues treated with 1-aminocyclopropane-1-carboxylic acid. *Horticultural Science*, **14**, 178–80.

Carlton, B. C., Peterson, C. E. & Tolbert, N. E. (1961). Effects of ethylene and oxygen production on a bitter compound by carrot roots. *Plant Physiology*, **36**, 550.

Chalutz, E. (1979). No role for ethylene in the pathogenicity of *Penicillium digitatum*. *Physiological Plant Pathology*, **14**, 259–62.

Chalutz, E., DeVay, J. E. & Maxie, E. C. (1969). Ethylene-induced isocoumarin formation in carrot root tissue. *Plant Physiology*, **44**, 235–41.

Chalutz, E. & Stahmann, M. A. (1969). Induction of pisatin by ethylene. *Phytopathology*, **59**, 1972–3.

Chou, T. W. & Yang, S. F. (1973). The biogenesis of ethylene in *Penicillium digitatum*. *Archives of Biochemistry and Biophysics*, **157**, 73–82.

Cronshaw, D. K. & Pegg, G. F. (1976). Ethylene as a toxin synergist in *Verticillium* wilt of tomato. *Physiological Plant Pathology*, **9**, 33–4.

Curtis, R. W. (1969). Effects of malformin on the major constituents of *Phaseolus vulgaris*. *Plant Cell Physiology*, **10**, 203–11.

Daly, J. M. & Deverall, B. J. (1963). Metabolism of indoleacetic acid in rust diseases. 1. Factors influencing rates of decarboxylation. *Plant Physiology*, **38**, 741–50.

Daly, J. M. & Knoche, H. W. (1976). Hormonal involvement in metabolism of host–parasite interactions. In *Biochemical Aspects of Plant–Parasite Relationships*, ed. J. Friend & D. R. Threlfall, pp. 117–33. London: Academic Press.

Dekhuijzen, H. M. & Overeem, J. C. (1971). The role of cytokinins in club root formation. *Physiological Plant Pathology*, **1**, 151–62.

Dekhuijzen, H. M., Singh, H. & Staples R. C. (1967). Some properties of hyphae isolated from bean leaves infected with the bean rust fungus. *Contribution to Boyce Thompson Institute*, **23**, 367–72.

Dekhuijzen, H. M. & Staples, R. C. (1968). Mobilization factors in uredospores and bean leaves infected with bean rust fungus. *Contribution to Boyce Thompson Institute*, **24**, 39–52.

Dimond, A. E. & Waggoner, P. E. (1953). The cause of epinastic symptoms in *Fusarium* wilt of tomatoes. *Phytopathology*, **43**, 663–9.

Dye, M. H., Clarke, G. & Wain, R. L. (1962). Investigations on the auxins in tomato crown gall tissue. *Proceedings of the Royal Society, London, B*, **155**, 478–92.

Evans, M. L. (1974). Rapid responses to plant hormones. *Annual Review of Plant Physiology*, **25**, 195–223.

Evans, M. L. (1973). Rapid stimulation of plant cell elongation by hormonal and non-hormonal factors. *Bioscience*, **23**, 711–18.

Evans, S. M. & Wilson, I. M. (1971). The anther smut of sea campion. A study of the role of growth regulators in the dwarfing syndrome. *Annals of Botany*, N.S., **35**, 543–53.

Fehrmann, H. & Dimond, A. E. (1967). Peroxidase activity and *Phytophthora* resistance in different organs of the potato plant. *Phytopathology*, **57**, 68–72.

Fowler, J. L. & Morgan, P. W. (1972). The relationship of the peroxidative indoleacetic acid oxidase system to *in vivo* ethylene synthesis in cotton. *Plant Physiology*, **62**, 161–2.

Freebairn, H. T. & Buddenhagen, I. W. (1964). Ethylene production by *Pseudomonas solanacearum*. *Nature*, **202**, 313–14.

Gentile, I. A. & Matta, A. (1975). Production of and some effects of ethylene in relation to *Fusarium* wilt of tomato. *Physiological Plant Pathology*, **5**, 27–37.

Gruen, H. (1959). Auxins and fungi. *Annual Review of Plant Physiology*, **10**, 405–40.

Hashimoto, T. & Tamura, S. (1967). Physiological activities of helminthosporol and helminthosporic acid. II. Effects on excised plant parts. *Plant Cell Physiology*, **8**, 35–45.

Helgeson, J. P. & Leonard, N. J. (1966). Cytokinins: identification of compounds isolated from *Corynebacterium fascians*. *Proceedings of the National Academy of Science, U.S.A.*, **56**, 60–3.

Herrero, F. A. & Hall, W. C. (1960). General effects of ethylene on enzyme systems in the cotton leaf. *Physiologia Plantarum*, **13**, 736–50.

Hislop, E. C., Archer, S. A. & Hoad, G. V. (1973). Ethylene production by healthy and *Sclerotinia fructigena*-infected apple peel. *Phytochemistry*, **12**, 1281–6.

Hyodo, H. & Yang, S. F. (1971). Ethylene-enhanced formation of cinnamic acid 4-hyroxylase in excised pea epicotyl tissue. *Archives of Biochemistry and Biophysics*, **143**, 338–9.

Imaseki, H. (1970). Induction of peroxidase activity by ethylene in sweet potato. *Plant Physiology*, **46**, 172–4.

Imaseki, H., Teranishi, T. & Uritani, I. (1968). Production of ethylene by sweet potato roots infected by black rot fungus. *Plant and Cell Physiology*, **9**, 760–81.

Jones, R. J. & Mansfield, T. A. (1970). Suppression of stomatal opening in leaves treated with abscisic acid. *Journal of Experimental Botany*, **21**, 714–19.

Kang, B. G., Newcomb, W. & Burg, S. P. (1971). Mechanism of auxin-induced ethylene production. *Plant Physiology*, **47**, 504–9.

Kazmaier, H. E. (1960). Some pathophysiological aspects of premature defoliation associated with rose blackspot. *Dissertation Abstracts* **21**, 21.

Ketring, D. L., Young, R. E. & Biale, J. B. (1968). Effects of monofluoroacetate on *Penicillium digitatum* metabolism and on ethylene biosynthesis. *Plant Cell Physiology*, **9**, 617–31.

Király, Z., El Hammady, M. & Pozsar, B. I. (1967). Increased cytokinin activity of rust-infected bean and broad bean leaves. *Phytopathology*, **57**, 93–4.

Klämbt, D. (1967). Nachweiss eines cytokinins aus *Agrobacterium tumefaciens* und sein vergleich mit dem cytokinin aus *Corynebacterium fascians*. *Wissenschaftliche zum Universitat Rostock*, **16**, 623–5.

Klämbt, D., Thies, G. & Skoog, F. (1966). Isolation of cytokinins from *Corynebacterium fascians*. *Proceedings of the National Academy of Science, U.S.A.*, **56**, 52–9.

Konze, J. R. & Elstner, E. F. (1978). Ethane and ethylene formation by mitochondria as indication of aerobic lipid degradation in response to wounding of plant tissue. *Biochimica et Biophysica Acta*, **528**, 213–21.

Kosuge, T., Heskett, M. G. & Wilson, E. E. (1966). Microbial synthesis and degradation of indole-3-acetic acid by *Pseudomonas savastanoi*. *Journal of General and Applied Microbiology*, **15**, 51–63.

Kuriger, W. E. & Agrios, G. N. (1977). Cytokinin levels and kinetin–virus interactions in tobacco ringspot virus-infected cowpea plants. *Phytopathology*, **67**, 604–9.

Lado, P., Rasi-Caldogno, F. & Colombo, R. (1974). Promoting effect of fusicoccin on seed germination. *Physiologia Plantarum*, **31**, 149–52.

Libbert, E. & Silhengst, P. (1970). Interactions between plants and epiphytic bacteria regarding their auxin metabolism. VIII. *Physiologia Plantarum*, **23**, 480–7.

Libbert, E., Wichner, S., Duerst, E., Kaiser, W., Kunert, R., Manicki, A., Manteuffel, R., Riecke, E. & Schroder, R. (1968). Auxin content and auxin synthesis in sterile and non-sterile plants, with special regard to the influence of epiphytic bacteria. In *Biochemistry and Physiology of Plant Growth Substances*, ed. F. Wightman & G. Setterfield, pp. 213–30. Ottawa: Runge.

Lieberman, M., Kunishi, A., Mapson, L. W. & Wardale, D. A. (1966). Stimulation of ethylene production in apple tissue slices by methionine. *Plant Physiology*, **41**, 376–82.

Lieberman, M. & Mapson, L. W. (1964). Genesis and biogenesis of ethylene. *Nature*, **204**, 243–5.

Lippincott, J. A. & Lippincott, B. B. (1976). Morphogenic determinants as exemplified by the crown gall disease. In *Encyclopedia of Plant Physiology, New Series*, vol. 4, *Physiological Plant Pathology*, ed. R. Heitefuss & P. H. Williams, pp. 356–88. Berlin: Springer-Verlag.

Lockhart, C. L., Forsyth, F. R. & Eaves, C. A. (1968). Effect of ethylene on development of *Gloeosporium album* in apple and on growth of the fungus in culture. *Canadian Journal of Plant Science*, **48**, 557–9.

Lovrekovich, L., Low, H. & Stahmann, M. A. (1967). The importance of peroxidase in the wildfire disease. *Phytopathology*, **58**, 193–8.

Lund, B. M. (1973). The effect of certain bacteria on ethylene production by plant tissue. In *Fungal Pathogenicity and the Plant's Response* ed. R. J. W. Byrde & C. V. Cutting, pp. 69–84. London: Academic Press.

Macko, F., Woodbury, W. & Stahmann, M. A. (1968). The effect of peroxidase on germination and growth of mycelium of *Puccinia graminis* f. sp. *tritici*. *Phytopathology*, **58**, 1250–4.

Magie, A. R. & Wilson, E. E. (1962). Expressions of virulence among isolates of *Pseudomonas savastanoi* from olive and oleander. *Phytopathology*, **52**, 741.

Magro, P. & Marciano P. (1974). Ricerche sull iperauxinia causata del *Ustilago maydis* (DC) Cda. su *Zea mays*. Nota 1. Variazioni postinfezionali del contenuto in composti fenolici ed in acido indolacetico (IAA). *Revista di Patoligia Vegetale*, **10**, 395–409.

Mapson, L. W. (1970). Biosynthesis of ethylene and the ripening of fruit. *Endeavour*, **39**, 29–33.

Marrè, E. (1979). Fusicoccin: a tool in plant physiology. *Annual Review of Plant Physiology*, **30**, 273–88.

Marrè, E., Colombo, R., Lado, P. & Rasi-Caldogno, F. (1974). Correlation between proton extrusion and simulation of cell enlargement. Effects of fusicoccin and of cytokinins on leaf fragments and isolated cotyledons. *Plant Science Letters*, **2**, 139–50.

Matsubara, S. & Nakahira, R. (1967). Cytokinin activity in an extract from the gall of *Plasmodiophora* infected root of *Brassica rapa*. *Botanical Magazine, Tokyo*, **80**, 373–4.

Miller, E. V., Winston, J. R. & Fisher, D. F. (1940). Production of epinasty by emanations from normal and decaying citrus fruits from *Penicillium digitatum*. *Journal of Agricultural Research*, **60**, 269–77.

Mills, L. J. & Van Staden, J. (1978). Extraction of cytokinins from maize smut tumours of maize and *Ustilago maydis* cultures. *Physiological Plant Pathology*, **13**, 73–80.

Misaghi, I., DeVay, J. E. & Kosuge, T. (1972). Changes in cytokinin activity associated with the development of *Verticillium* wilt and water stress in cotton plants. *Physiological Plant Pathology*, **2**, 187–96.

Mittelheuser, C. J. & Van Steveninck, R. F. M. (1969). Stomatal closure and inhibition of transpiration induced by (RS)-abscisic acid. *Nature*, **221**, 281–2.

Morgan, P. W. & Hall, W. C. (1964). Accelerated release of ethylene by cotton following application of indolyl-3-acetic acid. *Nature*, **201**, 91.

Mothes, K. & Engelbrecht, L. (1961). Kinetin-induced directed transport of substances in excised leaves in the dark. *Phytochemistry*, **1**, 58–62.

Moulton, J. E. (1942). Extraction of auxin from maize, from smut tumours of maize and from *Ustilago zeae*. *Botanical Gazette*, **103**, 725–39.

Muromtsev, G. S. & Globus, G. A. (1976). Adaptive significance of the ability to synthesize gibberellins for the phyto-pathogenic fungus. *Doklady Akademii Nauk. S.S.S.R.*, **226**, 204–6.

Nadolny, L. & Sequeira, L. (1980). Increases in peroxidase activities are not directly involved in induced resistance in tobacco. *Physiological Plant Pathology*, **16**, 1–9.

Patrick, T. W., Hall, R. & Fletcher, R. A. (1977). Cytokinin levels in healthy and *Verticillium*-infected tomato plants. *Canadian Journal of Botany*, **55**, 377–82.

Pegg, G. F. (1976a). The response of ethylene-treated tomato plants to infection by *Verticillium albo-atrum*. *Physiological Plant Pathology*, **9**, 215–26.

Pegg, G. F. (1976b). The occurrence of 1,3-β-glucanase in healthy and *Verticillium*-infected, resistant and susceptible tomato plants. *Journal of Experimental Botany*, **27**, 1093–101.

Pegg, G. F. (1976c). Endogenous auxins in healthy and diseased plants. In *Encyclopedia of Plant Physiology*, New Series, vol. 4, *Physiological Plant Pathology*, ed. R. Heitefuss & P. H. Williams, pp. 560–81. Berlin: Springer-Verlag.

Pegg, G. F. (1976d). The involvement of ethylene in plant pathogenesis. In *Encyclopedia of Plant Physiology*, New Series, vol. 4, *Physiological Plant Pathology*, ed. R. Heitefuss & P. H. Williams, pp. 582–91. Berlin: Springer-Verlag.

Pegg, G. F. (1976e). Endogenous gibberellins in healthy and diseased plants. In *Encyclopedia of Plant Physiology*, New Series, vol. 4, *Physiological Plant Pathology*, ed. R. Heitefuss & P. H. Williams, pp. 592–606. Berlin: Springer-Verlag.

Pegg, G. F. (1976f). Endogenous inhibitors in healthy and diseased plants. In *Encyclopedia of Plant Physiology*, New Series, vol. 4, *Physiological Plant Pathology*, ed. R. Heitefuss & P. H. Williams, pp. 607–16. Berlin: Springer-Verlag.

Pegg, G. F. & Cronshaw, D. K. (1976a). Ethylene production in tomato plants infected with *Verticillium albo-atrum*. *Physiological Plant Pathology*, **8**, 279–95.

Pegg, G. F. & Cronshaw, D. K. (1976b). The relationship of *in vitro* to *in vivo* ethylene production in *Pseudomonas solanacearum* infection in tomato. *Physiological Plant Pathology*, **9**, 145–54.

Pegg, G. F. & Selman, I. W. (1959). An analysis of the growth response of young tomato plants to infection by *Verticillium albo-atrum*. The production of growth substances. *Annals of Applied Biology*, **47**, 222–31.

Pegg, G. F. & Sequeira, L. (1968). Stimulation of aromatic biosynthesis in tobacco plants infected with *Pseudomonas solanacearum*. *Phytopathology*, **58**, 476–83.

Pilet, P. E. (1976). Fusicoccin and auxin effects on root growth. *Plant Science Letters*, **7**, 81–4.

Quetier, F., Huguet, T. & Guille, E. (1969). Induction of crown gall: partial homology between tumour-cell DNA, bacterial DNA and the G and C-rich DNA of stressed normal cells. *Biochemical and Biophysical Research Communications*, **34**, 128–33.

Radley, M. (1956). The distribution of substances similar to gibberellic acid in higher plants. *Nature*, **178**, 1070–1.

Rathbone, M. P. & Hall, R. H. (1972). Concerning the presence of the cytokinin N^6 (^{2}-isopentenyl) adenine in cultures of *Corynebacterium fascians*. *Planta*, **108**, 93–102.

Reddy, M. N. & Williams, P. H. (1970). Cytokinin activity in *Plasmodiophora brassicae*-infected cabbage tissue cultures. *Phytopathology*, **60**, 1463–5.

Riov, J., Monselise, S. P. & Kahan, R. S. (1969). Ethylene-controlled induction of phenylalanine ammonia lyase in citrus fruit peel. *Plant Physiology*, **44**, 631–5.

Rodrigues, C. J. & Arny, D. C. (1966). Role of oxidative enzymes in the physiology of the leaf spot of coffee caused by *Mycena citricola*. *Phytopathologia Zeitschrift*, **56**, 375–84.

Romanow, I., Chalvignac, M. A. & Pochon, J. (1969). Recherche sur la production d'une substance cytokinique par *Agrobacterium tumefaciens*. *Annals de l'Institute Pasteur*, **117**, 58–63.

Ross, A. F. & Pritchard, D. W. (1972). Local and systemic effects of ethylene on tobacco mosaic virus lesions in tobacco. *Phytopathology*, **62**, 786.

Sachs, T. & Thimann, K. V. (1967). The role of auxins and cytokinins in the release of buds from dominance. *American Journal of Botany*, **54**, 136–44.

Saltveit, M. E. & Dilley, D. R. (1978). Rapidly induced wound ethylene from excised segments of etiolated *Pisum sativum* L. cv. Alaska. 1. Characterisation of the response. *Plant Physiology*, **61**, 447–50.

Samborski, D. J. & Shaw, M. (1957). The physiology of host–parasite relations. IV. The effect of maleic hydrazide and IAA on the rust resistance of Khapli and Little Club wheat. *Canadian Journal of Botany*, **35**, 449–55.

Sassa, T., Togashi, M. & Kitaguchi, T. (1975). The structure of cotylenins A, B, C, D and E. *Agricultural Biological Chemistry*, **39**, 1735–44.

Schilperoort, R. A., Veldstra, H., Warnaar, S. O., Mulder, G. & Cohen, J. A. (1973). Formation of complexes between DNA isolated from tobacco crown gall tumours and RNA complementary to *Agrobacterium tumefaciens* DNA. *Biochimica et Biophysica Acta*, **167**, 523–35.

Seevers, P. M. & Daly, J. M. (1970). Studies on wheat stem rust resistance controlled at the Sr6 locus. II. Peroxidase activities. *Phytopathology*, **54**, 1642–7.

Sequeira, L. (1973). Hormone metabolism in diseased plants. *Annual Review of Plant Physiology*, **24**, 353–80.

Sequeira, L. & Steeves, T. A. (1954). Auxin inactivation and its relation to leaf drop caused by the fungus *Omphalia flavida*. *Plant Physiology*, **29**, 11–16.

Sequeira, L. & Williams, P. H. (1964). Synthesis of indoleacetic acid by *Pseudomonas solanacearum*. *Phytopathology*, **54**, 1240–6.

Shannon, L. M., Uritani, I. & Imaseki, H. (1971). *De novo* synthesis of peroxidase isoenzymes in sweet potato slices. *Plant Physiology*, **47**, 493–8.

Shaw, M. (1961). The physiology of host parasite relations. IX. Further observations on the accumulation of radioactive substances at rust infections. *Canadian Journal of Botany*, **39**, 1393–407.

Shaw, M. & Hawkins, A. R. (1958). The physiology of host–parasite relations. V. A preliminary examination of the level of free endogenous IAA in rusted and mildewed cereal leaves and their ability to decarboxylate exogenously supplied radioactive IAA. *Canadian Journal of Botany*, **36**, 1–16.

Shimakawa, K. & Kasai, Z. (1968). A possible incorporation of ethylene into RNA in Japanese Morning Glory (*Pharbitis nil*) seedlings. *Agricultural Biological Chemistry*, **32**, 680–2.

Smidt, M. & Kosuge, T. (1978). The role of indole-3-acetic acid accumulation by alpha methyl tryptophan-resistant mutants of *Pseudomonas savastanoi* in gall formation on oleanders. *Physiological Plant Pathology*, **13**, 203–14.

Smith, W. H., Meigh, D. F. & Parker, J. C. (1964). Effect of damage and fungal infection on the production of ethylene by carnations. *Nature*, **204**, 92–3.

Stahmann, M. A., Clare, B. G. & Woodbury, W. (1966). Increased disease resistance and enzyme activity induced by ethylene and ethylene production by black rot infected sweet potato tissue. *Plant Physiology*, **41**, 1505–12.

Steadman, J. R. & Sequeira, L. (1969). A growth inhibitor from tobacco and its possible involvement in pathogenesis. *Phytopathology*, **59**, 499–503.

Strugger, S. (1934). Beitrage zur physiologie des wachstums. 1. Zur protoplasmaphysiologischen kausalanalyse des Streckungswachstum. *Jahrbuche Wissenschaftliche Botanisch*, **79**, 406–71.

Tamura, S., Sakurai, A. Kainuma & Takai, M. (1963). Isolation of helminthosporol as a natural plant growth regulator. *Agricultural Biological Chemistry*, **27**, 738–9.

Thimann, K. V. & Sachs, T. (1966). The role of cytokinins in the 'fasciation' disease caused by *Corynebacterium fascians*. *American Journal of Botany*, **53**, 731–9.

Upper, C. D., Helgeson, J. P., Kemp, J. D. & Schmidt, C. J. (1970). Gas liquid chromatographic isolation of cytokinins from natural sources. 6-(3-methyl-2-butenylamino) purine from *Agrobacterium tumefaciens*. *Plant Physiology*, **45**, 543–7.

Van Steveninck, R. F. M. (1959). Factors affecting the abscission of reproductive organs in yellow lupins (*Lupinus luteus*). III: Endogenous growth substances in virus-infected and healthy plants and their effect on abscission. *Journal of Experimental Botany*, **10**, 367–76.

West, C. A. & Phinney, B. O. (1956). Properties of gibberellin-like factors from extracts of higher plants. *Plant Physiology*, **31**, Supplement XX.

Wiese, M. V. & DeVay, J. E. (1970). Growth regulator changes in cotton associated with defoliation caused by *Verticillium albo-atrum*. *Plant Physiology*, **45**, 304–9.

Williams, P. H. (1966). A cytochemical study of hypertrophy in club root of cabbage. *Phytopathology*, **56**, 421–4.

Williams, P. H., Reddy, M. N. & Strandberg, J. O. (1969). Growth of non-infected and *Plasmodiophora brassicae*-infected cabbage callus in culture. *Canadian Journal of Botany*, **47**, 1217–21.

Williamson, C. E. (1950). Ethylene, a metabolic product of diseased or injured plants. *Phytopathology*, **40**, 205–8.

Wolf, F. T. (1952). The production of indole acetic acid by *Ustilago zeae* and its possible significance in tumour formation. *Proceedings of the National Academy of Science, U.S.A.*, **38**, 106–11.

Wood, H. N. (1970). Revised identification of the chromophore of a cell division factor from crown gall tumour cells of *Vinca rosea* L.*Proceedings of the National Academy of Science, U.S.A.*, **67**, 1283–7.

Wood, H. N., Lin, M. C. & Braun, A. C. (1972). The inhibition of plant and animal adenosine $3^1 4^1$-cyclic monophosphate, phosphodiesterase by a cell-division promoting substance from tissues of higher plant species. *Proceedings of the National Academy of Science, U.S.A.*, **69**, 403–6.

Wright, S. T. C. & Hiron, R. W. P. (1969). (+)-abscisic acid, the growth inhibitor induced in detached wheat leaves following a period of wilting. *Nature*, **224**, 719.

Yang, S. F., Ku, H. S. & Pratt, H. K. (1966). Photochemical production of ethylene from methionine and its analogues in the presence of flavin mononucleotide. *Journal of Biological Chemistry*, **242**, 5274–80.

Yang, S. F. & Pratt, H. K. (1978). The physiology of ethylene in wounded plant tissue. In *Biochemistry of Wounded Plant Storage Tissues*, ed. G. Kahl, pp. 595–622. Berlin: de Gruyter.

Yu, Y. B., Adams, D. O. & Yang, S. F. (1979). 1-aminocyclopropanecarboxylate synthetase, a key enzyme in ethylene biosynthesis. *Archives of Biochemistry and Biophysics*, **198**, 280–6.

Yu, Y. B. & Yang, S. F. (1979). Auxin-induced ethylene production and its inhibition by aminoethoxyvinylglycine and cobalt ion. *Plant Physiology*, **64**, 1074–7.

J.FRIEND

Alterations in secondary metabolism

Introduction

In a review of secondary compounds as protective agents in plants Swain (1977) pointed out that there were at that time over 10 000 known low molecular weight secondary metabolites in higher plants. It is obviously impossible to cover all of them in this chapter which will therefore be very selective. Compounds which are present in healthy plants, either free or in a bound form and whose concentration does not change when the plant is either infected or challenged by a potential pathogen, and which have been reviewed recently by Overeem (1976) and Schönbeck & Schlösser (1976), will not be discussed. It is intended to concentrate on two types of compounds whose concentration alters upon infection and which have been implicated in the resistance of plants to pathogenic microorganisms. Chlorogenic acid and scopolin (or its aglycone scopoletin) (Fig. 1) will be used as examples of compounds of the first type which are present in healthy plants and whose concentration can increase after infection. The second type will include a range of compounds of different chemical classes which are known as phytoalexins. These compounds appear to be synthesized *de novo* by plants in response to infection and may well be involved in the limitation of the infection.

Fig. 1. Structure of chlorogenic acid, scopoletin and scopolin.

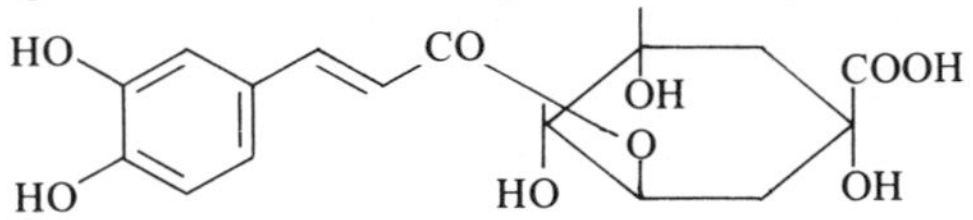

Chlorogenic acid

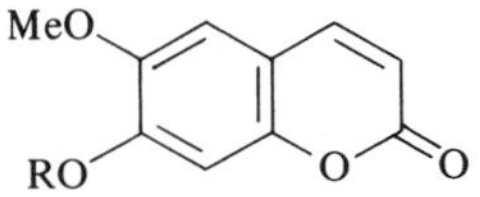

Scopoletin (R = H)
Scopolin (R = glucosyl)

Unfortunately the distinction between these two classes of compound has several times become blurred. For example, Kuć (1972) included chlorogenic acid in his list of phytoalexins although in a later review of phytoalexins (Kuć, 1976) he points out that 'the role of chlorogenic and caffeic acids in healthy and infected foliage is not clear'.

Apart from the fact that a distinction can be made between the increased accumulation of pre-existing compounds and phytoalexins synthesized *de novo,* it will be seen that their antifungal activities are quite different. In particular, attention should be drawn to the fact that the antifungal roles of phytoalexins are based primarily on the finding that phytoalexins accumulate rapidly to a fungitoxic level in resistant plants and that in susceptible plants there is either less or slower accumulation. It will be shown that the additional accumulation of pre-existing compounds does not necessarily follow a similar pattern; furthermore it will also be seen that they are not necessarily as fungitoxic as 'true' phytoalexins.

The increased accumulation of pre-existing compounds in infected plants: chlorogenic acid and scopolin in potato tissue as examples

Hughes & Swain (1960) reported large increases in the levels of both chlorogenic acid and scopolin in tubers of the potato cultivar Majestic infected with the compatible race 4 of *Phytophthora infestans*. However, further studies on the levels of these two compounds in infected tuber tissue show that there is little positive correlation between the accumulation of either compound and resistance to pathogens. In fact, Clarke (1973) has shown that greatest accumulations of scopolin in tuber disks of several potato cultivars inoculated with a complex race of *P. infestans* are associated with susceptibility to the fungus.

In the case of chlorogenic acid the changes in level depend both upon the potato cultivar and the pathogen (Table 1). In most cases shown the level of chlorogenic acid is far lower in inoculated than in uninoculated tissue and the difference is sometimes more marked in resistant than in susceptible reactions. In each case the control (uninoculated) disks show an increase in the two days after cutting. This will be related to wound healing reactions.

The levels of chlorogenic acid found in infected tubers are probably too low to have any appreciable antifungal activity (Kuć, 1957). Low levels of chlorogenic acid can stimulate the growth of such pathogenic fungi as *P. infestans* and *Fusarium solani* var. *coeruleum* (Farkas & Király, 1962; Waites, Reynolds & Friend, 1978). Since it seems that chlorogenic acid and scopolin are not involved as antifungal compounds, the possibility that they might be involved in the host–parasite relationship in other ways should be considered.

Table 1. Comparative levels of chlorogenic acid in inoculated potato tuber disks and in uninoculated controls. Values, for two days after inoculation, expressed as a percentage of the control level

Pathogen	Susceptible cultivar	Level of chloro-genic acid	Resistant cultivar	Level of chloro-genic acid	Reference
Phytophthora infestans (race 4)	King Edward	115	Orion Pentland Beauty	54 39	Henderson & Friend (1979)
P. infestans (race 1,3,5)	Orion Pentland Beauty	84 83	— —		Henderson & Friend (1979)
P. infestans (complex race)	King Edward	84	Stormont Enterprise	51	Y. A. Ampomah & J. Friend (unpublished)
Phoma exigua var. *foveata*	Ulster Sceptre	60	Roslin Castle	20	Calculated from graphs given in Gans (1978)
Fusarium solani var. *coeruleum*	Craigs Alliance	114	Homeguard	110	Waites (1979)

Chlorogenic acid, scopolin and scopoletin as modifiers of metabolic pathways.

Chlorogenic acid and scopolin or scopoletin can modify the action of enzymes isolated from plant tissues as shown in Table 2. It is possible, therefore, that the accumulation of chlorogenic acid or scopolin/scopoletin in infected plants, by modifying the action of enzymes *in vivo,* could alter important metabolic pathways in the infected tissue or hormone levels in such a manner that they would either help or hinder the progress of infection.

Chlorogenic acid as a possible metabolic intermediate in the
formation of insoluble phenolic compounds associated with resistance

Since it is now generally accepted that there is continual synthesis, turnover and degradation of phenolic compounds in plant tissues (Harborne, 1980), I should like to examine the possibility that the observed increase in accumulation of chlorogenic acid in infected plant tissues reflects its importance as a metabolic intermediate. It is known, for example, that radioactive chlorogenic acid can be metabolized by potato tuber disks to a lignin-like compound (Taylor & Zucker, 1966).

There is increasing evidence that deposition of phenolic barriers in potatoes seems to be an important part of the resistance mechanism of tuber tissue to a range of fungal pathogens. For example, cessation of fungal growth of *Phoma exigua* var. *foveata* and *Fusarium solani* var. *coeruleum* in resistant cultivars, and of a complex race of *Phytophthora infestans* in field-resistant varieties, is associated with the deposition of lignin or lignin-like materials including phenolic oxidation products. Phenolic deposition also occurs in the later stages of the resistance reaction of R-gene-containing potato tubers to incompatible races of *P. infestans.* The possible structures of the types of phenolic barriers which seem to be involved in the resistance of potato tubers to these pathogens are listed in Table 3.

As described above and shown in Table 1, in most cases examined the level of chlorogenic acid expressed as a percentage of that in inoculated tissue tends to be lower in resistant than in susceptible reactions. This is most marked in the resistant cultivar Roslin Castle infected with *Phoma exigua* where it arises because the uninoculated disks have the capacity to accumulate large amounts of chlorogenic acid. Gans (1978) found that in a range of cultivars, the resistance of the cultivar corresponded with the rate of accumulation of chlorogenic acid in uninoculated disks.

The lower accumulation of chlorogenic acid in inoculated compared with uninoculated disks could be due to either decreased synthesis or enhanced metabolism. The biosynthesis of chlorogenic acid is assumed to be via the pathway shown in Fig. 2. An important enzyme in the biosynthetic scheme is hydroxycin-

Table 2. *Effects of chlorogenic acid, scopolin and/or scopoletin on plant enzymes*

Enzyme	Source	Phenolic compound	Effect	Reference
Glucose-6-phosphate dehydrogenase (two isozymes)	Tobacco cell suspension culture	Chlorogenic acid Scopolin Scopoletin	Inhibited Inhibited Less inhibitory	Hoover, Wender & Smith (1977)
Peroxidase (two isozymes)	Tobacco cell suspension culture	Chlorogenic acid	Inhibited	Pickering, Powell, Wender & Smith (1973)
Two other isozymes	Tobacco cell suspension culture	Scopoletin	Stimulated (one isozyme only)	Schafer, Wender & Smith (1971)
Indol-3-yl-acetic acid oxidase	Sweet potato roots	Scopoletin	Stimulated at low concentration. Inhibited at high concentration	Imbert & Wilson (1970)
Catalase	Tobacco plants infected by *Peronospora tabacina*	Scopoletin	Inhibited	Hochberg & Cohen (1977)

Table 3. *Possible structures of insoluble phenolic compounds associated with resistance reactions of potato tubers to pathogens*

Compound	Structure	Reference	Pathogen or reaction causing accumulation	Reference
Lignin	Polymer of oxidized coniferyl (and *p*-coumaryl) alcohol units	Freudenberg & Neish (1968); Gross (1979)	*Phoma exigua* var. *foveata*	Walker & Wade (1976, 1978)
Feruloyl (and *p*-coumaroyl)-galactan	Ferulic (and *p*-coumaric) acid esterified to C_2 of hydroxyl groups of cell wall galactan (structure hypothetical)	Friend (1976, 1979, 1980)	*Phytophthora infestans* (major-gene-resistant tubers, reacting to incompatible races)	Friend (1973, 1976); Friend, Reynolds & Aveyard (1973)
Diferulate esters of cell wall polysaccharides	5,5'-diferulic acid and β,β'-diferulic acid esterified to hydroxyl groups of glycosyl residues of polysaccharides	Markwalder & Neukom (1976); Stafford & Brown (1976)	*P. infestans* (field-resistant tubers, reacting to complex races of the fungus)	J. McLauchlin & J. Friend (unpublished)
Chlorogenic acid oxidation products	Chlorogenoquinone coupled to NH_2- or SH-groups of cell wall protein	Pierpoint (1966); Pierpoint, Ireland & Carpenter (1977); Davies & Laird (1976)	*P. infestans* (field-resistant tubers, reacting to complex races of the fungus)	J. McLauchlin & J. Friend (unpublished); Y. A. Appomah & J. Friend (unpublished)
Suberin	Feruloyl and *p*-coumaroyl esters of hydroxy aliphatic acid polymer	Kolattukudy (1975)	Wound-healing compound; associated with resistance of tuber disks to *Erwinia atroseptica* and *Pseudomonas fluorescens*	Smith & Smart (1955); Zucker & Hankin (1970)

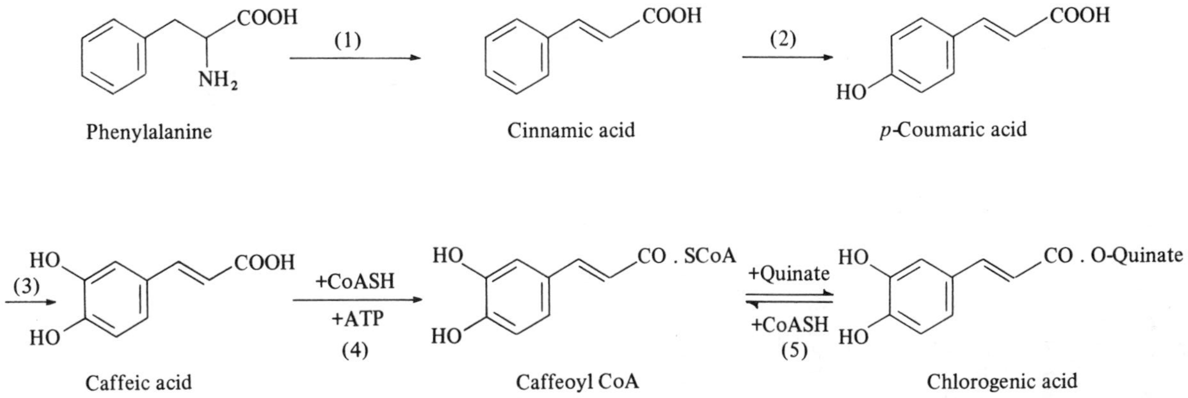

Fig. 2. Biosynthesis of chlorogenic acid. Enzymes: (1), phenylalanine ammonia lyase; (2), cinnamate-4-hydroxylase; (3), hydroxylating enzyme; (4), caffeoyl CoA ligase; (5), hydroxycinnamoyl CoA : quinate hydroxycinnamoyl transferase.

namoyl CoA : quinate hydroxycinnamoyl transferase (CQT). However, its activity is reversible (Rhodes & Wooltorton, 1976) and both the level of enzyme in potato disks and its activity *in vitro* can be modified by cinnamic acids (Lamb, 1977; Rhodes, Wooltorton & Lourenço, 1979). Furthermore the isoenzyme pattern of CQT extracted from potato tubers alters with the storage conditions (Rhodes *et al.*, 1979).

The conversion of chlorogenic acid to cinnamoyl CoA, by CQT, could lead to its further conversion to all the types of structure proposed for the phenolic barriers which seem to be associated with resistance. An outline of the sequence of possible reactions is shown in Fig. 3.

Decreased synthesis of chlorogenic acid in inoculated tuber tissue seems to be unlikely since there are increases in phenylalanine ammonia lyase (PAL) and in

Fig. 3. Possible metabolic reactions of chlorogenic acid in potato which can give rise to the range of phenolic derivatives found in infected tubers. OMT = *o*-methyl transferase; CQT = hydroxycinnamoyl CoA : quinate hydroxycinnamoyl transferase.

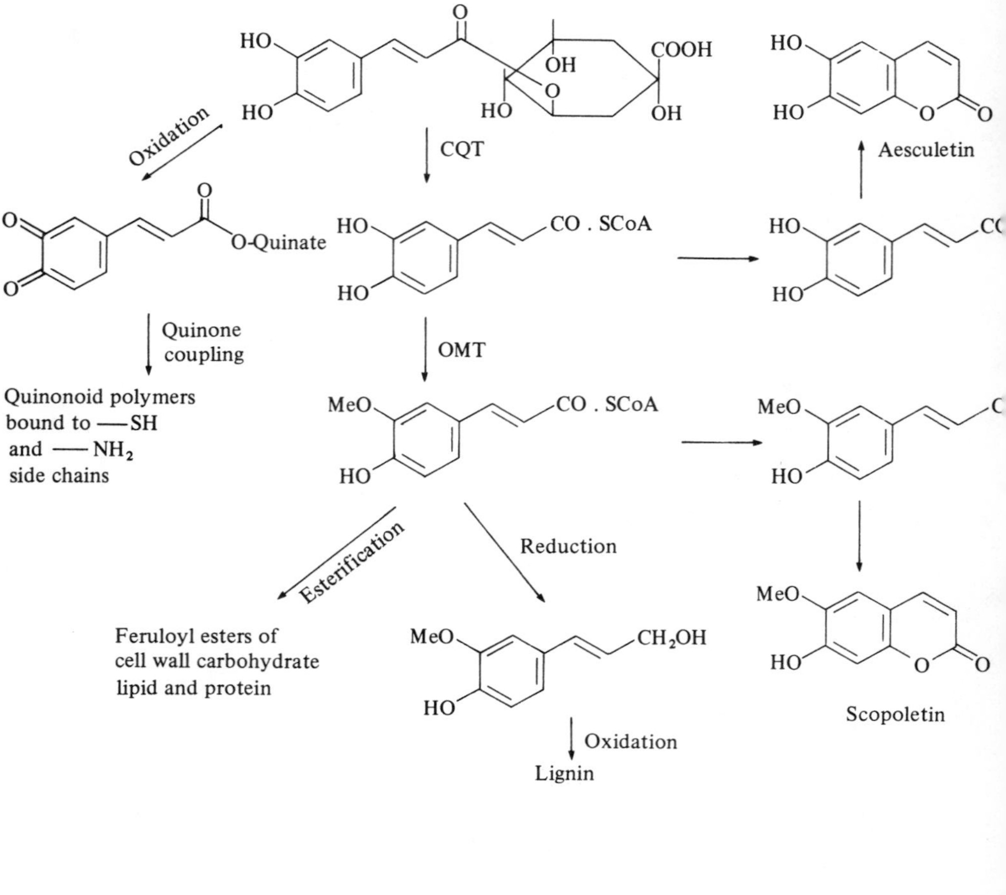

both PAL and *p*-coumaroyl CoA ligase in tuber disks inoculated with *Phyto-phthora infestans* or *Fusarium solani* respectively (Friend, Reynolds & Aveyard, 1973; Henderson & Friend, 1979; Waites *et al.*, 1978; J. McLauchlin & J. Friend, unpublished).

So far the activity of CQT in potato tubers has only been examined in relation to their resistance to *F. solani* (Waites *et al.*, 1978). It should be emphasized that in these experiments activity was measured as the conversion of chlorogenic acid to caffeoyl CoA, that is, in the metabolic rather than the biosynthetic direction. Its level, like that of chlorogenic acid, in the uninfected tuber disks is correlated with resistance of the tubers to *F. solani* (Table 4). Furthermore the level of the extractable enzyme rises in inoculated resistant tuber tissue.

If the levels of CQT were found to increase in potatoes inoculated with other pathogens, it would support the hypothesis that enhanced chlorogenic acid metabolism is an important biochemical reaction of potato tubers to fungal pathogens. I would further suggest that results obtained by Gans (1978) could be explained on the basis that a cultivar resistant to *Phoma exigua* has both the potential for a high rate of biosynthesis of chlorogenic acid and a faster rate of metabolism when it is infected. In other words the rate of turnover of chlorogenic acid may be the factor which determines the relative resistance of the tuber.

Phytoalexins

These antifungal compounds are produced by plants as a reaction to a variety of stimuli. This is taken into account in the most recent definition of a phytoalexin as, 'an antifungal compound produced by a plant in response to infection or attempted invasion by fungi or other microorganisms or by abiotic agents' (Harborne & Ingham, 1978).

Phytoalexins, as Kosuge & Kimpel (this volume) have pointed out, contain

Table 4. *Relative chlorogenic acid content and level of activity of CQT, measured in fresh tuber tissue, of several potato cultivars with different resistance or susceptibility to* F. solani *var.* coeruleum *(from Waites, 1979).*

Cultivar	Resistance to *F. solani*	Relative chlorogenic acid content	Relative CQT activity
Homeguard	Resistant	100	100
Pentland Crown	Intermediate	42.5	41.3
King Edward	Relatively susceptible	35.9	3.3
Craigs Alliance	Susceptible	44.6	0.0
Doon Star	Very susceptible	26.9	0.2

CQT = hydroxycinnamoyl CoA : quinate hydroxycinnamoyl transferase.

carbon, hydrogen and oxygen but come under several chemical classes such as phenolic, terpenoid and acetylenic compounds. The structures of some commonly-occurring phytoalexins are given in Fig. 4.

Four major generalized findings have been derived from phytoalexin research.

Fig. 4. Structure of some common phytoalexins.

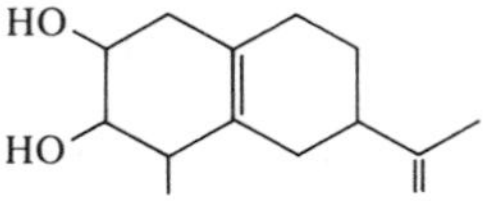

Rishitin (potato) 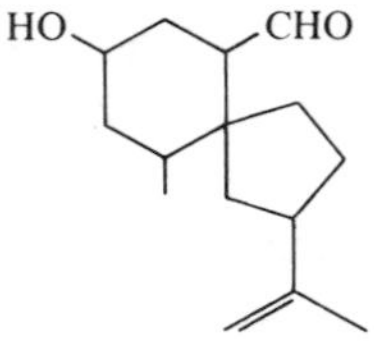   Lubimin (potato)

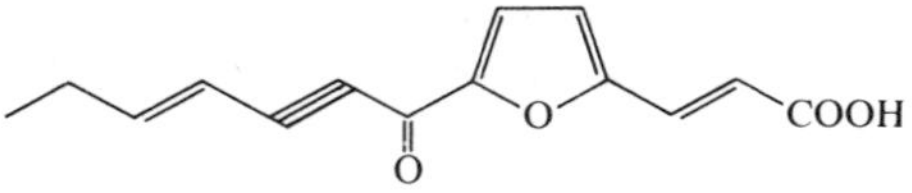

Wyerone Acid (broad bean)

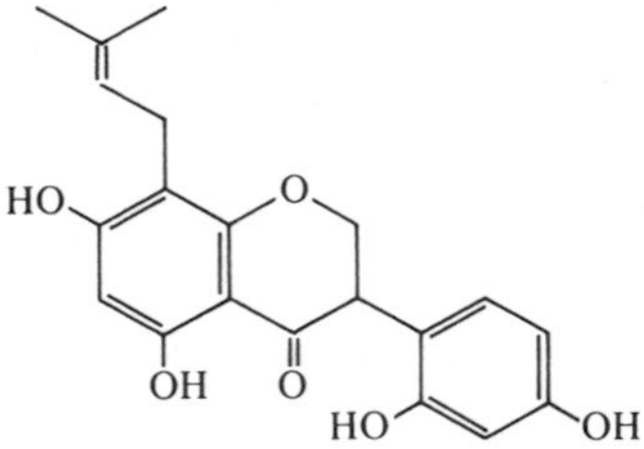

Kievitone (french bean) 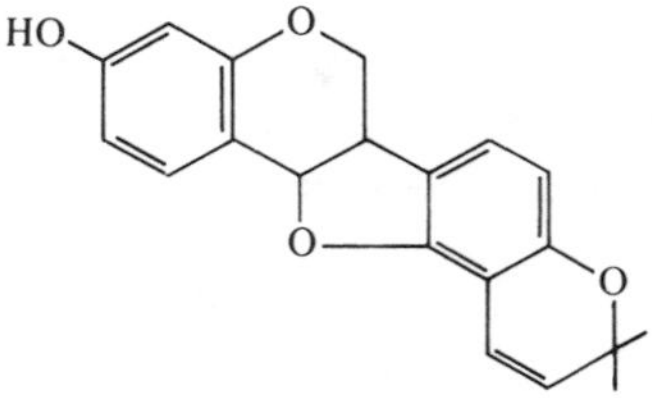   Phaseollin (french bean)

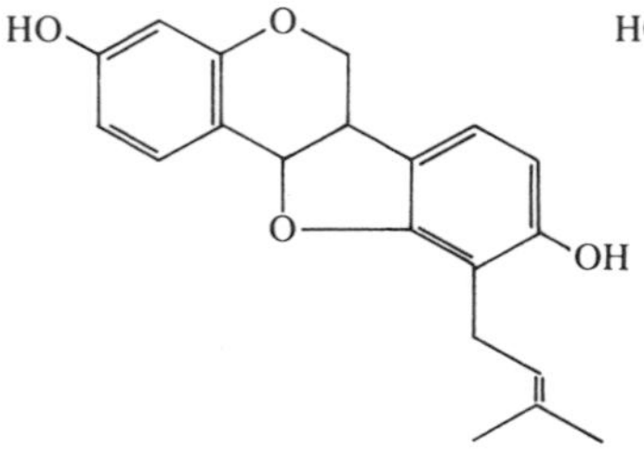

Phaseollidin (french bean) 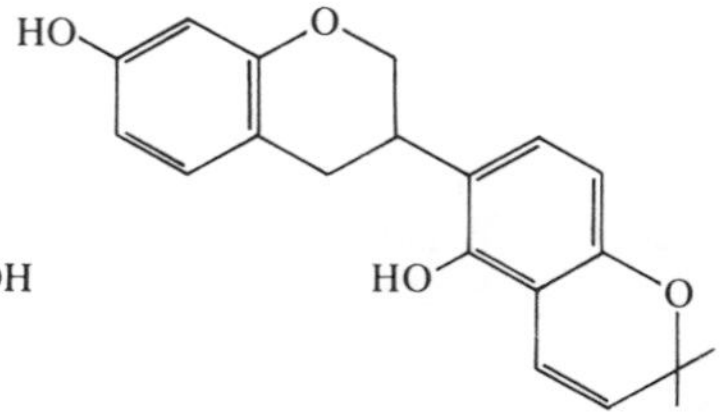   Phaseollinisoflavan (french bean)

First, which has already been mentioned, is that phytoalexins accumulate rapidly to a fungitoxic level in resistant plants and that in susceptible plants there is either less or slower accumulation. Second, non-pathogens are more susceptible to phytoalexins than are pathogens. Third, by increasing or decreasing phytoalexin biosynthesis plants can be made resistant or susceptible, respectively. Fourth, pathogenic fungi can metabolize phytoalexins to products which are less fungitoxic. In each of the host–parasite combinations which has been examined so far, at least one of these features, if not all four, has been demonstrated. These findings have emphasized the possibility that control of phytoalexin accumulation might be the most important factor in determining whether a host–pathogen interaction will be compatible or incompatible.

It is important to bear in mind that the accumulation of phytoalexins, like that of other secondary compounds, depends upon a balance between synthesis and degradation. It will be seen from the host–parasite combinations to be examined that phytoalexin degradation may be catalysed by either the host or the pathogen.

Phytoalexin accumulation and turnover in potato tuber slices and disks

Rogerson (1978) and Rogerson & Threlfall (1978) found that rishitin and lubimin seemed to be turning over at different rates even when they were both accumulating in tuber tissue of the cultivar Kennebec (R_1) challenged by the incompatible race 4 of *Phytophthora infestans* or a cell-free elicitor preparation derived from the fungus.

In slices inoculated with fungal spores the level of rishitin increased between 40 and 64 h after inoculation but the incorporation of radioactivity into rishitin from ^{14}C-mevalonic acid (MVA), given as a single pulse 40 h after inoculation, increased from 40–52 h but dropped to zero between 52 and 64 h. Fluctuations of ^{14}C incorporation were also observed even when incorporation was measured 3 h after application of the ^{14}C-MVA between 40 and 52 h after inoculation.

When a similar experiment was carried out with tuber slices and the cell-free elicitor, the levels of rishitin and lubimin both fluctuated as did the incorporation of ^{14}C into the compounds from ^{14}C-MVA. It was noticeable that the peaks of incorporation of radioactivity into the rishitin and lubimin did not necessarily coincide with the maximum levels of accumulation of the phytoalexins. It is assumed that phytoalexin degradation is catalysed by the host tissue, since after incubation of rishitin with potato tuber disks it was converted to hydroxylated derivatives and then to unidentified water-soluble products (Ishigura *et al.*, 1978).

Fungal metabolism of isoflavonoid phytoalexins in French beans

Inoculation of French beans with mycelium of *Rhizoctonia solani* gives rise to restricted lesions after penetration of hypocotyl tissue whereas inoculation with *Fusarium solani* f.sp. *phaseoli* to which they are susceptible gives spreading lesions. In the early stages of infection by *R. solani* the two major phytoalexins which accumulated were kievitone and phaseollin (Smith, Van Etten & Bateman, 1975). Kievitone increased in amount from young to intermediate to mature lesions (96 h after inoculation); the level of phaseollin was much lower in young and intermediate lesions but it increased considerably in mature lesions. Smith *et al.* considered that the levels of the two compounds, and particularly that of kievitone, were sufficient to cause the inhibition of mycelial growth of *R. solani* which is associated with the limitation of lesion spread. More recently Bull & Smith (1980) have found that kievitone will inhibit the polygalacturonase enzyme produced by *R. solani;* the inhibition of this enzyme may also restrict the pathogenesis of the fungus in the beans.

In *F. solani* infection, small amounts of kievitone were detectable at 24 h but fell to trace levels by 120 h while phaseollin continued to accumulate up to 120 h after inoculation (Morris & Smith, 1978). Van Etten & Smith (1975) had found that in other bean cultivars phaseollin was accompanied by an almost equal weight of 1a-hydroxyphaseollone, a smaller amount of phaseollinisoflavan and traces of 2'-methoxyphaseollinisoflavan and phaseollidin. 1a-Hydroxyphaseollone and 2'-methoxyphaseollinisoflavan are fungal detoxification products of phaseollin and phaseollinisoflavan respectively (Heuvel & Van Etten, 1973; Van Etten, 1973; Fig. 5).

Dr David Smith and his colleagues have carried out a series of experiments to determine whether the low level of phytoalexin accumulation in beans inoculated with *F. solani* is due to metabolism of phytoalexins by the fungus or to only a limited degree of elicitation of phytoalexin biosynthesis. Their results indicate that both these phenomena may be occurring. It was indicated earlier that *F. solani* can detoxify phaseollin to 1a-hydroxyphaseollone (Heuvel & Van Etten, 1973; Heuvel *et al.;* 1974). Kuhn & Smith (1976) found that when kievitone was added to a liquid medium in which mycelium of *R. solani* was growing, kievitone disappeared and was replaced by a less fungitoxic product, later identified as kievitone hydrate by Kuhn, Smith & Ewing (1977). The hydration reaction is catalysed by an extracellular enzyme isolated by Kuhn & Smith (1979) from culture filtrates of *F. solani*. This enzyme, kievitone hydratase, will also catalyse the detoxification of phaseollidin to phaseollidin hydrate (Smith, Kuhn, Bailey & Burden, 1980). The hydration of kievitone seems to occur during the progress of *F. solani* infections in French beans since Kuhn & Smith (1978) found low levels of both kievitone and kievitone hydrate in bean hypocotyls infected by *F. solani*.

The importance of phytoalexin elicitation in French beans by *R. solani* has been emphasized by the experiments of Morris & Smith (1978). They used, as their test system, excised hypocotyls from which the central core of tissue had been removed. They found that whereas cell-free mycelial extracts of *R. solani* would elicit the accumulation of high levels of kievitone in the de-cored excised hypocotyls, only trace amounts of kievitone were found when extracts from *F. solani*, prepared in a similar manner, were used as the eliciting agents. Furthermore the crude elicitor extracts from *R. solani* were partially purified by gel chromatography on Sephadex G75. No eliciting activity was found in any of the corresponding column fractions from *F. solani*. This finding lends further support to the hypothesis that *F. solani* is pathogenic on French beans because it does not elicit the putative defence mechanisms of the host in the same manner as *R. solani*.

Rates of biosynthesis and degradation of glyceollin in soybeans in relation to glyceollin accumulation

Yoshikawa, Yamauchi & Masago (1979) have examined the glyceollin accumulation, biosynthesis and degradation in Harosoy 63 soybeans inoculated with either compatible or incompatible races of *Phytophthora megasperma* var. *sojae*. Biosynthesis was measured as the incorporation of ^{14}C into glyceollin at various times after feeding a 'pulse' of ^{14}C-phenylalanine to the inoculated

Fig. 5. Structure of phytoalexin metabolites.

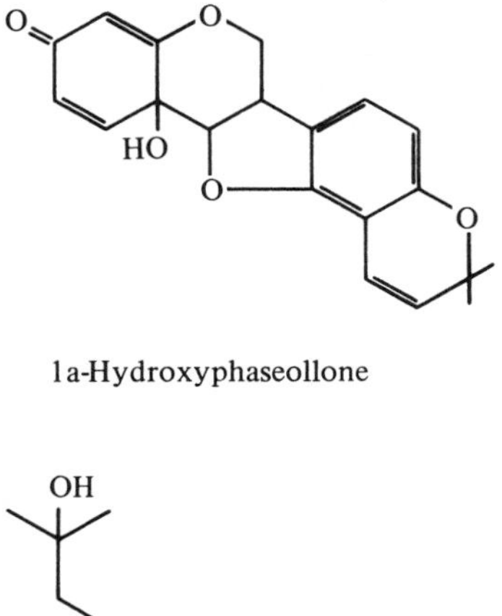

1a-Hydroxyphaseollone

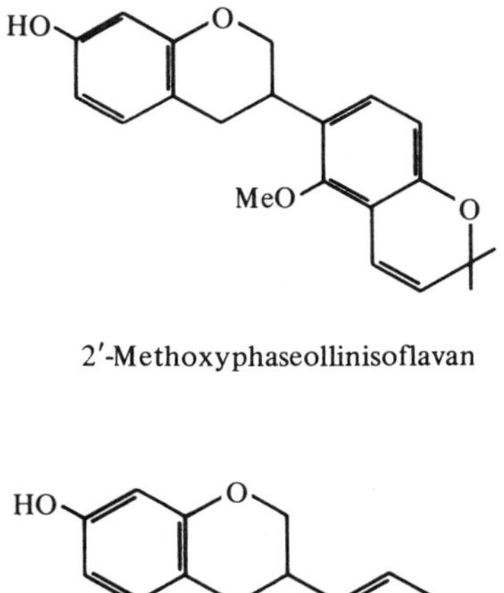

2'-Methoxyphaseollinisoflavan

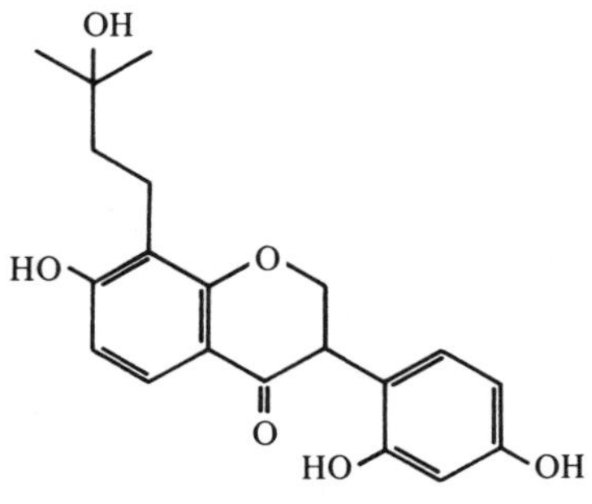

Kievitone hydrate

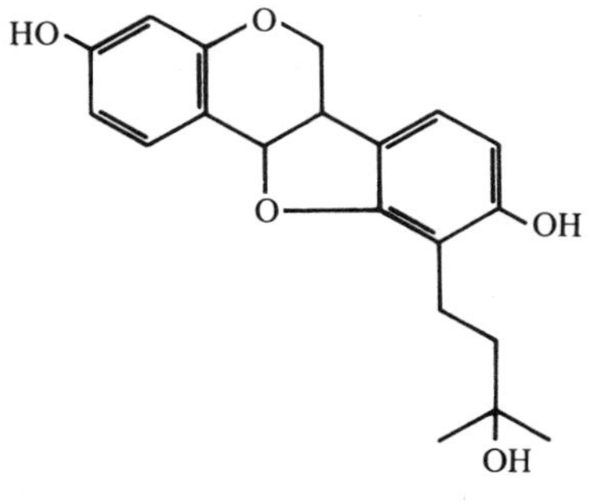

Phaseollidin hydrate

plants. Degradation was measured by determining the radioactivity in glyceollin at various times after feeding a 'pulse' of ^{14}C-phenylalanine followed by a chase with unlabelled phenylalanine. Race 1 of *P. megasperma* gives an incompatible reaction and caused accumulation of relatively large amounts of glyceollin but race 4 gives a compatible reaction – only small amounts of glyceollin accumulated. The rate of glyceollin biosynthesis after inoculation of the plants by either fungal race was identical but the rate of degradation in the plants inoculated with the compatible race 4 of the fungus was very much higher than that in the plants inoculated with the incompatible race 1.

Yoshikawa (1978) had earlier examined the effects of a 'biotic' elicitor, that is, one derived from cell walls of *P. megasperma* var. *sojae,* and compared them with those of a so-called 'abiotic' elicitor on the biosynthesis and degradation of glyceollin in soybean cotyledons. His results showed that whereas the biotic elicitor stimulated phytoalexin biosynthesis the abiotic elicitor inhibited phytoalexin degradation. Biosynthesis of glyceollin was measured by the ^{14}C method described above but degradation by a quite different method, as the disappearance of exogenous glyceollin added to the hypocotyl system. It is surprising, and perhaps unfortunate, that he did not measure phytoalexin degradation by the 'pulse–chase' method described above.

Since soybean is the only plant in which rates of phytoalexin biosynthesis and breakdown have been measured in response to different stimuli, it will be interesting to see whether similar results can be obtained with other hosts and in particular whether the differences between race specificity of phytoalexin accumulation in other host–parasite systems are related to biosynthesis or degradation. Furthermore, if the methods used by Yoshikawa are generally applicable to other host–parasite systems it should be possible to determine in more detail the relative importance of phytoalexin biosynthesis and metabolism in, for example, the reaction of French beans with *R. solani* and *F. solani* which was discussed earlier.

Changes of enzyme levels in infected legumes: control of biosynthesis of isoflavonoid phytoalexins

Kosuge & Kimpel (this volume) have already discussed in detail some of the fine control mechanisms involved in the biosynthesis of glyceollin and lignin. These are the requirements for NADPH and ATP at various stages, feedback inhibition by phenylpropanoid compounds and control of both PAL and cinnamate-4-hydroxylase by alteration of the oxidant–reductant levels.

There is also considerable evidence that the actual levels of some of the enzymes involved in phenolic biosynthesis alter following infection. The possibility that such alterations of enzyme levels are as, or more, important as control mechanisms than 'fine-tuning' of enzyme activities should not be ignored.

In a number of hosts where isoflavonoid phytoalexins are biosynthesized in response to infection or challenge inoculation, increases in the level of PAL activity have been recorded.

In both pea and French bean pods challenged by a range of pathogenic or non-pathogenic fungi, Hadwiger, Hess & von Broembsen (1970) found increases in PAL activity. In French beans the increase in PAL was gradual for the first 8 h after inoculation and then very rapid up to 32 h when *F. solani* f.sp. *pisi*, a non-pathogen, was used as the challenging organism. Phaseollin was first detected after 16 h, that is, 8 h after the increase in PAL. Rathmell (1973) found that when French bean hypocotyls were inoculated with *Colletotrichum lindemuthianum* there was a separation of about 24 h between the increase in PAL and increases in Folin-reacting material associated with the appearance of phaseollin. In soybean hypocotyls inoculated with *Phytophthora megasperma* and in French bean cell cultures plated with autoclaved ribonuclease (RNase), Partridge & Keen (1977) and Dixon & Bendall (1978) reported similar findings, namely that the PAL level increased and then fell to a basal level; the highest level of PAL occurred some time before the beginning of the relatively rapid rise in phytoalexin accumulation. Indeed, Dixon & Bendall (1978) point out that the time-course of PAL increases in their experiments was more closely correlated with the deposition of insoluble phenolic material in the French bean culture cell walls. These more recent findings therefore seem to confirm the earlier suggestion of Van Etten & Pueppke (1976) that the significance of increased PAL activity in the biosynthesis of isoflavonoid phytoalexins is debatable.

Nevertheless the importance of PAL in the control of isoflavonoid phytoalexin biosynthesis has been re-emphasized by the more recent experiments of Lamb & Dixon (1978) and Dixon & Lamb (1979). They elicited phaseollin accumulation in French bean cell cultures with either autoclaved RNase or with an elicitor preparation from cell walls of *C. lindemuthianum*. In each case PAL, which showed an early, transient increase, was demonstrated by density-labelling with D_2O to be synthesized *de novo*.

If similar experiments could be carried out on other enzymes which are possibly involved in the biosynthesis of isoflavonoid phytoalexins, it would be possible to obtain a better understanding both of the biosynthetic pathway and of whether it is controlled by enzyme synthesis or by modulation of the level of enzyme activity *in vivo*.

Partridge & Keen (1977) have measured the time-courses of increases in chalcone-flavanone isomerase and peroxidase in soybean hypocotyls inoculated with *P. megasperma* and in the case of each of these two enzymes there was no apparent correlation with the time-course of glyceollin accumulation. Dixon & Bendall (1978) found that flavanone synthase in French bean cell cultures treated with RNase showed a transient increase comparable with that of PAL; however, this enzyme only catalysed the synthesis of naringenin and not that of 4',7-dihydroxy flavanone which is the putative precursor of phaseollin. The change in levels of the chalcone-flavanone isomerase in French bean cell culture treated with either RNase (Dixon & Bendall, 1978) or with the *C. lindemuthianum* elicitor (Dixon & Lamb, 1979) did not give any indication that this might be a regulatory enzyme.

The major problem which seems to be facing investigators in the field of iso-flavonone phytoalexin biosynthesis is that the biosynthetic pathways to the phytoalexins often share many common reactions with those of the constitutive iso-flavonoids present in the plants before infection. An example is that of the chick pea (*Cicer arietinum*) which, when challenge-inoculated with *Helminthosporium carbonum,* accumulates two phytoalexins, medicarpin and maackiain (Ingham, 1976). The levels of the two constitutive isoflavones, biochanin A and formononetin, do not alter. It is interesting that formononetin is an intermediate in the biosynthetic pathway postulated for both medicarpin and maackiain (Dewick & Martin, 1979; Fig. 6). Biochanin A is not on this pathway. It is known that in uninfected *C. arietinum* plants the turnover of formononetin (measured as 'biological half-life') is much faster than that of biochanin A (Barz & Hoesel, 1979) and it seems therefore that after infection the relative rates of synthesis and degradation of formononetin must be the same as they were before inoculation. This is an interesting aspect of control since the route by which formononetin is metabolized in the uninoculated plant is presumably quite different from the route leading to the biosynthesis of medicarpin and maackiain. Does this finding mean that there is merely a diversion of formononetin metabolism by the 'switching-on' of a new pathway in which the turnover of formononetin is not altered?

Conclusions: summary and speculations

It can be seen, from the limited numbers of examples which have been described, that one of the effects of infection of a plant by a disease-causing organism is to cause an alteration, usually an increase, in the accumulation of secondary compounds in the plant. In the case of phytoalexins the nature of the compound which accumulates is characteristic of the host plant. Where several phytoalexins can be produced by a single host, the number of compounds which accumulate can be influenced by the pathogen. A similar situation exists for commonly-occurring compounds like chlorogenic acid in potatoes where the amount of accumulation seems to depend both on the genotype of the host and on the nature of the pathogen causing disease. Since all secondary products are turning over, even in healthy plants, an accumulation of any of these compounds means that the reactions causing its biosynthesis are proceeding more rapidly than those involved in its metabolism to other products or its breakdown. In order to explain the specificity of the accumulation of secondary products in a particular host–parasite interaction, it must be assumed that some biochemical reactions are stimulated or inhibited by specific control mechanisms. These control mechanisms will include the types of control of enzyme activity described by Kosuge & Kimpel (this volume), or the changes in enzyme level described above.

Several types of molecules, isolated from fungi, which may be involved in host–parasite interactions have been studied but their possible roles in the specific control of the accumulation either of phytoalexins or of other secondary products is unclear.

Fungal elicitors of phytoalexin production (Albersheim & Valent, 1978) are completely devoid of host-specific effects. Indeed it has been shown that the

Fig. 6. Probable biosynthetic reactions in chick pea (*Cicer arietinum*) leading to the constitutive isoflavonoids biochanin A and formononetin and to the phytoalexins medicarpin and maackiain. (Based on Dewick & Martin, 1979.)

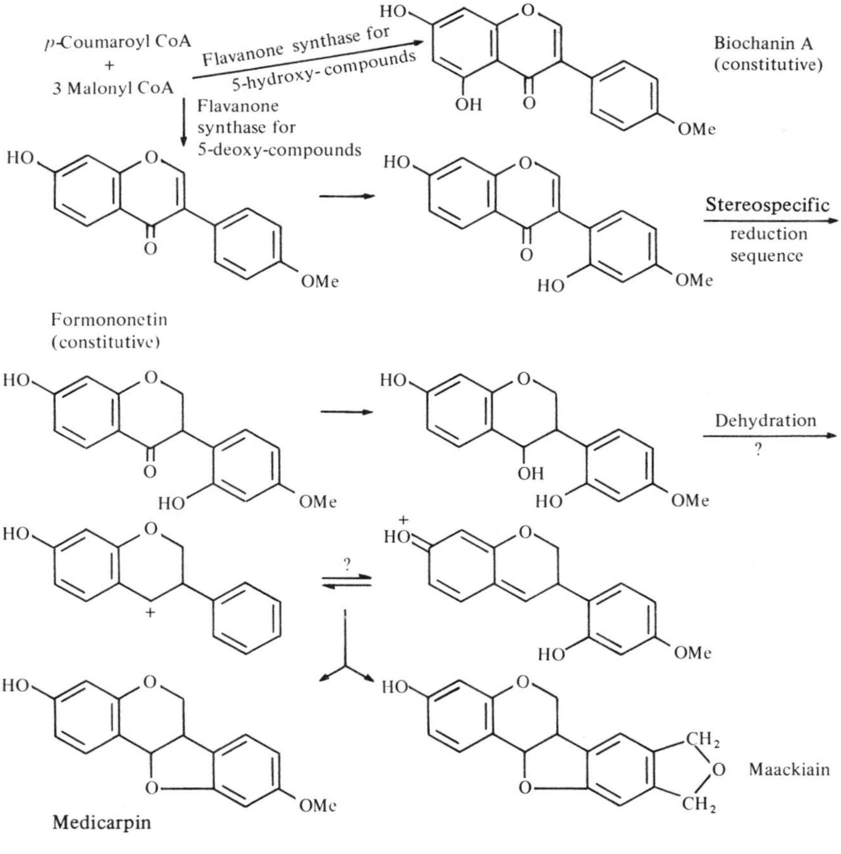

elicitor from *Phytophthora megasperma* which stimulated glyceollin accumulation in soybean would also elicit the accumulation of rishitin in potato and of isoflavonoid phytoalexins in French bean; similar effects were caused by an elicitor fraction isolated from yeast cell walls (Cline, Wade & Albersheim, 1978).

There is no evidence that the endogenous elicitors in host plants which are released by freezing, heat, or mercuric chloride treatment (Hargreaves & Bailey, 1978; Hargreaves & Selby, 1978; Hargreaves, 1979) are specific to that host plant. If they are, a specific effect caused by a pathogen would have to be explained by the pathogen having the ability either to modify the endogenous elicitor or to affect its mode of action.

The only fungal molecules which seem to be able to suppress the accumulation of phytoalexins caused by fungal elicitors are the mycolaminarin-like compounds isolated by Doke & Tomiyama (1980) from *P. infestans*. These are claimed to be race-specific in their effects on cells from potatoes of different genotypes, but there is no indication of their mode of action, particularly the means by which the fungus can control the secretion of elicitor and suppressor molecules. Wade & Albersheim (1979) found that race-specific extracellular glycoproteins (ECGPs) were secreted by cultures of *P. megasperma*. Partially purified ECGPs from incompatible, but not compatible, races of the fungus protected soybean seedlings from attack by compatible races. There was no evidence that these ECGPs acted by stimulation of phytoalexin production.

The only specific enzyme involved with phytoalexin metabolism which has been isolated from a fungus is kievitone hydratase, which is involved in the detoxification, and not the biosynthesis, of kievitone and phaseollidin (see above).

It can be seen that a great deal of research now needs to be carried out on the specificity of the control of biochemical pathways involved in the accumulation of specific phytoalexins and other secondary compounds in infected plants and to determine whether this control is exerted by the host, the pathogen, or a product or products of the host–pathogen interaction. Although this research will be difficult, the final answers should be intellectually highly rewarding.

References

Albersheim, P. & Valent, B. S. (1978). Host–pathogen interaction in plants. *Journal of Cell Biology*, **78**, 627–43.

Barz, W. & Hoesel, W. (1979). Metabolism and degradation of phenolic compounds in plants. In *Biochemistry of Plant Phenolics, Recent Advances in Phytochemistry*, vol. 12, ed. T. Swain, J. B. Harborne & C. F. Van Sumere, pp. 339–69. New York: Plenum Press.

Bull, C. A. & Smith, D. A. (1981). Pectic enzyme inhibition by the phytoalexin, kievitone. *Phytopathology* (Abst.), **71**, 206.

Clarke, D. D. (1973). The accumulation of scopolin in potato tissue in response to infection. *Physiological Plant Pathology*, **3**, 347–58.

Cline, K., Wade, M. & Albersheim, P. (1978). Host–pathogen interactions. XV. Fungal glucans which elicit phytoalexin accumulation in soybean also elicit the accumulation of phytoalexins in other plants. *Plant Physiology*, **62**, 918–21.

Davies, A. M. C. & Laird, W. M. (1976). Changes in some nitrogenous constituents of potato tubers during aerobic autolysis. *Journal of the Science of Food and Agriculture*, **27**, 377–82.

Dewick, P. M. & Martin, M. (1979). Biosynthesis of pterocarpan and isoflavan phytoalexins in *Medicago sativa:* the biochemical interconversion of pterocarpans and 2'-hydroxyisoflavans. *Phytochemistry*, **18**, 591–6.

Dixon, R. A. & Bendall, D. S. (1978). Changes in the levels of enzymes of phenyl propanoid and flavanoid synthesis during phaseollin production in cell suspension cultures of *Phaseolus vulgaris*. *Physiological Plant Pathology*, **13**, 295–306.

Dixon, R. A. & Lamb, C. J. (1979). Stimulation of *de novo* synthesis of L-phenylalanine ammonia-lyase in relation to phytoalexin accumulation in *Colletotrichum lindemuthianum* elicitor-treated cell suspension cultures of French bean (*Phaseolus vulgaris*). *Biochimica et Biophysica Acta*, **586**, 453–63.

Doke, N. & Tomiyama, K. (1980). Suppression of the hypersensitive response of potato tuber protoplasts to hyphal wall components by water soluble glucans isolated from *Phytophthora infestans*. *Physiological Plant Pathology*, **16**, 177–86.

Farkas, G. L. & Király, Z. (1962). Role of phenolic compounds in the physiology of plant diseases and disease resistance. *Phytopathologische Zeitschrift*, **44**, 105–50.

Freudenberg, K. & Neish, A. C. (1968). In *Constitution and Biosynthesis of Lignin*. Berlin: Springer-Verlag.

Friend, J. (1973). Resistance of potato to *Phytophthora*. In *Fungal Pathogenicity and the Plant's Response*, ed. R. J. W. Byrde & C. V. Cutting, pp. 383–96. London: Academic Press.

Friend, J. (1976). Lignification in infected tissue. In *Biochemical Aspects of Plant Parasite Relationships*, ed. J. Friend & D. R. Threlfall, pp. 291–303. London: Academic Press.

Friend, J. (1977). Biochemistry of plant pathogens. In *International Review of Biochemistry, Plant Biochemistry* II, vol. 13, ed. D. H. Northcote, pp. 141–82. Baltimore: University Park Press.

Friend, J. (1979). Phenolic substances and plant disease. In *Biochemistry of Plant Phenolics, Recent Advances in Phytochemistry*, vol. 12, ed. T. Swain, J. B. Harborne & C. F. Van Sumere, pp. 557–88. New York: Plenum Press.

Friend, J. (1980). Plant phenolics, lignification and plant disease. In *Progress in Phytochemistry*, vol. 7, ed. L. Reinhold, J. B. Harborne & T. Swain, pp. 197–261. Oxford: Pergamon.

Friend, J., Reynolds, S. B. & Aveyard, M. A. (1973). Phenylalanine ammonia lyase, chlorogenic acid and lignin in potato tuber tissue inoculated with *Phytophthora infestans*. *Physiological Plant Pathology*, **3**, 495–507.

Gans, P. T. (1978). Physiological responses of potato tubers to change and to infection by *Phoma exigua* f.sp. *foveata*. *Annals of Applied Biology*, **89**, 307–9.

Gross, G. G. (1979). Chemistry and biochemistry of lignin. In *Biochemistry of Plant Phenolics, Recent Advances in Phytochemistry*, vol. 12, ed. T. Swain, J. B. Harborne & C. F. Van Sumere, pp. 177–220. New York: Plenum Press.

Hadwiger, L. A., Hess, S. L. & von Broembsen, S. (1970). Stimulation of phenylalanine ammonia lyase activity and phytoalexin production. *Phytopathology*, **60**, 332–6.

Harborne, J. B. (1980). Plant phenolics. In *Encyclopedia of Plant Physiology, New Series*, vol. 8, *Secondary Plant Products*, ed. E. A. Bell & B. V. Charnwood, pp. 329–402. Berlin: Springer-Verlag.

Harborne, J. B. & Ingham, J. L. (1978). Biochemical aspects of the coevolution of higher plants with their fungal parasites. In *Biochemical Aspects of Plant and Animal Coevolution*, ed. J. B. Harborne, pp. 343–405. London: Academic Press.

Hargreaves, J. A. (1979). Investigations into the mechanism of mercuric chloride stimulated phytoalexin accumulation in *Phaseolus vulgaris* and *Pisum sativum*. *Physiological Plant Pathology*, **15**, 279–87.

Hargreaves, J. A. & Bailey, J. A. (1978). Phytoalexin production by hypocotyls of *Phaseolus vulgaris* in response to constitutive metabolites released by damaged bean cells. *Physiological Plant Pathology*, **13**, 89–100.

Hargreaves, J. A. & Selby, C. (1978). Phytoalexin formation in cell suspensions of *Phaseolus vulgaris* in response to an extract of bean hypocotyls. *Phytochemistry*, **17**, 1099–102.

Henderson, S. J. & Friend, J. (1979). Increase in PAL and lignin-like compounds as race-specific responses of potato tubers to *Phytophthora infestans*. *Phytopathologische Zeitschrift*, **94**, 323–34.

Heuvel, J. van den & Van Etten, H. D. (1973). Detoxification of phaseollin by *Fusarium solani* f.sp. *phaseoli*. *Physiological Plant Pathology*, **3**, 327–39.

Heuvel, J. van den, Van Etten, H. D., Serum, J. W., Coffen, D. L. & Williams, T. H. (1974). Identification of 1α-hydroxyphaseollone, a phaseollin metabolite produced by *Fusarium solani*. *Phytochemistry*, **13**, 1129–31.

Hochberg, M. & Cohen, Y. (1977). Scopoletin-induced catalase inhibition in tobacco leaves infected by *Peronospora tabacina* Adam. *Israel Journal of Botany*, **26**, 48.

Hoover, J. D., Wender, S. H. & Smith, E. C. (1977). Effects of phenolic compounds on glucose-6-phosphate dehydrogenase isoenzymes. *Phytochemistry*, **16**, 199–201.

Hughes, J. C. & Swain, T. (1960). Scopolin production in potato tubers infected with *Phytophthora infestans*. *Phytopathology*, **50**, 398–402.

Imbert, M. P. & Wilson, L. A. (1970). Stimulatory and inhibitory effects of scopoletin on IAA oxidase preparations from sweet potato. *Phytochemistry*, **9**, 1787–94.

Ingham, J. L. (1976). Induced and constitutive isoflavonoids from stems of chick peas (*Cicer arietinum* L.) inoculated with spores of *Helminthosporium carbonum* Ullstrup. *Phytopathologisch Zeitschrift*, **87**, 353–67.

Ishigura, Y., Tomiyama, K., Doke, N., Murai, A., Katsui, H., Yagihashi, F. & Masamune, T. (1978). Induction of rishitin-metabolizing activity in potato tuber tissue discs by wounding and identification of rishitin metabolites. *Phytopathology*, **68**, 720–5.

Kolattukudy, P. E. (1975). Biochemistry of cutin suberin and waxes – the lipid barriers on plants. In *Recent Advances in the Chemistry and Biochemistry of Plant Lipids*, ed. T. Galliard & E. I. Mercer, pp. 203–46. London: Academic Press.

Kuć, J. (1957). A biochemical study of the resistance of potato tuber tissue to attack by various fungi. *Phytopathology*, **47**, 676–80.

Kuć, J. (1972). Phytoalexins. *Annual Review of Phytopathology*, **10**, 207–31.

Kuć, J. A. (1976). Phytoalexins. In *Encyclopedia of Plant Physiology, New*

Series, vol. 4, *Physiological Plant Pathology*, ed. R. Heitefuss & P. H. Williams, pp. 632–52. Berlin: Springer-Verlag.

Kuhn, P. J. & Smith, D. A. (1976). The metabolism of the phytoalexin kievitone by *Fusarium solani* f.sp. *phaseoli*. *Proceedings of the American Phytopathological Society*, **3**, 261.

Kuhn, P. & Smith, D. A. (1978). Detoxification of the phytoalexin kievitone by *Fusarium solani* f.sp. *phaseoli*. *Annals of Applied Biology*, **89**, 362–6.

Kuhn, P. J. & Smith, D. A. (1979). Isolation from *Fusarium solani* f.sp. *phaseoli* of an enzymic system responsible for kievitone and phaseollidin detoxification. *Physiological Plant Pathology*, **14**, 179–90.

Kuhn, P. J., Smith, D. A. & Ewing, D. F. (1977). 5,7,2′,4′-Tetrahydroxy-8-(3″-hydroxy-3″-methyl-butyl)-isoflavanone, a metabolite of kievitone produced by *Fusarium solani* f.sp. *phaseoli*. *Phytochemistry*, **16**, 290–7.

Lamb, C. J. (1977). *Trans*-cinnamic acid as a mediator of the light-stimulated increase in hydroxycinnamoyl-CoA:quinate hydroxy-cinnamoyl transferase. *FEBS Letters*, **75**, 37–40.

Lamb, C. J. & Dixon, R. A. (1978). Stimulation of *de novo* synthesis of L-phenylalanine ammonia lyase during induction of phytoalexin biosynthesis in cell suspension cultures of *Phaseolus vulgaris*. *FEBS Letters*, **94**, 277–80.

Markwalder, H. U. & Neukom, H. (1976). Diferulic acid as a possible cross-link in hemicelluloses from wheat germ. *Phytochemistry*, **15**, 836–7.

Morris, A. J. & Smith, D. A. (1978). Phytoalexin formation in bean hypocotyls induced by cell-free mycelial extracts of *Rhizoctonia* and *Fusarium*. *Annals of Applied Biology*, **89**, 344–7.

Overeem, J. C. (1976). Pre-existing antimicrobial substances in plants and their role in disease resistance. In *Biochemical Aspects of Plant–Parasite Relationships*, ed. J. Friend & D. R. Threlfall, pp. 195–206. London: Academic Press.

Partridge, J. E. & Keen, N. T. (1977). Soybean phytoalexins: rates of synthesis are not regulated by activation of initial enzymes in flavonoid biosynthesis. *Phytopathology*, **67**, 50–5.

Pickering, J. W., Powell, B. L., Wender, S. H. & Smith, E. C. (1973). Ferulic acid: a substrate for two isoperoxidases from *Nicotiana tabacum* tissue cultures. *Phytochemistry*, **12**, 2639–43.

Pierpoint, W. S. (1966). The enzymic oxidation of chlorogenic acid and some reactions of the quinone produced. *Biochemical Journal*, **98**, 567–80.

Pierpoint, W. S., Ireland, R. J. & Carpenter, J. M. (1977). Modification of proteins during the oxidation of leaf phenols: reaction of potato virus X with chlorogenoquinone. *Phytochemistry*, **16**, 29–34.

Rathmell, W. G. (1973). Phenolic compounds and phenylalanine ammonia lyase activity in relation to phytoalexin biosynthesis in infected hypocotyls of *Phaseolus vulgaris*. *Physiological Plant Pathology*, **3**, 259–67.

Rhodes, M. J. C. & Wooltorton, L. S. C. (1976). The enzymic conversion of hydroxycinnamic acids to *p*-coumarylquinic and chlorogenic acids in tomato fruits. *Phytochemistry*, **15**, 947–51.

Rhodes, M. J. C., Wooltorton, L. S. C. & Lourenço, E. J. (1979). Purification and properties of hydroxycinnamoyl CoA:quinate hydroxycinnamoyl transferase from potatoes. *Phytochemistry*, **18**, 1125–9.

Rogerson, F. A. (1978). Biosynthesis of sesquiterpenoid stress compounds of potato. PhD thesis, University of Hull.

Rogerson, F. A. & Threlfall, D. R. (1978). Synthesis of stress metabolites in potato tuber tissue. *Annals of Applied Biology*, **89**, 351–4.

Schafer, P., Wender, S. H. & Smith, E. C. (1971). Effect of scopoletin on two anodic isoperoxidases isolated from tobacco tissue culture W-38. *Plant Physiology*, **48**, 232–3.

Schönbeck, F. & Schlösser, E. (1976). Preformed substances as potential protectants. In *Encyclopedia of Plant Physiology*, New Series, vol. 4, *Physiological Plant Pathology*, ed. R. Heitefuss & P. H. Williams, pp. 653–78. Berlin: Springer-Verlag.

Smith, D. A., Kuhn, P. J., Bailey, J. A. & Burden, R. S. (1980). Detoxification of phaseollidin by *Fusarium solani* f.sp. *phaseoli*. *Phytochemistry*, **19**, 1673–5.

Smith, D. A., Van Etten, H. D. & Bateman, D. F. (1975). Accumulation of phytoalexins in *Phaseolus vulgaris* following infection by *Rhizoctonia solani*. *Physiological Plant Pathology*, **5**, 61–4.

Smith, W. H., Jr & Smart, H. F. (1955). Relation of soft rot development to protective barriers in Irish potato slices. *Phytopathology*, **55**, 649–54.

Stafford, H. A. & Brown, M. A. (1976). Oxidative dimerization of ferulic acid by extracts from *Sorghum*. *Phytochemistry*, **15**, 465–9.

Swain, T. (1977). Secondary compounds as protective agents. *Annual Review of Plant Physiology*, **28**, 479–501.

Taylor, A. O. & Zucker, M. (1966). Turnover and metabolism of chlorogenic acid in *Xanthium* leaves and potato tubers. *Plant Physiology*, **41**, 1350–9.

Van Etten, H. D. (1973). Identification of a second antifungal isoflavan from a diseased *Phaseolus vulgaris* tissue. *Phytochemistry*, **12**, 1791–2.

Van Etten, H. D. & Pueppke, S. (1976). Isoflavonoid phytoalexins. In *Biochemical Aspects of Plant–Parasite Relationships*, ed. J. Friend & D. R. Threlfall, pp. 239–89. London: Academic Press.

Van Etten, H. D. & Smith, D. A. (1975). Accumulation of antifungal isoflavonoids and la-hydroxy phaseollone, a phaseollin metabolite, in bean tissue infected with *Fusarium solani* f.sp. *phaseoli*. *Physiological Plant Pathology*, **5**, 225–31.

Wade, E. M. & Albersheim, P. (1979). Race-specific molecules that protect soybeans from *Phytophthora megasperma* var. *sojae*. *Proceedings of the National Academy of Sciences, U.S.A.*, **44**, 33–7.

Waites, M. J. (1979). Aspects of phenolic metabolism associated with the defence reactions of potato tubers (*Solanum tuberosum* L.) towards a principal pathogen *Fusarium solani* var. *coeruleum* (Sacc.) Booth. PhD thesis, Wolverhampton Polytechnic.

Waites, M., Reynolds, S. B. & Friend, J. (1978). The metabolism of chlorogenic acid in tuber discs of a resistant and a susceptible potato cultivar after inoculation with *Fusarium solani* var. *coeruleum*. *Biochemical Society Transactions*, **6**, 441–2.

Walker, R. R. & Wade, G. C. (1976). Epidemiology of potato gangrene in Tasmania. *Australian Journal of Botany*, **24**, 337–47.

Walker, R. R. & Wade, G. C. (1978). Resistance of potato tubers (*Solanum tuberosum*) to *Phoma exigua* var. *exigua* and *Phoma exigua* var. *foveata*. *Australian Journal of Botany*, **26**, 239–51.

Yoshikawa, M. (1978). Diverse modes of action of biotic and abiotic phytoalexin elicitors. *Nature*, **275**, 546–7.

Yoshikawa, M., Yamauchi, K. & Masago, H. (1979). Biosynthesis and biodegradation of glyceollin by soybean hypocotyls infected with *Phytophthora megasperma* var. *sojae*. *Physiological Plant Pathology*, **14**, 157–69.

Zucker, M. & Hankin, L. (1970). Physiological basis for a cycloheximide induced soft rot of potatoes by *Pseudomonas fluorescens*. *Annals of Botany*, N.S., **34**, 1047–62.

R.RABBINGE & F.H.RIJSDIJK

Disease and crop physiology: a modeller's point of view

Introduction

Disease and pest management requires a knowledge of both the crops and the disease or pest. The interrelationships between host and parasite have a dynamic character, that is, they change with time, which has to be recognized in a proper description of the substrate and the environment of a parasitic organism. In the past, most studies of disease and pest management have emphasized the population dynamics of the disease and pest organisms, but their association with the growing crop has been virtually neglected. Elaborate studies on the population dynamics of pests or disease-causing organisms may be used in predicting future pest and disease intensity, but the value of these studies is limited when a reliable assessment of damage is not available. Models may help to develop management strategies.

Among dynamic models, various types can be distinguished according to the objectives of the study. When explanation is the aim, the corresponding explanatory models based on a systems hierarchy try to predict and explain integrated behaviour from a more detailed knowledge of the underlying physiological and morphological processes (De Wit & Goudriaan, 1978; De Wit et al., 1978). Much of the information presented in other chapters of this book illustrates studies of detailed plant physiological processes involved in crop–pathogen interrelations. To integrate this type of knowledge, and to determine the effects in terms of production ecology, a modelling approach of the explanatory type is needed. Of course, all knowledge of detailed processes becomes descriptive at the ultimate level of reduction, but one should nevertheless distinguish between descriptive and explanatory models. Descriptive models describe the behaviour of a system using only one level of integration. Descriptive models may be static or dynamic. In the latter case, the system and its behaviour may change in the course of time. Usually, descriptive models are static, as, for example, multivariate regression models, and their explanatory value is limited.

Explanatory models predict the behaviour of a system at the level to be explained using system-synthesizing elements, or subprocesses, at the next lower level of integration. These elements may be static (for example, light distribution in a canopy based on geometric and physical characteristics of the canopy) or dynamic (for example, crop growth, known in detail from plant physiology). Some comprehensive simulation models of pests and diseases have already led to simplified econometric models which can help decisions about 'spraying or praying'. However, the practical value of these models is limited as their reliability is low. Multivariate regression models have given better results in crop loss assessment; their superiority is mainly owing to the tuning procedure involved in the development of such models. These models accommodate better to average field conditions since they include data about the variations in plant stand, nutrient and water supply, and the level of injury by the disease or pest at a certain population density, which all together determine the yield. Regression models perform best in predicting the mean performance of a population of fields, whereas dynamic models may give better results when applied to the individual field.

Only a few combination models exist in which both crop growth *and* population dynamics of the pest or disease organism are based on detailed analysis. Such combination models are often of a dualistic nature, containing on the one hand a great number of descriptive elements, and on the other a great deal of detailed knowledge of subprocesses. When too many phenomena observed at the system level are introduced into the model, its behaviour is often governed by the descriptive relationships. In those cases the explanatory value of the models is limited and the modelling effort becomes a sophisticated method of curve fitting. Comprehensive models with a satisfactory compromise between completeness of basic data, time needed for experimental and modelling effort, and reliable output, are rare indeed.

In this chapter we will discuss two types of combination models. First we will discuss summary models. These models are designed to produce a shortcut to the objectives of the comprehensive model, without losing the sensitivity of the full analysis. Models of this type are used to calculate the effect of a pest or a disease on crop growth without further consideration of the nature of damage. Changes in crop–pathogen interactions are introduced in these models to compute the impact of the perturbations. The calculations give some insight into the relative importance of the nature of crop–pathogen interrelations. A complete explanation cannot be given as too many basic relations are neglected. Second, we will discuss an example of a comprehensive model of crop growth and a disease. This combination model is used to test hypotheses on the nature of the disease–crop interrelations.

Dynamic simulation of crop growth

During the last decade considerable attention has been paid to the development of procedures for the calculation of crop growth which are based on the process of photosynthesis. Some review articles summarize this effort (Waggoner, 1977; Loomis, Rabbinge & Ng, 1979; Penning de Vries, 1981). These calculations are usually based on the assumptions that photosynthetic activity is maximal and crop canopies are closed. The actual production of a crop is then found by accumulating this photosynthetic activity and multiplying this sum by the harvest index, the ratio of seed dry weight to total dry weight. Other methods, in which attention is paid not only to photosynthesis but also to respiration and the partitioning of assimilates between various plant organs, are scarce. Comprehensive models that incorporate all these aspects in sufficient detail are not yet available. The level of detail of some subprocesses depends mainly on the interest and knowledge of the model builder and his opinion on the relative importance of these subprocesses. A model with many details, simulating the assimilation, respiration and transpiration of crop surfaces (BACROS), has been developed by De Wit *et al.* (1978). However, the morphogenesis of the crop and the functioning of different organs are completely neglected in this otherwise comprehensive model; partitioning processes are only introduced as a functional balance between shoot and root that is independent of the relative water content of the canopy. This model is used later in an evaluation of the effects of stripe rust on crop productivity and in an effort to study the nature of stripe rust damage.

A summary model of crop growth may suffice in cases where the effect of disease or pests on crop growth is assessed. A summary model which is very suitable for this purpose has been developed by Van Keulen (1976) as a simple method for calculating potential rice production. In this model the considerable explanatory detail in the environmental and photosynthesis modules, which are presented in BACROS, is replaced by shortcuts and simple formulae which suffice to describe the dynamic character of these processes. The plant growth sections in the summary model are, on the other hand, more elaborate. Various plant organs are considered, so that it is possible to couple pathogenic infection to different parts of the plant. Crop development, i.e. initiation, growth and development of individual organs, is introduced into the model in a descriptive way, thus it contrasts with the photosynthesis model, which is based on explanatory models of assimilation, respiration and transpiration of crop surfaces. A temperature-dependent development rate is accumulated and this integral, called development stage, initiates changes in respiration and partitioning of carbohydrates to new growth centres. Van Keulen's summary model of crop growth and development is described in the next paragraphs, explaining in more detail that part involving photosynthate supply, which is extensively treated in De Wit *et al.* (1978).

Basic structure of summary model of crop growth

The basic structure of the summary model is presented in a relational diagram (Fig. 1). Shoot, root and grain (for example, of wheat) increase at a relative rate dependent on the developmental stage, which accounts for the partitioning of photosynthates. All plant organs grow from the assimilation stream, whose size depends on the incoming radiation and the leaf surface (leaf area index, LAI) participating in photosynthesis. Before partitioning of the carbohydrates to the plant organs, growth respiration (dependent upon growth rate) and maintenance respiration (dependent upon organ weight) are subtracted.

Ageing of plant organs is expressed as a relative rate of decrease of weight of these organs, which is governed by the developmental stage.

Photosynthesis

In the summary model the basis for the calculations is the photosynthetic rate of the canopy under optimal growing conditions. De Wit's (1965)

Fig. 1. Relational diagram of a summary model of crop growth. Rectangles represent state variables; rate variables are given by valves. Flows of material are presented by solid lines and flows of information by broken lines. ~ expresses a sink and ⌐ expresses a source.

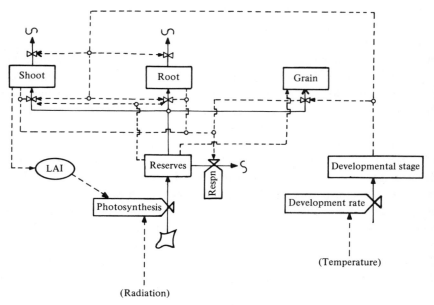

computation procedure, reformulated by Goudriaan & Van Laar (1978a), is used to find the photosynthetic rate of closed green crop surfaces. On the basis of the photosynthesis:light response curve of a single leaf in ambient air of normal temperature and carbon dioxide concentration, Goudriaan & Van Laar calculated a photosynthesis:light response curve for closed canopies without further knowledge of the geometric characteristics of the canopy. Only the total leaf mass needs to be known. Effects of chloroplast distribution, nitrogen content of the leaf blade, age of the leaf and environmental conditions such as carbon dioxide concentration and temperature are all expressed as changes in the efficiency with which the simple leaves use light, and these changes will result in changes in daily total gross photosynthesis. The distribution of radiation within the canopy can be determined from the radiation climate above the canopy, which is dependent on the position of the sun in the sky, the prevalent cloudiness and the way in which the incident radiation is absorbed by the leaves. With this method, Goudriaan & Van Laar calculated total daily gross photosynthesis as a function of the LAI and daily global radiation. Van Keulen (1976) used this method in his summary model to compute the daily gross photosynthesis of a canopy under the assumption that the actual rate of gross photosynthesis is proportional to the fraction of the total energy intercepted by the canopy.

The actual daily photosynthetic rate (BF) for a closed canopy in the summary model is found by calculating the fraction of the sky that is overcast during a day and multiplying the daily gross photosynthetic rate for overcast skies (PO) by this fraction, and then adding to this product the fraction of clear sky multiplied by the gross photosynthetic rate (PC):

$$BF = (1 - F) \times PC + F \times PO.$$

The fraction overcast (F) is calculated according to:

$$F = (DTRS - 0.2 \times HC)/(HC - 0.2 \times HC)$$

in which $DTRS$ = actual daily total global incoming radiation in J m^{-2} s^{-1} and HC = incoming radiation when the sky is completely clear. The incoming radiation on overcast days equals 0.2 of the amount of radiation at clear days. PC, PO, $DTRS$ and HC are introduced in the model as time- and location-dependent variables. Van Keulen (1976) calculates the gross photosynthetic rate of a crop ($GFOT$) by multiplying the gross photosynthesis of a closed canopy with a factor that accounts for the extinction of radiation in the canopy. This multiplication factor presumes radiation intensity decreases exponentially in a canopy, the relative rate of decrease being dependent on the LAI. The factor has considerable effect when the LAI $\leq$ 3, but becomes negligible with higher leaf areas.

Gross photosynthesis is now found from:

$$GFOT = BF \times (1 - \exp(-0.6 \times \text{LAI})).$$

In the summary model the LAI is not introduced as a driving force, nor simulated, but simply computed from the weight of the above-ground material, assuming a fixed specific leaf weight of 0.066 kg m^{-2}, a figure which seems to be representative for small grains.

In the comprehensive model of crop growth, the photosynthetic rate is computed on the basis of light-use efficiency, the maximum assimilation rate of individual leaves and stomatal behaviour. Within this latter model, C$_3$ and C$_4$ plants are distinguished and allowance is made for a stomatal regulatory mechanism that maintains a more or less constant carbon dioxide concentration in the stomatal cavity (Goudriaan & Van Laar, 1978b).

Respiration

The energy trapped in the photosynthetic process is immediately used in various ways, so that only a changing fraction remains in newly fixed compounds. The remainder is liberated in respiratory processes which support two distinguishable areas of activity.

First, *growth processes*, i.e. the synthesis of structural plant material, such as proteins, fats and carbohydrates. A variable amount of photosynthetic material is used to produce new material, depending on the composition of the plant material being synthesized. In a detailed study of growth respiration, which represents a sophisticated way of bookkeeping for all the processes involved, Penning de Vries (1975) calculated the efficiency of conversion for different structural compounds: this he called the production value (see Table 1). The percentage of photosynthetic compounds used for the construction of new plant materials is in the order of 40% for a fat- and protein-rich crop like soybean, and approximately 25% for a carbohydrate-rich canopy like sugar beet. In the summary model, calculations are made for small grains and the fraction of photosynthetic material invested in constructing structural material is then 30% of the total amount. Thus, all factors are lumped together to find one conversion factor.

Table 1. *Efficiency of conversion of substrate (glucose) into plant constituents*

Compounds	Production value (g material g^{-1} glucose)
Carbohydrates	0.826
Nitrogenous compounds	0.404
Organic acids	1.104
Lignin	0.465
Lipids	0.330

In the comprehensive model, the actual processes are simulated so that this lumping is not necessary. Penning de Vries showed that these conversion factors of photosynthetic material are virtually independent of temperature. Of course, this does not hold for the growth process itself.

Second, *maintenance processes* are the other sink for photosynthetic material. The structure of already existing cells must be maintained and this involves the turnover of protein and the sustaining of ionic gradients and membrane structures. Again the composition of the material determines the energy required, the main variable being the protein content. The complicated character of maintenance ensures that accurate quantitative estimates of these processes are rare. Although the size of maintenance respiration is low in comparison with growth respiration, its presence during the plant's entire life span means that its contribution to the total energy spent for respiration is comparable with that spent on growth processes (Penning de Vries, 1981). Maintenance respiration is directly affected by temperature and seems to have a Q_{10} value of 2 to 3.

Since maintenance of existing structures has a higher priority than synthesis of new structural material, the computations are done in such a way that growth respiration is calculated after the respiration needed for maintenance has been subtracted.

Development

As indicated in the relational diagram (Fig. 1), the developmental phase of the crop is used to govern relative partitioning rates and relative ageing rates. In most models of crop growth, development and morphogenesis are not considered. A major reason for this is that developmental processes are poorly understood; for example, explanation is virtually absent for processes such as the appearance of leaves, the transition between vegetative and reproductive phases, or the flowering and heading of plants. Still, the development of a crop greatly interferes with its growth, therefore development should be properly simulated in a realistic crop growth simulator. Development is affected by temperature and day length in most crops. These governing factors may be introduced to compute the rate at which the crop develops; this is usually done by defining crop development in terms of the temperature sum, i.e. the product of average temperature and time. A more flexible approach is used in this summary model in which development is mimicked by integrating a temperature and day-length-dependent development rate. The input relation of this rate should be determined from crop development experiments in which the average development period (for example, from germination until flowering) is determined at different temperatures. The development rate, integrated over different developmental stages, is one of the most critical variables in the model. It determines, for example, partitioning of assimilates and leaf duration.

Partitioning

The distribution of the newly formed photosynthetic products is greatly affected by the development of the crop. Early in the growth of the crop carbohydrates can only be transported to roots and shoot, but after flowering there is a considerable shift in partitioning. This may of course be different in plants whose growth is non-determinate, such as beans.

The proportion of material going to the different organs has been studied by plant physiologists in great detail, especially for small grains (Lian & Tanaka, 1967, Spiertz, 1978). To estimate the size of the various carbohydrate flows, labelling with ^{14}C is used. For rice it is estimated that 70% of stored carbohydrates are translocated to the grain, 30% being lost in respiration. Of the carbon fixed after flowering, 85% is accumulated in the grain, the remainder being used for the upkeep of other organs. Before flowering, only 10% of the photosynthetic products are stored in the stem, the other 90% being divided between root and shoot in the ratio of 1:3.

Each of the subprocesses described above may be affected by a pathogenic organism. To illustrate the effect of different pest or disease organisms in terms of production ecology, different pathogenic organisms have been connected to the summary model of crop growth.

Population dynamics of pests or disease-causing organisms

One of the most well known analytical formulae describing population growth rate is given by Van der Plank (1963):

$$\frac{dx}{dt} = R_c(x_{t-p} - x_{t-i-p})(1 - x_t)$$

in which x = fraction of visibly diseased foliage; t = time; R_c = the corrected basic infection rate; p = latent period; i = infectious period. This formula transforms into the well-known formula for logistic growth when the latent period approaches zero and the infectious period reaches infinity:

$$\frac{dx}{dt} = r \times x_t(1 - x_t)$$

where r = relative growth rate.

The occurrence of time-lags, such as latent periods, or finite multiplication periods, are normal in biology so that the logistic formula only holds in very exceptional cases, for example when yeast is grown under optimal conditions. However, it is difficult to solve the equation if terms are introduced to describe such time-lags. With numerical integration of the Van der Plank equation, dynamic simulation was introduced in botanical epidemiology (Zadoks 1971; Waggoner, Horsfall & Lukens, 1972). This new technique enabled the development of more realistic simulation models. Fig. 2 shows the flow diagram of a simple simulation model integrating Van der Plank's formula.

Infectious leaf area produces infective propagules, which can cause new infections leading to an increase of latent leaf area and a decrease of vacant leaf area. Thus, four conditions of leaf area are recognized

(1) not-infected, or vacant;
(2) infected but not-yet-infectious;
(3) infected and infectious;
(4) infected and no-longer-infectious.

The status of the non-vacant leaf area is indicated by rectangles, the vacant leaf area is absent in Fig. 2, as in Van der Plank's formula.

Time-lags between latent and infectious states, and between infectious and no-longer-infectious states, are governed by the latent period and infectious period respectively. The mathematical formulation for such processes is given by De Wit & Goudriaan (1978). The same model can be used for describing the population dynamics of pests. In that case the latent period is replaced by one or more developmental stages, and the infectious period is replaced by some adult developmental stage in the reproductive phase. Each of the rates is affected by environmental factors, so the model has to be modified appropriately. Models of this type give information on the total size of the population of pests or disease, and on the age distribution of populations.

Fig. 2. Relational diagram of a summary model of a fungus epidemic. IS = rate of infection; SIS = apparent infection rate; AS = rate of dying of infectious lesions; R = relative rate of infection; MI = potential number of lesions; LAT = latent; INF = infectious; REM = removed; P = latent period; I = infectious period.

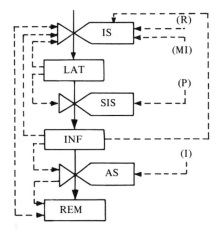

More elaborate population models may add more or less complicated sub-models to the basic model in order to allow calculation of the subprocesses in relation to climate, crop condition and natural enemies. Processes like lesion growth, spore dispersal and the geographical distribution of the population in crops have been studied in this way (Shrum, 1975; Waggoner, 1977; Kampmeijer & Zadoks, 1977; Rijsdijk, 1980). Elaborate studies describing parasite and/or predator population in relation to pest organisms have also been made (Gutierrez *et al.*, 1975; Rabbinge, 1976). Most models treat the crop as a qualitatively constant substrate for pests and disease-causing organisms. This limits the value of such models because opposite effects can be clearly demonstrated. Thus, resistance of barley to the leaf rust *Puccinia hordei* increased during crop development in both susceptible and more resistant barley cultivars, owing to an increase in latent periods and, thereby, a decrease in infection frequencies (Parlevliet, 1976). Last (1954) demonstrated the effect of differences in nitrogen fertilization on the growth of mildew on wheat. Rijsdijk (1980) presented data concerning the effect of nitrogen fertilization on stripe rust of wheat in field experiments and in detailed studies under controlled conditions. A wealth of data is available to demonstrate the influence of pests or disease-causing organisms on the host, and covers aspects ranging from changing rates of photosynthesis and respiration, to changing root:shoot ratios (Martin & Hendrix, 1966), to crop losses.

Host plant and disease-causing, or pest, organisms show mutual interference. In most cases only one side of the coin is shown and this gives a limited view of the effect of a pest on its host plant or vice versa. For example, the condition of a wheat plant affects the latent period and infectious period of stripe rust, but on the other hand the stripe rust may promote loss of water and affect the functioning of the crop in such a way that less nitrogen will be available for the shoot, thereby decreasing the infectious period.

To demonstrate the interactions for some pests and disease-causing organisms simple pest and disease models have been connected to the simplified crop model described above. In addition, one example of an interaction between a more elaborate crop model and disease model will be discussed.

Interactions between plant and disease or pest organisms
Mutilation of leaf mass
Many examples can be given of consumption of leaf mass by herbivores. However, the influence of leaf feeders seems limited unless their numbers become very high, or their consumption rate very large. For example, the effect of leaf hoppers on leaf mass is so high that sophisticated prediction and monitoring systems have been developed to prevent their disastrous effects. To demonstrate the effect of a leaf consumer on crop growth, a simplified simulator of

population growth of the cereal leaf beetle has been attached to the simple crop growth simulator discussed above and parameterized for winter wheat.

Larvae of cereal leaf beetles (*Lema cyanella*) consume leaf mass at a rate of about 250 cm^2 day^{-1} ($= 1.5$ g dry matter). Only the larvae consume leaves. After growth and development they pupate and later moult into adults that may give rise to another generation. The rate of increase of the numbers of cereal leaf beetle larvae mainly depends on the immigration rate of the adult beetles which lay their eggs on the leaves. After hatching, the larvae immediately start feeding. Their effect on crop growth is introduced into the model as a drain on the shoot weight. This rate of decrease of shoot weight is assumed to be proportional to the number of larvae of the beetle, lumping all developmental phases of the larvae together. Consumption of leaf mass by the adults is neglected, and age and reproduction rate (dependent on food quality and development rate) are not considered. The beetle population is introduced in a very simple way by distinguishing four morphological stages: eggs, larvae, pupae and adults. The adult population is assumed to be 50% male, so that after egg-laying only 50% (females) will grow and contribute to the next generation. Reproduction of the adult beetles is diminished when excessively high larval densities are reached, this depending on the ratio of number of larvae : weight of shoot.

Some results of calculations with the model are presented in Fig. 3. It is shown that when the population density of the larvae reaches a level of 15 000 ha^{-1}, or 1.5 m^{-2}, or 0.004 tiller^{-1} at flowering the effect on the yield loss will be less than 1%. It has also been shown that the time of introduction of the beetle is highly important. A late and heavy attack of the beetles scarcely affects the final crop yield, but an early and steady attack reaching a density of 0.04 tiller^{-1} may cause a severe decrease in yield (Fig. 3). In that case, 14% of the grain yield is lost and about 50% of the straw yield is not harvested.

Leaf coverage

To demonstrate the effect of a disease that covers the leaves with a thin layer and promotes leaf senescence, the powdery mildew *Erysiphe graminis* is coupled to the wheat simulator. The fungus is simulated with the Van der Plank equation (p. 208). Neither individual spores nor pustules are distinguished; instead, the sites are simulated, i.e. the leaf surface is represented in terms of potential sites, each site representing the minimum size of one lesion (a field of 1 ha, LAI $= 4$, contains about 10^9 sites).

The simple combination model used here only supplies information on the effect of the leaf-covering activity of mildew epidemics. This effect is introduced by multiplying the gross photosynthetic rate by the leaf area covered : total leaf area ratio. Some results of this model show that, when the assumption is made that the fungus is homogeneously distributed in the canopy, a considerable loss occurs (Fig. 4). However, in most cases the fungus grows from the bottom of the canopy towards the top, and is mainly located in the lower leaf layers. Losses are much lower if this location effect is introduced into the crop model. When the LAI ⩽ 3, effects are much greater than in crops with a higher LAI. In these crops with high leaf densities a large decrease or increase in respiration could affect the net assimilation rate, but in practice this seldom happens.

Extension of this model with the other effects caused by *E. graminis* is possible whenever more accurate knowledge of these effects on respiration rate or photosynthetic rate becomes available.

Stripe rust (Puccinia striiformis) *and winter wheat*

The examples of host plant–pathogen relations given above used a summary model of crop growth. This was possible since the objective was to show some of the effects in general terms. In most cases of pathogen–host plant rela-

Fig. 3. Simulated increase in weight of cereal grain. ● = beetles absent, × = beetle population at a maximum of 1 per 0.004 tillers, □ = beetle population 1 per 0.04 tillers at flowering, i.e. heavy attack.

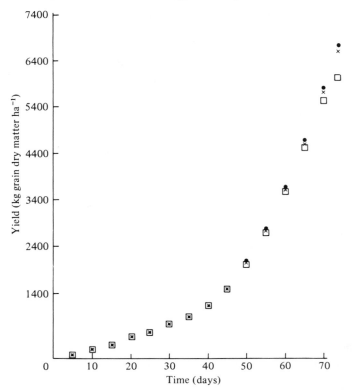

tions this is impossible as the interrelations are of a more complex nature. This is illustrated with stripe rust on winter wheat.

In an ecophysiological study of crop losses, exemplified in the infection of wheat by leaf rust, Van der Wal, Smeitink & Maan (1975) demonstrated that leaf rust infection increased the transpiration rate of spring wheat (also discussed by Ayres, this volume). Similar effects were shown for wheat with stripe rust (F. H. Rijsdijk, unpublished data).

The increased transpiration rate may have been due to an increase in leaf conductance or a shift in shoot:root ratio, a combination of both, or a chain of effects. Simulation studies may help to test the hypothesis that the sporulating

Fig. 4. Simulated increase in weight of cereal grain. ● = control, disease absent; × = mildew epidemic reaches a maximum of 80% leaf coverage, mainly concentrated in the lower leaf layers; ○ = mildew epidemic reaches a maximum of 80% leaf coverage, homogeneously distributed in the canopy.

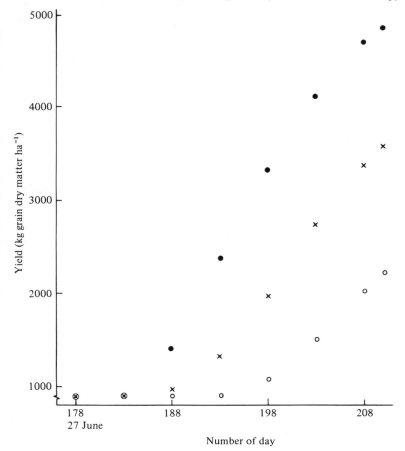

pustules of the fungus operate as holes in the leaf and to determine the conse-quences of such an effect. Summary models of crop growth with simplified re-lations for water balance and water use are insufficient to study this problem. An elaborate and detailed model of assimilation, transpiration and respiration of crop surfaces is needed to test the effect of stripe rust on crop behaviour.

De Wit's detailed simulation model (De Wit, 1978) is used to introduce this 'hole making' effect of rust. Within this model, transpiration is computed with a Penman-type formula in which leaf resistance is one of the most important variables. Leaf resistance can be found experimentally by measurements with a diffusion porometer (Stigter & Lammers, 1974). The dependence of stomatal resistance (the most important resistance for carbon dioxide and water diffusion) on environmental factors could be introduced into the model, but detailed anal-ysis of stomatal resistance in relation to assimilation rate and transpiration rate have shown that a linear relation exists in many cases between stomatal conduc-tivity and carbon dioxide assimilation rate (Goudriaan & Van Laar, 1978b). This indicates that stomata may regulate their aperture in such a way that a constant carbon dioxide concentration is maintained in the stomatal cavity (see also Raschke, 1975). Therefore, in the detailed crop simulator, this facultative regu-lation mechanism is introduced and the stomatal resistance (SR) is calculated from this equation:

$$SR = (68.4 \times (CO_{2_{ext}} - CO_{2_{int}}) - R_b \times 1.32 \times PHOT)/PHOT$$

where $CO_{2_{ext}}$ is the external carbon dioxide concentration; $CO_{2_{int}}$ is the regulated internal carbon dioxide concentration, R_b is the boundary layer resistance and PHOT is the actual photosynthetic rate, computed from a light response curve of carbon dioxide assimilation. The constants are necessary to transform the carbon dioxide diffusion resistance into a diffusion resistance for water.

The carbon dioxide regulation mechanisms may be overruled by regulation through the leaf's water balance, i.e. if a marked water shortage occurs, the stomata will close. The holes due to rust pustules may cause a continuous closing of stomata and thus, decreased photosynthetic activity. In the model the diffusion resistance of the holes is introduced by using the calculations for a membrane with cylindrical pores (e.g. Penman & Schofield, 1951; Monteith, 1973). For such a porous membrane made up of n cylindrical pores, of length l and diameter d, per unit of surface, the resistance R_m, is normally taken to be:

$$R_m = \frac{4l}{d^2nD} + 2 \times \frac{1}{2dnD}$$

in which D is the diffusion coefficient of carbon dioxide, which depends on temperature. The first term of this formula is the diffusion resistance of the tubes proper. The second term is the expression for the diffusional 'end effects' at both sides of the membrane. It represents the diffusion resistance of a semi-infinite half space, completely insulated at the free surface with the exception of n independent spots of given constant and uniform concentration. To compute the diffusion resistance for a canopy which contains a large number of these pores, the second part of the formula is used: $R = 1/nDd$.

The number of pores is calculated as follows: when the diameter d of a rust pore (= size of pustule) equals 1.6 mm, the potential number of pores per ha (n), in a canopy with LAI = 5, equals 5×10^8 cm^2/$\pi \times (0.08)^2 = 2.5 \times 10^{10}$ sites ha^{-1}. This means that when there is a 100% infection of the leaves, about 20% of the leaf area is replaced by pores, i.e. 20% $= 0.5 \times 10^{10}$ sites ha$^{-1} = 50$ sites cm^{-2}, and the diffusion coefficient $= 0.2$ cm^2 s^{-1}. Thus, the resistance of this canopy amounts to

$$R = \frac{1}{50 \times 0.2 \times 0.16} = 0.62 \text{ s cm}^{-1}$$

and the conductivity of the canopy is enlarged by 0.016 m s^{-1}; a considerable increase, indicating that the transpiration rate may be affected considerably. To test this, the assumption is introduced in a computer simulation that the maximum infection level is reached. The results of such simulation show that when the other effects of leaf rust on assimilation, etc. are neglected, the total production of dry matter is not much lower, but that there is an enormous shift in shoot:root ratio, so that the shoot weight is about 10% lower than that without rust attack and the root weight is about 1.5 greater than that without rust attack (Figs. 5, 6 and 7). The transpiration rate of the canopy is considerably higher, on average about two times the normal transpiration rate.

These results illustrate the influence of the functional balance, i.e. internal regulatory mechanisms of the plant, since, owing to an increase in transpiration, the root system has to be extended to keep up the relative water content of the crop and this lowers the amount of assimilates available for the shoot.

Although these results seem quite logical, they are not in agreement with results obtained from field and container experiments by Van der Wal *et al.* (1975). This is probably because it was unreal and incorrect to assume that the decrease in assimilation rate of the canopy, and the increase in respiration due to the production of rust material, could be neglected. When one of these processes is introduced into the model, there is again a change in effects.

The decrease in assimilation rate due to the absence of photosynthetic activity in the pustules is introduced by multiplying the net assimilation rate by the percentage of the total leaf area attacked. As a result of this change in the model, the total amount of above-ground dry matter simulated with the model is about

25% less in infected than in non-infected control plants, i.e. a yield loss of about 2500 kg ha^{-1}. Again the root weight is higher than in the control and this is probably owing to the functional balance, which causes an increase in root growth due to a higher transpiration rate. The decrease of assimilation rate caused by a loss in photosynthetically active leaf area resulted in the considerable decrease in crop growth found in these simulations.

Finally, the crop growth simulator is connected to a simulator of stripe rust epidemics, enabling latent, infectious and removed sites to be distinguished. The results of these calculations are also presented in Figs. 5, 6 and 7. A heavy attack of stripe rust causes a considerable decrease in shoot weight and a slight decrease in root weight, a result that confirms field observations. Still the model does not correspond completely with experimental results. Although the total loss in crop yield agrees rather well with the experimental outcome, the increase in root weight does not agree completely with some experimental results. This may be due to the incompleteness of the model, e.g. effects on maintenance respiration are neglected, or it may be caused by insufficient understanding of the way hormonal processes interfere with partitioning processes of carbohydrates. In spite of their imperfections, these simulations show how an effort is being made to gain a full understanding of the various processes which play a role in the crop–pathogen interrelations.

Fig. 5. Simulated increase in weight of shoot and ear with a comprehensive crop growth simulator. □ = unattacked crop; ○ = crop infected by a stripe rust epidemic, maximum leaf coverage of 20%; × = crop infected by a stripe rust epidemic, reaching maximum leaf coverage of 100%, i.e. 20% of leaf area replaced by holes, using a realistic simulator of the rust epidemics.

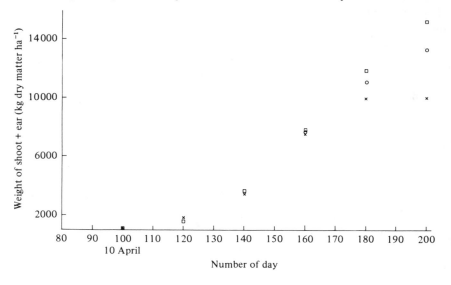

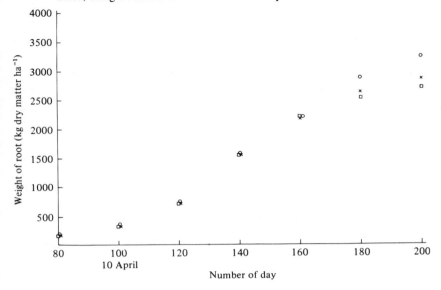

Fig. 6. Simulated increase in weight of root with a comprehensive crop growth simulator. □ = unattacked crop; ○ = crop infected by a stripe rust epidemic, maximum leaf coverage of 20%; × = crop infected by a stripe rust epidemic, reaching maximum leaf coverage of 100%, i.e. 20% of leaf area replaced by holes, using a realistic simulator of the rust epidemics.

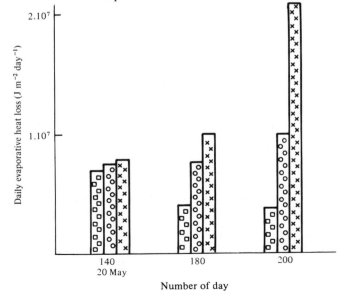

Fig. 7. Simulated daily evaporative heat loss in J m^{-2}. □ = unattacked crop; ○ = crop infected by a stripe rust epidemic, maximum leaf coverage of 20%; × = crop infected by a stripe rust epidemic, reaching maximum leaf coverage of 100%, i.e. 20% of leaf area replaced by holes, using a realistic simulator of the rust epidemics.

Discussion

Simple examples of host plant–pathogen models have been discussed. To design these models, well-known phenomena had to be formulated in quantitative terms. The quantification of processes compels the model builder to make his assumptions and hypotheses explicit. He can then find out what effects are of minor importance, and what effects are of major importance. Subprocesses which seriously affect the behaviour of the crop–pathogen system have to be studied in more detail than subprocesses which only cause small deviations from an optimal growth of the crop. In this way, model building may help to formulate research priorities.

Another important aspect of model building is the capacity of models to test hypotheses. A model reflects its architect's opinion on the way processes operate in the real world. By a continuous procedure of model building and testing, successive hypotheses can be rejected or accepted. In doing this the model operates as a communication tool between the generalist, who is urged by the model to study some processes in more detail, and the reductionist, who is able to recognize from the model the meaning of the subprocess studied by him within the total behaviour of the system. In this way models help to bridge the gap between scientists working in the laboratory on plant physiological processes and their colleagues in the field trying to understand the behaviour of crops under conditions of stress.

References

De Wit, C. T. (1965). *Photosynthesis of leaf canopies. Agricultural Research Reports, Wageningen,* No. 663. Wageningen: Pudoc.

De Wit, C. T. & Goudriaan, J. (1978). *Simulation of ecological processes. Simulation Monographs.* Wageningen: Pudoc.

De Wit, C. T., Goudriaan, J., Van Laar, H. H., Penning de Vries, F. W. T., Rabbinge, R. & Van Keulen, H. (1978). *Simulation of assimilation, respiration and transpiration of crops. Simulation Monographs.* Wageningen: Pudoc.

Goudriaan, J. & Van Laar, H. H. (1978a). Calculation of daily totals of the gross CO_2 assimilation of leaf canopies. *Netherlands Journal of Agricultural Sciences,* **26,** 373–82.

Goudriaan, J. & Van Laar, H. H. (1978b). Relations between leaf resistance, CO_2-concentration and CO_2-assimilation in maize, beans, lalang grass and sunflower. *Photosynthetica,* **12,** 241–9.

Gutierrez, A. P., Falcan, L. A., Loew, W., Leipzig, P. A. & van den Bosch, R. (1975). An analysis of cotton production in California: a model of Acala cotton and the effect of defoliators on its yields. *Environmental Entomology,* **4,** 125–36.

Kampmeijer, P. & Zadoks, J. C. (1977). *EPIMUL, a simulator of foci and epidemics in mixtures, multilines and mosaics of resistant and susceptible plants. Simulation Monographs.* Wageningen: Pudoc.

Last, F. T. (1954). The effect of application of nitrogenous fertilizer on powdery mildew of winter wheat. *Annals of Applied Biology*, **41**, 381–92.

Lian, S. & Tanaka, A. (1967). Behaviour of photosynthetic products associated with growth and grain production in the rice plant. *Plant and Soil*, **26**, 333–47.

Loomis, R. S., Rabbinge, R. & Ng, E. (1979). Models in crop physiology. *Annual Review of Plant Physiology*, **30**, 339–67.

Martin, N. E. & Hendrix, J. W. (1966). Influence of stripe rust on root development in wheat. *Phytopathology*, **56**, 149.

Monteith, J. L. (1973). *Principles of Environmental Physics*. London: Edward Arnold.

Parlevliet, J. E. (1976). Evaluation of the concept of horizontal resistance by the barley–*Puccinia hordei* host–pathogen relationship. *Phytopathology*, **66**, 494–7.

Penman, H. L. & Schofield, R. K. (1951). Some physical aspects of assimilation and transpiration. *Society for Experimental Biology Symposia*, V, 119–29.

Penning de Vries, F. W. T. (1975). Use of assimilates in higher plants. In *Photosynthesis and Productivity in Different Environments*, International Biological Programme 3, ed. J. P. Cooper, pp. 459–80. Cambridge: Cambridge University Press.

Penning de Vries, F. W. T. (1981). Modelling growth and production. *Encyclopedia of Plant Physiology*, New Series, vol. 14. Berlin: Springer Verlag. (In press.)

Rabbinge, R. (1976). *Biological control of fruit tree red spider mite. Simulation Monographs.* Wageningen: Pudoc.

Raschke, K. (1975). Stomatal action. *Annual Review of Plant Physiology*, **26**, 309–40.

Rijsdijk, F. H. (1980). Systems analysis at the cross roads of plant pathology and crop physiology. *Zeitschrift für Pflanzenkrankheiten und Pflanzenschutz*, **128**, 404–8.

Shrum, R. (1975). *Simulation of wheat strip rust* (Puccinia striiformis *West.*) *using EPIDEMIC, a flexible plant disease simulator. Pennsylvania State University, College of Agricultural Experimental Station Progress Report*, No. 371. Pennsylvania State University.

Spiertz, J. H. J. (1978). *Grain production and assimilate utilization of wheat in relation to cultivar characteristics, climatic factor and nitrogen supply. Agricultural Research Reports, Wageningen*, No. 881. Wageningen: Pudoc.

Stigter, C. J. & Lammers, B. (1974). Leaf diffusion resistance to water vapour and its direct measurement. III. Results regarding the improved diffusion porometer in growth rooms and fields of Indian corn (*Zea mays*). *Mededelingen Landbouwhogeschool, Wageningen*, **21**, 1–76.

Van Keulen, H. (1976). *A calculation method for potential rice production*, Contribution 21. Bogor (Indonesia): Central Research Institute for Agriculture.

Van der Plank, J. E. (1963). *Plant Disease, Epidemics and Control*. New York: Academic Press.

Van der Wal, A. F., Smeitink, H. & Maan, G. C. (1975). A crop physiological approach to crop losses exemplified in the system wheat, leaf rust and glume blotch. III. Effects of soil water potential on development, growth, transpiration, symptoms and spore production of leaf rust-infected wheat. *Netherlands Journal of Plant Pathology*, **81**, 1–13.

Waggoner, P. E. (1977). Simulation of modelling of plant physiological processes to predict crop yields. In *Environmental Effects on Crop Physiology*, ed. J. J. Landsberg & C. V. Cutting, pp. 351–63. New York: Academic Press.

Waggoner, P. E., Horsfall, J. G. & Lukens, R. J. (1972). *EPIMAY, a simulator of southern corn leaf blight. Bulletin of the Connecticut Agricultural Experimental Station*, No. 729. New Haven, Connecticut.

Zadoks, J. C. (1971). Systems analysis and the dynamics of epidemics. *Phytopathology*, **61**, 600–26.

INDEX

abscisic acid, in infected plants, 165–8
abscission, factors involved in, 153, 158
acacia, gall of, 60
acetyl salicylic acid, and tobacco mosaic virus, 8
acids, organic: efficiency of conversion of glucose into, 206
Agrobacterium tumefaciens, 74, 161
Albugo candida, A. tragoponis, 54, 58, 66
almond, canker of, 139–41
Alternaria helianthis, 70
Alternaria solani, 55
amino acids, free: increased in diseased plants, 20, 21, 22
1-amino-cyclopropan-1-carboxylic acid, probable precursor of ethylene, 151, 152
amylase of plant: fungal infection and, 70–1; increased by ethylene, 155, and by gibberellic acid ?, 164
antibiotics, for control of bacterial diseases, 7
apoplast: sucrose in, 48, 94; water movement in, 104
apple: canker of, 138; fireblight disease of, 6; *Gloeosporium* rot of, 155; scab of, 9, 54, 59
arabitol, induces 'green islands', 163
Arrhenatherum elatius, leaf rust of, 60
aspen, canker of, 56
Aspergillus wentii, 169
ATP: formation of, in photophosphorylation, 15–16; requirement for, in carbon dioxide assimilation, 13, 14, 16–17, 30, and in glyceollin and lignin synthesis, 32–3, 38, 192
ATPase: fusicoccin and, 169; in haustorial complexes, 95–8 *passim*
auxins (IAA, etc.), 156–7; in diseased plants, 5, 157–60; pathway of synthesis of, 157
avenacin, anti-infective toxin in plants, 41
avocado, *Phytophthora* infection of, 135–6

bacterial diseases, 7, 9; and carbohydrate metabolism, 74; and photosynthesis, 24–5
banana, bacterial wilt of, 154
barley: brown rust of, 59; dressing of seed of, 7; leaf blotch of, 139; leaf rust of, 210; losses from crops of, 3; net blotch of, 55; powdery mildew of, 6, 54, 58, 94, 143, 144; root cortex of, 104–5; root diseases of, 106
beans: anthracnose of, 60; ethylene, and enzymes in, 155; phytoalexins of, 186, 189–91, 193; rusts of, 55, 60, 70, 141; *Uromyces* infection of, 53, 98
benomyl, fungicide, 8
benzimidazole, systemic fungicides related to, 7
biochanin A, precursor of phytoalexin, 194, 195
Botrytis cinerea, 8, 9
Brassicae: club root of, 54, 58, 66, 162; white blister of, 54, 58

cabbage, Chinese, 9; virus infection of, 21
caffeic acid, precursor of lignin, 122, 185, 187
calcium: effect of root infection on shoot content of, 118, and on uptake of, 120
carbohydrates: accumulation of, at sites of infection, 57–64; efficiency of conversion of glucose into, 206; formed in photosynthesis, 13, 16–19; metabolism and transport of, in healthy plants, 47–52, and in plants with fungal infections, 52–7, and other infections, 73–4; processes of metabolism and transport affected in disease, 64–73
carbon dioxide: assimilation of, in photosynthesis, 16–19; stomatal apertures and concentration of, 214
carrot, antifungal compound in, 156
casbene, phytoalexin, 41
catalase of plant: ethylene and production of, 155, 156; inhibited by scopoletin, 183
catechol, anti-infective toxin in plants, 41
cauliflower, *Erwinia* infection of, 151
cell division, in root galls, 162
cell walls: of haustorial complexes, plant photosynthate in, 92, 93; of plants, (degradation of, by pathogens) 5, 110, (sucrose and invertase in) 48
cellulases: extracellular, of fungal root pathogens, 111, 114; of plant, increased by ethylene, 155
Cephalosporium gramineum, see Hymenula cerealis